D0202897

3 0700 11002 9294

Utopian Generations

TRANSLATION | TRANSNATION
EDITED BY EMILY APTER

Utopian Generations:

THE POLITICAL HORIZON

OF TWENTIETH-CENTURY LITERATURE

NICHOLAS BROWN

PRINCETON UNIVERSITY PRESS

PRINCETON AND OXFORD

Library of Congress Cataloging-in-Publication Data

Brown, Nicholas, 1971–

Utopian generations : the political horizon of twentieth-century literature / Nicholas Brown.

p. cm.—(Translation/transnation)

Includes bibliographical references and index.

ISBN 0-691-12211-3 (cloth : alk. paper) — ISBN 0-691-12212-1 (pbk. : alk. paper)

1. English literature—20th century—History and criticism. 2. Politics and literature—Great Britain—History—20th century. 3. Politics and literature—Africa—History—20th century. 4. African literature—20th century—History and criticism. 5. Literature, Comparative—English and African. 6. Literature, Comparative—African and English. 7. Modernism (Literature)—Great Britain. 8. Modernism (Literature)—Africa. 9. Politics in literature. 10. Utopias in literature. I. Title. II Series.

PR478.P64B76 2006

820.9'358—dc22   2005043926

British Library Cataloging-in-Publication data is available

FOR NORMA

IN MEMORIAM

CONTENTS

PART THREE: POLITICS

CHAPTER SIX

The Childermass: Revolution and Reaction

Wyndham Lewis, fascism, and the critique of liberalism—*The Childermass* and revolution: the embodied cliché—*The Childermass* and reaction: imperialism and the strong personality—The reaction in revolution and the revolution in reaction

CHAPTER SEVEN

Ngugi wa Thiong'o and Pepetela: Revolution and Retrenchment

The Trial of Dedan Kimathi and the ambivalence of Mau Mau— Kamiriithu, the Kenyan theater apparatus, and the neocolonial state— *A Geração da Utopia, I Will Marry When I Want*, and national tragedy—A new generation of utopia: the multitude and musical form

CHAPTER EIGHT

Conclusion: Postmodernism as Semiperipheral Symptom

The eidaesthetic itinerary continued—bossapósbossa—The aesthetic ideology of bossa nova—Four options for cultural production on the semiperiphery—1964 and the end of modernism—Tropicália, or bread and circuses?

ACKNOWLEDGMENTS

Special thanks for their more than generous guidance and support are due to Michael Hardt, Fred Jameson, Frank Lentricchia, and Valentin Mudimbe; Jamie Daniel, Madhu Dubey, Judy Gardiner, John Huntington, Lansine Kaba, Walter Michaels, Beth Richie, and Mary Beth Rose; Maria Elisa Cevasco; Ndinzi Masagara, Marjorie Perloff, and Sylvia Wynter; Alberto Moreiras; Neil Larsen and Ato Quayson; and the late Priscilla Lane. Throughout the writing of this book I have benefited greatly from my conversations with Kristin Bergen, Tim Choy, Jeremy Hermann, and Imre Szeman. The comments of those, known to me or anonymous, who read the manuscript and offered advice were invaluable in putting this book into its final form—which would not have been possible without the help of Kat McLellan, Mary Murrell, Linda Vavra, and Hanne Winarsky. My incalculable debts to Anna and to Lis and Steve and Nora are almost beyond mention; not so my debt to Eleazar Delgado and the staff at the Jumping Bean, who never kicked me off my table by the window. Parts of this book are printed with the permission of *Research in African Literatures*, the *New Centennial Review*, and *South Atlantic Quarterly*. This book was completed at the Institute for the Humanities at the University of Illinois at Chicago.

Utopian Generations

CHAPTER ONE

Introduction

> Whoever hasn't yet arrived at the clear realization that there might
> be a greatness existing entirely outside his own sphere and for which
> he might have absolutely no feeling; whoever hasn't at least felt ob-
> scure intimations concerning the approximate location of this greatness
> in the geography of the human spirit: that person either has no genius
> in his own sphere, or else he hasn't been educated yet to the niveau
> of the classic.
>
> —Friedrich Schlegel, *Critical Fragment* 36

Modernism and African Literature

This book argues for establishing the interpretive horizon of twentieth-century literature at capitalism's internal limit. In the classical Marxian conception this limit is the rift between capital and labor, but this rift knows many displacements, the most important of which is the division of the globe between wealthy nations and a much larger and poorer economic periphery. The literary texts primarily considered here come from each side of this divide: British modernism between the world wars, and African literature during the period of the national independence struggles. The following pages will insist that neither of these two literatures—each produced in a period of extraordinary political possibility—can be understood on its own; rather, the full meaning of each only emerges in relation to the other and to the rift, both internal and external, which they each try in different ways to represent.

But what does British modernism have to do with African literature? Provisional answers are not hard to come by. First, the prestige accorded modernist literary texts by colonial-style education at mid-century cannot be overestimated. The relationship to modernism of the African literature that emerged with the great national independence movements (a relationship not only to modernism proper but also to the entire new-critical canon, itself an enlarged and domesticated modernism then in full hegemonic bloom) is deeply ambivalent. The critical edge of the great modernisms presents a model, while their institutional weight as the vanguard of European culture presents both an obstacle and a formidable spur to new and sometimes aggressively oppositional literary production. One need only think here of the well-known kinship between *négritude* and European surrealism, but other examples come readily to mind.[1] Indeed, each of the African writers considered in this book was explicitly engaged in the vital refunctioning of modernist tropes and strategies to suit sometimes contrary representational ends. Cheikh Hamidou Kane takes over the central problems of French and German existentialism only to resolve them in a completely novel way; Chinua Achebe invests the apocalyptic visions of Yeats and Eliot with new meaning; and Ngugi wa Thiong'o begins from a Brechtian theory of practice with which North American critical theory has never quite come to terms.

In what follows, however, these direct and sometimes genetic connections cannot be the primary or even initial point of analysis. In the context of African literature and modernism, we have been permanently warned away from influence study by Ayi Kwei Armah's funny but devastating response to Charles Larson's *The Emergence of African Fiction*, which claims to show Armah's formal debt to James Joyce. Armah's intervention made it clear that the "language of borrowing and influence is usually a none too subtle way Western commentators have of saying Africa lacks original creativity."[2] In the case of Larson's analysis of Armah's *Fragments*, the evidence of influence was demonstrably flimsy; but it is not clear even what one is to do with a genetic relationship that can be definitely established.[3] The very language of "influence" is in any case misleading, since, as Borges once said, a writer creates his own precursors rather than the reverse. As Adorno put it in more agonistic terms, every act of imitation is at the same time a betrayal, and the mere fact of an "influence" is not enough to establish the movement of this dialectic in any particular case.[4] The point, then, is not that this kind of literary history is totally irrelevant, but rather that its meaning is wholly contingent on literary interpretation: "To become good literary historians, we must remember that what we usually call literary history has little or nothing to do with literature and that what we call literary interpretation—provided only it is good interpretation—is in fact literary history." [5] Our surest bet lies not with exploring empirical or genetic literary history but by asking what is historical about the works themselves. This book aims not simply to trace the common pathways that traverse modernism and African literature, though these are many, but to construct a framework within which these pathways make sense beyond mere similarity or influence, and within which the genuine difference they pass across will become apparent.

Considering the profound restructuring of African societies by the colonial economy—not least in the emergence of the class that will create the continent's new literature—we might, in a second approach, point to another, richer set of connections between both sets of texts and the societies from which they emerge. The mere fact that European imperialism names a key moment in the spread of capitalism as a global economic system already implies a certain baseline of universality. Amos Tutuola's radically deterritoralized English, Wole Soyinka's depiction of a social class deprived of its historical vocation, the emergent urban logic of Meja Mwangi's Nairobi—all these have ready equivalents in canonical European literature. From this perspective Achebe, for example, appears closest not to Yeats and Eliot (to whom the titles of his early novels refer), but to the

great nineteenth-century historical novelists, who also witnessed the long process of the "defeat of the gentile nations." And yet, as far as our practice in this
book is concerned, there can be no question of merely applying the methodological norms developed for one literature to the texts of the other. This is impossible for theoretical reasons—capitalism as a global economic system is also predicated on an uneven development that produces uncountable eddies and swirls
in historical time, the literally unthinkable complexity of contemporary history
that thwarts any overhasty universalizing gesture—but also on more empirical
grounds. The vast graveyard of forgotten new-critical readings of postcolonial
texts—not to mention the devastating blows dealt to such critical practice by
critics as different as Chinweizu and Chidi Amuta in the 1980s—attests to the
sterility of the transfer in one direction, and while the other has produced a
number of fruitful recent studies of, for example, James Joyce as a postcolonial
writer, the violence this approach inflicts on the Joycean text's internal norms
is palpable.

This book, then, reconstellates modernism and African literature in such a way
as to make them both comprehensible within a single framework within which
neither will look the same. This framework will hinge neither on "literary history"
nor abstract "universal history" but on each text's relation to history itself. In this
context—though the demonstration will have to wait until later—Achebe can be
considered most profitably in relationship with neither "The Second Coming"
nor, say, *Waverly*, but rather with the work of Ford Madox Ford, a writer with
whom he appears initially to have little in common. If African literature will
appear in a new light when thus set beside canonical modernism, then modernism, in turn, will look rather different from the perspective of the period of African independence. Readers expecting a "theory of African literature" or a theory
of canonical modernism are therefore bound to be disappointed. The wager of
this book is that every discussion that isolates a "modernist tradition" or an "African tradition" (the very incommensurability of these terms should warn us of
their insufficiency) carries with it an inherent falseness. Any attempt to discuss
the latter without accounting for the process by which previously autonomous
and hegemonic traditions assumed a position of subalternity (and therefore
changed meaning absolutely) is to mythologize cultural continuity while ignoring
the violence with which all cultural traditions have been violently opened up into
world history. On the other hand, any "theory of modernism" that fails to take
up this same history—the always encroaching movement of capital and the connection between this movement and colonialism, world war, and the containment
of socialism, which will be thematized more explicitly as we approach our chapter
on Wyndham Lewis—misses the very reason these texts are still so powerful today.

In any case, it is well known that attempts to produce a "theory of the tradition," rather than reconstructing an autonomous heritage, tend to construct tradition according to the more or less commonly held norms of one critical movement or another.[6] One could hardly do otherwise. The point is not to imagine
that one could produce a purely innocent descriptive discourse, but to be explicit
about the manner in which one is positing the contents of one's own language.

In this book, literature as such names a certain mode of approaching problems and possibilities that are endemic to the development of capitalism. In the last instance, our reading of literary texts, in all their richness and complexity, will take the history of this development as its frame of reference. Renouncing the claim to be explicating some relatively autonomous tradition does not, then, prevent us from asking fundamental questions about modernism and African literature; it does mean that we will not be asking them about one or the other without reference to the history that brings them into relation with each other.

The framework constructed in this introductory chapter is grounded in what is meant to be an orthodox interpretation of the Marxist revision of the Hegelian dialectic. This is in some sense a "European" trajectory (if this label still applies to a tradition whose most important development in the latter half of the twentieth century was its appropriation and revision by anticolonial and anti-imperialist movements in Asia, Africa, and Latin America), and it is customary at some point for the Western writer to "acknowledge his subject position"—a sign of good intentions that is meant to excuse any subsequent lapses. The subject position from which this book is written—a position that is intellectual, political, and classed as well as racial, geographical, and gendered—is obvious enough, but good intentions count for nothing if one genuinely wants not to be counted among Armah's "Western scholars, critics of African Literature included," who are "nothing if not Westerners working in the interests of the West . . . committed to the values and prejudices of his own society, just as much as any other Western expert hustling Africa, be he a businessman, an economic adviser or a mercenary wardog" (44). What is required, if only as a beginning, is rather the attempt genuinely to understand what it would mean to continue the colonial dynamic on cultural or theoretical territory.

We owe the most significant and rigorous analysis of what is commonly called cultural imperialism to Paulin Hountondji, who, in a remarkable series of interventions spanning nearly two decades, has demonstrated that theoretical production as such—even when it is apparently centered in the Third World—tends to be structurally oriented toward the interests of the First World.[7] Hountondji's materialist account of the circulation of knowledge between the periphery and the core economies—explicitly inspired by Samir Amin's account of the structural dependency of peripheral economies—primarily concerns scientific knowledge, but the thesis can be easily generalized.[8] In cultural as in directly economic production, the Third World tends to provide raw material (local knowledges, African novels, musical idioms) that are shipped to the research centers of the First World to be converted into finished products (anthropology and pharmaceuticals, literary criticism, Paul Simon albums) that are sometimes reimported to the periphery. Hountondji's argument, however, refuses to remain at the level of culture, ultimately referring this movement to the total functioning of the "worldwide capitalist system"[9] in which it is caught up and which determines the circulation of knowledge at every point. This step is absolutely indispensable. For it cannot, then, simply be a matter of altering the circulation of knowledge without first taking account of that other thing that determines this circulation. If, failing this, we were to take the vulgar logic of cultural imperialism to its limit, we would arrive at something like a practice of "import substitution," where weaknesses in First-World production are selectively exploited to develop a regional industry which, with a little luck, can eventually compete with the First-World product on the global market. While such a practice may have some positive effects, it mainly operates to the advantage of local owners of capital—cultural as well as economic. In other words, the struggle over who is entitled to appropriate local knowledge for his or her own theoretical discourse can easily become, as Chidi Amuta caustically puts it, "essentially an intra-class one, between bourgeois Western scholars and their African counterparts, over whose false consciousness should gain the upper hand."[10]

The point is not to imagine that one is somehow outside this cycle or immune to its effects. Rather, if we adopt Hountondji's goal as one of our own—"the collective appropriation of knowledge . . . by peoples who, until now, have constantly been dispossessed of the fruits of their labor in this area as in all others"[11]— then we have no choice but to address that other thing—Capital—that determines the circulation of knowledge. Instead of merely acknowledging the author's subject position or, on the contrary, perpetually worrying about the reaction of some imagined hysterical other, we will try to demonstrate that a Marxist framework is not only not Eurocentric, but the only conceptual framework that potentially avoids the pitfalls of both Eurocentrism and of the paradoxically Eurocentric refusal of Eurocentrism. This is not to say—far from it—that this potential has always been realized in Marxist criticism of postcolonial literature. But whatever objections there may be to the framework developed here, it seems unlikely that, at this late date, anyone will be particularly worried about the geographical origin of its basic conceptual tools.

How, then, to think capital and the relationship between modernism and African literature in a single thought? The most efficient way to broach this connection is through Marx's well-known appropriation of the Goethean notion of world literature. Goethe writes:

> For some time there has been talk of world literature, and properly so. For it is evident that all nations, thrown together at random by terrible wars, then reverting to their status as individual nations, could not help realizing that they had been subject to foreign influences, had absorbed them and occasionally become aware of intellectual needs previously unknown. The result was a sense of goodwill. Instead of isolating themselves as before, their state of mind has gradually developed a desire to be included in the free exchange of ideas.[12]

It is not difficult to discern the traces of this cosmopolitan multiculturalism in our own dominant discourse, where preexisting cultures develop a sense of goodwill in the "free exchange" of the mysteriously neutral ground of the university.[13] Goethe himself was more discerning than this, as can be seen from the continuation of this fragment (whose explicitly mercantile overtones are excised from the contemporary edition), where the purpose of developing a world literature is to "acquire from it, as must always from any kind of foreign trade, both profit and enjoyment."[14] For Marx, of course, the economic will be more than a metaphor when *Weltliteratur* puts in a surprise appearance in the *Communist Manifesto*:

> The need of a constantly expanding market for its products chases the bourgeoisie over the whole surface of the globe. It must nestle everywhere, settle everywhere, establish connections everywhere.
>
> The bourgeoisie has through its exploitation of the world market given a cosmopolitan character to production and consumption in every country. To the great chagrin of the Reactionists, it has drawn from under the feet of industry the national ground on which it stood.... And as in material, so in intellectual production.... [F]rom the numerous national and local literatures, there arises a world literature.[15]

Here the "peaceful coexistence" of nations, cultures, and texts is given definite historical content in the dynamic of imperial expansion. As plainly as we can see the legacy of the Goethean conception in contemporary multicultural discourse, it is just as clear that the Marxian narrative, where particular cultural forms colonize territory along with economic ones, represents the truth of Goethe's metaphor.

If world literature does not spring spontaneously from a host of freely developing cultural equals but rather represents the exploitation of geographic and cultural diversity by a limited ensemble of economic and cultural forms, we might ask to what extent "non-Western literature" is a contradiction in terms. The question would not be whether the most vital writing of the second half of the twentieth century was produced by Third World writers: it was. The question is rather what we mean by "literature" and what we mean by "West," what agendas reside in those words and whether they have any meaning at all. *Going Down River Road* by the Kenyan novelist Meja Mwangi presupposes the norms of European naturalism even where it works against them. Can we say of the *Inkishafi* (a verse meditation occasioned by the passing of the city-state of Pate in what is now Kenya, by the late classical Swahili poet Sayyid Abdallah bin Ali bin Nasir[16]) that we do not work a well-intended but nonetheless violent transformation by understanding it with reference to the concept of literature? What we usually call "non-Western" literature is rarely the expression (like the *Inkishafi*) of some other culture, if by that we understand some other set of norms and rules that has developed along its own internal logic; rather, it must be thought of in terms of the positions that economically, ethnically, sexually, and geographically differentiated subjects occupy within the single culture of global capitalism that has more or less ruthlessly subsumed what was once a genuinely multicultural globe.

All of this should be obvious, even if our entire mainstream multicultural discourse is built around its explicit denial. But the recognition of what multiculturalism denies should not be taken to signify a celebration of, or acquiescence to, the power of some henceforth inescapable "Western" tradition. Indeed, the capitalist monoculture dissimulated in multicultural discourse is not strictly speaking "Western" at all. It is true that the notion of a specifically "Western" hegemony has been useful as a heuristic for describing the Manichean superstructures of classical imperialism. But the concept of the "West" (except perhaps in its now outdated opposition to the communist "East") has no purchase in causality, no explanatory power. Now that these Manichean structures are generally under-stood to have dissolved in favor of more complex ones, the concept has outlived its usefulness. As Neil Lazarus reminds us in his *Nationalism and Cultural Practice in the Postcolonial World*,[17] the identification of capitalism with "the West"—the elevation of a heuristic into an explanatory concept—is a mystification that serves to moralize what is an essentially systemic phenomenon. The disequilibrium in-trinsic to the function of capital can be kept under control only by the expansion of capital itself: as Marx puts it in the *Grundrisse*, "the tendency to create the world market is directly given in the concept of capital itself. Every limit appears as a barrier to be overcome."[18] As industrial capitalism expanded from southeastern England it subjugated, incorporated (unevenly), or obliterated noncapitalist modes of production and ways of life, and this process continues not only on the terrain of the former colonies but over remaining enclaves of as yet unrationalized labor—cattle ranching, higher education—in the dominant countries.[19] Needless to say, some countries, classes, and economic sectors hold and attempt to main-tain far more advantageous positions than others. But this is not something the notion of the "West" helps to explain.

What this means for cultural analysis is that the forms imposed by global capital-ism frame the interpretive possibilities available for any concrete cultural contents, even contents of putatively ancient origin. One example of such a form would be the museum, which only becomes necessary in a society predicated on the tenden-tial annihilation of all other cultural forms—and which is therefore not only an institution for the preservation of a multitude of different cultural forms but, like the antiquities market it superficially opposes, also a symptom of one thing, namely their eradication.[20] It has been said that the Taliban's expressed reasons for destroying the statues of Buddha in the Bamiyan Valley paradoxically preserved them in their being as religious artifacts—which, like the Golden Calf, had to be destroyed.[21] We should go a step further, however, and insist that Unesco would have annihilated them just as surely by turning them into yet another monument to humanity's "cultural heritage." In this book, however, we are not primarily concerned with institutions of this sort but with concepts; not so much the mu-seum or Unesco as whole genera of discourses and mental structures that function in a similar way: "the novel," "criticism," and "culture"—in particular, "literature."

It will be objected that the methodological decision to begin from the monocul-ture implicitly invokes the discredited category of totality. One of the objectives of this book is to restore the respectability of this Hegelian concept—indeed of the dialectic itself—to postcolonial studies.[22] While the impact of Fredric Jame-son's work on this book will no doubt be felt by many readers, this book is devoted in part to undoing the damage done to the reputation of the dialectic for postcolonial criticism by Jameson's "Third World Literature in the Era of Multinational Capitalism"[23] and its infamous suggestion that "all third-world texts are necessarily . . . to be read as . . . *national allegories*" (69). Aijaz Ahmad's canonical critique of this position is astute and unassailable on many counts. Jameson's essay contains several bad, positivist reasons for reading literature pro-duced on the periphery of capitalism as national allegory, and indeed substantial parts of the essay—from a conflation of the process of the subsumption of older economic forms under Capital with the problems of the peripheral national economy all the way to rash assumptions about the "experience of colonized peoples" (76)—are indefensible.[24]

None of these problems, however, annuls the essay's one good, Hegelian argument, and in retrospect the failure of Jameson's essay seems really more rhetorical than theoretical: what was intended as a rhetoric of struggle—of precisely Ahmad's "ferocious struggle between capital and labour which is now strictly and fundamentally global in character"—is easily construed as a "rhetoric of otherness." As with the capital-labor relation, Jameson's First World-Third World distinction begins to evaporate as soon as one attempts to describe each side as a positive category. But this does not mean that the dash does not represent a real rift, the conflict between the two. The real ground of Jameson's article comes not at the beginning, with all its easily refuted generalizing about subalternity, but at the end, when he finally invokes the Hegelian master-slave dialectic. In order to make this part of the essay conform to his general critique, Ahmad has to arrest this dialectic at an early stage ("one is merely the *object* of history, the Hegelian slave"). Whether or not this is a justifiable reading of Hegel, it is certainly not the Lukácsian one favored by Jameson, who understands the difference between master and slave as one of subjectivity, and in particular of the superior consciousness of the slave: unlike the master, who is "condemned to idealism," "the slave can attain some true materialistic consciousness of his situation."[25]

In fact, the mode of reading recommended by Jameson for Third-World literature as "social allegory" (85) is not substantially different from the mode of interpretation as "socially symbolic act" that he recommends for European texts in *The Political Unconscious*.[26] Rather, the difference is one of consciousness, which Jameson's invocation of the master-slave dialectic is meant to establish as largely the positional matter of where one stands in relation to Capital. In this context it might be productive to give Jameson's "unconscious" its Hegelian rather than its more obvious Freudian referent, and recall the category of "unconscious symbolism" in the *Aesthetics*, whose forms are always inferior and inchoate next to those of "conscious symbolism," which contains allegory proper. Terms like "political unconscious" (and "postmodernism," which also makes an appearance in the "Third World Literature" essay) are cognate with unconscious symbolism and therefore privative next to the conscious symbolism of "national allegory"—not for sentimental reasons or because of an external political sympathy but because Jameson's theoretical coordinates demand it. One might wish after the fact that the essay had been worked into the introduction to *The Political Unconscious* as a final dialectical twist, where it would have made clear that Jameson did not have in mind a radically different theory for Third-World literature but rather a kind of completion of the theory he had laid out earlier. As it is, however, without the kind of detailed theoretical and exegetical work that sustained that earlier book, the charge of reductionism was all too easy to make.[27]

Further, there is no question that much criticism of Third-World literature at the time of Jameson's essay was (and continues to be, though often in less obvious ways) genuinely Eurocentric—what Chinua Achebe called "colonialist criticism"[28]—so that both alertness to the problem and the theoretical tools to combat it were at the forefront of postcolonial discourse when Jameson's essay emerged. In this context, and in light of the essay's real shortcomings, the dominant reading of "Third World Literature in the Era of Multinational Capitalism" as condescendingly reductionist was almost inevitable; the essay makes no attempt to preempt such criticism theoretically or to offer the kind of nuanced exegesis that would render it unthinkable. What is unfortunate is that an entirely salutary and productive reading within the micropolitics of the North American academy at the moment of the self-definition of postcolonial studies played directly into the macropolitics of the cold war: the description of Marxism (which, surely we do not need to be reminded, was appropriated by countless anticolonial struggles) as an intrinsically reductive and totalizing-totalitarian colonizer in its own right.

Micro- and macropolitics cannot, however, be kept rigorously separate. Although unfortunate and for the most part unintended—certainly so the case of Ahmad, whose work offers brilliant refutations of the anti-Marxism constitutive of mainstream North American postcolonial studies[29]—this conjuncture was hardly fortuitous. Before we address in detail the necessity of the concept of totality—which has nothing to do with reducing difference to similarity—it is worth asking what alternatives offer themselves, in the charge of "reductionism," to thinking the totality. The demand for a criticism that would do justice to the full complexity and contingency of contemporary social life functions in the main not as a methodology or even as an ideal but rather as an impossible demand whose stridency distracts us from other possible goals. And even if the charge of reductionism were justified at the level of any particular book, essay, or critic, it would still function as an hysterical repression at the level of its larger cultural context, in which the tendency is not to reduce cultural phenomena to the economic but, on the contrary, to take genuinely political phenomena (that is, conflicts that take place at capital's internal limit) as though they were purely cultural. When, from Rwanda to Bosnia to the potentially endless series of conflicts fantastically referred to as the "war on terror," we suppose that we are dealing purely with cultural phenomena like "ethnic conflict" or a "clash of civilizations" (though no doubt these diagnoses derive an element of truth from the very political manipulability of these categories), a dose of "economic reductionism" would be a welcome tonic.

At any rate, the charge of reductionism, supported by the leap (via a convenient but illegitimate paralogism) from the concept of totality to the assertion of a totalitarian will to power, is absolutely rejected here. There is a vulgar notion of totality that does indeed imply terror: the positive notion that every element in a set must conform to a single rule. The kind of "totalitarianism" that would submit certain ethnic traits or sexual practices to the rule of "revolutionary or counter-revolutionary" falls into this category. In this book, however, we will have a rather different totality in mind, one which, far from reducing contingency and complexity to a monotonous necessity, is in fact the precondition for understanding difference. Meanwhile, the hegemonic doctrine of difference, particularly in its vulgar form, falls prey to the most elementary Hegelian deconstruction. That the naïve notion of presence must everywhere give way before the operation of difference is unobjectionable as far as it goes, but at the same time the poverty of the concept of Difference is readily apparent. Any concept as universal as Difference (which, as the very medium of human cognition, is virtually synonymous with Being) necessarily lacks all specificity; it is empty as to content. But without content there can be no difference, and the concept of Difference turns into its opposite, the monotony of the Same.[30] This is not to say that Same and Different are really identical, which would be absurd, but that they share a certain ground; every mere difference exists by virtue of a field that stamps it with the character of the Same. This is easiest to see if one descends from the concept to its political application, where it is difference, not totality, that reduces the complexity of the world to the monotonous same, since the truly different (that is, what refuses to be seen as merely different) is excluded from the field of difference. As Alain Badiou puts it with characteristic vigor:

> Our suspicions are first aroused when we see that the self-declared apostles of the "right to difference" are clearly horrified by any vigorously sustained differences. . . . As a matter of fact, this celebrated "other" is only acceptable if he is a *good* other—which is to say what, exactly, if not *the same as us*?[31]

The primacy of difference in fact outlines an identity—the unacknowledged frame of the monoculture, global capitalism.

> The respect for differences applies only to differences that are reasonably consistent with this identity (which, after all, is nothing other than the identity of a wealthy—albeit visibly declining—"West").[32]

Meanwhile it must be understood that the social totality (the monoculture) is not One in the ordinary sense of positive identity; it is founded on a fundamental rift, an internal limit. Totality, that is, should be confused neither with unity nor with simple identity, but rather with the famous Hegelian "identity of identity and difference." The paradoxical formulation alone should make it clear that we are not talking about a reduction of difference to identity (difference remains part of the formulation), but rather the explicit placing of difference into a frame where it is made comprehensible.[33] The point is not that the master and the slave, to take up our previous example, are monotonously the same but that neither of them is anything at all outside of his relation to the other: the totality they comprise is constituted by the rift that opens up between them. What the concept of totality gives us is, paradoxically, access to the radical incompleteness of what appears spontaneously as solid and whole. Complete, self-evident things (say, a commodity, a democracy, a novel) are in fact incomplete and always derive their being from something else (the production cycle, the world economy, the concept and institution of literature). As Ato Quayson puts it in his defense of dialectical criticism, "any phenomenon, literary or otherwise and no matter how apparently innocent or irrelevant, can be made to speak to a wide ensemble of processes, relations, and contradictions."[34] In this book we will be taking this assertion a step further: the refusal to take account of these larger processes gives the phenomenon its innocence and in so doing utterly deforms it.

Not to acknowledge this fundamental incompletion (whether by asserting some transcendent plenitude or by insisting on the absolutely untranscendent plurality of differences, and we have already suggested that these are the same thing) is a good working definition of ideology. While we will insist, therefore, that totalization is necessary (and anyhow inevitable), what we must never lose sight of is not that conceptualizing the totality is in a rigorous sense impossible, always in some sense "wrong" and incomplete (though this is true enough), but that it is never innocent. The frame one constructs does not simply rearrange preexisting objects but intervenes directly in their being, even as one's own relation to them and therefore one's own being is constituted at the same moment. The manner in which one totalizes is therefore at base a decision, even if this decision is obscured when the act of totalization is disavowed. As such it is a matter of responsibility and, potentially, guilt. For this reason one should be as explicit about it as possible.

At a more concrete level, it is often said that the concept of totality allows no room for contingency: totalizing narratives neglect the openness of the struggles that constitute real history. Here one might repeat a gesture that seems facile yet unanswerable, namely that the narrative of the end of totalizing narratives is itself a totalizing narrative, which is why people can get excited about it and derive some satisfaction out of their participation in the great project of tearing down the old grand narratives. Further, this new narrative of the end of totality can only be made comprehensible in the light of the avowedly totalizing narrative of a continual segmentation and specialization of intellectual labor that makes conceptual totalization increasingly difficult. The imagined lack of a frame turns out to be a disavowed totalization whose truth only emerges when it is made explicit. What the critique of the Hegelian conception of history makes room for, then, is not some genuinely new way of thinking about time, so that events and struggles could finally appear in their radical contingency and particularity. Instead, we leap from the Hegelian fat only to find ourselves in the fire of a Kantian formalism: the contingency and particularity of "radical" historicism take place against an ahistorical set of silent a priori assumptions. What the rejection of the frame as such produces, paradoxically, is the reliance on one particular unacknowledged frame, namely capitalism as the ahistorical horizon of all history. As Omafume Onoge has observed, only from the perspective of totality can "social systems [be] accorded only temporary legitimacy";[35] only when capitalism is explicitly named as a totality can it itself be historicized.

More concretely still, a vivid example offers itself in the history of African independence. In every case, the independence most African nations achieved in the 1960s was won through countless individual heroic acts performed and lives sacrificed, every one of which deserves to be memorialized. Further, even if, as Immanuel Wallerstein has suggested, capitalism as a world economic system was well served by the ultimate conversion of settler economies into external markets for the core economies,[36] in no case was the anticolonial struggle guaranteed in advance to succeed. The protracted struggles in Lusophone Africa and the belatedness of black rule in Zimbabwe and South Africa attest to that. Nonetheless, the true dimensions of this struggle only emerge against a totalizing backdrop. The narrative of national independence, appearing spontaneously as complete in itself, in fact takes its historical meaning from what is excluded from it, namely the limitations placed on the liberation movements by their location in the world economy. Each of these countries, once independence was on the horizon, faced the same question: whether to dare genuinely to challenge the logic of capital and violently disturb property relations or, remaining within the context of a purely national liberation, to strike a bargain with the former colonizer (in the contemporary example of South Africa, with investment capital).[37] The question of the propertyless masses, as Zimbabwe and South Africa remind us today, is the irreducible limit of national liberation. Fanon—to whom this book owes the greatest intellectual debt—was able to see the pitfalls of national liberation precisely because he conceived of capitalism as a totality and because he therefore knew that the national narrative, however necessary, was limited by the foundational exclusion of that totality.[38]

All this is not to say that social life is not in fact unthinkably complex. Resistance—which is given in the concept of capital as one of its constitutive limits, always "to be overcome"—takes on an infinite variety of forms, some of which are refunctioned out of bits and pieces of older cultural pathways. But these can be as easily refunctioned in the service of capital as its resistance, and to take resistance to capital as a basis for discussion is very far from multiculturalism as it is generally practiced, which functions in the main to discourage any attempt to theorize the monoculture. To begin, then, with an analysis of this striated capitalist monoculture is not (unlike discourses from either Left or Right that fetishize "the West," for ill or for good, as the fundamental source of "modernity" or "development") Eurocentric. To the contrary, such a beginning provides the only ground for discussing cultural differences without turning them into fetishized substances.

The global expansion of capitalism, with all of its social, psychological, and cultural effects, is obscured when we speak of modernism as a product of "Western culture" and of African literature as "non-Western." Indeed, when the boundary between the two is bracketed, the differential movement of capital emerges not as one kind of content among many, but as the fundamental content of both modernism and African literature. One might say it emerges as the content of literature itself. What do modernism and African literature have to do with each other? The obvious answer—both are literature—tells us nothing until we reconsider what we mean by "literature" in the first place.

The Eidaesthetic Itinerary

It is often said that "literature" in its current sense, with all the privilege and ontological weight it now enjoys or is burdened with, is not much older than the nineteenth century. Dr. Johnson's *Dictionary of the English Language*, completed in 1755, mentions only its older and more general meaning, defining literature as simply "Learning, skill in letters."[39] Alain Badiou, who maintains that literature in the modern sense is constituted by the emergence in the poem of problems that philosophy was unable to solve, traces its emergence to Nietzsche.[40] Jean-Luc Nancy and Philippe Lacoue-Labarthe, referring to literature's new philosophical calling as its "eidaesthetic" vocation, place the emergence of the modern concept of literature somewhat earlier, almost exactly at the turn of the nineteenth century.[41] That literature as we know it is invented in the nineteenth century does not mean that the literary tradition begins then; rather, it is precisely the retroactive invention of a literary tradition that makes the romantic conception so powerful. Like the terms labor, life, and language that define the epistemological mutation Foucault pursued almost obsessively to precisely this historical moment, the instant literature comes to exist, it is discovered always to have existed.[42] It should come as no surprise that in Foucault, too, literature, "constituted and so designated on the threshold of the modern age," appears with the dawn of the nineteenth century.[43] Nancy and Lacoue-Labarthe's *The Literary Absolute*, however, is considerably more specific than Foucault about the origins of literature (even if this specificity does not alone do anything to explain it), tracing literature's origins primarily to the philosophical fragments produced by Friedrich Schlegel between 1797 to 1804. What is at stake here is not simply German romanticism or even romanticism in the sense of a literary period or a closed set of texts. Rather, romanticism is "our *naiveté*," the very ground of postromantic thought, even as its later mutations—modernism and postmodernism—continue to define themselves against it. "A veritable romantic *unconscious* is discernable today, in most of the central motifs of our 'modernity.' "[44]

Nancy and Lacoue-Labarthe point out that this henceforth "romantico-modern" conception of literature as it develops in Schlegel's writings is not simply a mutation in a preexisting field, but a complex and dramatic reshuffling of discourses:

> It is precisely what determines the age we live in as the *critical* age *par excellence* or, in other words, as the "age" (almost two hundred years old, after all) in which literature . . . devotes itself exclusively to the search for its own identity, taking with it all or part of philosophy and several sciences (curiously referred to as the *humanities*) and charting the space of what we now refer to, using a word of which the romantics were particularly fond, as "theory."[45]

Literature here emerges as the middle term in a temporal and logical series, sandwiched between two apparently extra-literary discourses as it *takes up* philosophy on one hand and *opens up* the space for theory on the other. Schlegel expresses the first moment quite clearly in his *Ideas*: "Where philosophy stops, poetry has to begin."[46] The second moment emerges from Schlegel's *Athenaeum* fragments: "poetry should describe itself, and always be simultaneously poetry and the poetry of poetry."[47] In other words, poetry (understood in the broadest sense) must also always be a theory of poetry. Conversely, however, critique must always be "poetical through and through and at the same time a living, vibrant work of art."[48] Thus theory and anti-theory are generated at a single stroke: poetry is to produce the most adequate theory of poetry, but a subtle reflexive bifurcation is now required of poetry, so that poetry itself cannot exist without the critical moment, either immanent to the text itself or exiled to an initially intimate symbiosis.

This series—philosophy, literature, theory—can be given a more concrete history. To begin with, it is specifically Kant who opens up the possibility of the first moment, the emergence of poetry from philosophy, the peculiar philosophico-artistic or eidaesthetic hybrid of literature in the modern sense. The critique of aesthetic judgment—this is typically said of the analytic of the beautiful, but it can be shown equally of the analytic of the sublime—is originally meant to mediate between the "otherwise irreconcilable opposites" that characterize the Kantian impasse: the well-known antitheses of subject and object, phenomenon and noumenon, and the ever-widening circle of antinomies this fissure produces.[49] But as Georg Lukács argued decisively, these antithetical moments do not originate purely in philosophy, reflecting rather "antinomies of bourgeois thought" whose ultimate determinants are the segmentation of the labor process and the dominance of the commodity form, which sever subjectivity from matter at all points, from the assembly line to legal procedure all the way to the philosophy of science. Therefore, it is not surprising that an *aesthetic principle*, originating from within thought—the integrative notion of aesthetic pleasure developed in the third *Critique*—should be elevated beyond the sphere of aesthetics as such. The aesthetic, philosophically resolving antinomies whose origin lies outside philosophy, emerges to bear the responsibility for overcoming contradictions produced by capitalism itself: for "salvag[ing the contents of life] from the deadening effects of reification."[50] After Kant, the aesthetic sphere becomes necessarily philosophical and, within the limited sphere of thought, utopian. And indeed, this dual exigency, to "realize the kingdom of God on earth"[51] precisely through the philosophical operation of literature, is present everywhere in Schlegel's fragments: "The French Revolution, Fichte's philosophy, and Goethe's *Meister* are the greatest tendencies of the age."[52]

As for the second moment, the emergence of theory, it is easy enough to see that the subtle, reflective bifurcation of literature itself—the demand that each work develop along a purely internal dynamic of which it must in some sense also be aware—has a built-in tendency to become an absolute rupture and to engender theory as a separate discourse. The concept of literature demands, at one and the same time, both what is commonly called romantic "organicity" quite apart from external determinants, and a distinct discourse that would be able to recover that organicity from the necessarily fragmentary nature of any particular literary work—which then becomes merely an occasion, incidental to the project of recovery itself. But this logical exigency for theory, as we know, unfolds in history, and Fredric Jameson has described the "emergence of Theory, as that which seemed to supplant traditional literature from the 1960s onwards,"[53] as completing an earlier Hegelian premonition of the "end of art" that had appeared hopelessly wide of the mark. (This subsumption, of course, cannot be attributed solely to the autonomous unfolding of the idea of criticism; we will have to return later to its precipitating determinants.) This late "end of literature," postponed for two centuries by the romantic epicycle, would not refer to the actual disappearance of literature, which would maintain itself in a kind of decorative afterlife, perhaps with occasional isolated re-efflorescences of its original power. Rather, the "end" of literature would refer to the migration of its philosophical excess, the absolute to which each work refers without ever managing to contain, over into theory once and for all.

For reasons we have already touched on, this philosophical excess emerges after Kant, and indeed the account of the absolute that was most decisive for literature was the Kantian sublime, which subjectively mediates the fundamental Kantian antinomy of noumenon and phenomenon. In what follows we will be developing a theory of a certain modernist sublime.[54] It might well be asked why we need another sublime on top of the pile of sublimes that have accumulated in recent decades. The point here is not to produce yet another variation on the theme, but to identify modernism as such with a certain mode of the sublime. Luckily, Jean-François Lyotard has already made this equation for us, and probably the best way to go about establishing the peculiar qualities of the modernist sublime is to turn to Lyotard's essay as a point of departure—even if ultimately Lyotard's revision of the sublime will have to be abandoned in favor of a more orthodox reading of the Kantian sublime and of its Hegelian deconstruction.[55]

For Lyotard, the basic problem of modernism follows the familiar Frankfurt School analysis: "Capitalism inherently possesses the power to derealize familiar objects, social roles, and institutions to such a degree that the so-called realistic representations can no longer evoke reality except as nostalgia or mockery. . . . Classicism seems to be ruled out in a world in which reality is so derealized that it offers no occasion for experience but one for probing and experimentation."[56] Kant's sublime is a similarly structured failure of representation, the inability of the understanding to compass a reality that nonetheless demands to be conceptualized. But the sublime names something else as well: the experience of such failure strangely brings with it a kind of elation. Therefore the Kantian sublime involves two moments: the first being the (painful) experience of failure, while the second (pleasurable) moment comes with the recognition that the very awareness of failure implies some further, heretofore unrecognized capacity.

Simplifying Lyotard's argument, we may say that he assigns the name "modernism" to the first moment of failure and "postmodernism" to the second, ecstatic moment where the failure itself is registered on another level. But at this point, something happens that initially seems rather strange: "Postmodernism thus understood is not modernism at its end but in the nascent state, and this state is recurrent."[57] Two things have happened here. First, a double inversion: not only the modernism-post-modernism sequence but the temporality of the sublime itself has been turned around, as the ecstatic moment precedes the experience of the loss of the signified. Lyotard arrives at the first reversal by the simple expedient of taking the word "postmodern" absolutely literally: every genuinely modern work must follow some older modernity. Cézanne had to break with impressionism, Picasso had to reject Cézanne, Duchamp had to leave behind what was left of painting after Picasso. Thus the experimental impulse itself is always "postmodern," while the complacent repetition of an older modernity is simply a matter of style, modern in the sense of fashion, *mode*. The second inversion, however, presents a difficulty Lyotard resolves by flattening out the temporality of the Kantian sublime and repositing it spatially: the difference between modernism and postmodernism is a difference in emphasis between the two poles of the sublime—from which it follows that a work can be both modern and postmodern at the same time. But this flattening leads to the second, and more important transformation: Lyotard—while keeping faith with the temporal etymology of all the words deriving from "modern" (from *modo*, just now)—effectively abandons their periodizing function. Surprisingly, the postmodern "slackening" (*relâchement*) Lyotard criticizes in the "just now" of the opening pages of the essay turns out not to be postmodern at all but rather modern in the new sense, while the modernism to which he fantastically wishes to return was in fact the postmodern. It is obvious that at this point "modern" and "postmodern" name more or less eternal possibilities. It might come as no surprise that Proust is modern and Joyce is postmodern—but then it might be less obvious that Montaigne is also postmodern while Schlegel is modern.[58] The implication is that this play of the modern and the postmodern could be pushed back indefinitely: one might think of Rome as a merely modern repetition of postmodern Greece.

Lyotard's distinction, in fact, is so fundamental that the game begins to impose itself everywhere one looks. (In the context of the works currently under consideration, one would have to argue that they are all "postmodern" in Lyotard's sense, while our current middlebrow explosion and the institutionalization of the market in postcolonial literature would be "modern," a term that now becomes almost derogatory.) But we cannot go along with Lyotard so easily. For if the distinction is now conceptual and therefore more or less outside history (or everywhere the same in history, which is the same thing), we cannot forget that the very impetus away from a naïve or cynical realism (that is, toward the postmodern in Lyotard's sense) was, in Lyotard's account, historical: namely, capitalism, and a particular early twentieth-century moment at that, one which was able to grasp aesthetically the "derealization" imposed by the commodity form. The concept of modernism, it turns out, cannot shake off its empirical referent so easily, and this leads us back to the same old question we never started with, which is that of modernism in the literary-historical sense, although we can no longer ask it in the same way.

Meanwhile, we are confronted with another fundamental issue. In the final paragraph of the essay Lyotard suddenly brings in a whole new set of questions having to do with totality in the Hegelian sense: "Let us wage war on totality; let us be witness to the unrepresentable; let us activate the differences (*différends*) and save the honor of the name."[59] Lyotard is here attacking both official or genteel realism and *transavangardisme*, or facile pastiche, both of which fundamentally fail to ask any difficult questions of reality itself. So much is unobjectionable. But the passionate last-minute assault on "totality," while hardly unexpected in itself, is puzzling in this context. It is clear enough that Lyotard's equation of the failures (or evasions) of current art with Hegelian totality involves a very different interpretation of Hegel than our own, and there is no point in repeating our earlier comments on the subject. The problem for us, however, is not Lyotard's reading of Hegel but his reading of Kant.

Lyotard's distinction may well be the same one identified in Thomas Weiskel's classic *The Romantic Sublime* as that between the sublime proper and the "secondary or problematic sublime" which, like Lyotard's bad "modernism," is essentially nostalgic.[60] Weiskel, however, understands something that Lyotard explicitly rejects: the sublime proper requires the notion of totality; without it we are left with what Lyotard condemned as the merely modern. At the very outset of Kant's discussion of the sublime, when he begins to draw the distinction between the sublime and the beautiful, he emphasizes the importance of totality: "But the sublime can also be found in a formless object, either [as] in the object or because the object prompts us to present it, while yet we add to this unboundedness the thought of its totality."[61] The last phrase here is essential. Unrepresentability alone doesn't constitute the sublime. The sublime, rather, requires the capacity to recognize that the sublime object is conceptually totalizable—in fact, it positively requires that we do so totalize it—at the same time as we fail to totalize it aesthetically as we do with ordinary objects. The sublime could be summarized as the simultaneous experience of aesthetic unboundedness and conceptual totalization. Now is not the time to explore the relevant passages in Kant in detail, but it would not be difficult to show that at every stage, totality ("the infinite as *a whole*," "the idea of the absolute whole")[62] is absolutely central to the sublime as such. "Unboundedness" and "totality" are the fundamental conflict at the heart of the sublime. Without this conflict there is no sublime, only conceptual failure.

Our long digression on Lyotard thus leads us back to two things: first, to some less naïve conception of modernism as a moment in literary history and, second, to the original Kantian presentation of the sublime as the conflict between totality and unrepresentability. But while we will want to retain Lyotard's observation that modernism (now in the vulgar literary-historical sense) is intimately bound up with a certain mode of the sublime, we cannot fail to note that we have gotten far ahead of ourselves. We began this section with Nancy and Lacoue-Labarthe's account of the first emergence of the "literary absolute" in the post-Kantian moment of early German romanticism, a full century prior to the emergence of a distinctively modernist literature. Indeed, the genre of the fragment, as practiced by Schlegel's circle at Jena, mobilizes precisely the same logic that we will see in the modernist sublime. Nonetheless, there is plainly a difference between literary romanticism and modernism, one which surely has something to do with the "derealization" of the object world cited by Lyotard. The terms by means of which this transition can be understood are to be found within the Kantian sublime itself. The difference between romanticism and modernism—within the single, romantico-modern conception of literature—might be identified, perhaps too schematically, with the difference between the mathematically and the dynamically sublime, the shift from the thought of the infinite itself to the confrontation with its embodiment in the sublime object.[63]

Criticism, unsurprisingly, registers this shift. T. E. Hulme's 1914 "Romanticism and Classicism," for example, repudiates the "spilt religion" of romanticism in favor of a literature of "small, dry things."[64] It almost goes without saying that the terms of Hulme's repudiation are thoroughly romantic. The philosophical excess carried by art in Hulme's antiromanticism is precisely that put into play by the Kantian impasse: if reality "could come into contact with sense and consciousness, art would be useless and unnecessary. . . . [T]he function of the artist is to pierce through here and there . . . the veil placed between us and reality."[65] (It may serve as a measure of the ubiquity of this movement to modernism that Victor Shklovsky's rejection of symbolism—almost exactly contemporary with the Hulme essay—in favor of a practice that would, famously, "make the stone *stony*," unfolds along lines that are congruent with Hulme's.[66]) The metaphor of the veil is, also, of course, unmistakably romantic.[67] What occurs here is not a radical break with romanticism but a more subtle shift in emphasis onto matter as such as the means of access to the absolute experience beyond the veil: Hulme's poetry of "finite things," John Crowe Ransom's "physical poetry," or Shklovsky's poetry of the "artfulness of an object."[68]

This critical tendency, whose philosophical counterpart would be phenomenology's Husserlian slogan "To the things themselves!"[69] resonates profoundly with a tendency that was already deeply inscribed in modernist practice. In James Joyce's *Stephen Hero*, written just after the turn of the twentieth century, Stephen's aesthetic theory hinges precisely on the apprehension of the thing-in-itself: first as something discrete, then as something with a form, and finally as something that is, mutely, stubbornly, and infungibly, "*that* thing which it is."[70] Ezra Pound wrote that the first "principle" of modern poetry was "the direct treatment of the 'thing.' "[71] William Carlos Williams's famous line from *Paterson* can be taken as a manifesto-in-miniature: "no ideas but in things"[72] reaffirms the value of "seeing the thing itself without forethought or afterthought but with great intensity."[73] And so on.

What is clear, then, is that while the absolute as such becomes in the modernist period an object of ridicule—Hulme's "circumambient gas"—the problematic of the absolute, of the fragmentary representation of the unrepresentable, remains as central as ever, only now condensed into matter. This historical shift, the movement from the mathematically to the dynamically sublime, runs from the ability to postulate the infinite without being able adequately to present it to a kind of shock at the confrontation with brute materiality, from the radical inaccessibility of the supersensible Idea to the radical inaccessibility of the *Ding an sich*, from symbolism to defamiliarization, from romanticism to Hulme's "classicism" or modernism. Doubtless the dynamically sublime undergoes a certain domestication, however, as it makes its way into modernism: from "shapeless mountain masses piled on one another in wild disarray, with their pyramids of ice, or the gloomy raging sea"[74] to, say, a red wheelbarrow.

Or perhaps not. In Joyce's *Ulysses*, Stephen Dedalus condenses in a phrase what is presumably something like Joyce's early theory of the epiphany: "God is a shout in the street."[75] This is, on one hand, a reformulation of the romantic theory of the fragment.[76] But it might also remind us, in its equation of altogether incommensurate registers of being, of a well-known similar paradox in Hegel: "the being of Spirit is a bone."[77] Here (in the discussion of phrenology in *Phenomenology of Spirit*) the representational problematic of the sublime is understood differently than it had been in Kant's *Critique*. It is not that the skull somehow actually embodies the truth of the subject (that the "sublime object" somehow allows us to be aware of an essence that cannot be represented); rather, the skull represents the fact that there is no subject in the positive sense that phrenology dreams of— the inertness and absurdity of the skull only reminds us that it might as well be the skull as anything else. If we read the modernist sublime in this way—as Žižek puts it, converting "the lack of the signifier into the signifier of the lack"[78]— then the privileged signifier of the modernist *thing*, rather than presenting in the humbleness of objects an unrepresentable Being, signifies a lack, the absolute absence of a certain kind of content.

But what is this lack, and why the *thing*? With the Hegelian example, the movement between the lack of the signifier and the signifier of the lack is metonymic: the skull assumes the dimensions of Spirit just because it happens to be convenient and suitably empty. If we remember that in the modernist era, the "age of mechanical reproduction," the *thing* has acquired a whole new and mystified mode of being on the assembly line, it may not be too much to say that the unassuming *thing* comes to represent metonymically the entire system of productive forces, the social totality. Or rather, as we saw in the phrenology example, it precisely does not represent this system—which does not in any case exist as a positive substance, as a One—but stands in for the lack of any concept of it. The real object of (representational) desire is—as in the Lacanian explication of the " 'perverse' fixation"—metonymically displaced.[79] As with the skull, there could not be a less promising signifier than the mass-produced thing, which, as is well known, is systematically deprived of all traces of its production. It should come as no surprise, therefore, that self-conscious attempts to theorize the *thing*—in Heidegger, for example—are led into a marked nostalgia for an older form of production, and for the set of cultural pathways that went along with this older mode and whose modern analogs are steadfastly refused. (In fact, compared to the subjectivities born with the mass-produced object world, the old feudal master of the Hegelian narrative, whose distinguishing trait was utter alienation from the reality of his material existence, appears positively earthy by comparison—as will be seen in our readings of Ford Madox Ford's novels in chapter 4.) The *thing* does not represent or provide some kind of mystical quasi-representational access to this new productive totality; instead, merely convenient metonymically to the great mutation in productive power, it signifies the impossibility of representing the field of productive forces from within the field of commodities.

Needless to say, this representational dilemma is not faced uniformly by everybody; in its modernist form it is proper to a certain mode of subjectivity and a certain position within the economic order. And with this realization we find ourselves suddenly free of the claustrophobic atmosphere of the logic of modernism and able to consider a different set of approaches to the same problem, namely—to get ahead of ourselves—the literature of decolonization, where, in a rather different sense than Fanon had in mind, "the Third World . . . faces Europe like a colossal mass whose aim should be to try to resolve the problems to which Europe has not been able to find the answers."[80] No doubt it would be possible to think of other, European late avatars of the romantico-modern conception of literature, not least in the postmodern condensation of the newly global and instantaneous forces of production into the relatively puny figure of the individual body, its pains and pleasures, and its decay. But this would be a relatively static and essentially external mutation, in every way less dramatic than the seizure of the literary itself at the very moment that the colonized world breaks free of the colonial yoke.

But first, we must remember that the modernist sublime was, within the terms set out by Lukács, utopian. It fulfilled the function of uniting, at the level of thought, the intellectual antinomies opened up by the rift that runs through capitalism—subject and object, noumenon and phenomenon—by means of the sublime object that was supposed to represent the unrepresentable totality: the shout that signifies God, the wheelbarrow that signifies "so much." But the trick lurking in the aesthetic is that it is utopian "only *in so far* as these [contradictions] become aesthetic."[81] This is not a quibble but an absolute reversal, a cancellation that repeats, in quite other terms, the Hegelian reduction of the sublime outlined above. The secret truth is that the Kantian noumenon is fictional through and through; that the very condition of access to the Idea is that it originate in ideology; that aesthetic utopia comes into being only at the expense of aestheticizing the problems it resolves; that the Being or totality to which modernism promises access is a mystification. At this point it might occur to us that, historically, modernism's aesthetic utopia has a counterpart in the quite different (specifically, socialist) political utopia imagined by the great wave of European political struggles following the Soviet revolution. Precisely to the extent that canonical modernism puts into practice the Lukácsian structure outlined above, it becomes, regardless of any particular politics, antagonistic to politics as such. Modernism is utopian only in so far as it refuses utopia.

As Lukács makes clear, this antagonism is a kind of complementarity in that both aesthetic and political utopia represent solutions, incommensurate with each other and originating from different positions within the economic order, to the same set of problems. (That this structure is explicitly inscribed in the idea of literature from the very beginning can be clearly seen in Schiller's *Letters on the Aesthetic Education of Man*.)[82] If the deep bifurcation between aesthetic and political utopia in modernism marks the radicalization of a more ambiguous dual impulse in the romanticism of Schlegel's circle[83] (which develops, quite consciously, in the shadow of the French Revolution and the Napoleonic reorganization of feudal space), then we should not be surprised to discover this ambiguity once more in the literature of decolonization, which unfolds in a third revolutionary moment.

Four overlapping series: within the larger series (philosophy-literature-theory, to which we will return shortly), a narrower literary sequence (romantic-modernist-postcolonial), which corresponds to a representational shift (mathematically sublime to dynamically sublime to, as we shall see shortly, the evacuation of the sublime), and ultimately to a series of historical crises (the French, Russian, and anticolonial revolutions). It needs to be remembered of this third and final moment that postcolonial literature is literature in precisely the romantico-modern sense: postcolonial literature bears a specific ontological burden that differentiates it both from other art forms in formerly colonized countries (it is no accident that there is no such field as "postcolonial music," for example, even though much of the world's most interesting and culturally important music is produced on postcolonial territory), and from the status that quite "literary" texts like *Al Inkishafi* would have had in precolonial times. That postcolonial literature is literature should go without saying. But, as Gayatri Spivak has pointed out in a quite different context, the "theoretical sophistication" that is taken for granted in European texts, which demands that a specific hermeneutic be devised for each work (this exigency is precisely what is implied by the romantic invention of theory), is all too often denied to postcolonial cultural production, which is reduced— not only for a relatively naïve audience but also in academic multicultural discourse—to mere raw material, "the repository of an ethnic 'cultural difference' ": or, one might add, of the specifically local or subjective effects of a "clash of cultures."[84] Works from the independence period, no matter how complex, are perpetually submitted to a hermeneutic that mines them for primarily ethnographic and sometimes historical evidence. Such a literal-minded mode of reading is, of course, possible as one approach among others; one could easily read, say, Joyce's *Dubliners*, Ford's *Parade's End*, or Lewis's *Tarr* in precisely this way. As the dominant approach to postcolonial literature, however, the assumption that one already knows how to read it inflicts a flattening violence. More important, this violence, as benevolent as it may believe itself to be, cannot be innocent: it is not merely a blindness but a refusal of the properly eidaesthetic project of postcolonial literature, a refusal to recognize its appropriation of the problem of the absolute, understood explicitly now as the social totality.

But with this we are prepared to understand the real difference imposed by the anticolonial *prise de parole*. It is perfectly reasonable to anchor this difference initially in the Hegelian master-slave dialectic and the epistemologically mutilating position of the master vis-à-vis his laboring bondsman (which mutilation would also explain the metropolitan containment of postcolonial writing within a hermeneutic of cultural expression), as long as we understand that this dialectical unity is the totality that each seeks to represent, though in quite different ways and with quite different possibilities of success. The "mimetic purchase" or apparent representational immediacy of much postcolonial literature may also be situated in this dialectic, but this does not then allow us either to mistake representational urgency for naïveté, or to abdicate the responsibility, having felt Schlegel's intimation that one "might have absolutely no feeling" for the resonance of the text before one, to search patiently for further allegorical registers. It was suggested earlier that as postcolonial literature takes over the project of the literary, it also takes over and refunctions many of the tropes and topoi of European modernism. It does not seem very useful, therefore, to describe the difference between modernism and the literature of decolonization in terms of some relative lack of interest in form or in some real representational immediacy, if this is understood as a kind of naïveté or obstinacy—however bracing or salutary. Instead, we might think of this difference as marking the emergence of a new kind of consciousness, a shift similar in form to Hegel's "end of art" but within the literary itself: a shift from the "poetry of the imagination to the prose of thought."[85] What is new in the anticolonial *prise de parole* is its refusal or evacuation of the whole problem, central to modernism, of the thing-in-itself: the evacuation, that is, of the whole structure of the sublime.

We remember that this problem, the mainspring of modernist defamiliarization and so-called difficulty, is ultimately the symptom of a certain position in the economic order and represents a mutilated but real striving after the utopian representation of the absent totality.[86] The literature of decolonization takes over this striving, the eidaesthetic project itself, but from a quite different position within the global division of labor; in so doing, it hollows out the equivocal structure of the sublime (which, meanwhile, begins to be supplanted in the First World by the category of the beautiful, embodied in advertising and the "serious" book market).[87] The totality is no longer to be thought of as a mystical substance, accessible in quasi-religious form through the fetishized "host" of the fragment or the thing-in-itself, but rather as no more than a necessary fiction in a globalized world; a world, that is to say, where the truth of any event (or any "culture") resides more or less outside itself. To fail to attempt a strategic map of the totality, to pretend that one could possibly narrate the particular without providing some account of the universal, would be more profoundly ideological than any (necessarily) flawed attempt. Could we imagine, for example, Achebe's brilliant *Arrow of God*, the story of what might be called the "nervous breakdown" of a village priest, without a simultaneous narration of the intimate rhetorical interference offered by the Christian narrative?[88] This narrative, in turn, could not be introduced without depicting the conflicted ideology of the British imperial project; which could not be depicted without representing capitalism in the form of extraction of raw materials and the introduction of a cash economy; which itself entails a sketch of the crisis in capitalism occurring in Europe concurrent with the narrative; which itself leads back to the (secret) delicacy and impermanence of cultural forms in general and to a genuinely utopian possibility.

But it should be clear that utopia no longer takes its positive, potentially totalitarian form—the mystical City of God, the ideal of the Harmonious Man, the impossible, totalitarian solution to a world of conflicts, which would only be, at best, an idealization of our own world anyhow. Instead, utopia is understood here, in keeping with Hegel's critique of Plato's *Republic*,[89] precisely as something negative, nothing other than a lack or contradiction in the actually existing social totality whose presence hints at an as yet unimaginable future. The future, insofar as this word is used in a nontrivial way, cannot be represented except as a lack: as the Mozambiquan writer Mia Couto puts it in his story "The Flags of Beyondward," "the destiny of a sun is never to be beheld."[90] Positive utopias—like Plato's *Republic*, the cyber-utopias of our own recent past, or the popular futurisms of the 1950s—cannot think the future; they can only rearticulate the actual in futuristic form. The negative version of utopia, only available in genuinely political moments, is utopia stripped down to its naked essence. It is the bare thought, emerging from the nearness of the rift or set of contradictions that characterize social life under capitalism, that things might really be otherwise.[91]

As we all know, the utopian trajectory suggested by the writings of the period of decolonization was hijacked, as Fanon feared it might be, by national bourgeoisies only too happy to profit through the old economic relationships and to celebrate their private wealth as a collective triumph. The great period of utopian anticolonial literature in Africa is followed in the postcolonial moment by a literature of corruption, of stagnation—to a surprising degree, a literature of feces.[92] It is tempting to say that with the disillusionment of the post-independence period, the utopian energies contained in modernism by its own conditions of possibility are, in the case of the literature of decolonization, contained by history itself. But history is not external. The literature of decolonization, as literature, does not come with an epistemological or ideological guarantee merely because it is written from the relative position of the bondsman—which is in any case only an allegorical figure whose geographic representational value was already receding with the postcolonial reorganization of accumulation. The colonizer/ colonized dialectic, indispensable for understanding the historical dynamics of post–World War II global politics, cannot be given foundational authority or be understood to describe even that period without excess: the domain of the colonized, like that of the colonizer, has its own "lords" and its own "bondsmen," with greater or lesser degrees of collusion among homologous groups in each space. (If "hybridity" can be thought without contradiction it must refer to something like this structure.) The literature of decolonization, in turn, mystifies its own conditions of possibility and dissembles its interest in the ascendancy of a national bourgeoisie. In his extraordinarily insightful work on postcolonial disillusion, Neil Lazarus has said of the generation of African anticolonial intellectuals that their optimism was "so naïve . . . as to seem culpable in retrospect."[93] More often than not the utopian element in the African literature of independence, while anything but a mere aesthetic compensation, is nonetheless purely abstract. As long as utopia is only the abstract negation of the colonial system, everyone can agree on it because it lacks the concrete content—the radical reorganization of property relations—that would necessarily impose division and dissent. Neither is this lack of specificity innocent: in the political realm it allows the national bourgeoisie, without apparent contradiction, to pursue its own goals under the cover of revolution. Merely by being literature, moreover, the literature of decolonization presupposes a certain division of labor which it does nothing concrete to oppose, even as it is genuinely critical of many of its effects. If modernism can be considered, in a sense, "genuinely" utopian after all because it does finally yield up the secret of its own failure, the genuinely utopian literature of decolonization already contains within itself the seeds of its own defeat.

This seemingly brings us to a kind of dead end. But we should keep in mind that the First World 1960s, and postmodernism more generally, are the direct inheritors of the decolonization movement. The apparently independent and quintessentially U.S. phenomena of the civil rights movement and the protest against the war in Vietnam, for example, are coordinated through and take their meaning from the worldwide expansion of the struggle against colonialism. The pan-African aspect of the civil rights movement is misunderstood if it is considered to be based solely on the valorization of common cultural roots; fundamental to such identification is the possibility of political solidarity with the decolonizing world. And we are so used to thinking of Vietnam in cold war terms that we have all but forgotten that the Viet Minh was first an independence movement and only later a communist party; the refusal to serve in Vietnam, played out in other contexts and other territories in Europe, is a refusal to recognize the legitimacy of colonial domination.[94] In more general terms, we might think of the relationship between the Third World 1960s and our own postmodern, globalized moment as exemplifying a Marxian insight that Michael Hardt and Antonio Negri have radicalized in *Empire* and *Multitude,* namely that "resistance precedes power."[95] Rather than seeing capital's positive side as its dynamism, Hardt and Negri place that dynamism in the hands of living labor, which has at every step forced capital to reorganize. In this model, the current reorganization of capital called globalization is an essentially reactive regrouping after the disintegration of classical imperialism at the hands of the anticolonial movements.

Which returns us to our original, larger series: philosophy-literature-theory. For the utopian impulse that recedes in postcolonial writing reappears with the emergence of theory: Foucault's disappearing face in the sand or the "as yet unnameable" that marks Derrida's writings testify, if not to any particular future, then at least to the decisive end of the present. On the surface, however, nothing could seem as parochially European as theory, and indeed Edward Said and others have criticized theory for not engaging sufficiently with the postcolonial world.[96] But all theory is postcolonial theory: it owes its very existence to the struggle against colonial domination and its echo in the political urgency of the First World 1960s. The initial designation "poststructuralism" refers to Saussure's legacy to be sure, but also and more importantly to Lévi-Strauss and a crisis in French anthropology that V. Y. Mudimbe has identified as part of a more general moment of European cultural doubt when confronted with the illegitimacy of the colonial venture.[97] Derrida's classic "Structure, Sign, and Play in the Discourse of the Human Sciences"[98] is an exegesis of this crisis—the inability to posit any longer the difference between engineer and bricoleur, an inability that is itself the symptom of the impossibility of legitimizing the colonial project in the face of anticolonial resistance. The very possibility of imagining "Western Culture" as no more than "myth today"—and it is no accident that Barthes's primary example of contemporary myth is the image of an African soldier saluting the French flag—emerges from the fissure opened up by this crisis.[99] We should not forget either that the secret determinant of everything in Foucault's *The Order of Things* turns out to be anthropology. To be sure, a specifically philosophical meaning is given to this word, but we must remember that the climax of Foucault's text, the emergence of theory and the end of humanism, arises precisely out of a crisis in ethnology, which is understood not as a purely epistemic phenomenon but in its relationship to French imperialism, the "relation that can bring [European thought] face to face with all other cultures as well as with itself."[100] Foucault's introduction to Deleuze and Guattari's *Anti-Oedipus* draws the connection between the Vietnamese anticolonial struggle and European political developments on the first page; the decisiveness of this connection for theory is pointed to everywhere in *Anti-Oedipus* itself, where colonialism becomes a key to understanding the imposition of both the Oedipal figure and capitalism everywhere.[101] No doubt there are other examples—indeed, even Pierre Bourdieu, whose work perennially arouses the suspicion of a parochial Frenchness, begins from a critique of ethnography motivated directly by the Algerian war, which is also the occasion for Fanon's *The Wretched of the Earth*—but these will suffice to sketch the point. Our own present—from the reorganization of Capital all the way up to the reorganization of knowledge, not to mention the boomeranging effects of decades of disastrous U.S. foreign policy—is the product of a history of anticolonial struggle.[102]

Totality, Allegory, and History

This does not bring us to the end of the eidaesthetic itinerary, and we will return in our final chapter to the contemporary history of the eidaesthetic. In the intervening chapters, our aim will be to capture this dual project—the grasping toward the representation of the rift or set of contradictions that produces the social totality, a representation that at the same time discloses a utopian desire—as it plays out between modernism and African literature. Insofar as our work in these chapters will be interpretive, it will be methodologically useful to translate the structure we have been discussing into more explicitly hermeneutic terms. Here we might note, no doubt too quickly, that the position maintained in different forms of the absolute throughout the eidaesthetic itinerary is congruent with that occupied by the *anagogic* in the allegorical tradition.

This identification may initially seem more problematic than useful. The canonical illustration of the fourfold method of allegorical reading—the successive derivations of the literal, allegorical, moral, and anagogic meanings of the biblical text, referring respectively to the historical meaning of the Hebrew Bible, its prefiguration of the New Testament, its ethical import, and finally to its disclosure of "eternal glory"—is Dante's reading of Psalm 114:

> Now if we look at the letter alone, what is signified to us is the departure of the sons of Israel from Egypt during the time of Moses; if at the allegory, what is signified to us is our redemption through Christ; if at the moral sense, what is signified to us is the conversion of the soul from . . . sin to the state of grace; if at the anagogical, what is signified to us is the departure of the sanctified soul from bondage to the corruption of this world into the freedom of eternal glory. And although these mystical senses are called by various names, they all may be called allegorical.[103]

The key element of this interpretive machine, as we will shortly see more clearly, is that not only this verse but ultimately any biblical passage, no matter what path it takes through the infinite possibilities generated by the literal, allegorical, and moral levels, is ultimately to be understood in the light of eternal glory. Both the biblical anagogic meaning and the postromantic absolute, the totality to which fragmentary representation refers, are the ultimate resting points of all signification within their respective systems, the absent signifieds that guarantee the meaning of a signifier that in itself would be merely fragmentary and infinitely interpretable. Like the anagogic, totality is a "nodal point" that binds the signifier to the signified for the subject caught up in the signifying machine.

We have learned to be wary of such ultimate significations, and we will return to this problem shortly. Meanwhile, the logic of allegory contains peculiarities that will clarify aspects of the current project. The Greek *allêgoria*, "speaking otherwise," implies not only a complex symbolic act but also a social one: *agoreuô* is not only to speak but to speak publicly or politically: *agorêphi*, in assembly. Allegorical language is charged with social effectivity. If the relevance of this etymological moment to the seemingly hermetic fourfold scheme that comes down to us through Aquinas and Dante seems obscure, we might recall that in its original formulation in Saint Augustine's *On Christian Doctrine*, Christian allegory has a specifically missionary purpose: it is a means by which "the Church of Christ is able to destroy all sorts of superstitions in those who come to it and to incorporate them into itself."[104] Allegory serves the socially integrative function of subsuming whole signifying systems into its own regime of meaning, turning them into mere fragments of a signifying machine oriented toward eternal glory. As can be seen in Dante's reading of Psalm 114, for example, allegory manages to preserve the truth of the Hebrew Bible while bringing it within the narrative of Christian redemption. The exodus is not any less factual for being the sign of something else, but the nature of its truth has fundamentally changed. The utility of this hermeneutic machine for evangelization is tremendous: nothing has to be made false for it to mean something else, too. Allegory, then, is not a machine that interprets merely for the sake of interpretation or even for the revelation of theological truth. Rather, it interprets in the service of a social agenda—in this case, the expansion and maintenance of the community of believers. Missionary discourse can expand this community not simply by destroying other beliefs—though of course it does this, and sometimes crudely—but by bringing other narratives into itself, by subsuming their truth into the anagogic truth of Christian allegory.[105] This social activity is the *effective truth* of Christian allegory, as distinct from the *interpretive truth* it wishes to reveal.

We might pause here to take note of a logical structure essential to the allegorical machine. If the original function of allegory is to animate the words of the Hebrew Bible with the spirit of the New Testament so that the former comes to signify the coming of Christ in advance, then in missionary discourse, traditions seemingly in competition with Christianity can turn out to have been obscurely about Christian salvation all along. This temporal quirk gives us a clue to a deeper constitutive structure that would seem to rule out allegory as a viable mode of reading for a secular text: the allegorical meaning that seems to emerge from the reading of a text must instead have been posited in advance. What emerges from the allegorical reading, in other words, is precisely the interpretive a priori (prior with regard to any particular reading, but belated in relation to the text itself), which has miraculously circled around to become the endpoint of interpretation. Augustine is actually quite frank about this:

> Whoever, therefore, thinks that he understands the divine scriptures or any part of them so that it does not build the double love of God and of our neighbor does not understand it at all. Whoever finds a lesson there useful to the building of charity, *even though he has not said what the author may be shown to have intended in that place*, has not been deceived, nor is he lying in any way.[106]

The biblical text must always "turn out" to mean something that was programmed in advance. Only faith prevents allegory from collapsing into tautology.

The scandal here is not for Christian allegory, for which the centrality of faith was hardly a secret. Instead, what is unmasked by Augustine's exposition is fundamental to interpretation itself. And in fact it is hardly a revelation today that interpretation is no more than the strategic—one might substitute "political" or "pedagogical"—arrest of the movement of signification, the attempt to center the infinite play of the chain of signifiers, to stem the flow of meaning in a way that is never justified by the text "in itself." But to leave things at this, to return to this fact anxiously, repeatedly, to pile precautions on top of hesitations, to try at all costs to avoid the accusation of naïveté (ultimately, to seek escape from this breathless interior through an unjustifiable leap that then must assume monstrous proportions), betrays a certain fear. Not a fear of error, of accidentally making a claim that cannot be rigorously justified, but a fear of truth. Here again we might turn to Hegel's critique of Kant in *Phenomenology of Spirit*. The rigorous exclusion of the thing-in-itself from cognition, the limiting of experience to the phenomenal realm in the interest of avoiding the naïve trap of mistaking the phenomenon for the thing-in-itself, all bespeak a fear of error. But what is in fact excluded here, since the procedure "presupposes that cognition which, since it is excluded from the [noumenal realm], is surely outside of the truth as well" is even the possibility of an encounter with truth.[107] The absence of the guarantee of truth is made over into the guarantee of the absence of truth. For the same reason, it is not enough to point to the strategic function of the transcendental signified while limiting oneself rigorously to the interior of a signifying system whose subordination to that signified demands constant vigilance. In this way the error of confusing the signifier with the signified can be avoided. But what is ruled out in advance is not only naïveté but what truth naïveté might encounter.

This critique of interpretive skepticism does nothing, however, to resolve the dilemma of interpretive tautology—a problem for all interpretation, brought to a level of self-consciousness by the allegorical tradition. For a solution we must return to the notion of effective truth derived above from Augustine's discussion of allegory. As we have seen, the anagogic truth put into question by interpretive skepticism is not the only truth of the allegorical machine. Faith seems to be a mere prop supporting the production of interpretive truth, preventing the allegorical circle from collapsing into tautology. But the production of faith is in fact the very truth of that circle. A signifying system that seems to be supported by an external belief is in fact oriented toward producing that belief as its effective truth. The paradox lies in the fact that the truth is in the process (the production of faith) only to the extent that truth is believed to be in the product (the produced interpretation). The effective truth toward which the system is oriented can only be generated if quite a different (interpretive) truth is aimed at by the subject caught up in it. The lesson here is that the anagogic truth, which appeared in relation to the effective truth to be merely a secondary and mystified truth, cannot be simply abandoned once its essentially unjustifiable nature is recognized. Without it, the effective truth becomes a mere demand and ultimately an appeal to force. Allegory is in the end nothing more than a rhetoric, but a rhetoric whose logic is founded on a commitment to Truth.

In spite of everything, we imagine ourselves to live in one of those eras when, in Hegelian terms, "antithesis is in abeyance."[108] History, in the form of the contradictions and tensions that threaten to rupture a social totality from the inside and emerge from its ruins as a new form of ethical life, is successfully kept at bay, and subjectivity exists at a remove from the possibility of history as anything other than the static passage of time punctuated by disaster, the aimless flipping of blank pages interleaved with unrelated and inexplicable atrocities. There is no way of knowing, from within the present, if our current experience of history reflects a real stasis or whether, on the contrary, the famously ahistorical or antihistorical character of the postmodern age is no more than a fantasy, a defense against a history that lurks on the edge of consciousness, against a nightmare that has taken refuge just beyond the streetlamps of neoliberal discourse.[109] Readers will recognize in what follows an approach, generally in line with a tradition in which Theodor Adorno and Fredric Jameson mark pivotal moments, that challenges this apparent separation of the subject (to make explicit what is often assumed, the First-World subject) from history. As Adorno bluntly puts it, "History is the content of artworks."[110] This dictum should not be confused with historicism in the ordinary sense, which often pretends as if it were enough simply to situate literary works in their own moment in empirical history, as though in themselves literary works were merely existent and absolved from becoming.[111] But the meaning of any literary work that is still vital remains fundamentally open to history. This is the meaning (quite aside from any preference for a certain incompletion of form, what Schlegel called *Härte* or roughness) of Schlegel's pronouncement that the "real essence" of "the romantic kind of poetry"—that is, literature in the modern sense—is that it "should forever be becoming." The Brazilian critic Roberto Schwarz points out, for example, that the great nineteenth-century novelist Machado de Assis had not been a particularly important writer before 1964. But nothing new was discovered in 1964 about Machado's "context" that had not been known before; rather, the military coup of 1964 intervened directly in the meaning of Machado's great late novels.[112] The method for drawing out this continuous historical sedimentation of meaning in Jameson's introduction to *The Political Unconscious*—possibly the last word in the allegorical tradition—cannot simply be applied as a guarantee of truth, nor can it establish, for those who are inclined against it, an "ultimately determining instance" that could justify interpretation once and for all.[113] But the anagogic truth of the Hegelian tradition—narrative as the symptom of history—will here be aimed at with all sincerity. The effective truth will have to be sought elsewhere.

It might still be objected that this framework for the readings that follow—no matter how aware of its own functioning—is merely a secularization of a Christian hermeneutic. Indeed, it would not be the first time that a Marxist perspective has been derided as secretly religious. Without wanting to enmesh ourselves too deeply in Slavoj Žižek's attempt to rescue the Christian legacy from "fundamentalist freaks,"[114] we might concede an element of truth in the accusation while pointing out that its basic falseness resides in the word "merely." To say that this framework "merely" secularizes Christian allegory implies that what constitutes Christianity is not a particular faith but rather a rhetorical structure whose content might as well be temporal politics as eternal glory—a gesture that empties out the content of Christianity to the point that one might as well accept the accusation as refute it. Further, the whole structure becomes something other than it had been once the relationship between effective and anagogic truth is made explicit and fully assumed—though one may always, in retrospect, see that the new structure was fully present in the old, just as one now reads Hegel through Marx. In the readings that follow, the paradox of the framework laid out above is fully operative; we have tried to show that it is also inevitable. It is legitimate, finally, to insist on calling this structure "secularized Christianity," but only if one is willing to admit that all interpretation is, in this sense, fundamentally religious: aiming at Truth, but producing a community of agreement.

One senses, however, that the objection "Marxism = secularized religion" goes beyond simple questions of method. One might treat this equation as a misperception to be dispelled or, with Žižek, to be endorsed in a particular way, but for the moment we can restrict ourselves to pointing out that with regard to the particular problems such an equation means to imply (a rigid teleology, a myth of salvation, a corruptible priesthood, a cult of infallibility, recourse to a "greater good" that justifies atrocities carried out in its name), market liberalism (with its teleology of development, the "sin" and "redemption" of Third-World corruption and structural adjustment programs, a technocracy acting entirely in the interests of the core economies, a discourse that automatically represents its own failures as pathological rather than structural, and an utter indifference to human suffering inflicted in the name of "open markets" and "economic efficiency") has much more to worry about than Marxism. Recent work by Third-World-oriented theologians has begun to notice that in terms of its formal procedures, "the discourse of the World Bank's analysis and policy prescriptions for Africa closely resembles the discourse of fundamentalist theology."[115] If Marxism retains anything at all from the Christian tradition, it is precisely what is lacking in market fundamentalism: the Pauline doctrine of universal love.[116]

Utopian Generations

The last moment of the analysis begun here has to be completed anew in each chapter: so little can there be a gapless theory of literature that at this point even the relatively few works addressed in this book refuse to be theorized in precisely the same terms. This apparently innocuous warning might be radicalized into a thoroughgoing questioning of the categories that organize this book. Certainly it would not be hard to find examples of what is commonly called modernism and of literature written during the heyday of the African independence movements that would fit into our schema uncomfortably at best. Just as surely, the dynamic elaborated above can be discerned in other contexts altogether. It seems we are presented with two incompatible options. The first, nominalist option would be to identify the problem with categorization as such: there is no such thing as modernist literature or African literature; there are only works. The other, stereo-typically idealist one, would be to say that any work is modernist or African only if and insofar as it conforms to the ideas sketched out above. Caught between these two unsatisfactory options, we might then find ourselves in the predicament of Paul de Man, whose title "Literary History and Literary Modernity" contained "no less than two . . . absurdities—a most inauspicious beginning."[117] One of the lessons of that essay and its sequel, "Lyric and Modernity," was that once a partic-ular tendency is established as constitutive of a literary-historical entity (say, mod-ernism, or postcolonial literature), not only will exceptions immediately spring to mind, but the tendency in question will suddenly be found at work in one form or another throughout literary history. Isn't the dynamic laid out above as constitutive of modernism a feature of literary language more generally (Herrick's "careless shoestring," for example, reproducing the logic of the fragment, of the humble thing as the little piece of the Real)? And isn't the "postcolonial" refusal or evacuation of this logic an equally perpetual impulse, indeed virtually implied by the first? Our own theorization, after all, was authorized by a reference to Hegel, for whom postcolonial literature did not exist and who had rather discred-itable things to say about Africa.

There are several ways to answer this. The easiest would be to take refuge in the dialectic of quantity and quality: at the point where an occasional feature becomes an organizing principle we must establish some sort of break. A more interesting solution is suggested by Fredric Jameson's recent suggestion that "the canon, or Literature as such . . . is simply modernism."[118] This is to say that the canonization of high modernism in the United States after World War II effec-tively decided the terms by which all literature was to be evaluated, so that "liter-ary history" in effect becomes the prehistory of modernism. The new critics, in other words, effectively repeat the founding gesture of the romantics with regard to literature itself: the moment modernism comes to exist, it is discovered always to have existed. But this second option—which has the advantage of both preserv-ing and trumping de Man's insights, since the features he finds throughout liter-ary history are precisely those associated with "literary modernity"—in fact relies on the first. As we saw in our discussion of Lyotard and modernism, it is only in the light of the break that the break can be deconstructed. Horkheimer and Adorno's *Dialectic of Enlightenment,* for example, which traces that dialectic back to Homer, could not have been written without the prior isolation of the Enlightenment as a discrete object of analysis and critique. That the deconstruction of literary history relies on literary history is trivial and quasi-tautological; more consequent is the fact that the conclusions drawn from the deconstructive moment continue to presuppose what has been deconstructed. The point here is that while literary-historical categories cannot be rigorously sustained, neither is there any perspective that is rigorously free of dependence on them. We must, in other words, be vigilant in our use of literary categories even as we have little choice but to use them. The tendencies we have theorized under the names of modernism and African literature from the moment of independence may in fact be only two strands in a much more complex history and may, as the title of this book implies, be discernible at other times and other traditions entirely. When we try to be rigorous about defining them as positive entities, modernism and African literature tend (like capital and labor or the First and Third Worlds) to evaporate before our very eyes. But what the preceding pages have attempted is not a description of two positive entities but the exploration of a negative one, the rift that separates them. What we have outlined, in other words, is a relationship, one that exists not only between modernism and African literature but within modernism (between, say, Proust and Dos Passos), within African literature (say, Mia Couto and Sembène Ousmane), and within individual national literatures (Wole Soyinka and Femi Osofisan, or Dos Passos and Mike Gold). Further, when viewed from the perspective of the postmodern recedence of the utopian horizon, as we shall have the opportunity to do in the conclusion, both strands currently under consideration appear thoroughly modernist. This is not, however, a hopeless situation. Instead, the caution it recommends is the best justification for the practice of literary interpretation.

But to which texts does one turn? The works that appear here do so not because of their canonicity or potential canonicity, but according to a logic that will unfold from chapter to chapter. While it would be foolish to claim, given the above, that there will no arbitrariness in our selection of texts, it should be equally clear that we are not interested in "typical" works, good positive examples of this or that literary tendency: any "good example" is necessarily inadequate, only imperfectly embodying an ideal whose existence is only notional. Rather than looking for good examples, we will turn first to works that constitute an "event" in the sense proposed by Alain Badiou—the exception that breaks out of and reorganizes an existing order and is therefore at one and the same time both absolutely particular and (with regard to the field it pertains to) absolutely universal.[119] The procedure is therefore not one of scanning the literary order for representative works but of seeking out those texts which, in reconstituting the field of possibilities at a single blow, constitute an event. Under this criterion the choices of Joyce and Achebe are nearly unavoidable—so much so that, as will have not escaped notice, our "theory of modernism and African literature" is, thus far, at least partly a theory of Joyce and Achebe.[120]

So fundamental, in fact, was the impact of each of these authors that the difficulty now becomes finding texts that manage to escape the dominion their most revolutionary works exerted once they became institutionalized—and it should be kept in mind that this dominion extends as much into a work's past (under the sign of its "precursors") as it does into the future of its "influence." The first thing to look for would be texts that self-consciously attempt such a break, and we find ready examples in the most adventurous work of Ngugi wa Thiong'o, whose theater experiments explicitly reject every element of Achebean decorum up to and including the use of European languages, and in the work of Wyndham Lewis, possibly the only of Joyce's contemporaries to have been unimpressed with him in an interesting way. It is not surprising that the most successful of their works—Lewis's *The Childermass* and Ngugi's Kamiriithu theater projects—are decidedly marginal texts in our contemporary canon. They are not only directly partisan works, which itself accounts for part of their marginality, but they reject the very coordinates on which critical common sense is founded. Further, we should note that while there is no direct antagonism between the works of Joyce and Achebe (indeed, they seem to share the same project, even the same "postcolonial" canon; their opposition only emerges at the formal level outlined in the foregoing pages), something different happens at the level of their opposites: Ngugi's Marxism and Lewis's proto-fascism, each the force behind their respective literary projects, are radically opposed.

If there is no obvious antagonism between Joyce and Achebe, however, the reason now becomes easier to discern: while Ngugi and Lewis occupy the same terrain of the political, the Joycean and Achebean projects are marginal with regard to each other. Subjectivity, whose centrality to Joycean language is obvious on even the most superficial reading, is precisely the problem that Achebe deliberately and rigorously excludes—in fact, as we shall see, the rigorous bracketing of subjectivity is one of Achebe's most essential stylistic decisions. On the other hand, historical movement (as Abiola Irele has emphasized, the heart of Achebe's works)[121] is marginalized in Joyce's work—in *Ulysses* by the formal limitations imposed by the single day. We will return to this phenomenon in the next chapter, but for now it may suffice to imagine that Lukács, as suspicious as he was of *Ulysses*, would have been able to work *Arrow of God* into the genealogy of the historical novel with little difficulty. The antagonism between Joyce and Achebe lies not at the level of the texts themselves but in what terrains they ground themselves in.

We find, then, that we have generated three categories: politics, subjectivity, and history. These three possible axes, whose centrality to a particular text determines the possibilities open to it, are in some degree incommensurate with each other; the relationships among them cannot be entirely symmetrical. The first thing one would say from a Hegelian perspective is that history is transcendent in relation to the other two categories: subjectivity and politics exist only within history. In that case it would seem that subjectivity and politics are history in mediated form. However, this same move could be made from the perspective of the other two categories as well. From a psychoanalytic perspective, history and politics are only possible on the basis of the structure of subjectivity, however minimal this structure may be; and politics as such, the structure of social antagonism, occupies much the same position in the theory of hegemony. Which of the three categories is transcendent with regard to the others is therefore a choice, and one of some moment. Having cast our methodological bet with history, it remains to be seen how these categories are to be ordered. Simply saying that history is transcendent with regard to the other two categories is insufficient, since subjectivity and politics can evidently not be reduced to the same genus. While subjectivity only exists in history, politics in a sense *is* history. History only acquires content through human practice; politics is history concretely mediated. It is not, then, that politics and subjectivity are history in mediated form, but that politics is the mediation between the subject and history, and thus "higher" (that is, more concrete) and more likely to display antagonisms that are latent in more abstract moments. The antagonism we have been charting in this introduction will therefore deepen as we move across our three categories: from subjectivity to history to politics.

Our grid, however, is incomplete. We are lacking both a text that performs the Achebean evacuation of the sublime on the terrain of subjectivity—in other words, one that, paired with Joyce, would reproduce the dialectic between subjectivity and history within the realm of subjectivity—and one that, conversely, embodies the structure of the modernist sublime on the terrain of history. Whatever we find will be anomalous: since part of the very problem of the sublime as a utopian moment is that it confines itself to the realm of a subjective compensation, what kind of text will break with the sublime while remaining on the ground of subjectivity? And, conversely, what on earth could we call an "historical sublime" when the sublime itself is predicated on the suppression of history? Here must we turn neither to canonical nor to marginal works but to two "minor masterpieces" which, while tangential with regard to the dominant concerns of modernism or the literature of African independence, nonetheless bring out possibilities that went unnoticed in the dominant works: the novels of Ford Madox Ford, "historical" in a way that Lukács surely would not have recognized, and Cheikh Hamidou Kane's *L'aventure ambiguë*, which replaces the sublime with the notion, itself highly ambivalent, of authenticity.[122] It must be emphasized once more that the procedure here has not been to juxtapose or compare works that are in some obvious way similar or that have evident genetic relationships with each other. What would that show? Rather, the pairings—Joyce and Kane, Ford and Achebe, Lewis and Ngugi—will construe each of their texts as part of a larger totality. More precisely, each pairing will play out, with increasing intensity, the dialectic sketched out above, which ultimately hinges on the status of utopia. Along all three axes, utopia is a space opened up only in the end to be foreclosed. But what is impossible for modernism (what can be understood only by entering into each work's particular mode of the sublime, its mystified or inarticulate expression of an inchoate representational and political desire) appears more or less clearly as a possibility in African literature of the independence period—but a possibility that contains its own negation, the seeds of its own failure.

The historical situation of neither of these periods is our own: that the utopian longing embodied in each of these texts seems naïve from a perspective that takes in the actual futures of both of these literary moments—World War II and neocolonial Africa—is an index of this fact. The unique danger of our present moment, with the disintegration of the Second World and the apparently secure victory of capitalism over all points on the globe, is that the globalization of the "free market" threatens to dress a unique historical moment in the raiment of an anthropological universal, canceling in advance any discussion of social, economic, or political alternatives. As Hardt and Negri suggest in *Empire*—a text which, despite limitations we will turn to in our final chapter, suggests the possibility of a new utopian generation—we may be witnessing the construction of a new form of global sovereignty whose domain would extend infinitely, not only geographically over the entire globe, but also temporally, ideologically projecting itself backward and forward into eternity. But the question of the future is still an urgent one, or ought to be; in our final chapter we will return to the question of our own future. In the meantime, it is good to remember that the future has sometimes seemed quite near. On the longest view—say, on the scale of Benjamin's "Messianic time," where each moment brings the possibility of revealing "a secret agreement between past generations and the present one"[123]—perhaps the longing of the texts examined here will turn out to have been prophetic after all.

PART ONE

Subjectivity

CHAPTER TWO

Ulysses: The Modernist Sublime

Each of the African works we will be addressing in this book holds a more or less explicit dialogue with its own contemporary history and maintains before it the horizon of the future—the "future citadel" that will fascinate Cheikh Hamidou Kane's characters—as a question to be kept open. Meanwhile the problem of Ford Madox Ford's novels is a mode of narration that would do full justice to historical trauma, and Wyndham Lewis, apparently in spite of himself, keeps introducing history into the eternal afterlife. But while Irish history is explicitly thematized in James Joyce's *Ulysses* (and of course characters, events, and places in *Ulysses* cannot help but be historical in the banal sense), any sense of historical movement is foreclosed. The infamous early Marxist commentaries on *Ulysses*, like those of Lukács and Karl Radek, though they expressed it in the form of a criticism, were surely right in pointing to the static quality of *Ulysses*, whose single-day form, as Franco Moretti has observed, finally insists that all days are the same.[1] *Ulysses* deliberately frustrates any attempt to speculate beyond the last page. The absence of any hint of the political future—a violent struggle for Irish independence from the Easter Rising of 1916 to the Anglo-Irish treaty of 1921—is all the more astounding when one considers that much of *Ulysses* was actually written during that period.[2] If Achebe's writing (which oriented us toward our second axis of History) develops its historical perspective in part from a third-person viewpoint whose circumspection with regard to individual subjectivity is strictly enforced, *Ulysses* takes a diametrically opposite approach: the "end of a meta-language" forces language from history back into the subject—initially and finally the identifiable fictional subjects Stephen, Bloom, and Molly, but also the increasingly abstract and unstable subject positions that proliferate from "Aeolus" to "Ithaca."[3]

This very ahistoricism or stasis—paralysis, to use Joyce's own word for it—can and should be read historically, and recent writing on Joyce has benefited from a reintroduction of historical specificity that was missing from much earlier criticism. In a well-known talk he gave in 1907, Joyce informed his audience that "for so many centuries the Englishman has done in Ireland only what the Belgian is doing today in the Congo Free State."[4] It speaks volumes about the history of Joyce criticism that it was unable to engage substantially with the colonial context of *Ulysses* until the 1970s, a blockage that was not really broken until a substantial literature on a postcolonial Joyce emerged in the mid-1990s. This is all the more remarkable in that the British occupation and its effects are explicitly present throughout *Ulysses*; recent Joyce criticism has had no trouble finding virtually endless affinities between Joyce's work and postcolonial literature or in reading Joyce through postcolonial theorists.

But historical content is not the same as historical movement, and such an approach can only go so far: Fanon the critic of the nationalist bourgeoisie is perfectly applicable, while Fanon the theorist of revolutionary violence is considerably less so.[5] Enda Duffy's ingenious decision to read question-and-answer form of the "Ithaca" episode absolutely literally, as a kind of "police interrogation" that reveals a "massive regime of surveillance of the colonial state" (palpably present elsewhere in *Ulysses*), is a case in point.[6] On one hand, this startling perspective gives new significance to a number of important passages in the episode. On the other, the conceit does not illuminate uniformly. In the schema Joyce circulated, the episode's technique of "catechism" is not a particular content but a form for which all kinds of content can be supplied, of which police interrogation, medical exam, bureaucratic inquiry, charismatic pedagogy or textbook quiz, psychoanalysis, legal cross-examination, sociological questionnaire, opinion poll, marketing research, or religious catechism are among the possible candidates. The more or less "vulgar" or thematic postcolonial approaches to *Ulysses*, while absolutely welcome as a corrective to the hasty universalism of much earlier criticism, tend eventually to rub up against the text's own universal ambitions. The "Ithaca" example, to which we will return, is as much "about" the reification of language as it is about the particular uses to which language is put in the Dublin of 1904, though these are often crucial.[7]

All this is not to say that the semiperipheral condition of Joyce's Ireland is not decisive but that its determination is more mediated and formal than thematic readings would suggest. A number of possibilities arise, none of them mutually exclusive. One might point here to Seamus Deane's reading of the violence done to the form of the English novel as a symbolic reconquering of colonized territory.[8] Or to the way in which the palpable incompleteness on the Irish semiperiphery of processes that are already completely hegemonic in the metropole (an example thematized in *Ulysses* is the way gossip still competes with mass communication as the dominant medium of communication) produces frictions between institutions and ways of behaving that tangibly interfere with and defamiliarize each other in everyday life, rendering any cozy realism unrealistic. Or one might see in the imposition of external unities—the day, the Homeric parallel, the system of correspondences—a sign that there can be no internal unity to a story set in colonized territory; that is, territory whose history is determined from the outside. And while one might well, along with Moretti, see the recycling of advertising imagery (that is, the fetishization of the commodity and of consumption to the near exclusion of production and labor) as symptomatic of a general crisis or internal contradiction in Capital itself, it must also be seen as symptomatic of a situation where local industry, as Joyce was well aware, had been systematically gutted by the colonizing power.

But this reversal works in the other direction as well. Since the peculiarities of cultural, economic, and political life on the semiperiphery are rooted in its marginal relationship to Capital, the choices faced by writers on the semiperiphery are symptomatic of Capital itself as well as of the semiperipheral situation. The coexistence of residual and emergent cultural forms, for example, is more intense in the periphery but not unique to it. Similarly, the need to impose external unities is symptomatic not only of a colonized history but also of the dominance of the market. Under capitalism the market is the external finality of any and all endeavors, which themselves become arbitrary as to their particular content; therefore verisimilitude and internal narrative coherence become less and less compatible.[9] We shall have more to say in the final chapter about the choices imposed on writers on the semiperiphery by this movement back and forth between capitalism as a totality and its local effects. Meanwhile, while both moments need to be taken into account, the emphasis in our current chapter will be on the former, on historicizing *Ulysses* within the history of capitalism as a whole rather than in the history of Irish colonialism. The latter, however, will be assumed rather than demonstrated to be a condition of possibility of Joyce's modernism, a degree of dislocation with regard to hegemonic structures—expressed negatively in Stephen's famously bitter charactarization of Irish art as the "cracked looking-glass of a servant"—that is essential for the production of the kind of defamiliarizing language we find in *Ulysses*.

Let us take it as axiomatic, then, that any consequent historicization of *Ulysses* must begin from the question of form. But this imperative is not sufficient; to Fredric Jameson's list of the three "boring" ways to read *Ulysses* (the mythical, which mistakes an organizational framework for an interpretation; the psychoanalytical, which neglects to historicize the Oedipal situation even as *Ulysses* itself does not; and the ethical, which reduces *Ulysses* to a banal personal and familial drama)[10] we must add a fourth, what we might call the subversive or carnivalesque approach, which views the stylistic explosion of *Ulysses* as primarily disturbing the limits of univocal language or the phallogocentric subject. This mode of criticism is precisely boring rather than false or illegitimate for two reasons. First, while *Ulysses* is subversive of these things, this does not in itself mean it is subversive of anything else. The past twenty or so years have demonstrated that the critique of the subject is coincident with the movement of contemporary Capital, not contrary to it; the decentered subject needs to go shopping even more than the old centered one did. In fact, Moretti draws precisely the opposite conclusion that the proliferation of styles implies the absolute irrelevance of the aesthetic sphere to the social world, even as compensation: "*Ulysses* is not, therefore, a work 'bristling with possiblities,' as Eco would have it: the idea of 'possibility' that it communicates has lost all concreteness and objectivity . . . and has become a subjective and merely formal phantasm. In *Ulysses*, everything is possible because everything is indifferent."[11] The second problem is that this approach flattens the differences among the episodes, which all now appear to do the same thing, even if some of them do it better than others. (This is of course true of Moretti's counterargument as well; if the proliferation of styles primarily functions as a kind of premonitory parody of the postmodern withdrawal of the signifier, then Joyce could have accomplished the same thing using a whole different set of styles.)[12] But given the entirely distinct pleasures to be derived from immersion in each episode, surely it is not sufficient to speculate about the function of style as such in *Ulysses*; rather, the function of style is a question to be opened up anew with every episode.

"Eumaeus" and "Ithaca" initially appear to be parodies along the lines of the "Nausicaa" episode. But, unlike "Nausicaa," what they are supposed to be parodying is far from clear. "Ithaca," as we suggested earlier, evokes several different genres simultaneously without being reducible to any one of them, while "Eumaeus" has been taken as a parody of anything from Bloom's own language (first suggested by Hugh Kenner) to Jameson's whimsical decision to see in it an indifferent parody of Henry James.[13] The difficulty in finding an original for the respective styles of these two episodes derives from the fact that while both can be tremendously funny, neither is genuinely parodic. Both the humor and the poignancy of these episodes derive from the decision to isolate not a particular style or author but a tendency inherent in language itself at a particular historical moment and to turn this tendency into a principle that is then taken to its own limit. What these principles might be for "Eumaeus" and "Ithaca" is not immediately clear, although they are evidently diametrically opposed. Where the style of "Eumaeus" is elaborately flabby, that of "Ithaca" is deliberately terse; if "Eumaeus" takes inaccuracy to absurd levels, then "Ithaca" satirizes precision; while "Eumaeus" delves into a language that indefatigably assimilates events to its own idiosyncratic everydayness, the language of "Ithaca" flees from the phenomenal level to narrate events at registers as foreign as possible from everyday experience. The schema, which give "narrative (old)" for "Eumaeus" and "catechism (impersonal)" for "Ithaca," don't tell us anything we don't know from a first reading of the text. "Error" and "accuracy" are possible candidates, it being understood that in "Eumaeus" error names a path toward meaning while accuracy in "Ithaca" often produces none. Cognate with these, "subjectivity" and "objectivity" are more banal but have the advantage of not only conforming well to the formal tendencies of the episodes but also naming precisely the gap that the sublime itself was to bridge—in its modernist variant, in the subject's momentary encounter with, in "Ithaca"'s words, "the presupposed intangibility of the thing in itself."[14]

We recall from the introduction that Lukácsian reification describes a process by which subjectivity comes into being by way of its own constitution of the object-world as absolutely external to itself. The object-world can then be marshaled and manipulated by construing it as a system of laws. At the moment that subject and object are thus constituted as external to each other, any possibility of intervening directly in the being of the object-world is foreclosed—even though its original constitution as a system of laws was just such an intervention. As we saw in the introduction, the sublime in all its variants is an attempt to leap over this divide while leaving its terms unaffected. Rather than by placing the commodity (exchange value) into the cycle of production and consumption, the modernist sublime turns to the thing in itself which, as infungible use value—Stephen Hero's ecstatic recognition of "*that* thing which it is"—gains a utopian valence. The characteristic movement of the modernist sublime was from the apparent concreteness of a mutely infungible particular thing to a totality that is abstract and therefore empty. This emptiness, however, is not simply false but testifies to the actual abstractness of immediate experience, which can no longer sustain the more concrete conception of the social totality that underlay classical realism. The various modes of modernist defamiliarization jolt the experience of the meaningless material fragment onto the plane of the sublime, where it comes to signify the immediate presence of Being itself. But since the Being thus conjured is empty of any content save the arbitrary one of the fragment that conjured it, this quintessential modernist gesture is a failure. Rather than signifying totality, modernist defamiliarization stands in for the lack of a concrete conception of the social totality, and its ideological nature is revealed in its infinite repeatability.

The allegorical content of both "Eumaeus" and "Ithaca" is reification itself. In the context of these episodes it will be useful to recall briefly Heidegger's idealist account of modernity (itself readily subsumed within Lukács's materialist presentation), which usefully theorizes reification under different aspects. Two of the most important of these are *Gerede* and *Gestell*. *Gerede*, "idle talk," language unmoored from any relation to truth, is a symptom of the estrangement of subjectivity from what determines it, and *Gestell*, "enframing," names the conversion of Being, to which human subjectivity was still essential, into a dead world of manipulable objects. *Gerede*, to put things even more crudely, names reification from the side of the subject; *Gestell*, from the side of the object.[15] The languages of "Eumaeus" and "Ithaca," rather than parodying the idiolect of some particular subject, dramatize these two possibilities and bring each of them to a kind of linguistic limit. Nevertheless, against these reified backdrops, meta-events—the narrative revelations that give *Ulysses* its affective charge—continue to assemble themselves into the text's sublime objects, temporarily bridging the very divide that the episodes' language represents. The subjective error-language of "Eumaeus" fumbles for the object, while the rigors of "Ithaca" reach from objectivity to the subject—with what success and what consequences remains to be seen. Ultimately, however, the machinery that produces these meta-events takes its revenge, laying bare the emptiness of the sublime gesture.

In the introduction, we took a shortcut by identifying Stephen Dedalus's aesthetic theory with Joyce's understanding of his own early practice—hardly an indefensible move given the overtly autobiographical nature of Stephen's character, but one that ultimately must take account of the ironies produced by the literary frame.[16] What is certain is that this understanding cannot be simply applied to *Ulysses*, which subsumes the epiphanic method within a grander strategy. For a formal description of the peculiar excitement of reading *Ulysses* one probably cannot do better than Kenner's well-known formula of an "aesthetics of delay" in which narrative temporality is superseded by the pace at which the narrative is reconstructed by a reader. The real events in *Ulysses* do not take place at the level of narrative: however interesting we may find the narrative of Stephen, Bloom, and Molly, our interest does not derive primarily from the events themselves, which would be banal if arranged into a linear narrative, but from the intensity of the movement in which we discover them.[17] The canonical example would be the shadow of a cloud that passes over Stephen in "Telemachus" and the one that darkens Bloom's morning in "Calypso"; neither has particular narrative significance, but the discovery that this is the same cloud constitutes a major event in the reading of *Ulysses*. Similarly for a sentence in "Telemachus" describing Stephen's mother's death, repeated with minor modifications a few pages later; the sentence is insignificant in itself, but its repetition reveals to us that Stephen is not simply obsessing about his mother's death but also about how to make a nice sentence out of it—and indeed, the first version turns out, on a second reading, to have been awkward and tentative. The space mapped out in "Wandering Rocks," the fact that Corny Kelleher is a police informer, the famous seconds of missing time in Bloom's morning after the shock of seeing Boylan's letter; none of these is particularly interesting in itself.[18] What we learn from the cloud could have been accomplished with the word "meanwhile." But in *Ulysses* each of these acquires the status of a revelation.

In *Ulysses* the modernist sublime is taken to its limit. Not just any object or scene or event, but the entire narrative fabric is defamiliarized, jolted onto a plane where, quite aside from any naïve symbolism, it seems to signify beyond itself. The narrative of *Ulysses* is arbitrary in its details (even Bloom's decision to pee is determined by a Homeric parallel) and insignificant in its broad outline. If Kant's sublime drives us toward an apprehension of the absolute, then in "Eumaeus" the modernist sublime offers us an "experience"—incredibly, the word is an overstatement—in a cabman's shelter. But as with Williams's wheelbarrow, we experience it as having tremendous import—and indeed a great deal of Joyce criticism, reading this experience of the text back into the narrative itself, has taken it for granted that this particular day is tremendously significant. But like the famous question that seems to haunt Stephen ("What is that word known to all men?"), any particular significance would be banal—only in its emptiness does the mystery have any allure.[19] The great scramble after Ulyssean facts is a testimony to the surcharge of signification that attaches to the narrative details; the general failure of these facts to add much to our understanding of the book is a symptom of their emptiness.

That the sought-after signification is ultimately empty, however, does not mean that it is simply false, and it is not nearly enough to say that *Ulysses* ultimately refuses such grand signification because it demands it at the same time. In this chapter we will not be primarily interested in adding to Joyce scholarship in the usual sense but in demonstrating how contradictory tendencies in *Ulysses* can be composed into a single thought. From this perspective, essentialist readings that seek in *Ulysses* a profound meaning and anti-essentialist ones that find in *Ulysses* primarily the lack of a unifying meaning—a lack of closure that can be seen as either liberating or ideological—only assume their dimensions of truth in relation to each other. In a first, utopian moment, *Ulysses* short-circuits the rift between subjectivity and the object-world, miraculously imbuing the accidents of daily life with inscrutable significance. For all the reasons touched on in the introduction, this Utopia fails to bear on an actuality for which it can only compensate. But in a second moment this failure makes itself manifest. "Needs," the dreaded old verb of ethical criticism, applies properly in *Ulysses* not to characters but to formal events. As mentioned a moment ago, Bloom "needs" to urinate in "Ithaca" because of the parallel with Odysseus drawing his bow; therefore he needs to sit tight rather than "moving a motion" in "Eumaeus" so that he might later pee in "Ithaca"; this in turn produces what, as we shall see in a moment, appears to be one of the more poignant moments in *Ulysses*. The same process that imbues the narrative with significance (Bloom isn't just peeing in "Ithaca," he's drawing Odysseus's long bow, about to slay the suitors, etc.) turns out, from a different angle, to take it away, highlighting the arbitrariness of events in the narrative that are as they are and not otherwise only to satisfy an external demand. As we shall see, this contradiction—*Ulysses* as a deep well of meaning as against a *Ulysses* that refuses all final meanings—plays out in several other ways as well, from the external correspondences to the internal symmetries to the tremendous layering and cross-referencing of narrative detail that is one of the book's great achievements. An immense engine of meaning or a fascinating indexing machine? A profound meditation on the modern condition or a colossal joke? Both sides of this contradiction are partly correct, and in what follows we will try to be parallactic (or dialectical) in composing them into a single object.

"Eumaeus" used to be the most boring episode in *Ulysses*. But "Eumaeus" is one of the most stylistically intense episodes in *Ulysses*, one whose drama is in the movement of the modernist sublime and its self-deconstruction. As in many of the later episodes, the exact point of this particular style is not immediately apparent. It is difficult to convey piecemeal a quality that consists in the gradual accumulation of page after page of solecisms and painful flourishes, but the marvelous opening passage contains many of the elements that animate the "Eumaeus" style:

> Preparatory to anything else Mr Bloom brushed off the greater bulk of the shavings and handed Stephen his hat and ashplant and bucked him up generally in orthodox Samaritan fashion, which he very badly needed. His (Stephen's) mind was not exactly what you would call wandering but a bit unsteady and on his expressed desire for some beverage to drink Mr Bloom, in view of the hour it was and there being no pumps of Vartry water available for their ablutions, let alone drinking purposes, hit upon an expedient by suggesting, off the reel, the propriety of the cabman's shelter, as it was called, hardly a stonesthrow away near Butt Bridge, where they might hit upon some drinkables in the shape of a milk and soda or a mineral. But how to get there was the rub. For the nonce he was rather nonplussed but inasmuch as the duty plainly devolved upon him to take some measures on the subject he pondered suitable ways and means during which Stephen repeatedly yawned. (612–13)

Thus begins the comedy of errors that is "Eumaeus." "Preparatory to anything else" is in fact preparatory to nothing in particular, and it is not clear what would distinguish the bulk of shavings from "the greater bulk." "Orthodox Samaritan" is a contradiction in terms. The clarification "His (Stephen's) mind" serves rather to obfuscate, since the clarification is unnecessary in the first place and misplaced, since there are plenty of other confusing pronouns in the episode. When there is no water available for their "ablutions, let alone drinking purposes," this is supposed to be funny, and in fact it is, but only through a second-order optic that watches the first-order joke fail. "Expedient" and "propriety" are joco-pretentious, as are the literary touches "was the rub" and "for the nonce." "Off the reel" and "as it was called" are useless language, describing nothing that is not understood without them; "ways and means" is redundant, and, due to a misplaced modifying phrase, it seems that Stephen yawns during these means rather than during Bloom's pondering. And so on, for fifty-one more pages. The fact that the text pursues its own banality with such extraordinary energy gives the text its curious duplicity: nearly every sentence can be read as, on one hand, merely a somewhat facile pastiche of some unidentified but plainly irritating narrative style, or, on the other hand, a tour de force in which every pause (a study could be made of the commas in "Eumaeus") is followed by precisely the wrong word; where every explicit punch line fails to come off—but fails so completely and so pathetically that it is simultaneous with the actual punch line, which is precisely the foundering of the first:

> The face of a streetwalker, glazed and haggard under a black straw hat, peered askew round the door of the shelter, palpably reconnoitering on her own with the object of bringing more grist to her mill. (632)

As a jocose locution for business custom, "grist to her mill" falls flat. But as a grotesque sexual metaphor it is funny precisely because it is so obviously beyond the reach of this obtuse language, whose native humor does not extend beyond forced jocularity. In the voice of the Nameless One of "Cyclops," the prostitute seeking "grist to her mill" would be gutter humor; here it is much finer than that because it is not a joke at all, only an unnecessary circumlocution. Jokes in "Eumaeus" are not funny: "[It] threw a nasty sidelight on that side of a person's character—no pun intended" (665). But their failure is. The "Eumaeus" language is a Peter Sellers clown: every sophisticated flourish turns out to be an impeccable failure. A minor character has a "strong suspicion of nosepaint about the nasal appendage" (631). The last phrase is funny, not because "about the nasal appendage" is a witty circumlocution but because it is so preposterously unnecessary coming directly after "nosepaint." An ersatz sailor, after having taken several items out of an inner pocket, whose voluminousness has already been jocosely alluded to, "snapped the blade to and stowed the weapon as before in his chamber of horrors, otherwise pocket" (629). This time the real joke runs backward, to the same effect: explaining the epithet "chamber of horrors" ruins whatever was slightly funny in it, but this anticlimax itself is quite funny. In the same paragraph that began with the prostitute finding grist for her mill, the late edition of the *Daily Telegraph* is described in a circumlocutory embellishment—not with a straight face, which implies a purposeful deadpan, but with perfect ingenuousness—as the "pink . . . Abbey street organ." Later, describing Parnell's affair with Kitty O'Shea:

> First, it was strictly platonic till nature intervened and an attachment sprang up between them, till bit by bit matters came to a climax. (650)

The precise shape of this intervening nature, this "attachment" that "sprang up between them" and "bit by bit . . . came to a climax" will be obvious to everyone (and it is well within the ken of Bloom's habitual idiom), but any hint of reflexive awareness of this double entendre is carefully excised from the "Eumaeus" language which, far from mastering the art of double entendre, has enough trouble just keeping adjectives in the vicinity of the nouns they're supposed to modify.

Indeed, in "Eumaeus," where mistakes attain the status of rhetorical figures, the misplaced modifier is a privileged trope: there are at least five misplaced clauses in the first paragraph of the episode, and modifiers crop up in places even the most incompetent writer wouldn't put them: "The queer suddenly things he popped out with" (656). The effect can best be described as "Funny very" (629). (This tendency of adjectives to float free of their referents, of qualities to float free of any material substratum in a haze of language, is already a kind of allegory of the gap between subject and object.) The resulting temporary confusions that litter "Eumaeus" are the episode's mode of narrative defamiliarization. The texture of the "Eumaeus" language—otherwise smooth like the surface of chatter to which one is only half attentive—is constantly disturbed by misplaced fragments of language, which produce absurdities. The "Eumaeus" sentence often registers first as nonsense; it is only a moment later that the meaning resolves itself:

> He [Bloom] personally, being of a sceptical bias, believed, and didn't make the smallest bones about saying so either, that man, or men in the plural, were always hanging around on the waiting list about a lady, even supposing she was the best wife in the world and they got on fairly well together for the sake of argument, when, neglecting her duties, she chose to be tired of wedded life, and was on for a little flutter in polite debauchery to press their attentions on her with improper intent, the upshot being that her affections centred on another, the cause of many *liaisons* between still attractive married women getting on for fair and forty and younger men, no doubt as several famous cases of feminine infatuation proved up to the hilt. (655–56)

Beyond typical "Eumaeus" absurdities like "up to the hilt" (which, like "grist for her mill," is funny precisely because it's not a double entendre), the language is so garbled it is difficult to know where to begin, and yet the sentence is intelligible. Rather than enumerating all of the displacements that take place here, let us look at more or less grammatical version of the same sentence:

> Being of a sceptical bias, Bloom believed, and didn't make any bones about saying, that men were always hanging about with improper intent to press their attentions on a lady who, neglecting her duties, chose to be tired of wedded life, and was on for a little flutter in polite debauchery; the upshot being that her affections centred on another—even supposing, for the sake of argument, that she was the best wife in the world and they got on fairly well together: this, as several famous cases of feminine infatuation proved up to the hilt, was no doubt the cause of many liaisons between younger men and women getting on for fair and forty.

Like the larger narrative, "Eumaeus" would be boring indeed without its deformations. Several phrases in the original passage make no sense without a moment's pause to sort out the pieces and put them where they belong. In "Eumaeus," error's paradoxical function is to give us a new and potentially more profound mode of access to narrative events, even as it threatens initially to withhold them altogether. For this error-language to be understood a reader must posit a text that "means to say" something else: surely they didn't really get on "fairly well together for the sake of argument"; rather, we must be "supposing, for the sake of argument," that they get on fairly well. The text we understand is a hypothetical one, a negation of the language printed on the page; only in a third moment do we reconnect the two, and it is in this disjunction that both the humor and the meaning of the episode originate.

With the relentless flabbiness of the "Eumaeus" language as backdrop, narrative events that would pass by unnoticed in an overtly competent text suddenly assume tremendous importance. The content that assembles itself beneath the "Eumaeus" language is revealed in a series of glances—a guarded look, a furtive glance, a glimpse sideways; a choreography of gazes that never manage to connect—that, rather than leaping to us from the vestment of its appearance in the "Eumaeus" language, emerges with slow clarity, deriving its poignancy from its immersion in that language, which continues its delightful absurdity:

> The guarded glance of half solicitude, half curiosity, augmented by friendliness, which he gave Stephen's at present morose expression of features did not throw a flood of light, none at all in fact, on the problem as to whether he had let himself be badly bamboozled. (621)

There are more qualities here than a glance divided into halves can hold; the clause that begins "which he gave" seems to modify "friendliness" but instead modifies the glance; the lack of a "flood of light," which turns out to be no light at all, is shaped like an understatement but turns out to be an overstatement: all these are typical "Eumaeus" bloopers. But the complex "guarded glance" is all the more touching for that; the gesture (to which "solicitude," "curiosity," and "friendliness" still stick, even when the verbiage around them is discarded) almost gets lost in the absurdity of the language. But that "guarded glance" (not a careless phrase) remains, forcing us to take seriously, at the illusionistic level of our reading, Bloom's desire to understand the riddle that Stephen represents.

Soon afterward Bloom attempts another look:

> Mr Bloom determining to have a good square look at him later on so as not to appear to ... for which reason he encouraged Stephen to proceed with his eyes while he did the honours by surreptitiously pushing the cup of what was temporarily supposed to be called coffee gradually nearer him. (622)

"A good square look at him ... so as not to appear to": in other words, anything but a good square look. This (along with the misplaced modifier in "he encouraged Stephen to proceed with his eyes" and the imperfect fit of the two halves of the sentence) is more "Eumaeus" speak: but this error is not pure accident. The square look is only a determination; it never takes place. Each of Bloom's glances is furtive, indirect: if the "Eumaeus" language uses too many words, some of them are nonetheless telling. The "solicitude" of the earlier glance manifests itself here as Bloom tries to get Stephen to eat, but pushing the coffee cup is also a ruse: he wants Stephen to concentrate on something so that he can observe him more directly. Hence the "surreptitious" movement of the cup, while his eyes, not focused directly on Stephen, invite him to take it up. Stephen does not take the bait.

Bloom's first (solicitous, curious, friendly) glance is repeated, with a difference, several pages later. Bloom has just finished narrating the events of the "Cyclops" episode to Stephen, somewhat changing the tone of his retort to the citizen:

> Christ [. . .] was a jew too, and all his family, like me, though in reality I'm not. That was one for him. A soft answer turns away wrath. He hadn't a word to say for himself as everyone saw. Am I not right?
>
> He turned a long you are wrong gaze on Stephen of timorous dark pride at the soft impeachment, with a glance also of entreaty for he seemed to glean in a kind of way that it wasn't all exactly. . . (643)

The complex adjective "of timorous dark pride," though it is misplaced so that it seems at first to describe Stephen rather than Bloom's glance, is not what one expects here among the awkward phrasing of this sentence and its faltering indirection that finally falls off into ellipses. In fact, a reconstructed phrase "a long gaze of timorous dark pride, also of entreaty," with its precise description of the complex meanings behind a fleeting gesture, sounds more like the language of a *Dubliners* story than that of "Eumaeus." Stephen responds noncommittally, in language Bloom will not understand:

> — *Ex quibus*, Stephen mumbled in a noncommittal accent, their two or four eyes conversing, *Christus* or Bloom his name is, or, after all, any other, *secundum carnem*. (643)

Stephen's Latin confirms Bloom's point, and their "two or four eyes" are "conversing." But this is more likely a meaningless cliché than an indication of communication: regardless of whether their eyes are conversing, Bloom and Stephen are not. Bloom, with his "small smattering" of classical knowledge (644) will not—as is apparent from the Latin proverb (*Ubi bene, ibi patria*) that Bloom immediately flubs—understand Stephen's Latin. Once rescued from the lazy syntax, the details are telling. Timorous Bloom asks a question with a glance of entreaty, afraid that Stephen will disagree; Stephen mumbles an answer, in Latin, noncommittally. And then it is not clear where "you are wrong" belongs in this sentence: is it that Bloom expects that Stephen will think him wrong, or is it Bloom's gaze that says "you are wrong" to Stephen, thus adding an element of challenge to the "timorous dark pride" of Bloom's glance? Or, at a further remove, does "you are wrong" still refer to Bloom's attitude toward the citizen? In any case, the communion hinted at by their "conversing" eyes is everywhere negated by the details: that "they didn't see eye to eye" (656) is more literally than figuratively the truth.

In fact, Stephen, who had been "staring and rambling on to himself" (637) before Bloom's narration of his retort to the citizen, continues to be inattentive: "listening to this synopsis of things in general, Stephen stared at nothing in particular" (644). He does finally look up, and what he sees is Bloom's gaze:

> Then he looked up and saw the eyes that said or didn't say the words the voice he heard said—if you work.
>
> Count me out, he managed to remark, meaning to work.
>
> The eyes were surprised at this observation, because as he, the person who owned them pro. tem. observed, or rather, his voice speaking did: All must work, have to, together. (644)

But this still does not amount to an exchange of glances, a genuine nonverbal communication; on this level, too, Stephen remains uncommunicative. For Stephen, Bloom's expression begins and ends with his eyes: "The eyes were surprised." An expression is registered, nothing more; the same is true for the sound of Bloom's "synopsis of things in general," which is simply a "voice speaking." What is behind the eyes (and the voice) is, to Stephen, either beyond his capacities at the moment or simply of no particular interest.

The one potential candidate for a real exchange of glances is intriguing. The proprietor of the cabman's shelter is reputed to be James Fitzharris or "Skin-the-Goat," a conspirator in the assassination of a high-level Irish collaborator in Phoenix Park. Someone brings up the "park murders" and Bloom and Stephen seem to share a moment of mutual recognition:

> At this remark, passed obviously in the spirit of *where ignorance is bliss*, Mr Bloom and Stephen, each in his own particular way, both instinctively exchanged meaning glances, in a religious silence of the strictly *entre nous* variety however, towards where Skin-the-Goat, *alias* the keeper, was drawing spurts of liquid from his boiler affair. (629)

It is tempting to read this "instinctively" at face value. The anonymous comment accidentally touches on something real. Language stops. Stephen and Bloom reveal what really unites them—Irish history—in a revealing mutual glance. But Stephen has only learned of this (false) rumor a few moments earlier from Bloom (621). The "instinctively" and the "meaning glances" are only taken from stereotype (though it is possible that Bloom participates in this fantasy), and once more we are disappointed.

If glances tend to pass from Bloom to Stephen and not the reverse, Bloom does not always look toward Stephen; when he shows Stephen a photo of Molly, he looks away:

> Nevertheless, he sat tight, just viewing the slightly soiled photo creased by opulent curves, none the worse for wear, however, and looked away thoughtfully with the intention of not increasing the other's possible embarrassment while gauging her symmetry of heaving *embonpoint*. (653)

Again we have misplaced modifiers, and here the ambiguities they produce are telling. Which is "none the worse for wear": Molly's opulent curves or the soiled photo? For that matter, Molly's curves are collapsed with the creases in the picture itself ("the slightly soiled photo creased by opulent curves"); it is plain that this photo, more than a representation of Molly, is somehow transubstantiated into Molly herself. It is hard not to see Bloom's willful inattention to Stephen's presumed ogling of Molly's cleavage in relation to his earlier willful inattention (willful inattention being, of course, no inattention at all) to Boylan's visit.

However one wants to read this passage, it is clear that Bloom's immediate motive is to connect with Stephen by sharing Molly's photo as an object of desire. Although he purposefully does not watch Stephen looking at the photo, neither does he want to leave his side even though he needs to urinate: "The spirit moving him, he would much have liked to follow Jack Tar's good example . . . and satisfy a possible need by moving a motion. Nevertheless, he sat tight, just viewing the slightly soiled photo" (653). If he can arouse Stephen, he will finally have gotten a reaction out of him beyond the noncommittal. Soon after, he briefly entertains the idea of Stephen and Molly having an affair: "And why not? An awful lot of makebelieve went on about that sort of thing" (654). But this, too, fails: Stephen finally only says that "the picture was handsome" (653); there is no indication that by this Stephen means, as Bloom takes him to mean, that he finds Molly attractive.

The sexual content of Bloom's gaze—the furtiveness of Bloom's glance translating into a kind of coyness, a shy desire for Stephen's desire—is plain enough, but the desire here is more than sexual. Bloom is a man of wide acquaintance, but genuine sociability is closed off to him. The relationship with Molly is intense but attenuated. The only person in the book who could qualify as a friend of Bloom's is Richie Goulding, but Bloom seems to meet Goulding more with irritation than anything else ("Rhapsodies about damn all. Believes his own lies" [272]). In "Ithaca," we are able to discover that Bloom has not had an actual conversation in the eleven years since his son's death: a sequence of dates marking interesting discussions ends in 1893 (667). The language of the later episode—which, as we shall see, always strives toward a surface of affective flatness—registers his dismay at this fact only as a reflection on "the restriction of the . . . domain of interindividual relations" (667). But Bloom's day, no matter how many people he meets or how thoroughly and amusingly he manages to occupy himself, is profoundly lonely, making his failure to connect with Stephen, which we understand as the illusionistic content of the episode, all the more unbearable.

Bloom gives Stephen one more glance before the episode ends:

> He looked sideways in a friendly fashion at the sideface of Stephen, image of his mother, which was not quite the same as the usual blackguard type they unquestionably had an indubitable hankering after as he was perhaps not that way built. (663)

Once more error-language covers up the meaning of the gesture only that it be finally registered more profoundly. It appears at first that it is Stephen's mother "which was not quite . . . the usual blackguard type"; then perhaps it is Stephen; then we realize that it is his "sideface" that merits the impersonal "which." Then the adverbial clause "as he was perhaps not that way built" seems mysteriously to explain the hankerings of women for blackguards before we can see that it instead refers to Stephen's lack of a "blackguard type" face. Once the content of the glance is uncovered, this turns out to be a pivotal moment: Bloom has decided that Molly would not find Stephen attractive anyway. Immediately before, the positions of Bloom and Stephen had been reversed: while the episode opens with an inattentive Stephen ("who up to then had said nothing whatsoever of any kind" [615]) interrupting a voluble Bloom, it ends with an inattentive Bloom interrupting a voluble Stephen:

> These timely reflections anent the brutes of the field occupied his [Bloom's] mind, somewhat distracted from Stephen's words, while the ship of the street was manoevring and Stephen went on about the highly interesting old . . .
>   — What's this I was saying? Ah, yes! My wife, he intimated, plunging *in medias res* . . . (662)

Initially Stephen, absorbed in his own thoughts, had suddenly interrupted Bloom with a word from his obsession with betrayal: "Judas." Bloom returns the favor with his own obsession: "My wife." The positions have flipped, but Bloom and Stephen have still not managed to communicate. Bloom has constructed a new fantasy world where Stephen becomes a professional singer; Stephen answers direct questions, but goes off on tangents that Bloom imperfectly understands and to which he is imperfectly attentive.

The effect of the entire episode is played out in miniature in a brief passage:

> The vicinity of the young man he certainly relished, educated, *distingué*, and impulsive into the bargain, far and away the pick of the bunch, though you wouldn't think he had it in him . . . yet you would. (653)

This is the language of the salesman's pitch: "educated, *distingué*, and impulsive into the bargain, far and away the pick of the bunch." At a certain level one cannot help but take literally that word "bargain," and the list of Stephen's attributes is an utterly conventional collection of adjectives that, like an advertisement, carries a positive tone without saying anything about the person or product: words are chosen for their market value (*distingué*) rather than their meaning. This is commodified language in a rather more immediate sense than we usually mean. And yet underneath this language is the profoundest content of the episode, for Bloom really does, in a deeper way than its banalized expression would seem to suggest, "relish" Stephen's presence. If one can see "Eumaeus" as dramatizing what Heidegger formulated as *Gerede*, "idle talk," then it is much closer to Heidegger's interpretation of meaningless language than the stereotype of his position. While "idle talk" is useless as a discourse on truth, it nonetheless has its own truth, which is the Being-with-one-another that Bloom seeks when he tries to engage Stephen in conversation. By wallowing in a degraded language, a language that must be negated before its content appears, "Eumaeus" attempts to recover, from within the safety and complacency of an utterly reified language, the shock of this desire.

"Eumaeus" first appears as a thoroughly subjective error-language that fumbles for and fails to reach its object; in a second, ecstatic moment this failure is overcome and the content of the episode is registered all the more profoundly. This movement is what we have been calling the modernist sublime, and the tremendous significance that attaches to the recovery of an everyday experience is in line with what we earlier theorized under that name. As we suggested at the beginning of this chapter, however, it is not only an example but, together with "Ithaca," a reflexive radicalization of the modernist sublime. The ultimate failure of the sublime is not a judgment we can, invoking the critique of the sublime worked out in the introduction, impose on "Eumaeus" from the outside; it is instead inscribed in the episode itself. In "Eumaeus," the sublimity of the banal transforms unbidden into the banality of the sublime. Hegel pointed out of the supposedly ultimate and unreachable realm of the noumenon, the supersensible Idea, that there is in fact nothing more commonplace and familiar since it is in fact only a product of the thought that imagines itself unable to reach it. The banality of "Eumaeus" is of a similar order. The recovered content of the episode, rather than emerging pure and luminous from a sea of stereotypes, turns out itself to be a stereotype, a fetishized "theme," though brilliantly elaborated, of the most naïve and insipid kind: none other than a trite and entirely expected "failure to communicate" between Stephen and Bloom.[20]

The form, taking its revenge on the commonplace material on which it is forced to work, makes this all the clearer. The symmetry we noticed between the beginning of the episode (Bloom rambles; Stephen is silent; blurting out one of his obsessions, Stephen finally interrupts Bloom) and the end (Stephen rambles; Bloom is silent; blurting out one of his obsessions, Bloom finally interrupts Stephen) is neat but in conventional terms unmotivated; Stephen becomes voluble rather than taciturn simply to produce the symmetry. This is not to criticize Joyce for failing to produce Stephen's motivation; on the contrary, nothing would be more boring than to discover that somewhere Joyce had indeed managed to "motivate the device." Indeed, it would not make much difference if such a motivation were discovered. The most intense expression of Bloom's desire for Stephen is, as we noted earlier, motivated by the Homeric parallel and not by Bloom's character: Bloom "sits tight" rather than peeing in "Eumaeus" so that he might later draw Odysseus's long bow in "Ithaca." Bloom's "motivation" for resisting the urge to urinate (to sit and gaze at Stephen gazing at Molly) is from this perspective nothing more than an epiphenomenon of the form. Similarly for the elegant symmetries of the text, which appear at first to give the narrative a kind of classical inevitability; as more and more of these symmetries pile up, operating at every conceivable organizational level (without resorting to a word-counting exercise it is difficult to confirm, but it seems that many grammatical errors and lexical quirks in "Eumaeus" are repeated precisely twice), it becomes clear that their determination is, once again, wholly external to the narrative. A moment after Stephen suggests in "Eumaeus" that "Sounds are impostures. . . . Like names . . . Shakespeares were as common as Murphies" (622), a suspicious stranger, an impostor, claims to know another Simon Dedalus (not a name as common as Murphy). No sooner can Bloom say "curious coincidence" (624) than the stranger himself turns out to be named Murphy. (W. B. Murphy in the older editions, and no doubt someone has pointed out that William B. Murphy would, in the form of a bad joke, confirm the identification implied in Stephen's proleptic observation about Shakespeares and Murphies.) This is the kind of symmetry that we might find in a magical realist text, where it would be full of portent. Here, we know that it will not give up its secret, because there is none; this is the kind of symmetry the text is made of, that is all. And of course the elephant in the room is that the meeting of Stephen and Bloom, the crux of the entire episode, is also motivated only by the Homeric parallel. There is not much reason for Bloom and Stephen to end up in the same place, nor much effect either can have on the other once they do. The drama of glances itself begins to seem schematic and artificial, and ultimately even "Bloom" and "Stephen," two of the most realized characters in English-language literature, fall apart into the *actants* from which they are constructed. The fact that Joyce can produce a profound illusionistic effect out of such unpromising formal requirements is yet another testament to his genius— but eventually the logic of these requirements overpowers the illusion of meaning. This illusion, carefully constructed and hidden within the haze of "Eumaeus," is broken by that same careful construction.

The rambling, intensely subjective error-language of "Eumaeus" is followed by the mysteriously disembodied catechism of "Ithaca." Bloom boils water twice in *Ulysses*, both times in his own kitchen. The first time is in "Calypso":

> He turned from the tray, lifted the kettle off the hob and set it sideways on the fire. It sat there, dull and squat, its spout stuck out. Cup of tea soon. Good. Mouth dry. (55)

This description takes place in a comfortable and familiar temporality, more or less in real time; the action is interrupted only by Bloom's internal speech, which represents a familiar bodily desire ("Good. Mouth dry."). When Bloom makes cocoa in "Ithaca," however, we are confronted by something quite different: a reader is suddenly at sea in a mass of seemingly irrelevant data assimilated only with difficulty:

> What concomitant phenomenon took place in the vessel of liquid by the agency of fire?
>
> The phenomenon of ebullition. Fanned by a constant up-draught of ventilation between the kitchen and the chimney-flue, ignition was communicated from the faggots of precombustible fuel to polyhedral masses of bituminous coal, containing in compressed mineral form the foliated fossilized decidua of primeval forests which had in turn derived their vegetative existence from the sun, primal source of heat (radiant), transmitted through omnipresent luminiferous diathermanous ether. Heat (convected), a mode of motion developed by such combustion, was constantly and increasingly conveyed from the source of calorification to the liquid contained in the vessel, being radiated through the uneven unpolished dark surface of the metal iron, in part reflected, in part absorbed, in part transmitted, gradually raising the temperature of the water from normal to the boiling point, a rise in temperature expressible as the result of an expenditure of 72 thermal units needed to raise 1 pound of water from 50° to 212° Fahrenheit. (673–74)

In an illusionistic mode this could still be rescued as a colossal euphemism: the phenomenon of ebullition is yet another way to avoid Boylan (boiling). But what is typical in this answer is its absolute refusal of the illusionistic "initial style," the enormous distance between "Mouth dry" and the quantification of energy, expressed in thermal units, expended in heating the water to boiling. "Calypso" is a humid interior of "warmbubbled milk" and the smells of tea, frying kidney, and Molly's body; "Ithaca" is a desolate landscape, arid, devoid of smells, populated by familiar yet alien objects that only manifest themselves at the request of a mysterious and powerful voice.

The initial movement is to withhold narrative content altogether in favor of a literally objective language, a language of objects strangely independent of their narrative function. A complementary pair of passages exemplifies the dominant tendency of "Ithaca":

> With what meditations did Bloom accompany his demonstration to his companion of various constellations?
>
> Meditations of evolution increasingly vaster: of the moon invisible in incipient lunation, approaching perigee: of the infinite lattiginous scintillating uncondensed milky way, discernible by daylight by an observer placed at the lower end of a cylindrical vertical shaft 5000 ft deep sunk from the surface towards the centre of the earth: of Sirius (alpha in Canis Major) 10 lightyears (57,000,000,000,000 miles) distant and in volume 900 times the dimension of our planet: of Arcturus: of the precession of equinoxes: of Orion with belt and sextuple sun theta and nebula in which 100 of our solar systems could be contained: of moribund and of nascent new stars such as Nova in 1901: of our system plunging towards the constellation of Hercules: of the parallax or parallactic drift of socalled fixed stars, in reality evermoving wanderers from immeasurably remote eons to infinitely remote futures in comparison with which the years, threescore and ten, of allotted human life formed a parenthesis of infinitesimal brevity. (698)

As the last phrase ("human life formed a parenthesis of infinitesimal brevity") only emphasizes, this description (nominally of Bloom's thoughts) spins out by orders of magnitude from the limits of the experienceable.

> Were there obverse meditations of involution increasingly less vast?
>
> Of the eons of geological periods recorded in the stratifications of the earth: of the myriad minute entomological organic existences concealed in cavities of the earth, beneath removable stones, in hives and mounds, of microbes, germs, bacteria, bacilli, spermatozoa: of the incalculable trillions of billions of millions of imperceptible molecules contained by cohesion of molecular affinity in a single pinhead: of the universe of human serum constellated with red and white bodies, themselves universes of void space constellated with other bodies, each, in continuity, its universe of divisible component bodies of which each was again divisible in divisions of redivisible component bodies, dividends and divisors ever diminishing without actual division till, if the progress were carried far enough, nought nowhere was never reached. (699)

Here the movement is toward the microscopic rather than the macroscopic; but in both cases the movement is centrifugal, tending away from the level at which the narrative is playing out. If the landscape of "Eumaeus" is relentlessly subjectivized (our only access to it being through the error of a language that assimilates everything to itself), then the language of "Ithaca" is objective in a strangely literal sense, spinning away from human experience in directions where "human life form[s] a parenthesis." From this perspective the language of "Ithaca" is the language of the things in themselves, majestically unconcerned with the narrative unfolding among them.

But in a secondary movement, corresponding to the ecstatic moment of sublime, meaning is suddenly recovered. As in "Eumaeus," a kind of negation of the text on the page must take place before the language registers as sense. It takes a moment's thought to recompose

> the natural grammatical transition by inversion involving no alteration of sense of an aorist preterite proposition (parsed as masculine subject, monosyllabic onomatopæic transitive verb with direct feminine object) from the active voice to its correlative aorist preterite proposition (parsed as feminine subject, auxiliary verb and quasi-monosyllabic onomatopæic past participle with complementary masculine agent) in the passive voice (734)

into "he fucked her, she was fucked by him, it makes no difference." And once again, what is to be reconstructed is the very narrative and affective content of the episode. For example, Bloom spends a great deal of time puttering around the house at two o'clock in the morning, and while this gives us an interesting and revealing tour of his house it is not at all clear why until we arrive at this question:

> What selfimposed enigma did Bloom about to rise in order to go so as to conclude lest he should not conclude involuntarily apprehend?
> The cause of a brief sharp unforeseen heard loud lone crack emitted by the insentient material of a strainveined timber table. (729)

The reason for Bloom's rising, rescued from the convoluted syntax, is not the sound the table makes but rather a decision to get things over with: Bloom is "about to rise in order to go" in to Molly, "lest he should not conclude." The enigma Bloom puts to himself of why the table makes a crack can only be answered by the commentaries, which tell us that it is the reassuring thunderclap Zeus sends Odysseus out of a cloudless sky. As usual, this doesn't tell us much about the "slaughter of the suitors," since the irony of this identification cannot be definitely determined, but it does confirm this moment as a kind of turning point that reminds us of all the empty time that has passed since Stephen's departure. Suddenly this intervening time—which until now has registered primarily as boring and during which, we realize, Bloom's thoughts have been reverting with increasing frequency to the possible consequences of Molly's infidelity—is retroactively endowed with unexpected affective charge. Bloom has spent the time since Stephen left idly looking into drawers and flipping through books, dreading the moment when he goes in to see Molly.

The relation of form to content in "Ithaca" is not as arbitrary as it might seem. For Bloom, the transformation of the comfortable "Calypso" world into "Ithaca" has a specific meaning. The familiar furniture reappears as evidence:

Describe them.

One: a squat stuffed easychair with stout arms extended and back slanted to the rere, which, repelled in recoil, had then upturned an irregular fringe of the rectangular rug and now displayed on its amply upholstered seat a centralized diffusing and diminishing discolouration. The other: a slender splayfoot chair of glossy cane curves, placed directly opposite the former, its frame from top to seat and from seat to base being varnished dark brown, its seat being a bright circle of white plaited rush.

What significance attached to these two chairs?

Significances of similitude, of posture, of symbolism, of circumstantial evidence, of testimonial supermanence. (706)

We and Bloom encounter a surprising amount of circumstantial evidence of Molly's liaison in "Ithaca," from a conveniently scarlet pair of betting tickets to Molly's discarded gloves and "two discoloured ends of cigarettes" (706). The furniture is not only arranged in a suggestive manner, pantomiming the seduction itself, but also bears a suspicious stain: "a centralized diffusing and diminishing discolouration." As we find out in "Penelope," Molly had sat in this chair as Boylan "pull[ed] off his . . . trousers there on the chair before me" (776).

In a first moment "Ithaca" 's relentless spinning away from narrative continuity was seen to gesture toward a noumenal realm to which the narrative activity of the episode was strictly irrelevant. In a second moment, against all expectations, that narrative and affective content is recovered. At this point we realize that what had appeared as an attempt to represent a noumenal realm beyond human structuration in fact already has a structure: the structure of evidence. This reversal at the level of narrative also functions at the level of the text, which no longer operates primarily as narrative but as information. What we see in movement from "Calypso" to "Ithaca" is the linguistic form of reification itself, the becoming-information of meaning. If we think of reification as cognate with *Gestell*, Heideggerian "enframing" of Being into manipulable objects (leaving aside for the moment that at the level of causality these two concepts are diametrically opposed), then the content of the "Ithaca" language appears neither as illusionistic narrative nor as a trace of the noumenon but rather as a kind of standing reserve or raw material.

This becoming-information or becoming-raw-material is not yet total. There are in fact two distinct "Ithaca" languages. The first is the terse, invariant, institutional question-language. The second is the variable language of the responses, a mode of speech that perpetually struggles to maintain its equilibrium, to match the tone and demands of the question-language—and which consistently falls short, finally falling silent altogether. The answers veer from absurd scientistic technicality (burning being described as "releasing the potential energy contained in the fuel by allowing the carbon and hydrogen elements to enter into free union with the oxygen of the air" [670]) to Dedalus-like poetry ("The heaventree of stars hung with humid nightblue fruit" [698]) to the dream-language of Bloom's last waking thoughts ("Sinbad the Sailor and Tinbad the Tailor and Jinbad the Jailer and Whinbad the Whaler" [737]), while long answers in "Ithaca" often begin as lists and end as poems. The answer to the question about Bloom's admiration of water (671–72) begins obediently with abstract and geographic matters like its "universality" and the depth of the Sundam trench, and ends with "pestilential fens, faded flowerwater, stagnant pools in the wandering moon" (672). The contrast between the unitary language of the questions and the variable language of the answers then becomes important, for it dramatizes the reification of language at the more particular level where languages belong to institutions. Once again, both Lukácsian and Heideggerian examples come to mind, but the most obvious referent for the catechistic form is the Church. As we have seen, however, the "Ithaca" language has a much more general significance than any particular example would suggest. One of Foucault's great insights was that power lies not so much in the right to speak as in the right to elicit speech. The "calm violence" of such power is felt on every page of "Ithaca," where the answer-language perpetually seeks to escape the constraints placed on it by the question-language, which commands it into usefulness.[21] "Ithaca" is inscribed throughout with the unequal relationship between the massive, inert institutional language of the questions and the more fragile speech it elicits. The patient, commanding language of the questions is clipped and formal; the answer-language, constrained to follow in kind, replies with alacrity, with promptitude, with self-abnegating docility. And yet the answer-language, as we saw above, digresses from the demands placed on it, tending to drift into reverie.

We saw that the "Eumaeus" language, nervous and complacent at the same time, performs reification from the side of the subject without any possibility of substantial encounter with being or participation in history, emptied of the fear imposed by genuine otherness and yet full of the anxiety produced by the uncomfortable awareness that the thoroughly anthropomorphized world is at the same time constituted as paradoxically beyond human intervention—that is, from the side of the subject *tout court*. The extreme objectivism of "Ithaca" brings this uneasiness home. Put dramatically, "Ithaca" is the truth of "Eumaeus." To use Heideggerian language once more, "the 'not-at-home' " ("Ithaca") "must be conceived as the more primordial phenomenon" in relationship to the "tranquilized self-assurance" of average everydayness ("Eumaeus").[22] "Ithaca" dramatizes reification "from the side of the object," something that sounds less paradoxical when we consider that human potential is also converted into standing reserve, from labor power as human resource to desire as consumer demand. That is, the individual is as much on the side of the object as on the side of the subject (a fact that describes the fragmenting of the subject rather than a bridging of the gap between the two) while "objectivity" is as much a function of human activity as external to it (a fact that describes reification rather than overcoming it).

As in "Eumaeus," the utopian aspect is not in the "Ithaca" languages themselves but in the way they must be negated to produce meaning out of information. Once again, the language of *Ulysses* manages, against the odds, to produce meaning—not by pretending that meaning in the old sense is still possible, by telling a "meaningful story," but by taking reified language to its limit and producing meaning within it. In the Adornian dictum that the "complete presentation of false consciousness is ... itself truth content" the emphasis is on the word "complete."[23] "Ithaca" takes the reification of language to its limit, hence its power. The experience of "Ithaca" is one of compensation: the more total our experience of reification, the more intense the experience of the recovery of meaning, which may be one reason why we find "Ithaca" more appealing than Joyce's contemporaries did.

But the question Adorno asks of art's utopian vocation also applies: "Whether the promise is a deception—that is the enigma."[24] This is another way of expressing the problem of an aesthetic solution to real problems, which we explored in its general form in the introduction. On one hand, a total exposure of a rift at the heart of the actual; on the other, a purely imaginary leap over it. In "Eumaeus" this problem, without being solved, arrived at a kind of self-consciousness: the procedures that imaginatively bridged this gap also reveal the apparent short circuit as only a special kind of illusion. In "Ithaca" we must first of all note an intensification of the same dynamic. "Ithaca" is the episode most heavily and arbitrarily determined by the Homeric parallel, where the correspondences reach a kind of fever pitch: from Bloom's corrugated brow when he sees the betting tickets (like Odysseus entering his suitor-infested hall), to his knock on the head (Antinous's stool), to the urination scene (Odysseus's bow), to the loud crack from the table (Zeus's thunder), to Bloom's lighting of incense (Odysseus's fumigation). If a shooting star points to a constellation, it has to be Leo; Bloom's income and expenditures for the day are identical down to the pence (yet another confirmation that nothing can happen in Bloom's day) and so on. While these correspondences are often funny, they also point to something else, which is that the narrative has reached a height of pointlessness where the correspondences can be given free reign. As in "Eumaeus," the correspondences and coincidences both give meaning and take it away. When the shooting star points to the constellation Leo, one's first reaction is that the Universe is speaking to Leopold Bloom. But the entire rhetoric of the episode, not to mention the book as a whole, speaks against this, and by now we are used to this kind of coincidence, which is, once again, part of the fabric of *Ulysses* and nothing more.

But of course "Ithaca" itself is far from pointless. We learn a great deal from "Ithaca" aside from the narrative: the details of Bloom's father's suicide; who his friends were; his height, weight, age, and other measurements; his religious and educational history; his financial situation; his two encounters with a younger Stephen and their respective links to Mrs. Riordan; the history of the Blooms' relationship with Boylan; a well-nigh ethnographic account of the petty-bourgeois furnishings of the Blooms' house and cupboards; and so on—the kind of background, carefully suspended until now, which might comprise the bulky exposition of the kind of novel satirized in "Nausicaa." In addition, we get confirmation of information (like the bee sting we may have missed in "Hades," "Nausicaa," and "Cyclops") that has already been presented obliquely. All of this is essential for our understanding of *Ulysses*. But here, without realizing it, we have already arrived at a reversal. For while the progress of the narrative has to be reconstructed out of the information-language of "Ithaca," this narrative is itself entirely superfluous—except as information. As with "Eumaeus," the relation of motivation to technique must be read absolutely ambivalently. On one hand, the technique—the quasi-forensic investigation of Bloom's house—is motivated by Bloom's procrastination. On the other hand, Bloom's procrastination is motivated by the need to show us what is in Bloom's desk drawers. The reading of "Ithaca" becomes a huge marshaling of evidence, a mining of the superabundance of information for scraps that will bear on our understanding of the previous episodes. And it can't be ignored that this mode of reading is essential to *Ulysses* as a whole and the foundation of the "Joyce industry." What was to be overcome—language as information rather than meaning—unexpectedly turns out to be that on which the text depends, making "Ithaca" not only a supreme example but the reflexive representation of the modernist sublime.

CHAPTER THREE

Ambiguous Adventure: Authenticity's Aftermath

Novels are the Socratic dialogues of our time.

—Friedrich Schlegel, *Critical Fragment* 26

Cheikh Hamidou Kane's 1961 *L'aventure ambiguë*[1] is generally read in two ways: as a commentary on the paradoxes of cultural conservation in the face of the hegemony of mainstream European cultural norms (in other words, in terms of contemporary North American or European cultural politics) and as an allegory of the subjective experience of a generation of African intellectuals (as proclaimed on the back of a French edition, of "l'angoisse d'être noir," which is immediately subsumed as merely a special case of "l'angoisse d'être homme"). The first approach is ethnographic; it mines the text for testimony about cultural pathways and raises valuable but by now expected questions about cultural difference, thereby refusing to think the largely material and historical difference between two societies. The second forcibly maintains the protagonist's anguish at the level of the merely subjective—something at every moment refused by the text—only to subsume it under a universality that refuses the positional difference that is the cause of that very anguish.[2]

While both of these themes are clearly operative in the text, a different sort of content emerges when the book is jolted out of its usual critical context. The relationship to modernism described in the introduction, the evacuation of the structure of the sublime, can be illustrated concretely by way of a passage whose significance in the text we will return to later. A man called simply the fool, who has returned to Senegal from the European war, describes things he has seen to the teacher, who has never been to Europe:

> "I have seen the mechanisms. They are shells. It is a rolled-up expanse, which moves. Well, you know that expanse has nothing inside it; therefore it has nothing to lose. It cannot be wounded, like the form of man, but only unrolled. Also, it has forced back man's form, fearful that it, in being wounded, will lose what it contains."
>
> "I understand you. Go on."
>
> "This expanse moves. . . . Its movement is more finished than the fitful progression of man's hesitant form. It cannot fall—where would it fall to?" (92–93, translation modified)

The narrative technique here will be familiar to readers of Faulkner:

> Through the fence, between the curling flower spaces, I could see them hitting. They were coming towards where the flag was and I went along the fence. Luster was hunting

in the grass by the flower tree. They took the flag out, and they were hitting. Then they put the flag back and went to the table, and he hit and the other hit. Then they went on, and I went along the fence.[3]

Like the golf game Benjy witnesses at the opening of *The Sound and the Fury*, in *Ambiguous Adventure* the simple descriptive content of a European street is defamiliarized through the perspective of a naïve eyewitness. The fool's naïveté in fact makes a difference only of degree; we are given to understand that it is the extreme form of a perspective shared in varying degrees by all of the African characters in the novel, even a woman born in Paris. In Faulkner this technique is part of a larger, well-nigh cubist perspectivism that is another mode of the modernist sublime: multiple fragmented and incomplete representations are meant to provide access to a reality that would otherwise be inaccessible. Here a similar technique is immediately given geopolitical content, for it is only narratively possible on the basis of a radically uneven development between the metropole and the colonies, of which it then becomes a thumbnail sketch. The noumenal excitement of Faulkner's prose is completely missing in Kane's, which, however, is endowed with more consequence.

Similarly for the Joycean interior monologue when it appears—here in the precocious intellectual mode of a Stephen Dedalus—as the hero of the novel, Samba Diallo, walks the Boulevard Saint-Michel:

These streets are bare. . . . No, they are not empty. One meets objects of flesh in them, as well as objects of metal. Apart from that, they are empty. Ah! One also encounters events. Their succession congests time, as the objects congest the street. Time is obstructed by their mechanical jumble. . . . I walk. One foot before, one foot behind: one-two, one-two. No! I must not think: one-two, one-two. I must think of something else. One-two, one-two. . . . Malte Laurids Brigge. . . . Look! Yes—I am Malte Laurids Brigge. Like him, I am walking down the Boulevard Saint-Michel. There is nothing, nothing but me, nothing but my body, I mean to say. I touch it. Through the pocket of my trousers I touch my thigh. I think of my right big toe. Otherwise, their street is empty, their time is encumbered, their soul is silted up down there, under my right big toe, and under the events and under the objects of flesh and the objects of metal—the objects of flesh and—. (128–29)

Here the literal content of this stream of consciousness—a street in Paris—is the same as the fool's naïve account, and the allegorical content—the historical basis upon which such a technique can register as realistic—is not very far removed from that of the earlier passage. The main distinction between the two passages is that Samba Diallo's distance from this scene is vastly reduced, as the Bergsonian flux of his own thought ("one-two, one-two") cannot be separated from what he describes as the succession of events that "[congest] time, as the objects congest the street."

Since the modernist structures Kane transforms most effectively are philosophical rather than literary, our direct comparison to Joyce will not be extended beyond these introductory pages. Nonetheless, *Ambiguous Adventure* shares something with Joyce in that both illustrate quite literally the maxim that heads this chapter.[4] The extended dialogue in *Stephen Hero* we cited in the introduction works out the modernist sublime through the notion of the epiphany, while the dialogues of *Ambiguous Adventure* directly concern the futurity of a social totality that has rapidly subsumed formerly autonomous and wildly disparate cultural forms: "We have not had the same past, you and ourselves, but we shall have, strictly, the same future. The era of separate destinies has run its course" (79). The dialogues of *Ambiguous Adventure* are philosophical in a more literal sense than Joyce's: Kane, who earned a degree in philosophy from the École de la France d'outre-mer, was accused by a contemporary French reviewer of letting all his characters "speak in the language of a philosophers' congress."[5] The truth of this critique is descriptive rather than normative. The extended dialogues of *Ambiguous Adventure* are scattered throughout the text, flattened into a single, consistent, limpid, classical register, and fragmented in time to the point that they can almost be said to constitute one extended dialogue. In keeping with the *Ambiguous Adventure*'s internal norms, our procedure in this chapter will be to put it in dialogue with its philosophical interlocutors. As frustrating as this approach may be to some readers, it keeps faith with a central difference between *Ulysses* and *Ambiguous Adventure*.

Of course the differences between *Ulysses* and *Ambiguous Adventure* are obvious and many, but once again their meaning is only registered in the light of a similarity. Since what most profoundly unites *Ulysses* and *Ambiguous Adventure* is the investment of subjectivity with a utopian energy, it comes as no surprise that Kane's evident philosophical coordinates are closely related to those we brought to bear on Joyce. If "Eumaeus" embodies, in narrative form, something like the relationship between *Mitsein* and *Gerede*, Kane's narrative puts into play a critique of the "West" quite in line with Heidegger's *Gestell*—which, as we have seen, can also be brought to bear on "Ithaca." As a notion of utopian subjectivity crosses a geopolitical fault line, however, it fundamentally changes character: where the Joycean text brings the social totality into itself in mystified form, the mode of subjectivity evoked by *Ambiguous Adventure* is conceived as an agenda for that totality—though this agenda is not without its own mystifications. In Kane's novel, subjective utopia—the reunification of the subject with the object-world and simultaneously with itself—is not to be found in the aesthetic object: *Ambiguous Adventure* was not originally intended for publication and has no intention of producing Joycean pleasure.[6] Rather, it is to be sought in a mode of experience that would directly cross the gap between the subject and a luminous Being. The origins of this experience lie not directly in the individual but in a social totality, in the memory of a genuinely "non-Western" way of life that must somehow be reintroduced into the new totality that has subsumed it. The position occupied by various permutations of the modernist sublime in *Ulysses* is, in short, taken over in *Ambiguous Adventure* by the notion of authenticity.

The concept of authenticity as it appears in representations of precolonial worldviews has a condition of possibility in what has been called "ethnophilosophy," and we will turn shortly to both Placide Tempels's foundational text on

"Bantu philosophy" and also to Heidegger, a thinker with whom Kane's deliberately ontological language engages and who is both a modernist and an ethnophilosopher *avant la lettre*. (To discourage any misunderstanding it should be emphasized that despite an unavoidable detour through Heidegger, we are not embarking on a Heideggerian reading of Kane; on the contrary, what is most Heideggerian in Kane is what is most problematic.) But whereas Heidegger's and Tempels's philosophies are in their own ways properly nostalgic, valorizing older values and practices as a project for the future, Kane's narrative attempts to refigure authenticity in such a way as to cancel this nostalgia. The hero's geographical and metaphorical "retour au pays natal" is no return at all but a movement that shows precisely the impossibility of any return. At the same time, however, the space opened up by the memory of authenticity freewheels on as the very desire it stimulates for this impossible return. This delicate moment is neither self-sustaining nor the end of the story of authenticity in Africa, which returns in a substantial sense quite in line with the concept's proto-fascist connotations in Heidegger. But here, for a brief moment, "authenticity" names the possibility of imagining an experience outside the ever-expanding "investiture of the actual" (151) that names what we now call "economic development" or, more precisely, the real subsumption of labor under capital.

Ambiguous Adventure initially appears to be an autobiographical novel. (Indeed, the protagonist's name, Samba Diallo, is none other than Cheikh Hamidou Kane disguised through Tukolor naming conventions and a Tukolor-Fula translation.)[7] *Ambiguous Adventure* is apparently unexceptional in its narrative structure, and its basic plot follows a now familiar line. And yet what Kane hangs on this plot, threadbare but not without drama, is nothing less than a confrontation between Western modernity, a technological episteme that construes the thing as object on the way to its conquest of the object-world, and what we will initially, keeping faith with the Francophone African discourse of the period, call an African experience of Being: what Sartre called "l'être-dans-le-monde du Nègre," the being-in-the-world of the Black.[8] We can no longer, of course, take this essentialized opposition or the generalization on which it is founded seriously, nor must we grant final authority to Kane's image of the "West." Kane's narrative, however, only brings forth the image of such a primordial experience of Being and such a stark distinction in order to dramatize the extinction of both.

The intensity of this experience of Being is dramatized in the opening chapters of *Ambiguous Adventure*, which narrate scenes from the life of a young Samba Diallo before he has any explicit awareness—but already a "vague prescience" (39)—of the European presence that has begun to reorganize the space inhabited by the fictional Diallobé.[9] This intensity is registered on the very first page with the complex and lyrical violence of the unforgettable scene of Samba's recitation for the Koranic teacher:

> The teacher had let go of Samba's thigh. Now he was holding him by the ear and, cutting through the cartilage of the lobe, his nails met . . .
> "Repeat it! Again! Again!"

The teacher had shifted the grip of his fingernails, and they were now piercing the cartilage at another place. The child's ear, already white with scarcely healed scars, was bleeding anew. Samba Diallo's whole body was trembling, and he was trying his hardest to recite his verse correctly. (3–4)

The apparent sadism of Samba's Koranic teacher is at the same time an expression of his admiration for Samba and the verses he recites: "What purity! What a miracle! Truly, this child was a gift from God" (5). We do not need to gloss over the cruelty of this scene—the contradiction between the teacher's esteem and its violent expression is part of a much larger ambiguity—in order to characterize the intensity of this episode as something that both separates it from and privileges it over the narration of events outside the immediate sphere of the Diallobé country of Samba's childhood, which are narrated in a much more straightforward, even consciously banal style: "June was drawing to a close, and already the heat in Paris was oppressive" (128). In Paris there is no sweat running down cheeks, no shirt clinging to flesh, but only an abstract "oppressive heat" that is barely registered as more than an annoyance. How different is the language of Paris—tending toward pure exposition, where the language of the body is flattened to matters of "comfort" (143)—from the bodily language of the earlier chapters, with their visceral descriptions of the brutality of the teacher's lessons, the trembling of Samba Diallo at his experience in a graveyard, the scintillating night that greets his recitation of the Koran, the grotesquely painful animation of the aging body of the teacher of the Diallobé; chapters where an impending quarrel can be registered as "an odor of brush fire which was tickling his nostrils" (19). In Paris, Samba Diallo is "benumbed by the heat" (128) on a summer afternoon, but he tells a Parisian friend that his numbness is more thoroughgoing:

"I should have wished that the heat of the sun would suddenly abate, that the sky would become a little more blue, that the water of the river would flow more swiftly and make more sound. The universe ought to scintillate all around us. Lucienne, is that not possible? When I was a child I was a master of all that." (143)

The affective flatness of the second half of the book is not, then, purely formal, but is endowed explicitly with meaning: the contrast between the intensely physical prose of the opening chapters and the flattened language of the Paris chapters reflects back on a new lack in Samba Diallo's experience of the world:

"It is difficult," Samba Diallo began at last. "It might be said that I see less fully here than in the country of the Diallobé. I no longer feel anything directly. . . . In former times the world was like my father's dwelling: everything took me into the very essence of itself, as if nothing could exist except through me. The world was not silent and neuter. It was alive. It was aggressive. It spread out. No scholar ever had such knowledge of anything as I had, then, of being."

After a short silence he added:

"Here, now, the world is silent, and there is no longer any resonance from myself. . . . I have the impression that nothing touches me anymore." (148–50)

Here we see dramatized within a single life a process that appears in Joyce as a metaphysical background: the creation of subject and object as external to each other seems to take place before our very eyes. The nostalgic note is unmistakable; the world animated by this precolonial "knowledge of being," in which there is no solid line demarcating world from self, evokes a palpable desire for return. But this nostalgia, already undercut by the violence with which the novel opened, faces a more substantial challenge from what, with the economic and technological changes brought to the region by the French, appears as the material poverty of the Diallobé.

Meanwhile, we might take note of the peculiar language in which this precolonial experience is couched: a language of "being," of "essence," in which the *world* itself (as "dwelling") comes to "exist through" the activities of the "I." Indeed, both Anglophone and Francophone African literature of the 1950s and 1960s often makes use of existential, and particularly Sartrean situations and terminology, from Camara Laye's incorporation of the Look in *Le regard du roi* to the postcolonial nausea of Ayi Kwei Armah's *The Beautyful Ones Are Not Yet Born*. In particular, the significance of Sartre's "Orphée noir"—the introduction to Senghor's 1948 *Anthologie de la nouvelle poésie nègre et malgache* which figures *négritude* as a particular mode of being-in-the-world—cannot be ignored. In this context one cannot help but be intrigued by Samba's prayerful invocation of an older, apparently Diallobé wisdom:

> the human being is quartered from nothingness, is an archipelago of which the islands do not remain underneath, drowned as they are by nothingness. They say that the sea, which is such that everything not itself floats there, is nothingness. They say that the truth is nothingness, and being, a multiple avatar. (127)

This prayer, proclaiming that the "human being" (but in French simply "l'être," *being* [139]) "is quartered from nothingness" ("le néant"), is a lyrical invocation of the Sartrean dialectic. The "nothingness," "abyss," or "shade" that come up so often in *Ambiguous Adventure* is what guarantees the difference between what is human and what is not; both in phenomenology and in Kane's novel, the human being is founded on the nothingness of the "not-yet." This difference—which technological development, as the "investiture of the actual" (151), of that which *is*, is unable to compass—separates the human from things that are merely present-at-hand.

Similarly with Samba's father's insistence on the experience of "anguish" ("*l'angoisse*" [89]) as the essential mood:

> Then from the bottom of my heart I wish for you to rediscover the feeling of anguish in the face of the dying sun. I ardently wish that for the West. (77)

Again, there is nothing new in unearthing Sartrean thematics in Francophone African literature, much less this particular novel.[10] However, the specificity of this "feeling of anguish" can be further fixed. Samba Diallo is speaking:

"It seems to me . . . that in the country of the Diallobé man is closer to death. He lives on more familiar terms with it. His existence acquires from it something like an aftermath of authenticity. Down there, there existed between death and myself an intimacy, made up at the same time of my terror and my expectation. Whereas here death has become a stranger to me. . . . When I search for it in my thought, I see only a dried-up sentiment, an abstract eventuality, scarcely more disagreeable for me than for my insurance company."

"In sum," said Marc, laughing, "you are complaining of no longer living your own death."

They all laughed, and Samba Diallo, wholly acquiescent, laughed with them. Then he went on, seriously. (149)

Samba's laugh, it should be clear, is only polite, "wholly acquiescent": his interlocutor has summed up in jest precisely what Samba was saying in earnest. The intensity of the earlier episodes has little to do with conspicuously vivid prose, a proliferation of adjectives, or self-conscious lyricism. Instead, this attitude toward death provides the passionate undertone of scenes set in the Diallobé country, from Samba's resort to a mortuary as a place of refuge, to the contrasting attitudes of Samba Diallo's father and M. Lacroix to the dying sunset, to Samba's reaction to a flower: " 'It smells good. . . . But it is going to die' " (57). The lyric tone, when it appears, alerts us to the presence of death.[11]

Samba Diallo's attitude toward death is most profoundly reflected in the begging verses he composes, reminding the Diallobé to donate to the disciples because their own lives are short:

"Men of God, reflect upon your approaching death. Awake, Oh, awake! Azrael, Angel of death, is already breaking the earth for you. It is about to rise up at your feet. Men of God, death is not that sly creature it is believed to be, which comes when it is not expected, and conceals itself so well that when it has come there is no longer anyone there. . . . [D]eath is not that night which traitorously floods with darkness the innocent and lively ardor of a summer day. It warns, and then it mows down in the full mid-day of the intelligence." (13–14)

What is invoked here is not a mere fear of death but an admonishment to live one's life in perpetual consciousness of death. Although we have seen that Sartrean nothingness—the guarantee of the particularity of the human being, which is never simply an object that is what it is but is always oriented toward what it is not-yet—is operative in the novel, it cannot be forgotten that the Sartrean relation is a reformulation of Heidegger's altogether grimmer expression *Sein zu tod*, Being-towards-death. Samba Diallo's insistence on "living your own death" paraphrases rather precisely the Heideggerian expression as theorized in the beginning of division two of *Being and Time*—indeed, the reference to the calculable and statistical "abstract eventuality . . . for my insurance company" would hardly be out of place in Heidegger's contemptuous sections on the everyday conception of death.[12] In particular, Being-towards-death is central to both works as the attitude that attunes the subject most purely to his or her own "potentiality-for-Being." Being-towards-death, "living your own death," is the guarantor of authentic experience: "existence acquires from it something like an aftermath of authenticity." As bizarre as it might initially seem given Heidegger's political enthusiasms, *Ambiguous Adventure*'s existential affinities are more Heideggerian than Sartrean.[13] (Indeed, Sartre himself returned to explicitly Heideggerian terminology when referring to an African context: "la négritude, pour employer le langage heideggerien, c'est l'être-dans-le-monde du Nègre": "négritude, to employ Heideggerian language, is the being-in-the-world of the Black."[14] For reasons that shall become clear, Heidegger's terminology is better tuned to a certain conception of precapitalist collectivities than is Sartre's more agonistic language.)

What initially appeared, then, as an African and Islamic conception of Being bears the unmistakable traces of a European, indeed modernist conception of Being. (Kane's unproblematic identification of Sufism with African spirituality generally, both in the text and outside it, also probably owes something to a conventional modernist conception of the absolute alterity of African cultures with regard to the "West," a conception that implies a certain homogeneity both within and among African cultures—and which, as we shall see in a moment, is not a mere ethical lapse of modernism but is instead determined by the relationship between capitalism and the societies it encounters. In fact, however, even within Tukolor society the relationship between Islamic spiritual authority and a temporal authority with pre-Islamic roots was historically not an easy one.)[15] The outline of affinities between Kane's novel and the thought of Sartre and Heidegger is not intended, however, to expose an "African" worldview as all too Western. As tidy as it would be to show that "authenticity" is itself culturally inauthentic, such critiques are probably no longer necessary. It is important to understand, moreover, that in the previous sentence "authenticity" already has two distinct meanings: "cultural" or ethnic authenticity on one hand, and the more philosophical notion of authenticity as the experience of Being on the other. And it is true that what is at stake in *Ambiguous Adventure* does not seem to be some authentically African mode of being at all but this latter possibility, which is for some reason only felt as its own aftermath (*regain*, resurgence or revival). On the other hand this authentic experience of being stands against a mode of thought that is clearly marked as belonging to a particular culture—the "West"—and so the question needs to be asked: what precisely is the relationship between authenticity in the "good" (or at least in the apparently ethically neutral) sense and authenticity in the "bad" sense of ethnic or racial purity? Is ethnic authenticity necessarily implied in the idea of an "authentic experience"?

Heidegger is not generally thought of as an "ethnophilosopher," a label that would surely have scandalized him. As we suggested in the introductory chapter, Heidegger's thought is intimately connected with the "thingly" aspect of modernism, from the Husserlian slogan of *Being and Time*—"To the things themselves!"—all the way to his 1950 meditation on a jug, "Das Ding." It is Heidegger's 1935 lecture "The Origin of the Work of Art," however, which most interestingly interprets the *thing*, an emphasis that is always, though sometimes in a highly sublimated way, bound up with the new status of things as mass-produced commodities.[16] This relationship between the thing and productive technology is central to *Ambiguous Adventure*, where it appears as the dilemma of accepting "the mastery of the object" (154) (but in French "la maîtrise de la chose" [167], mastery of the thing) at the cost of losing an authentic "knowledge of being." "The Origin of the Work of Art," however, has another object: not only does it theorize the thing for modernist poetics, it also, though more obscurely, posits the *ethnos* as the origin of Being.

Like any of the great hermetic modernist works, the essay on the work of art is a language game that imposes rules to which a reader must accede before the text's meaning makes itself available. Throughout Heidegger's writings, the pun— homophony, homography, etymologies philological, folk, and false—plays a privileged role, as critics have never been slow to point out.[17] But to acknowledge that Heidegger's "argument" (such a word is already inappropriate) sometimes proceeds by means of etymologies, themselves dubious, whose relevance to the truth of the matter at hand is questionable, is not so much to criticize it as to recognize the mode of reading it demands. True, a commentary on Dürer's use of the word "wrest" ("Reissen heisst hier Herausholen de Risses und den Riss reissen mit der Reissfeder auf dem Reissbrett"[18]) loses all of its force and much of its meaning when translated to English: " 'Wrest' means here to draw out the rift and to draw the design with the pen on the draftboard." Throughout the essay on the work of art, much depends on there being an essential relationship between words having to do with inscription (such as *Aufriss* [sketch] and *Grundriss* [ground plan]) and *Der Riss*, a rift. It might be said that Heidegger's argument hinges on the contingent and wholly arbitrary outcome of a particular language's history. From another angle, however, this criticism is simply an explication: Heidegger's thought presumes an essential relationship between language and Being. The ways in which this presumption plays out are infinitely questionable, as Adorno demonstrated without a doubt when he laid bare the particular social origins of a terminology that had claimed to reveal a primordial truth.[19] But within Heidegger's own frame of reference, what guarantees this relationship?

In the famous reading of a Van Gogh painting of some peasant shoes in "The Origin of the Work of Art," what is revealed in the painting is the equipmental nature of those shoes, their status as the original kind of thing—equipment— viewed from a position outside their *zuhandenheit* (availability for use) but fundamentally different from their *vorhandenheit* or availability for abstract contemplation. But this is only one work of art. What of a lyric poem, or a Greek temple? What Van Gogh's shoes reveal is not just their equipmentality but what lies behind that equipmentality: the world of the peasant woman who wears them. The fundamental opposition of the essay is between this *world* and *earth*, a tension that synthesizes such older dichotomies as form and content, culture and nature, idea and materiality, the historical and the transcendental, and so on. As such, it brings together aesthetics, philosophy, ethnology, and history under a single opposition. We might think we have a fairly good idea of what Heidegger means by "world," but in this essay his own formulation is startling:

> A world is the self-opening openness of the broad paths of the simple and essential
> decisions in the destiny of a historical people. (174)

Suddenly, into this seemingly universal language that had appealed only to the
structure of Dasein itself, slips the formulation, slyly repeated throughout the rest
of the essay, of the "historical people." The appearance of this phrase in its historical context—the Germany of 1935—cannot but be troubling. But is there anything fundamentally new here, or is this merely an explicit reformulation of a
structure that had already been implicit in Heidegger's thought? "World," here, is
not so much a universal—the individual's subjective *Umwelt*—as it is a collective
average everydayness that *Being and Time* had already undertaken to explicate
existentially. This undertaking has had the profoundest consequences for professional ethnology. But *Being and Time* was also, already, secretly, an ethnology,
seeking as it did to uncover an implicit philosophy, an implicit set of attitudes
toward Being and of interpretations of the Being of the human being, behind
everyday practice, which is only a fallen form of (but nonetheless the only path
to) this forgotten, prior, authentic experience. Implicitly throughout *Being and
Time*, but increasingly explicitly in later work, the privileged form of practice
through which these truths are revealed is in actual language, and the guarantor
of the relationship between truth and language—in other words, the guarantor
of the relationship that underpins Heidegger's method—is none other than the
"historical people," historical experience of the ethnic community:

> Actual language at any given moment is the happening of this [poetic] saying, in which
> a people's world historically arises for it. . . . In such saying, the concepts of a histori-
> cal people's essence, i.e., of its belonging to world history, are performed for that
> people. (199)

In order to draw out the importance of the concept of the "historical people"
and to bring it into relation with Kane's own intellectual milieu, we will bring
in a quite different text: Father Placide Tempels's *La philosophie bantoue* (*Bantu
Philosophy*), a book that acquired tremendous importance after it was reissued in
1949 as the first book to be published by Présence Africaine.[20] Tempels was neither
a professional ethnographer nor a professional philosopher but a cleric whose
mission among the Baluba in what was then the Belgian Congo had begun in
1933. *La philosophie bantoue* claimed to discover, in the same region that Conrad's
Heart of Darkness had represented as embodying the most atavistic of human
possibilities, an advanced folk wisdom, complete with an ontology, a criteriology,
a psychology, a system of jurisprudence, and an ethics. *La philosophie bantoue*
represents, as V. Y. Mudimbe has pointed out in *The Invention of Africa*, a moment
of "cultural doubt," when the civilizing mission of the Belgian colonial project
wavers before the possibility of indigenous civilization, and in particular of an
autochthonous relation to God.[21] It also became the foundational text of ethnophilosophy, a philosophical school that has sought to describe local worldviews in
terms of systematic philosophy. Doubtless Tempels could not have foreseen such
a possibility; *Bantu Philosophy* neither invents a methodology nor outlines a proj-

ect that would serve as a foundation for a philosophical school. It is only with Alexis Kagame's systematic checking and revision of Tempels's work, in his 1956 *La philosophie bantu-rwandaise de l'être*,[22] that the ethnophilosophical project gains an explicit methodology. Nor does *Bantu Philosophy* represent the first time that non-Western worldviews had been sympathetically rendered by European observers: it is preceded by the work of both Lévy-Bruhl and Marcel Griaule. Indeed, the book, whose African edition had been repressed by the clergy, would probably have been forgotten entirely had not Alioune Diop run across a copy in Leopoldville. It is, as Mudimbe remarks, possibly the name of the book itself, the prestige suggested by a Bantu *philosophy*—as well as the division of this philosophy into such (presumably) Western categories as ontology, criteriology, ethics, and so on—that initiated a discourse and controversy that continued through the end of the twentieth century.

Nothing seems further from *Bantu Philosophy* than the thought of Heidegger, which is eminently philosophical, which is as systematic as it chooses, which takes little interest in the "primitive stage of Dasein," and which is scornful of ethnology, which "already presupposes as its clue an inadequate analytic of Dasein."[23] On the other hand, we have seen that something like an ethnic community appears from time to time in a structurally important position, and so it is worth asking if there may be deeper affinities between Heidegger and Tempels. To be sure, when Heidegger is explicating the same language in which we know he writes, the ethnological aspect of his philosophy is easily passed over: nothing would seem more natural and legitimate than a reflexive awareness of the pathways by which thought is determined by one's own language. We can even dismiss the references to an "historical people" as extrinsic, traces perhaps of a proto-fascist obsession with the *volk*—if dismissal is indeed how such traces are to be met. But when we turn to his explications of Greek texts, Heidegger's essentially ethnophilosophical method becomes much easier to discern.

Indeed, Heidegger's 1946 "The Anaximander Fragment"[24] has much in common with Tempels's work on Bantu philosophy, published the year before. Doubtless, there are many connections between the two that could be passed off as accidental. Both explicate and, to differing degrees, advocate an anthropomorphic conception of being (as against a static conception of being as substance and property)—which each takes pains to explain is in fact *not* anthropomorphic but only seems so from the perspective that experiences things as *substantia* and *accidens*. For Heidegger, the Greeks experienced the Being of beings as *energeia* (activity); for Tempels, the Bantu experience such Being as *bukomo* (force). Both hinge on the exegesis of relatively few, isolated words (*eonta, logos, moira, aletheia; muntu, bukomo, vidye*). Both posit a society whose radical difference from Western modernity is seen as temporal priority and from which the current state of affairs is a "fallen" one. Both reject "correct" and "literal" professional understandings of their material—Heidegger rejects scholarly translations of Anaximander as Tempels rejects the "objective study" of the "actual state of affairs" by ethnologists—in order to arrive at some other kind of truth; both take pains to distinguish their interpretations from the condescension into which "objective" interpretations, failing to take account of their own history, necessarily fall. Each author conceives the "historical people" under discussion as a society that had not yet developed separate conceptual systems—and therefore separate languages—for what must seem to us to be disparate fields of life. In particular, juridical language—in which the word is for the first time divorced from the thing, "letter" distinguished from "spirit"—has not yet come to exist.[25] Thus each society is seen to be both integral and to have a purer relationship with Being as such, having not yet carved Being into separate spheres.

In *Bantu Philosophy*, Placide Tempels makes an audacious claim, one professional ethnology has been too ashamed to make for some time: "The Bantu psychology which we are going to study is that which is found in the minds of the Bantu themselves, not that which would result from the observation of Bantu by Europeans" (63). This is precisely the claim Heidegger makes when, in the exegesis of a pre-Socratic fragment, he demands that we bypass every "correct" translation, all accepted philological methods, every lexical nicety—in essence, that we forget the entire history of the European interpretation of Greece—in order first to translate "our thinking . . . into what is said in Greek." How is one to translate oneself to "what is said in Greek" without first translating the Greek (or what is said in Luba without first translating the Luba)—without, that is, using the very tools that lock us into a "Western" viewpoint from which early Greek thought is inaccessible? Heidegger phrases his claim as a paradox, indicating that he is more aware than Tempels of the difficulty; but the problem is fundamentally the same for both. The paradox is not to be resolved by particularly brilliant methodology but through the authority of the author himself. Both texts depend upon the conviction that the writing offers what Heidegger calls a "vibrant rapport" (14) with the material—what Mudimbe, in reference to Tempels, calls a "vivid *Einfüh-lung*."[26] That the methodology can in no way serve as a guarantee of the truth of the project, however, does not mean that there is no method at all.

We have seen that language itself is the key to both writers'thought. But language is only a privileged instance of average everydayness itself. Tempels:

> We could begin by a comparative study of the languages, modes of behavior, institutions and customs of the Bantu; we could analyze them and separate their fundamental ideas; finally we could construct from these elements a system of Bantu thought.
>
> This, as a matter of fact, is the method that I followed myself. . . . Speaking their language, one . . . attains the ability to think like the Bantu and to look upon life as they do. (28)

If his language is more subtle, Heidegger's method is fundamentally the same. In order to "cross over" to what is expressed in Greek by *ta onta*, Heidegger turns not to later Greek thinkers who explicitly name *ta onta* as a subject for philosophy but to Homer's use of the word. It is not discourse on the word, theorizing about beings, but the simple, ordinary use of the word that determines Greek thought and later philosophy: "This word [*ta onta*] indicates the source from which the fragment speaks, not merely that which it expresses. That from which it speaks is already, before any expression, what is spoken by the Greek language in common everyday parlance as well as in its learned employ." Language already embodies all that can be thought within it: language "lies outside philosophy, and . . . from every point of view precedes the pronouncements of thinking."[27]

The task of thinking, then, is to make explicit what had already been experienced by an "historical people" and had been set inchoately into their language. This is what qualifies both *Bantu Philosophy* and Heidegger's writings on Greek thought—implicitly, much of Heidegger's thought—as ethnophilosophy. Both seek, through an interpretation of average everyday behavior (language first but also ritual, art, work, and institutions), to abstract an original relationship with Being from the conduct of the everyday life of an "historical people." Further, the ethnos is the only foundation capable of sustaining this relationship, which cannot survive translation or contamination. The relationship to Being that characterizes Heidegger's Greece is lost the moment Greek thought is translated into cosmopolitan Latin: "Meanwhile an epoch of being soon comes in which *energeia* is translated as *actualitas*. The Greek is shut away."[28] In another context, speaking of the same event, Heidegger had written "The rootlessness of Western thought begins with this translation."[29] The anti-Semitic overtones of Heidegger's contempt for this "rootlessness" are well known, but the contempt it registers most profoundly is for any cosmopolitanism, any set of cultural norms and habits not rooted in a particular ethnic life world. Tempels is more circumspect with regard to cultural purity; after all, as a missionary his project is one of conversion. But the true measure of Tempels's ethnologic nostalgia can be found in his disgust and contempt for the "evolués," Africans who had absorbed Western learning, whom he prefers to call "les déracinés et les dégénérés" (19), "rootless and degenerate people." The *evolués*, it need hardly be noted, represent the first generation that will be able to confront the contradictions of the colonial project on its own terms. At least in these two texts, authenticity in the "good" sense—a nonreified relationship to Being—is grounded in authenticity in the "bad" sense—the purity of an "historical people."

The strangely similar appearance of the early Greeks and the Baluba when considered from the perspective of authenticity should come as no surprise since, in spite of appearances, its origins lie first not in any positive conception of being but in a purely negative rejection of reification, the relationship to being that characterizes Capital. As in Heidegger, though less subtly, Tempels's nostalgia for an "original simple philosophy" (105) is a reaction against "mechanical, material, [and] industrial . . . progress [which] has scarcely aided the progress of humanity at all; that, on the contrary . . . has contributed largely to make modern man less happy" (112). Other social forms, whatever their original positive content, are transformed on contact with Capital into its limit, that is, its negation, and appear as nothing other than the "other" of a "West" that now determines their contents. Neither Heidegger nor Tempels, however, explicitly thematizes or has a conception of Capital, which would tend to lead away from the notion that any space outside Capital could be simply preserved. Instead, both figure modernity as a technological episteme that severs the connection between subject and object, word and Being. These words, spoken by Tempels of the Baluba, could just as easily have been spoken by Heidegger of the Greeks: "Their words lead to the real nature of things. They speak 'ontologically' " (67). While on one hand it is tempting to sympathize with a conception of authenticity that stands against the baleful effects of reification, it seems to lead, even in the best interpretation, to a mere ethnographic nostalgia.

At least this is the case with Heidegger and Tempels. Initially *Ambiguous Adventure* seems caught in this ethnographic impasse as well. During one of a series of philosophical dialogues that take place in various settings in and around Paris, Samba Diallo addresses another African expatriate and his family:

> This feeling of exile which weighs upon us does not mean that we should be useless, but, on the contrary, establishes the necessity for us, and indicates our most urgent task, which is that of clearing the ground around nature. (153)

The import of this passage is far from transparent: what does it mean, for example, to "clear the ground around nature?" Both the "we" of this sentence and "nature" itself are similarly open to question. The figure of "ground-clearing," however, is already familiar from "The Origin of the Work of Art":

> In the midst of beings as a whole an open place occurs. There is a clearing. Thought of in reference to beings, this clearing is more in being than are beings. This open center is therefore not surrounded by beings; rather, the clearing center itself encircles all that is, as does the nothing, which we scarcely know. (178)

The metaphor of the "open place" or "clearing," translated into vulgar terms, refers to the space in which people interact with things. One of the things revealed in this clearing is, indeed, nature—or rather "earth," of whose manifold connotations nature is one: "To set forth the earth means to bring it into the open region" (173). Other connotations of "earth" include materiality as such, "soil" both as the ground of peasant labor and as the political basis of nationalist politics, whose analog in *négritude* poetry, particularly Senghor, is a kind of pan-African feminine principle. We have already touched on the relation between *world* and *earth* and the relationship between *world* and the concept of the "historical people," which, though latent in Heidegger's earlier writing, turns out to be a kind of idée fixe in the essay on the work of art: "The world is the self-opening openness [another formulation of the ground-clearing around being] of the broad paths of the simple and essential decisions in the destiny of a historical people" (174). Once again *world* is immediately brought back to the "historical people," now explicitly in the context of a people's "destiny," or "historical task": "Whenever art happens— that is, whenever there is a beginning—a thrust enters history; history either begins or starts over again. History here means not a sequence in time of events, of whatever sort, however important. History is that transporting of a people into its appointed task" (202). What is the difference between this passage—where ground-clearing as an essential expression of the ways of knowing of any particular culture is easily read as the aggressive expression of "ground-clearing" as the destined task of a particular nation as a new beginning to history—and the one that began this paragraph? It is not enough simply to point out that Kane's ground-clearing is "from below," with neither opportunity for nor intention of global hegemony. As the history of postcolonial Africa demonstrates, there is no "from below" that is not from another perspective a coercive "from above."

The "nature" and the "we" of our last passage from *Ambiguous Adventure* also seem to follow a familiar trajectory: a negative stereotype of "the African" as closer to animal nature is enunciated from a new position with a positive valence, an equally stereotyped African who is more authentically in touch with the earth, free from the technological encumbrances of modernity. This is the "returned gaze" of Sartre's existential version of *négritude*, where an identity that had been borne in shame is now assumed with pride: as Aimé Césaire put it, "Eia pour ceux qui n'ont jamais rien inventé!" "A cheer for those who have never invented anything!"[30] (We will discuss this moment in more detail in chapter 5.) The narrative of the fool—the "authentic son of the countryside" (86)—with whom we began this chapter, tends to support this initial appearance. Where European spaces are characterized by the clatter of "monstrously hardened . . . terminal conches" on pavement, African spaces are represented by "the soft upheaval of earth from a naked foot" (91): the same earth that clings to Heidegger's peasant's shoes. It seems as though the nostalgic impulse toward agrarian simplicity in Heidegger's writings—which as we saw in the introduction is virtually required of any thought that tries to conceptualize production without an account of Capital—is simply translated into an African context. (In a very Heideggerian move, "le regain," translated as "aftermath" in the key phrase we noted earlier, "un regain d'authenticité," also means a "second crop.")[31] The notion of a discrete people with an historical task in Heidegger simply seems to be taken over by Kane, one form of ethnic authenticity answered by another.

There is no point in denying that these overtones are present in the novel. In the fool's narrative what characterizes Europe is technology: "In man's own dwelling place I have seen these deadly spaces. Mechanisms are reigning there" (92). Indeed *Ambiguous Adventure* could be considered a meditation on the meaning of productive technology—once again, also the central concern of literary modernism, though in a much more inchoate way—as a particular orientation toward "earth" or the material world, an orientation characterized by the "investiture of the actual" (151), the "mastery of the object" (167), the "proliferation of the surface" (78), and so on. The central feature of technology (figured as "the West" in Kane's story) is, as might be gathered by the title, its ambiguity: "can one learn *this* without forgetting *that*" (34); can one conquer the *thing* without converting the human being into an object among objects? In more Marxian terms, can the tremendous expansion in productive power brought about by the increasing "organic composition of Capital"—that is, technology—be retained or even accelerated without maintaining the larger capitalist dynamic that sustains it? This ambiguity, though conceived in quite other terms, is the very "question concerning technology" in Heidegger's essay of that name.[32]

In Heidegger's terminology, "ambiguity" (*Zweideutigkeit*) is itself ambiguous. In *Being and Time* it refers to a fundamental feature of *Gerede*, "idle talk": namely, that one can never tell if, in "average everydayness," what looks like truth is indeed truth, or what looks like falsehood is indeed falsehood: "Everything looks as though it were genuinely understood, genuinely taken hold of, genuinely spoken, though at bottom it is not; or else it does not look so, and at bottom it is."[33] This ambiguity takes two forms. The first is in tune with the stereotype of "idle talk" and refers to the idea that what is taken up in idle talk quickly loses its ground and becomes mere gossip. But a more interesting possibility, which is present throughout *Being and Time*, is represented by the "or else": the outworn ideas, the sedimented thoughts that repeat themselves in idle talk might, if closely examined, prove to involve an intuitive apprehension of the truth.

In the technology essay, however, we encounter another kind of ambiguity: "The essence of technology is in a lofty sense ambiguous. Such ambiguity points to the mystery of all revealing, i.e., of truth" (338). This lofty ambiguity is quite different from that which characterized idle talk: it is a world-historical ambiguity in what Heidegger understands as the essential unfolding of the West itself. It refers to technology's potential for (in the terms of the essay from which it comes) both "the danger" and "the saving power." The stakes are higher than the uses to which any particular technology may be put. The danger inherent in *Gestell* is that it may come to colonize all knowledge, eclipsing all other modes of truth: "On the one hand, enframing challenges forth into the frenziedness of ordering that blocks every view into the propriative event of revealing and so radically endangers the relation to the essence of truth" (338). The other side of this ambiguity is Heidegger's "saving power," the simple fact of the enormous increase in productive power: "On the other hand, enframing propriates for its part in the granting that lets man endure—as yet inexperienced, but perhaps more experienced in the future—that he may be the one who is needed and used for the safekeeping of the essence of truth. Thus the rising of the saving power appears" (338). What is at issue is whether technology will eventually reduce the human to mere raw material or standing reserve; or whether, on the contrary, it will free humanity to pursue its authentic being—*poiesis* which, as we have seen, is the expression of "an historical people."

Kane's narrative is ambiguous in both senses. What appears in *Ambiguous Adventure* as simple cliché or outmoded ideology is not entirely what it seems. Africa as a zone of authenticity, as a place where people are closer to the earth, more alive or more human, and so on: these are guidebook clichés, but they also point to *Ambiguous Adventure*'s more original concerns. With a slight change in perspective we might stop asking what all this—in short, the "nature" of our earlier quotation—represents positively and ask to what extent the materialist perspective we have begun to suggest emerges in the text itself. As in Heidegger's essay, what is at issue is not the effect or the potential for good or ill of any particular technology but the "meaning" of technology itself.[34] If we take seriously the Heideggerian overtones of Kane's text, we can say that Kane's "nature" (a concept Heidegger generally avoids) has no positive content in itself. Instead, "nature" is best understood as a negative category: it names what gets enframed, what is converted into standing reserve, what is dominated by technology's "investiture of the actual," whether this refers to the rationalization of production, of knowledge, or of African space. "Nature" is that which resists and is overcome by the "mastery" of technological thought. In *Ambiguous Adventure* the sign of authenticity represents the external boundaries of Capital: that which has yet to be "checked by census, divided up, classified, labeled, conscripted, administrated" (49): in other words, what has not yet been or for structural reasons cannot be assimilated into "standing reserve."

This brings us to the "lofty ambiguity" of the novel, what Kane, in explicating the title, has called the "two paths open to humanity."[35] Once again Kane appears to operate on Heideggerian ground. The danger is that technology—as dramatized by the fool's tale of a Europe where humanlike beings clatter about in insectile machines on asphalt spaces—will be able to "pass by" (153) other modes of being, obliterating them completely in the process of colonization. But here Kane also begins to supersede Heidegger, for while Heidegger's idealism expresses this danger purely as a blocking of *poiesis*, Kane's narrative construes this epistemic blockage as part and parcel of material history, namely colonization and the material benefits it both promises and withholds:

> The West is possessed by its own compulsion, and the world is becoming Westernized. Far from men's resisting the madness of the West at a time when they ought to do so, in order to pick and choose, assimilate or reject, we see them, on the contrary, in all latitudes, a-quiver with covetousness, then metamorphosing themselves in the space of one generation. (69)

But it is in the "saving power" that *Ambiguous Adventure* decisively evacuates the modernist structure set in place by Heidegger. For if Heidegger's *poiesis* marks an apex in the theorization of the eidaesthetic, a pivotal moment in what Badiou has called philosophy's "age of poets,"[36] it also names the attempt to elevate the poetic principle (a subjective solution to objective problems) immediately back into the realm of the objective—either through a politics of authenticity or, when that investment proves disastrous, in the deus ex machina of "only a god can save us."

In *Ambiguous Adventure* the "saving power," the utopian possibility inherent in the "aventure occidentale" (170), is not quite what one might think: the utopian alternative to total colonization by the "madness" of Western technology does not follow the nostalgic lines sketched out by Heidegger, where an autonomous technology would free up the space for a return to older experiences of being. As we saw earlier, Being-towards-death as the guarantor of authenticity passes through a specifically Diallobé "average everydayness." But the possibility of a return to this mode of authenticity is rigorously foreclosed. When Kane could so easily have taken refuge in a nostalgic notion of cultural authenticity, preferring the depth of Diallobé culture to the arid effectivity of European technology, the possibility of such a choice is everywhere denied, not only in the figure of Samba Diallo himself, but in the prophecy his father makes to a Frenchman in his country:

> We have not had the same past, you and ourselves, but we shall have, strictly, the same future. The era of separate destinies has run its course. In that sense, the end of the world has indeed come for every one of us, because no one can any longer live by the

simple carrying out of what he himself is. But from our long and varied ripenings a son will be born to the world: the first son of the earth. (79–80)

"The end of the world has indeed come for us" in more ways than one. Each world, each "separate destiny" has come to an end, but more significantly "world" itself, the very possibility of authenticity as "the simple carrying out" of one's own being is no longer possible. The *world*, the Heideggerian category that refers to the "pathways" of an historical people, is henceforth at an end; after the "strange dawn" of the colonial moment, there are no more discrete cultural worlds.

The prophecy is not that a return to authenticity is possible, but that the experience of the colonized has the potential to contribute decisively to a new form of ethical, political, and economic life—the "future citadel" (in French simply *la cité future* [92]) that "will open its wide windows on the abyss" (80)—which we cannot presently conceive. Technology as an epistemic form is to be superseded by something that preserves the possibility of the "not-yet," by a mode of subjectivity that will lie behind this future city, a social totality oriented toward the possibilities of the human being. How, then, is this city of ends to be reached? Who is the "we" whose "urgent task" is to "clear the ground" for this future? "In the city which is being born such should be our work—all of us, Hindus, Chinese, South Americans, Negroes, Arabs, all of us, awkward and pitiful, we the underdeveloped, who feel ourselves to be clumsy in a world of perfect mechanical adjustment" (80). Once again what is occluded in Heidegger's poetic thought emerges into the light of day in Kane's prose. As with the "compulsion" to assimilate Western attitudes, the experience of "nothingness" is not allowed to sever its links to the material history that produces it. This "we" is then transformed: rather than standing for an ethnic or racial identity, it refers to an historical and economic experience. The "we" who are to "clear the ground around nature" are those who are systematically excluded from the benefits of technology: the experience of Being constituted by the cultural "world" is transformed into the experience of underdevelopment.

Meanwhile, the "ground-clearing" around nature refers to the possibility that the mastery of the object-world could be advanced while preserving the bar between the potentialities of the human and the potentialities of the object:

> The West . . . masters the object and colonizes us at the same time. If we do not awake the West to the difference which separates us from the object, we shall be worth no more than it is, and we shall never master it. And our defeat will be the end of the last human being on this earth. (154)

The "mastery of the object" is not to be rejected in favor of some imagined or remembered prior relationship to the object-world. In *Ambiguous Adventure* the notion of authenticity attenuates its links to the *ethnos* to the point where it becomes no more than a memory, the mere sting of nostalgia for a nontechnological episteme. Whatever its origins, the difference that imposes this necessity is ultimately material and positional, not ethnic and essential. The insight Kane reaches here is that imperialism had in fact already transformed positive differences into positional ones. On one hand, the internal cohesion or interchangeability of "African" or "non-Western" cultures is ideological, a stereotype of the non-Western other. On the other hand, this very stereotype is based on something real, the conversion of all noncapitalist ways of life to tributaries of Capital—and therefore alerts us to the possibility of a real political identification. If a return to a genuinely non-Western episteme is impossible, its memory nonetheless is to serve as an impetus toward a social totality that would preserve capitalism's "mastery of the thing" without orienting itself toward the final conversion of human possibilities into standing-reserve. The equivalent of the "saving power" in Kane's narrative is a leapfrogging, through the experience of underdevelopment, of the technological episteme toward some other mode of being that would preserve both the mastery of the object-world and the specific potentialities of the human being.

But this is simply a wish. The question "can one learn *this* without forgetting *that*" is quietly transformed into an abstract imperative: "one must learn *this* without forgetting *that*." It becomes then simply a matter of how one should "pick and choose, assimilate or reject" rather than "metamorphosing [oneself] in the space of one generation." But does this option exist? "If I do not tell the Diallobé to go to the new school, they will not go. Their houses will fall into ruins, their children will die or be reduced to slavery. Extreme poverty will be entrenched among them" (34). As with, for example, the decision to borrow money from the IMF, there is really not much of a choice to be made; whatever cultural pathways are worth preserving, presumably poverty is not one of them. But once made, this non-choice severely restricts the field of action. If the good (technology as the mastery of the thing) and the bad (technology as the mastery of the human being) are dialectically related then the imperative to have one without the other is simply empty, like the liberal wish for a market economy that doesn't produce poverty. In the introduction we argued that both the development of technology and colonialism were a function of capital, something Samba Diallo approaches abstractly when he notes that the "West . . . masters the object and colonizes us at the same time" (154). Imperialism, technology, and the reification of experience are all manifestations of the same thing, the tendency of Capital to overcome all external limits. The aggressivity and "compulsion" of colonization belong not to the West but to Capital, for which perpetual expansion of the market is a precondition of its continued existence. Similarly for technology: the major impulse behind the increase in productive power has not been the autonomous unfolding of the Idea of technology: on the contrary, technological advances arise from the conflict between maximizing profit and the limit represented by the cost of reproducing labor.[37] Technology's "aggressivity" is only the anthropomorphized image of the restlessness of Capital and its tendency to construe subjectivity as well ("demand") as a limit to be overcome. The principle of rationalization is itself the expression of the fact that calculability is a precondition for speculation and investment; the very "fall" into the segmentation of Being and the diremption of spirit and letter are aspects of the organization of society around the commodity form. And the conversion of anything and everything into standing-reserve, up to and including the reserve army of the (increasingly Third World) unemployed, may very well be a feature of the technological episteme, but only if we ultimately refer it to the imperative to keep production costs down.

Referring to existentialism's elaboration of the concept of "nothingness," Adorno wrote, "The public is . . . learning to understand their nothingness as Being, to revere actual, avoidable, or at least corrigible need as the most humane element in the image of man."[38] As we have seen, *Ambiguous Adventure* brings this relationship to self-consciousness: "Strange, Lacroix was thinking, the fascination of nothingness for those who have nothing" (78). Resistance to assimilation into the radically inhuman notion of the person as a "human resource"—that is, what resists the conversion of human power into the infinitely manipulable "standing-reserve"— is attributed to those who are in fact systematically excluded from the material benefits that derive from such notions. While this contains the seeds of a real insight, the elevation of Heideggerian language to a level of self-consciousness does not alone solve its problems, and four decades of hindsight give us license to suspect a note of bad faith here. Samba Diallo's "having nothing"—the "having nothing" of the anticolonial intellectual—is of a different order than that of the propertyless African masses who, far from being able to choose their own nothingness, are what Neil Larsen, after the German political economist Robert Kurz, calls "monetary subjects without money": individuals who have neither recourse to the remnants of noncapitalist production nor access to the capitalist cycle of production, even at the lowest level.[39] In this situation "those who have nothing" cannot be made to represent directly a utopian possibility; rather, any such possibility would have to be mediated through the potential crisis in the world system they represent and through a politics that could organize them into a political subject.

From this perspective, it appears that by elevating the subjective experience of underdevelopment to a utopian principle, the processes of actual economic underdevelopment are occluded and *Ambiguous Adventure* cedes everything decisive to that which it hopes to overcome. The choice raised by the novel is then different than it originally appeared. Is authenticity—understood now in its most sympathetic interpretation, the surpassing or overcoming of reification—a project for humanity, for the social totality? If so, the abstraction of this project is its ideological content. As we saw in the introduction with regard to anticolonial utopias in general, anyone can endorse Kane's "future city" because there is no program for getting there: the unanimity it inspires is a spurious one whose historical referent is the populist euphoria that accompanied the accession to power of the first independent African governments. Mediated by a politics that would in fact mobilize "those who have nothing," and therefore given concrete content, Kane's project would become a much more contentious thing. If authenticity cannot project itself immediately onto the social totality, it can, on the other hand, still be maintained (in religious or other private experience) in the face of "Western values." The channeling of resistance to reification into a compensatory private sphere, however, is rather different than the promise of creating a whole new society that had seemed to be at stake. The possibility raised by *Ambiguous Adventure* sinks back into the same compromise that characterized modernism's aesthetic utopia: a purely private compensation for problems whose origins lie at the level of the social totality.

But the point here is not to accuse *Ambiguous Adventure* of an idealism which, like that of Heidegger's *Gestell*, is the very source of its fascination. The remarkable thing, rather, is that *Ambiguous Adventure* already embodies its own critique. At the end of the novel, Samba Diallo, the potential "first son of the earth" (80) is called back to the land of the Diallobé, where he is mistaken by the fool for the reincarnation of his old Koranic teacher. But one day the fool recognizes that the returned son no longer embodies the promise he held out on his departure. Scandalized, he strikes down Samba Diallo, who is received by a mysterious voice who promises that all ambiguity has been dispelled. We must of course take Kane's Sufism seriously. But in a final ambiguity, what appears to be a solution for Samba Diallo is not a solution for anybody else; his private destiny finally takes precedence over the communal aspirations it had seemed to represent. As we shall see played out repeatedly in the novels of Wyndham Lewis, a resolution that has to wait for the afterlife tends to imply a contradiction that cannot be resolved on earth. As Kane says himself, Samba's death is "a way of resolving problems which haven't found a solution down here."[40] At the moment of Samba's death the abstract utopian hope of the anticolonial intellectual ("the first son of the earth") is converted into its postcolonial opposite, which in comparison can only seem like the defeat of "the last human being on this earth."

PART TWO

History

CHAPTER FOUR

The Good Soldier and *Parade's End*: Absolute Nostalgia

It will not have escaped notice that in the previous chapter we already made the transition from the terrain of subjectivity to that of history—without, however, a mediating concept that could have rendered this transition anything but self-defeating. The nostalgia and elegiac tone of Ford Madox Ford's most accomplished novels resonate with *Ambiguous Adventure* because they occupy the same aporia, but from the side of history. *The Good Soldier* and *Parade's End* derive their power not from any particularly surprising or profound exploration of subjectivity but from a mode of narration in which history is approached in the mode of the sublime, as the unnameable. Faced with the onslaught of a history that cannot be conceptualized and therefore appears wholly external to them, Ford's characters can only recoil.

Every decade since the 1930s has discovered Ford, not as refreshed by the experiences of a new generation but as a neglected treasure picked out of someone else's trash. Since his death in 1939 he has been the subject of occasional brief blasts lamenting public and critical ignorance of his work: Ezra Pound, Graham Greene, William Carlos Williams, and W. H. Auden each wrote such pieces in successive decades. Rebecca West's 1915 review of *The Good Soldier* testifies that this was already the case even at the height of Ford's creative period:

> Mr. Ford Madox Hueffer [Ford changed his name in 1919] is the Scholar Gypsy of English letters: he is the author who is recognized only as he disappears around the corner. . . . [U]nfortunately [this recognition] usually takes the form of enthusiastic but belated discoveries of work that he left on the doorstep ten years ago.[1]

Surely the defensive pose of sixty years of Ford criticism, always insisting on greatness but never taking it for granted, has done more harm than good to Ford's reputation. Nonetheless, it might be useful to review the familiar list of reasons ordinarily given for Ford's neglect, though no one of them is sufficient, if only to remind ourselves of some aspects of Ford's work that do stand in the way of his appreciation by contemporary readers.

The first offense of Ford's work is to be unassimilable to any canon. The best work is too late, too convoluted, and too much influenced by early French modernism to be included with his nineteenth-century British forebears. But despite the appearance of the initial chapters of *The Good Soldier* between the puce-colored covers of Wyndham Lewis's first *Blast*[2]—a publication where it does not look nearly so out of place as one might have thought, sharing as it does Lewis's preoccupations with the vices and virtues of The Englishman, roundly Blasted and Blest in the Vorticist "Manifesto"—it is too much in the tradition out of which it arises to take part fully in the *bellum omnium contra omnes* that was literary modernism. Ford's masterpiece, the tetrology collected under the title *Parade's End*, despite its ambition and scope, is too diffuse to be compared favorably with modernisms such as Eliot's or Woolf's by the terms their work imposed on literary judgment.

Second, Ford's oeuvre is both impossible to master and not worth the trouble. Ford published more than eighty books during his lifetime, and he left behind masses of uncollected essays and unpublished manuscripts. Over a productive life of forty-seven years, it would be impossible to produce eighty brilliant books or even eighty readable ones, and even Ford's best work, with few exceptions, suffers from a dilution of his energy. Acquaintance with Ford's minor works has the odd effect of lessening rather than amplifying the impact of *Parade's End* and *The Good Soldier*; as with a television actor in a cinematic role, the ubiquity of a characteristic gesture can cheapen its monumentalized performance.

Further, Ford, like Joyce and Kane, drew from life; but unlike either of them, Ford's life was in the public eye, and often a public scandal: for example, his irregular marriage to Violet Hunt was made public in a lawsuit over his name pressed by legal wife, Elsie Hueffer.[3] At the time of the publication of *Parade's End*, the relationship of Christopher Tietjens to his wife, Sylvia, might have seemed too transparently drawn from his affair with and estrangement from Hunt, which had several times made the newspapers. His portrayal of Sylvia Tietjens's vindictive sexuality was in this context taken to be a self-serving embellishment of personal history rather than a deliberate reworking of subjective experience into a fragmentary representation of the social totality.

All of this has been said many times before. One has only to glance at the introduction to any one of the biographies or critical studies of the last sixty years to find similar explanations for Ford's neglect—a neglect that also has its positive side in that it makes possible a constant rediscovery that is closed off to more solidly canonized modernists. None of these extrinsic explanations is sufficient to account for Ford's relative obscurity, although no doubt they all have played a part. Other authors have been rescued from the gap between modernism and its antecedents; other canonical authors have written unread novels; and, whatever degree Ford may in fact have been guilty of a propensity to self-exculpation in his work, the passage of time has succeeded where Ford may have failed: any scandalous autobiographical reference is long forgotten to all but scholars. But there is another element, perhaps more consequent than all the others, that keeps Ford's great novels out of currency. They can only be read once.

Certainly, one may read *Parade's End* as many times as one pleases, and it remains an entertaining read. But the first reading of a novel like *The Good Soldier* or the books of *Parade's End* is fundamentally different from any subsequent reading, and the intensity and utter uniqueness of that first reading is something nearly impossible to recover. For the primary effect of Ford's best sustained writing is bewilderment. The techniques used to achieve this effect we shall return to later, but for now it is enough to point out that never, at any point during either *The Good Soldier* or *Parade's End*, does one truly have a grasp of what is going on; and yet nothing is secretly omitted or archly withheld, and no mysteries have been inserted for posterity. Pastoral idylls turn to hysterical visions—and back again within the space of a sentence—without one having the vaguest idea why. Morbid similes introduce a pleasant luncheon, hands clutch desperately at wrists, a wife hesitates significantly before sitting, "as if her horse had checked";[4] the explanation is out of reach, but only barely out of reach, like a movement perpetually caught in peripheral vision. There is not a sentence in Ford—nor indeed a passage or scene—that is not, despite an occasional Jamesian tendency toward knotty grammatical subordination, readily intelligible. But there are sentences of seemingly great import that refuse to give up their meaning, and passages that provoke, with an utter lack of gothic mystery, the kind of deep uneasiness that Conrad was generally limited to describing. Unlike the major effects of *Ulysses*, which are engineered to reward the sifting and resifting of repeated reading, the foreboding of the Fordian sentence is completely lost on a second reading. For by the time one reads *The Good Soldier* again, a sentence like "Heavens! There doesn't seem to have been the actual time" (8) becomes mere foreshadowing, since one is no longer desperate to know "time for what?"

The sublime, reconnecting the subject with an object that is universal, abstract, and empty, is predicated on a suppression of its own historical content—in the Kantian case, the constitution of the noumenon as external to phenomena and in the general modernist case the substitution of the abstract *thing* for a more concrete conception of the social totality. What, then, would a historical mode of the modernist sublime look like? Better known than the published fruits of Ford's years of collaboration with Joseph Conrad (for example, *The Inheritors*, a political allegory concerning the takeover of the British government by usurpers from the fourth dimension) are the technical and formal innovations developed during their collaborative years. Conrad seems to have been readier to accept the label "impressionism" for these developments, writing as early as 1897 in his preface to *The Nigger of the Narcissus* that fiction "must be, like painting. . . . an impression conveyed through the senses."[5] Conrad's remarks, which precede Ford's statement of literary method, "On Impressionism," by nearly two decades, is more polemical, more concise, and clearer about the representational and epistemological claims it is making; but Ford's mode of "impressionism," though closely related to Conrad's and plainly influenced by it, is both more complex and more ambitious. Conrad's theory of the impression therefore provides an ideal jumping-off point for understanding the Fordian mode of the modernist sublime, which extends impressionist method into the actual fourth dimension: time and, ultimately, history.[6]

In the well-known preface to *The Nigger of the Narcissus*, Conrad outlines a form of the modernist sublime more basic than what we found in *Ulysses* but quite congruent with Stephen's theory of the epiphany:

> Art itself may be defined as a single-minded attempt to render the highest kind of justice to the visible universe, by bringing to light the truth, manifold and one, underlying its every aspect. It is an attempt to find in its forms, in its colors, in the aspects of matter and the facts of life, what of each is fundamental, what is enduring and essential—their one illuminating and convincing quality—the very truth of their existence. (vii)

Conrad's "truth, manifold and one, underlying . . . every aspect" of sensory experience glosses the Kantian noumenon, the inaccessible substratum of experience that can only be intuited indirectly by means of the sublime object. The object cannot be merely itself; if it is to provide access to "what is enduring and essential," it must be shaken loose from the concept that anchors it in its self-evidence. Conrad's impressionism seeks to arrive at the "very truth" underlying experience by means of mere sensory perceptions freed from the mediation of the concept. But as with the languages of *Ulysses*, the first effect of impressionistic language is not to reveal the truth but to withhold it. A purely sensory language need not have a content at all; it could be a pure record of sense data that never congeal into things and events. *Heart of Darkness*, for example, has been accused by critics as diverse as F. R. Leavis, Chinua Achebe, and E. M. Forster precisely of having no content beneath its surface:

> But suddenly as we struggled round a bend there would be a glimpse of rush walls, of peaked grass-roofs, a burst of yells, a whirl of black limbs, a mass of hands clapping, of feet stamping, of bodies swaying, of eyes rolling under the droop of heavy and motionless foliage. The steamer toiled along slowly to the edge of a black and incomprehensible frenzy. . . . We were cut off from comprehension of our surroundings.[7]

The actual content of this image (singled out by Achebe in his critique of Conrad) cannot be reconstructed from the fragments given in the image.[8] We are not given a description, only isolated sense impressions, cut off from any consciousness of what these impressions might represent. Here the device is explicitly motivated by the narrative: "We were cut off from comprehension of our surroundings" (42). This refers to Marlowe and his crew, but it could be a description of impressionistic language itself. Rather than being given together at the outset, intellection is suspended in favor of sense impressions which, although they may retroactively be given a name, can never be completely reconstructed. What the Marlowe of *Lord Jim* called "jumbled bits of color like a damaged kaleidoscope" are not to be restored into recognizable objects.[9] We are left with Eliot's "heap of broken images"; or, as the narrator of Ford's *The Good Soldier* says, "a picture without a meaning" (254). What we are given in the sense-language of impressionism is not the thing itself but a list of its properties.

The epistemological claim of Conrad's preface, that a pure record of sensory impressions will provide that "glimpse of truth for which you have forgotten to ask" (xi)—that the thing can be brought closer by foregoing the mediation of the concept—involves a contradiction. The recognition of an object—a human face or the ring of a telephone—is immediate; sense impressions can only be separated from this recognition by an act of abstraction away from the object. Paradoxically, what appears to be less mediated (sense data, from a commonsense or computational point of view, must be registered by sense organs before they can be interpreted by consciousness) is, from the viewpoint of consciousness, more mediated. Sense data can only be arrived at through a further process of mediation away from the thing itself, which has always already been interpreted, that is, mediated through a concept. What Conrad's impressionist language registers is not a truth prior to interpretation but the purely negative refusal of a prior, implicit claim to truth made by the preexisting universal that is named by "village," "street-scene," and so on. If any content at all is to be reconstructed from impressionist language, it can only be delivered by the concept that was to be avoided.

This contradiction within the representational structure of impressionism is matched by the political ambiguity that we have seen as a general feature of the modernist sublime. Science, says Conrad sarcastically, concerns itself with "weighty matters: with . . . the proper care of our bodies, with . . . the perfection of the means and the glorification of our precious aims" (vii–viii). The languages of science and philosophy "make their appeal" by "speaking authoritatively to our common sense" (vii)—which appeal is in fact "always to our credulity" (vii). The sensory language of Conradian impressionism, opposed to the "common-sense" language of prefabricated meaning, already follows the general form of modernist utopia: it is both the explicit negation of the world to which "common sense" is an adjustment, and, in its refusal of intellection altogether, an accommodation to what it rejects.[10] Once again the sublime object, rather than providing a mystical access to the Truth, is the symptom of the absence of a certain kind of truth. Rather than competing with self-evidence, the content of Conrad's literary impressionism can only be provided by that common sense it opposes—and indeed, usually is, in the form of the moral stories that Conrad's narratives are still often taken to be.

Ford's statement of method must be considered in relation to this Conradian impressionism, compared with which it is both more modest and more sophisticated. On one hand, "On Impressionism" (published in 1914, when Ford was working on *The Good Soldier*) is a much more workmanlike affair than Conrad's, largely concerned with writerly advice on achieving particular effects, and relatively free of claims about the truth content of impressionist language. On the other hand, it tremendously complicates the idea of the "impression," which is bifurcated between writer and reader, and, more important, shifted from the instantaneous moment of sensory perception to the diachronic space of memory.

Ford's explicit concern is not so much with truth as with verisimilitude, not so much with the justice language may do to sense impressions as the impression language may produce in a reader: how to introduce a character so that his subsequent actions will bear the stamp of his or her first sentence, how to render a speech without producing endless dialogue, or how to time a suicide to maximum effect. The justification of Fordian impressionism is to synchronize descriptive language with the rhythms of remembered experience. Impressionistic language is to be as "true to life" as possible, not through doing justice to the surface of things, but through a reproduction of the way "impressions" are remembered. The decisive split between Conrad's and Ford's impressionisms is that Ford's is temporal. Diachronic events rather than synchronic images are broken up and allowed to associate freely with one another, giving the illusion of being "the record of a recollection" (41). Thus, on a certain level Fordian impressionism is theoretically illusionistic: "to produce an illusion" of memory is its ultimate justification (44). But Ford's impressionism duplicates, at the level of the event, the dialectic implicit in Conrad's descriptive language: impressionism's reality-effect is only achieved through a further mediation.

This can be demonstrated by way of two meanings of "impression" in Ford's text: "impression" stands not just for the fictional set of recollected impressions to be conveyed illusionistically by the text, but the actual effect of the text on the reader. Ford's impressionism does not primarily attempt to represent the sense data that intellection ordinarily composes into the object-world, but to represent the jumbled memories that recollection ordinarily composes into an event. But verisimilitude in the Fordian sense (justice to the way "impressions" are recollected in memory) and effect (the "impression" made on a reader) cannot be unproblematically identified. Much closer to us than the process of memory are the memories themselves. As with Conradian impressionism and the object-world, the representation of the process of memory in Fordian impressionism requires an act of abstraction away from the event itself; the first meaning of "impression" names a process that tends away from the goal named by the second. If anything, Ford was more concerned in practice with effect, with the impression produced in the reader, than faithfulness to the structure of impressions in his "analysis of the human mind" (48). "If the final province of art is to convince, its first province is to interest" (46). The Conradian dialectic is brought a degree nearer to self-consciousness, as the nonequivalence of these two provinces broaches the surface. As with Conrad's impressionism on another plane, the effect of unmediated recollection is achieved only through a double mediation. In Ford, however, the process of mediation produces not a fragmentation of the image in a doomed attempt to escape the tyranny of the concept, but a fragmentation of memory in a parallel attempt to escape the mediation of history.

The formal procedures by which this is carried out are worked out in their most thoroughgoing form in *The Good Soldier*. In what is ostensibly a review of the novel, Theodore Dreiser explains how he would have written it:

> Personally I would have suggested to Mr. Hueffer that he begin at the beginning . . . [and] once begun . . . go forward in a more or less direct line. . . . The interlacings, the cross references, the re-re-references to all sorts of things which subsequently are told somewhere in full, irritate one to the point of one's laying down the book.[11]

Despite what must seem to twenty-first-century readers an inane criticism of a book whose every sentence is so obviously directed at not telling the story in a "direct line," Dreiser's frustration is a reminder of the distance traveled between the memory-language of *The Good Soldier* and what it is designed to escape, of the violence that has been done to what Dreiser called "the makings of a fine story" (50).[12] It is useful to imagine what *The Good Soldier* might be like if it were rewritten as a chronological narrative, if only as a step toward clarifying how drastically the narrative has been rearranged. An American, John Dowell, marries a somewhat reluctant younger woman, Florence. Her guardians seem to have some reservations, and the couple elopes; during their flight to Europe, the bride feigns a heart attack and lives thenceforth as an invalid. She continues an affair with, and is subsequently blackmailed by, a young man in Paris with whom she had traveled on an earlier European trip. Dowell is preposterously unaware, believing that her condition precludes any sexual activity, marital or otherwise. Florence begins another affair, of which Dowell is again pathetically unaware, with Edward Ashburnham, one of a wealthy couple they had met at a European spa. A former lover of Ashburnham dies of a broken heart when he falls for Florence; when he falls for yet another girl, or perhaps for some other reason, Florence commits suicide. But the girl is Ashburnham's ward, and he slits his throat because he cannot have her. Ashburnham's wife, Leonora, remarries. The girl goes mad with grief over Ashburnham's suicide, and Dowell, who has fallen in love with her, buys the Ashburnhams' ancestral home and becomes the girl's caretaker.

Written thus, the plot of *The Good Soldier* looks like high melodrama. And yet there is not a dramatic moment in the book; every narrative climax is carefully converted into an anticlimax. To take an obvious example: the actual narration of Edward Ashburnham's suicide—slitting his throat with a penknife—appears as an afterthought. By the second page of the book we are aware that Ashburnham will die before the end of the novel; that his death will be a suicide is revealed not much later. But the event itself is not narrated until five pages after the novel has ostensibly ended; Leonora is remarried, the girl has gone mad; Dowell, living in the house, has proclaimed, as narrator, "Well, that is the end of the story" (252). The story even has an edifying moral, or antimoral. Then: "It suddenly occurs to me that I have forgotten to say how Edward met his death" (255). In fact, Dreiser's review is insightful, even if his expectations were anachronistic:

> Every scene of any importance has been blinked or passed over with a few words or cross references. . . . Every conversation which should have appeared, every storm which should have contained revealing flashes, making clear the minds, the hearts, and the agonies of those concerned, has been avoided. . . . You are never really stirred.[13]

This is all true: it is not just that the narration is passionless: *The Good Soldier* is "A Tale of Passion" (the novel's subtitle) from which every ounce of passion has been deliberately bled. And yet while a reader may not be "stirred" by the drama of events as they unfold, the novel is hardly affectively flat. The text is still furiously driven by narrative tension and resolution, but the tension is not provided by the anticipation of events, nor is resolution afforded by the events themselves.

Instead, the reader is thrown into a state of confusion. A close rereading of the remarkable first chapter of *The Good Soldier* reveals that reference is made to nearly every event in the novel: the blackmail of Teddy Ashburnham and the disintegration of the Ashburnhams' marriage; Florence's affair with Ashburnham and her insinuation into the Ashburnhams' lives; Dowell's comical nine-year ignorance of this affair; the deaths of Florence and Ashburnham; Dowell's purchase of their estate—not, of course, in such a logical order. By the end of the second chapter, we have references to the rest of it: Dowell's strange marriage to Florence and Ashburnham's final doomed love affair. On a first reading, these passing references are frustratingly oblique: the reference to Ashburnham's final affair is simply the mention of "the girl" as an intermediary between Ashburnham and Leonora (20). Her importance is marked by a sentence that gets its own paragraph, stopping the flow of language both before and after it: "The girl was out with the hounds, I think" (20). But that is all we get of Nancy Rufford for the next seventy-five pages, and even then we don't get much. This is foreshadowing; but when images, phrases, and emotions from a ten-year history flash before our eyes—sometimes for not more than a phrase or a sentence—in the space of twenty pages, the effect is bewildering. Thereafter, each page throws a little light on this history; but, until the end, only enough to deepen the shadows behind it. The tug of narrative tension is provided not by anxiety over what happens next, but by the desire not to lose track of the threads one already has in hand.

This effect is brought about in several ways. The first is this super-foreshadowing, where the entire plot is given in advance but in such a way as to leave a reader entirely in the dark. The second is a kind of hypertrophied digression. We do not hear of Nancy Rufford, who is really the central element in the story, for seventy-five pages after her original, fleeting, portentous entrance. When we do hear of her again, her narrative continues—interrupting and interrupted by the narrative of Florence's affair with Ashburnham—for some forty pages before being interrupted for sixty pages of reflection—with interruptions—on the story of Leonora's marriage. The technique is first introduced in the second chapter: Dowell has us "Consider the lamentable history of Peire Vidal"; but we have to wait four pages for it. The narration of the Ashburnhams' first meeting (or is it the first?) with the Dowells is suspended for six pages, and then for twenty-two, and then for ten more. Sometimes a strand is interrupted for good: the statement that a speech of Leonora's told Dowell "almost more than I have ever gathered at any one moment—about myself" (46) is never picked up. The narration seems to promise an explanation, then turns to other things, and we are left to conjecture what it is that Dowell gathered about himself. This would be digression except that what is interrupting the narrative is not extraneous material but all the other strands of the plot, which are in turn interrupted by this one and all the others, so that a reader must try to hold onto one strand while others are being introduced and dropped; when the narrative picks up that strand it drops another, virtually in mid-sentence, keeping the reader in perpetual suspense.

Again, this is not suspense as to what will happen next, but to what is really happening now. The narration is always clear enough as to what it is saying at the moment. But the valence of an event changes constantly as its narration is picked up at various moments throughout the text. A central event is introduced in the third chapter of part 1: the Ashburnhams walk into a dining room and, rather than sit at their assigned table, choose to dine with the Dowells, who are complete strangers. Is this merely because Ashburnham doesn't like the sun in his eyes? Or, as Dowell later insinuates, because Ashburnham already has his eye on Florence? Or has Florence already decided to "annex" Ashburnham? Is it because they were all "good people"? Or is it precisely because Leonora found Florence vulgar? Or is it, finally, because Leonora wants to impress upon Florence, who had witnessed an earlier scene in a hallway, what a happy couple the Ashburnhams are? At one time or another Dowell attributes responsibility for this event to each of the "four-square coterie" (5)—except himself.

The effect of each of these techniques is a kind of double vision. Both techniques—relentless foreshadowing and suspension of narrative—guarantee that the narration under one's eyes never commands full attention: one or more lost strands always hover in the background. But this is not actually so much a background in a painterly sense as a scrim through which the action is perceived. The structure of *The Good Soldier* is precisely that described by Ford, with a metaphor more apt than many critics' attempts to characterize it, in "On Impressionism":

> Indeed, I suppose impressionism exists to render those queer effects of real life that are like so many views seen through bright glass—through a glass so bright that whilst you perceive through it a landscape or a backyard, you are aware that, on its surface, it reflects a face of a person behind you. (41)

The action narrated at the moment is always taking place on the other side of the glass; what is fainter, yet closer to us as though reflected on it—and also menacing, like a person sneaking up behind—is the fate of all the other strands that are left in suspense.

From the perspective of any particular point in the narrative, the flitting appearances of all the plot elements that must unfold over a ten-year narrative are flashes from the future. The vague uneasiness that accompanies our reading of a passage that has interrupted a more important one is a presentiment of the latter's disastrous return; the interrupted fragment, the dimly perceived face on the glass, is a harbinger of what is to come. Events must constantly be reinterpreted in terms of a truth that is always about to be revealed. Dasie Maidan dies "quite quietly—of heart trouble" (51). Later, for no reason that is yet apparent, her death has become "pretty awful . . . when you figure out what it means" (67). But we have no idea what this means: this statement points toward a future moment that (we suspect) will reveal the meaning of the previous ones. Characteristically, this moment is kept in suspense yet longer, until we discover that Dasie had indeed died of a heart attack, brought on by rage at the discovery that she had been essentially bought for Edward from her husband—information given to her by Florence (73–76): "She died so grotesquely that her little body had fallen into [a] trunk, and it had closed upon her, like the jaws of a giant alligator . . . sticking out . . . [was] a small pair of feet in high-heeled shoes" (75–76, quotation rearranged). Only pages ago, Dasie had died "quite quietly." The quiet death (51) is converted to an awful one (67) by a moment further down the road (76).

A bravura passage near the beginning of the novel establishes the mode of the novel as a whole:

> Our intimacy was like a minuet, simply because on every possible occasion and in every possible circumstance we knew where to go, where to sit, which table we unanimously should choose; and we could rise and go, all four together, without a signal from any of us, always to the music of the Kur orchestra, always in the temperate sunshine, or, if it rained, in discreet shelters. . . .
>
> No, by God, it is false! It wasn't a minuet that we stepped; it was a prison—a prison full of screaming hysterics, tied down so that they might not outsound the rolling of

our carriage wheels as we went along the shaded avenues of the Taunus Wald.

Yet I swear by the sacred name it was true. It was true sunshine; the true music; the true plash of the fountains from the mouth of stone dolphins. (6–7)

The central sentence, running from minuet abruptly to madhouse and then gently turning back, on a trochaic internal rhyme, to the shaded avenues of Taunus Wald, is a small masterpiece in itself; the brief irruption of a nightmare perspective into the temperate world of fashionable resorts is not a paranoid fantasy but none other than the sublime crashing through the edifice of the beautiful. The vision of the rolling carriage as prison van is no less than a glimpse of the inconceivable truth: a truth whose brief appearance, in turn, can only be neutralized and re-contained by an almost tangible effort of will on the part of the narrator.

On second and subsequent readings, all of the bewildering ambiguity of passages like the above can be read without dissonance or resistance as oscillating between "appearance" and "reality." It is no accident that the hermeneutic possibilities of the text are rigorously grouped in pairs. It is difficult to find a statement in *The Good Soldier* that has not its precise opposite. This equivocation begins in the first paragraph: "My wife and I knew Captain and Mrs. Ashburnham as well as it was possible to know anybody, and yet, in another sense, we knew nothing at all about them" (3). Such passages, containing both a statement and its negation, pervade the text: "Her eyes had made a favorable answer. Or, perhaps, it was not a favorable answer" (33). And so on. Is Florence, or Ashburnham for that matter, a heart patient or not? Is the "mainspring" of Florence's behavior fear (93) or vanity (117)? Does Dowell love Leonora (32) or dislike her (252)? Was Florence "[not] for one minute out of my sight" (8) or was she "out of my sight most of the time" (88)?

What this means is that in the story being told by the narrator Dowell, each event is subjected simultaneously to two competing horizons of interpretation which, on a second reading, are collapsed into one. The first horizon is that of the continual present: events are interpreted in real time and seeing is believing. The second horizon is the future (that is, the truth of the present): events are interpreted with reference to the "four crashing days at the end of nine years and six weeks" (6)—the two suicides and the collapse of the entire web of lies that had held together the "four-square coterie" (5)—that comprise the chronological end of the story. On a second reading the whole narrative is oriented toward this second horizon, which becomes simply the truth, and the passages that do not register the truth testify to a delusion.

Up to a certain point, this narrative structure exemplifies, in a more intimate register, key features of the historical dialectic in Hegel. Hegel's famous owl of Minerva "spreads its wings only with the falling of the dusk."[14] This means that the significance of an historical period, the synthesis of all the partial truths and the meaning for us of all the contingent events that populate it, is never given with the events themselves, but can only be constructed as a totality from a perspective for whom that period is past. Hegel's impressive-sounding and much maligned Absolute Spirit is, formally, no more than the projection of the perspective of the historian onto the material of the past, a totalization of narrative matter that has constantly to be remade in the light of events that are, for the moment, immediate and inassimilable. If the "plash of . . . fountains from the mouth of stone dolphins" is the immediate experience of the present, the intrusion of the paranoid voice is historical consciousness, the present mediated through history.

We earlier theorized the sublime as the conflict between the inability to totalize and the necessity of totalization. If the uneasiness that characterizes a first reading of *The Good Soldier* has its origins in the former, the excitement of the latter accounts for the energy of the text, which constantly presents us with hints of a totalizing perspective. This process is what makes the book interesting and not merely Dreiser's "fine story." But where we would ordinarily find in this formal movement the utopian moment in this text, here we unexpectedly find something different happening at the level of content, which seems to invest the other moment (the failure of representation that characterizes Lyotard's bad "modernism") with utopian desire. While the text's every energy is devoted to presenting the terrifying possibility of totalization, Dowell's every energy is devoted to keeping totalization at bay. The passage we looked at earlier continues:

> For, if for me we were four people with the same tastes, with the same desires, acting—or, no, not acting—sitting here and there unanimously, isn't that the truth? If for nine years I have possessed a goodly apple that is rotten at the core and discover its rottenness only in nine years and six months less four days, isn't it true to say that for nine years I possessed a goodly apple? (7)

In the first instance the desire of this passage is oriented toward the past. But what is wished for is not so much any particular point in the history of this little social circle as a holiday from history itself, a return to a condition of immediate experience. In this sense Dowell's nostalgia is absolute, completely independent of any content. Dowell doesn't want to go back to the moment when he possessed a goodly apple; he wants to return to the condition where he could regard the rotten apple as goodly. Having woken up into history, Dowell wants to go back to sleep.

All that we have said so far is complicated by another possible reading whose historical resonance is emphasized by a last-minute revision of Ford's. So far we have been taking the significance of these two possible horizons—that of the immediate present and of the present mediated by history—at face value. But one can imagine a reading of *The Good Soldier* in which Dowell himself, against all expectations, becomes the malevolent spirit behind events, pulling the strings in this history without lifting a finger. Formally, this points to the existence of a third horizon of interpretation: not either of Dowell's two horizons but an ironic horizon from which the oscillation between the two is visible and comprehensible. Dowell everywhere presents himself as a chump, a foolish bystander living in "absolute happiness" and "absolute ignorance" of the tangled mess of tragic affairs unfolding under his nose. But Dowell is not entirely to be trusted; he makes the occasional slip—and another kind of history assembles itself under the text:

> Well, there you have the position, as clear as I can make it—the husband the ignorant fool, the wife a cold sensualist with imbecile fears—for I was such a fool that I could never have known what she was or was not—and the blackmailing lover. (93)

This is the situation; but the phrase "as clear as I can make it" takes on an ambiguous cast. There are several moments throughout the text where Dowell's statements about his own actions make no sense within either of the two dominant horizons of interpretation. Why, for example, if Dowell has no idea of his wife's dalliances or, it follows, of her uncle's knowledge of these affairs, would it occur to him to send him "only the most glowing accounts of her virtue and constancy" (90)? Why would he defend something which, according to him, it had never occurred to him might have been impugned? Such an action cannot be interpreted consistently either with reference to Dowell's past naïve perception of the present or the real machinations that lead on to a calamitous future—at least not the machinations and future we have been given by Dowell.

It is true that Dowell never seems to act on his own behalf; he does nothing for a living, and seems to have no other particular ambitions: "I did nothing. I suppose I ought to have done something, but I didn't see any call to do it. Why does one do things?" (15). In this sense Dowell is, throughout the book, singularly passive. But this seeming passivity is itself effective. Without doing more than referring to the orders of Florence's doctors, for example, Dowell prevents a channel crossing that would have allowed her to continue her dalliance with Ashburnham on a new footing. The ostensible reason for his refusal is the very heart trouble that is her excuse for keeping Dowell out of her bedroom and her affairs, and Dowell turns her own lie against her simply by maintaining it. "I would not have let her cross the steamer gangway to save her life," he begins; but his justification undermines itself, since the reason he gave for *not* letting her go was ostensibly to save her life. "I tell you it fixed her" (90).

Dowell claims that a late interview with Leonora was "the first knowledge I had that Florence had committed suicide. It had never entered my head. You may think that I had been singularly lacking in suspiciousness" (106). Dowell's incredulity—complete innocence of, among other things, a nine-year affair taking place under his own roof—stretches the bounds of believability. The question of whether this lapse in verisimilitude is Dowell's or Ford's does not resist an answer for long. Dowell claims to have thought that the bottle of prussic acid Florence carried about with her was some kind of heart remedy and that she had, in the moments before her suicide, simply been running upstairs to get it. (But according to Dowell, Florence's heart is "unable to stand the strain of . . . running" [107; see also 48–49]). But when he sees her running he refuses to stop her, exhibiting none of the solicitude he showed when it was useful in hindering her affair with Ashburnham. There is even a hint that he had some idea what was in the bottle: "It is even possible that if that feeling had not possessed me, I should have run up sooner to her room and might have prevented her drinking the prussic acid. But I just couldn't do it. It would have been like chasing a scrap of paper—an occupation ignoble for a grown man" (121). It is by a refusal of action—with a gesture of contempt—that he accomplishes his aims: two hours after Florence's death (though characteristically narrated before it) he announces, "Now I can marry the girl" (104), meaning Nancy.

Dowell similarly refuses to prevent Ashburnham's death. In a moment of high comedy, Ashburnham, a parody of the country gentleman that Ford is supposed to have worshiped, pulls an absurd penknife out of his pocket, and asks Dowell to take a message to Leonora:

> I guess he could see in my eyes that I didn't intend to hinder him. Why should I hinder him? . . .
>
> When he saw that I did not intend to interfere with him his eyes grew soft and almost affectionate. He remarked:
>
> "So long, old man, I must have a bit of a rest, you know." (256)

Dowell's wide-eyed appreciation of Ashburnham's Dr.-Livingston-I-presume sang-froid is apparently naïve. But his behavior is considerably less naïve: with the death of Ashburnham, Dowell acquires not only Nancy, mad though she has become, but also what he claimed never to have wanted: Branshaw, Ashburnham's estate.

Dowell studiously avoids any discussion of his own motivation: "I don't know that analysis of my own psychology matters at all to this story" (103) he says, moments after revealing that he wanted to marry Nancy. Dowell's claim to motivelessness is itself sinister:

> I suppose you will retort that I was in love with Nancy Rufford and that my indifference [toward Florence's death] was therefore discreditable. . . . I don't mean to say that I sighed about her or groaned; I just wanted to marry her as some people want to go to Carcassonne. (121)

But this is the same language he used to narrate his desire for Florence: "Why does one do things? I just drifted in and wanted Florence" (15): "I first met Florence at the Stuyvesants', in Fourteenth Street. And from that moment I determined with all the obstinacy of a possibly weak nature, if not to make her mine, at least to marry her" (78). On this perspective, *The Good Soldier* unexpectedly transforms itself into one of Browning's dramatic monologues.

If the motives behind Dowell's inaction—not only in allowing the suicides of Ashburnham and Florence but in standing by while the situation became intolerable enough to drive them each to suicide—are unclear, its consequences are not. Dowell's name has been seen as ironic on two levels: as "dowel" he is supposed to be remarkably inefficient, letting the story fall apart into a mass of contradictions; he is also supposed to be a bumbler named "do-well." But, as we have seen, the story is precisely in what Dowell cannily withholds; the story hangs together at all only through the narrative thread that connects Dowell to all of the events in the story. Further, Dowell, inheriting Florence's uncle's fortune (only settled on her because of the otherwise inexplicable letters he had sent concerning her "virtue and constancy" [90]) and buying Branshaw, manages to do well for himself.

This brings us back to the historical content of *The Good Soldier*. The foreboding of the Fordian sentence, the uncanny presence of the future, has something like an objective correlative in the actual future of the Europe of 1914. *The Good Soldier* sets itself up in its opening pages, in a passage that immediately precedes that of the carriage of screaming hysterics, as an allegory of World War I as the definitive end to a belle epoque of high profits, labor retrenchment, and financialization not unlike our own recent past:

> You may well ask why I write. And yet my reasons are quite many. For it is not unusual in human beings who have witnessed the sack of a city or the falling to pieces of a people, to desire to set down what they have witnessed. . . . Someone has said that the death of a mouse from cancer is the whole sack of Rome by the Goths, and I swear to you that the breaking-up of our little four-square coterie was such another unthinkable event. . . .
>
> Permanence? Stability! I can't believe it's gone. I can't believe that that long tranquil life, which was just stepping a minuet, vanished in four crashing days at the end of nine years and six weeks. (6)

There is a term missing from the analogy set up in the first paragraph. The death of a mouse is the sack of Rome; the breakup of the foursome is . . . ? The existence of Ford's great tetrology *Parade's End*—which in a more obvious way concerns World War I as the decisive end of permanence, stability, and so on—would tend to confirm the notion that the collapse of the social minuet, like the sinking of the *Titanic* in 1912, comes in retrospect to signal something sinister about the course of European history itself. The mouse is to Rome as the four-square coterie is to Europe.

This allegorical reading might seem a little odd for a text that was, by some accounts, completed before the outbreak of hostilities. In *The Sublime Object of Ideology*, Slavoj Žižek refers to a text by Morgan Robertson called *The Wreck of the Titan; or, Futility*.[15] Written several years before the sinking of the actual *Titanic*, *The Wreck of the Titan* tells the story of the future event with remarkable precision, right down to the April iceberg, the size of the passenger manifest, and the proportion of lifeboats to passengers. Žižek is not of course claiming that Robertson (or Ford) could predict the future; the point is that the space for such supposedly "unthinkable" or "inconceivable" events is in fact prepared in advance. And it is a commonplace that the sinking of the *Titanic* (a floating embodiment of Europe's self-image quite as much as the resort culture of *The Good Soldier*) derives its symbolic weight from the calamity that was shortly to overtake European civilization itself.[16]

A reading of *The Good Soldier* as an allegory of World War I is confirmed to a degree by the fact that Ford did himself, it seems, come to see it that way in retrospect. As can be seen by comparing the 1914 *Blast* chapters with the completed version, chapters of *The Good Soldier* underwent relatively little revision once they were completed. Ford did, however, according to his biographer Max Saunders, choose to accentuate one element throughout the text in revision, a revision that constitutes the only radical violation in the novel of Ford's canon of verisimilitude. Ford emphasized the date August 4, on which Florence, improbably, was born, died, married Dowell, and began all her affairs; that date also marks "the last day of my absolute ignorance—and, I assure you, my perfect happiness" (100). The passage that overdetermines August 4 as a fateful day (77–78), added in revision, sticks out rather starkly as precious and unlikely.[17] But August 4, 1914 is, of course, the date England declared war and Wilson declared American neutrality. *The Good Soldier*—complete with the American finally coming to lord it over the English manor—has to be reinterpreted in terms of the calamitous historic events that followed August 1914. The new title (in Ford's own mythology, chosen from the battlefield)[18] and the newly emphasized date project this dystopic future back out into history. The fact of an American coming to possess the English manor can no longer simply signify itself: indeed, it foreshadows an American economic hegemony (Dowell buys Branshaw) figured in *Parade's End* by the imagined death of cricket and its replacement by that "beastly yelping game . . . baseball."[19]

The ascendance of cold, "greedy" (118) John Dowell over the stereotypical country gentleman elevates national stereotypes to a symbolic level. Here we are solidly in the realm of "national allegory" as Jameson first used that term, in reference to Wyndham Lewis's *Tarr*, also written in 1914. That Ford concludes *Parade's End*, his "war tetrology," with the same allegorical structure of the American occupying the ancestral home only confirms this intuition. But if the war was ultimately fought over competing pretensions to empire—the claims of France and England against the ambitions of Germany—then the economic mode of Dowell's accession to Branshaw is particularly apt; the transfer of Branshaw from the aristocratic Englishman who soldiered in India to the American businessman prefigures the decline of the Western European empires in favor of a global American economic hegemony.

In *The Good Soldier*, then, nostalgia is first of all an investment in the immediacy of experience, an investment which must constantly refuse the second horizon of formal historical mediation. From this perspective the sublime object of *The Good Soldier* is the Disaster around which it perpetually circles and whose meaning Dowell continually tries to escape. A third possible horizon of interpretation, in ironizing a nostalgia that now seems to be false, reintroduces History in a more literal sense as the ultimate horizon of interpretation. But the poverty of this historical allegory—which is in any case wholly external to the characters, laid over the narrative fabric rather than woven into it—cannot pass without comment. As with the more general case of modernism's sublime object, the historical Disaster to which *The Good Soldier* promises access is empty of all content—how empty can be seen by comparing it with Chinua Achebe's *Arrow of God*, which we will turn to in the next chapter. While Achebe's great historical novel takes place in an area geographically remote from Ford's, it is not far removed either in historical time or in its final allegorical content of a crisis in the social totality. But while *Arrow of God*, without any fanfare or apparent didactic effort, manages to sketch a remarkable multilevel representation of Disaster, Ford's is empty of any content save possibly a kind of American conspiracy that is surely not to be taken seriously. Doubtless this has partly to do with the jury-rigged nature of this allegory, which as we have seen appears to have been conceived after it was too late to hint at more concrete historical content. Nonetheless the major element of this allegory will be repeated in Ford's masterpiece, *Parade's End*, where, in the face of this abstract disaster, the only reaction can be a conventional nostalgia that can be no more innocent than Dowell's. The absolute nostalgia that had been ironized by the third, properly historical horizon is reinstated on another level, where it reappears as an elegy for the belle epoque.

The first novel of *Parade's End* (awkwardly titled *Some Do Not . . .*) begins with extraordinary placidity:

> The two young men—they were of the English public official class—sat in the perfectly appointed railway carriage. The leather straps of the windows were of virgin newness; the mirrors beneath the new luggage racks immaculate as if they had reflected very little; the bulging upholstery in its luxuriant, regulated curves was scarlet and yellow in an intricate, minute dragon pattern, the design of a geometrician in Cologne. The compartment smelt faintly, hygienically of admirable varnish; the train ran as smoothly—Tietjens remembered thinking—as British gilt-edged securities. (3)

The complacency of the world of the "official class" is matched perfectly by the tranquillity of the narrative, which runs every bit as smoothly as the train on which Tietjens and Macmaster ride: the very mirrors reflect the insulation of this class, "immaculate as though they had reflected very little." Sentences are lovely in such a way as to be barely noticeable of themselves; paragraphs tend to be overwrought, but slightly and without ostentation—admirably varnished, one might say. The flow of narrative is never jolted by shifts in time or perspective; flashbacks are plainly marked both by explicit cues and by the use of the pluperfect. It is not until the second half of the novel that events are fragmented into shards of conversation and flattened into the perfect. As we cannot know as part 2 of *No More Parades* begins, the disastrous conversation between Tietjens and his wife that introduces this second part is separated from what precedes it by the beginning of world war. As Sylvia and Tietjens each try in different ways to inflict as much pain as possible on the other, the events that precede part 2—the beginnings of the war; Tietjens's commission, brain injury, and imminent return to the front; Macmaster's affair, marriage, and social rise; the deaths of Tietjens's brothers and sister at war, his mother's in grief, and his father's suicide; his semi-betrayal at the hands of his only remaining brother—as well as earlier events like the circumstances of the Tietjens' marriage and of the birth of their son; Tietjens's trip to Germany to retrieve his errant wife; and the occasions of her liaisons with a man called Perowne and a man called Drake must be divined from the spilled and flattened entrails of the intervening time. The emergence of the same narrative structures we saw in *The Good Soldier* at a specific point in the text points to the fact that they can no longer be thought of merely in terms of stylistic devices that may or may not have a certain social content, but must instead be explicitly invested with historical meaning. It is too early to specify with precision what this meaning might be, but it is difficult not to see this narrative fragmentation in the same way that Adorno saw the fragmenting of cubism's visual planes, which "anticipated something real, the aerial photographs of bombed-out cities during World War II."[20]

We might begin looking for a clue to this relation by turning to a letter Ford wrote to Conrad from the Western front. Ford describes the sounds made by artillery shells blowing up buildings:

> Shells falling on a church: these make a huge "*corump*" sound, followed by a noise like crockery falling off a tray—as the roof tiles fall off. If the roof is not tiled you can hear the stained glass, sifting mechanically until the next shell. (Heard in a church square, on each occasion, about 90 yds away.) Screams of women penetrate all these sounds— but I do not find that they agitate me as they have done at home (Women in cellars round the square. Oneself running thro' fast.)[21]

Here, writing to Conrad, ostensibly providing him with potentially useful raw material for some future story, it is unsurprising that the mode of impressionism is Conradian. However, it is significant that *No More Parades*, the first novel of the tetrology to take place at the front—and the only one whose action is entirely shifted there—opens in precisely this Conradian mode:

> When you came in the space was desultory, rectangular, warm after the drip of the winter night, and transfused with a brown-orange dust that was light. It was shaped like the house a child draws. Three groups of brown limbs spotted with brass took dim high-lights from shafts that came from a bucket pierced with holes. . . .
> An immense tea-tray, august, its voice filling the black circle of the horizon, thundered to the ground. Numerous pieces of sheet-iron said, "Pack. Pack. Pack." . . . Catching the light from the brazier as the head leaned over, the lips of one of the two men on the floor were incredibly red and full and went on talking and talking. (291)

This is primitive, Conradian impressionism, very much like the passage referred to earlier from *Heart of Darkness*. Here the brown limbs belong not to the residents of Conrad's Congolese village but to British officers sitting in a tent in France. The first sentence is a mass of mutually conflicting impressions: the space is "desultory, rectangular, warm"; these juxtaposed adjectives do not in themselves invoke any particular thing but name isolated aspects that are as yet meaningless. The brown-orange dust that "transfuses"—a word that would naturally apply to light better than dust—turns out to be not dust but light after all. And this space is located not in place but in time: it comes "after" the winter night, not within it, as though its presence only existed for the "you" who came into it from the cold. The winter night itself is evoked only by a sound, its "drip."

The second paragraph gives the motivation for this jumbled sensory language: this heap of broken images represents a world that is only provisionally not a heap of broken things. The tent is not so much a tent as a space that serves, for a brief time, as a warm inside against a cold outside: it is only a temporary dividing line between the most basic of phenomenal states. The "three groups of brown limbs" refer—for the time being—to three people. But in a moment they could really become just that: "three groups of brown limbs spotted with brass," or the later "collections of tubular shapes in field-grey" (550) that litter a battlefield. The shrapnel shell that interrupts the first paragraph is itself only a *thing* provisionally, a thing that, in becoming a non-thing, breaks up other things. It, like the tent and the officers, registers not as a named object, a "shrapnel shell," but as a sensory trace, which it leaves behind in disappearing: the "Pack. Pack. Pack" of sheet iron. In this case, then, impressionist language which, rather than capturing the thing in language, parades fragments and traces across the page, is used to reflect a situation where it could at any moment become straightforward representation. Here, the apparently static Conradian impressionism is Fordian and temporal after all, taking its meaning, like the impressionism of *The Good Soldier*, from the horizon of a calamitous future. Things are described with reference to a future in which they are blown up.

But while in *The Good Soldier* the desire to retreat into the immediacy of experience was Dowell's particular madness, in *Parade's End* the situation is apparently reversed: madness is the name for recognizing the truth. Tietjens's shell-shocked superior, Captain McKechnie, is afraid of nothing—except sound. For everyone else, including the narrative voice that mainly follows Tietjens's thinking, the clamor of exploding shells becomes mere sound, a pure sensory stimulus inducing a response. But throughout the wartime segments of both *No More Parades* and *A Man Could Stand Up—*, artillery does not merely make sound, it speaks. The shrapnel "said, 'Pack. Pack. Pack'" (291); a cannon "said . . . something sulky" (544); flying shells drop "saying 'Wee . . . Ee . . . ry. . . . Whack!'" (551); another cannon "remarked: 'Phohhhhhhhhh'" (575). In this strange language modern weaponry speaks to everyone, but only McKechnie understands. The artillery strafe that opens *No More Parades* is in fact narrated twice in quick succession. The first time makes up the first two paragraphs of the book, quoted above. The second follows it immediately, narrating the same event in greater detail. The scene concentrates on five figures: Tietjens and McKechnie (still called McKenzie, the name Tietjens mistakenly assigns him), a sergeant-major, and two runners squatting on the floor. One of the runners is talking about a cow, the other is talking about his laundry business; the sergeant-major is worrying about dinner for a draft of men; Tietjens and McKechnie are in desultory conversation. The shell bursts for a second time:

> An enormous crashing sound said things of an intolerable intimacy to each of those men, and to all of them as a body. After its mortal vomiting all of the other sounds appeared a rushing silence, painful to ears in which the blood audibly coursed. (293)

What this sound says is plain enough: the sound, a "mortal vomiting" whose aftermath is an awareness of the coursing of blood, is the sound of death, whispered with "intolerable intimacy to each of these men, and to all of them as a body." But only McKechnie hears this truth, what it is that the crashing sound "says." The runners continue talking about the laundry and the cows; the sergeant-major suggests to Tietjens that he should indent for suppers for the draft; Tietjens himself continues to worry about, by turns, the draft and his domestic troubles. But every time the artillery begins its "beastly row," McKechnie stands "violently up on his feet," screaming fantastic obscenities in order to block the sound from his ears, and continues talking in circles until Tietjens can calm him down. This is madness, shell-shock; but it is a strange madness that consists in hearing a truth that is spoken, and a strange sanity that consists in reducing it to babble. For these machines really do say "death": the runner obsessed with his wife's sale of his laundry business is killed by the next shrapnel shell. The line between sanity and insanity has become blurred: sanity exhibits all the symptoms of madness, and delusion looks like calm rationality. The rationality that reduces the language of artillery to mere sound is the same impulse as Dowell's desire to burrow into the immediacy of his "goodly apple": a retreat from the mediation of time.

If, in the preface to *The Nigger of the Narcissus*, the languages against which impressionism sets itself—the languages of science and philosophy—exist essentially to outfit us for the "warlike conditions of existence" (viii), then Ford's use of Conradian impressionism here reveals that this sensory language always existed in contrast to a dystopic environment in which sensory input already overpowered the capacity to interpret it. The truth of Conrad's impressionist dream emerges from Ford's lurid nightmare of the senses. This is, once again, the standard Frankfurt school interpretation of modernist language: that capitalism's power to deterritorialize and decompose what had been solid and familiar had rendered "realistic" representation unrealistic. In *Parade's End* the history from which Ford's absolute nostalgia retreats acquires a concrete content much more substantial than the artificial one imposed on *The Good Soldier*: history is reification itself, the progressive alienation of rational means from irrational ends, of which war—particularly this war, more straightforwardly than most the intensification of a worldwide crisis in capitalism—is only a special case. We are once again in the neighborhood of Weiskel's "secondary or problematic sublime" or Lyotard's nostalgic modernism, whose investment is not in the moment that grasps for totalization but in the loss of the signifier. However, even this secondary sublime has its utopian aspect. Absolute nostalgia is not homesickness for any particular home but merely for abstract escape from the march toward the future. As Horkheimer and Adorno put it in their reading of Odysseus's nostalgia, "Homeland is the state of having escaped."[22] In *A Man Could Stand Up—*, the desire for such escape is figured as the urge, impossible to fulfill in the trenches, to stand upright. The innermost impulse of nostalgia is liberatory. On the other hand, as a purely abstract negation of history, it is powerless. Supplied with a content that could oppose the movement of history, it becomes conventional nostalgia, which is ultimately a reactionary and brutalizing wish to recover lost privilege. The nostalgia for a certain range of action open to the talented individual, figured by Tietjens's "nobility," testifies to the real pain—as we saw in the previous chapter, not a pain unique to Europe or the First World—experienced in the rationalization of older and at least retrospectively more humane modes of existence. At the same time, it is just as clear that this nobility itself, quite apart from any particular historical referent, is bound up inevitably and from the outset in a brutalizing class structure—as was the prewar belle epoque in which noble

Tietjens still felt relatively at home—to which there can be in good faith no wish to return.

This second, conventionally nostalgic moment is not long in coming, and here, unlike *The Good Soldier*, the nostalgia of the novel's hero cannot be so easily separated from the nostalgia of the text for that hero, Christopher Tietjens, the "last Tory." *Parade's End*'s apparent mourning for aristocratic paternalism and stiff upper lips is self-evident and seems to need little elaboration. The wartime novels of *Parade's End* exhibit a longing for prewar England, conventionally figured as the eternal English countryside with its "plough land, the heavy groves, the slow high-road above the church that the dawn was at that moment wetly revealing" (566). And indeed this nostalgia for homeland is easily mingled in Tietjens's thoughts with conventionally jingoistic sentiment:

> What a handful of frail grass with which to stop an aperture in the dam of—of the Empire! Damn the Empire! It was England! It was Bemerton Parsonage that mattered! What did we want with an Empire! It was only a jerry-building Jew like Disraeli that could have provided us with that jerry-built name! The Tories said they had to have someone to do their dirty work. . . . Well, they'd had it! (591)

Beneath the surface opposition between England and the jerry-building Jewish Disraeli is an opposition between the emergence of the British Empire and an imagined earlier moment in British history, signified by a fantasy of George Herbert's parish:

> . . . in a seventeenth-century street. . . .
>
> The only satisfactory age in England! . . . yet what chance had it to-day. Or, still more, tomorrow. In the sense that the age of, say, Shakespeare had a chance. Or Pericles! Or Augustus!
>
> Heaven knew, we did not want a preposterous drum-beating such as the Elizabethans produced—and received. Like lions at a fair. . . . But what chance had quiet fields, Anglican sainthood, accuracy of thought, heavy leaved, timbered hedge-rows, slowly creeping plough-lands moving up the slopes? . . . Still, the land remains. . . .
>
> The land remains. . . . It remains! (566)

This passage, with its multiple exclamation points, ironizes itself, and yet it harmonizes with the nostalgic thrust of the entire tetrology.

But the land doesn't remain in any substantial sense. It has become an imitation of itself. Actual England (as perceived here by Valentine Wannop in a passage that recalls the irruption of the sublime into the beautiful avenues of Taunus Wald) is quite different from Tietjens's idyll, a "sham country, with sham lawns, sham avenues, sham streams. Sham people pursuing their ways across the sham grass. Or no! Not sham! In a vacuum! No! 'Pasteurized' was the word! Like dead milk" (273). Long before 1914, the yeoman farmer had been replaced by poorly paid agricultural laborers, his cottages had been converted into villas for urban white-collar workers, former cottage industries had been rationalized in factories, and ancestral estates had been bought by Americans and nouveaux-riches. Even estates that remained in the hands of their ancestral owners were maintained for their prestige value at a financial loss, supported by industrial investments.[23] Seventeenth-century England had become, by the beginning of the twentieth century, essentially what it is on television, namely scenery.

Absolute nostalgia—nostalgia as pure escape from history, without any definite content of its own—is dramatized in *The Good Soldier* by Dowell's constant drive to escape the mediation of an historical horizon. But the Disaster that threatens to restore this horizon is empty; if history can be reintroduced at all into this narrative, it is only as a mechanical and external allegory that serves to emphasize rather than bridge the chasm between the novel's characters and a history to which they apparently have no relation. In *Parade's End* history begins to acquire a more concrete content in the intensified derealization of the modern battlefield. But against this more concrete historical horizon absolute nostalgia can do nothing but retreat before the advancing conditions it opposes. Since the escape from history can have no impact on history itself, which soldiers on regardless, nostalgia is forced to acquire concrete content of its own. But as we have just seen, this very movement converts its utopian moment to a reactionary one.

Of course, this concrete content can be purged of its brutalizing political implications, but only at the cost of becoming nothing more than a new form of aesthetic compensation. Tietjens does go back to England, ensconced finally in his beloved English countryside. Despite Valentine Wannop's flash of intuition, there is not much indication that the nostalgic, soft-focus, Merchant-and-Ivory ending to *Parade's End* is anything other than what it seems. But at the last moment, and so subtly as to be almost unconscious, the text insinuates an irony that both reveals the falsity of the text's nostalgia and reintroduces its real, if limited, historical content. Tietjens's new profession is symptomatic of the status of this "England," as his nobility is converted into exchange value: a talent for appraising furniture. Like the gunner who toys with an anonymous German soldier in *A Man Could Stand Up—*, history is merciful in the end: by the last novel, Tietjens is not dead, but petty bourgeois. The aristocratic figure who, in the first book, had entertained an antipathy for antiquities, had "hated . . . disinterred and waxed relics of the past" (43), becomes, by the last book, an antiques dealer: a purveyor of the simulacrum of his own desire.

CHAPTER FIVE

Arrow of God: The Totalizing Gaze

Chinua Achebe's village novels reinvent "the classic form of the historical novel" in the precise Lukácsian sense.[1] Placing Achebe's spare masterpieces in a genre with Sir Walter Scott's *Waverly*, James Fenimore Cooper's *The Leather Stocking Saga*, or Gogol's *Taras Bulba*—a genre which, moreover, has been moribund for well over a century—sounds more reasonable when we consider that its thematic core is, like these earlier novels, what Lukács called the "downfall of gentile society" (58)—the collapse of autonomous noncapitalist ways of life, a collapse that is progressive and continues today. As we have seen, this collapse is also, though in a more obscure way, the core of Ford Madox Ford's novels. This thematic connection is important not for its own (minimal) content but for the difference it highlights. In Ford, history is conceived as absolutely external to the characters caught up in it, who must cope with it as best they can. Faced with a social life predicated on the "the social eccentricity and superfluity of the best and sincerest human talents" (33), the only option is to long both for a past that gave such talents scope and for the barbarous material basis on which that scope was predicated. In Achebe, on the other hand, history is imagined with astounding concreteness; the disaster that faces village life is no abstract and external predicament approached in the mode of the sublime and then recoiled from in horror, but rather the outcome of "certain crises in the personal destinies of a number of human beings [that] coincide and interweave with the determining context of historical crisis" (41). Unlike Ford's novels, which invest the past with utopian desire, the narration of the past in Achebe's work, like that of the great European bourgeois historical novelists, is unexpectedly oriented toward the future: as Lukács commented of Alessandro Manzoni's *The Betrothed*, *Arrow of God* is "a real historical novel, that is, one which would rouse the present" (70). And as with the great European historical novels, this orientation toward the future has everything to do with the emergence of a new and progressive social class: the anticolonial African bourgeoisie whose "hopes and impediments," to use the Achebean phrase, have been a recurrent theme in this book.

Not that *Arrow of God* is a mere repetition of the classical historical novels; far from it, as we shall see. Easily the most read African writer in the English-speaking world, Chinua Achebe is best known for his first two novels, *Things Fall Apart* and *No Longer at Ease*, and for his scathing critique of Conrad's *Heart of Darkness*.[2] *Things Fall Apart* in particular, though written before Nigeria's independence, is many high school and first-year college students' introduction to "postcolonial" literature; the critique of Conrad, "An Image of Africa: Racism in Conrad's *Heart of Darkness*," is often assigned along with *Heart of Darkness* in first-year great works courses as a critique of the tradition under study. Both of these works are, in different ways, victims of their own success. Achebe's stylistic innovations—*Things Fall Apart* is, despite the limpid clarity of its sentences and deceptive simplicity of its structure, quite different than anything that had come before it—have become so naturalized, so internalized by a whole generation of African novelists, that nothing seems more natural than Achebe's style. Indeed it sometimes seems as though Achebe's style were the only way its kind of content could be represented. The thematic substance of Achebe's rural novels might appear inevitable to us now; but it is hard to say how much this appearance of inevitability owes to the power of Achebe's work. *Things Fall Apart* was adopted very quickly as a school text in West Africa from the early 1960s, in advance of new postcolonial histories, so that the very conception of colonial history shared by many younger writers derives directly from Achebe.[3] The same might be said about Achebe's primary stylistic innovation, the subtle modulation and contrast of multiple styles of English, some "translated" from other idioms, to represent various positions within colonial, village, and postcolonial society. Again, this may not any longer, nearly fifty years after the publication of *Things Fall Apart*, seem like a startling narrative discovery. But one has only to compare the output of Nigerian writers like Cyprian Ekwensi and Amos Tutuola, two novelists whose early published work precedes Achebe's, to the generation of writers whose first novels emerged after *Things Fall Apart* (for example, Clement Agunwa, Flora Nwapa, and Nkem Nwankwo) to see how profoundly Achebe's first novel determined the style and content of at least a generation of writers. While Tutuola's comically dystopic narratives seem to derive from an intuitive fusion of Yoruba folktales and widely available European forms like *The Pilgrim's Progress* (but in fact also emerge from a Yoruba-language novelistic tradition represented by D. O. Fagunwa),[4] and Ekwensi's early works appear unreflectively to transpose wholesale the tropes and narrative schema of British and American popular novels to suit an urban Nigerian market, the next generation of Nigerian novelists turns virtually unanimously to Achebe's central themes and to his primary technical innovations.[5] Even older novelists (such as Onuora Nzekwu) dramatically altered the form of their novels with the discovery of what might be called the Achebe style. Faced with the explosive success of this style—though it is more than a style, since it also involves both narrative architecture and dramatic and allegorical content—it is difficult to regain a sense of Achebe's early novels as they appeared at the time (as indeed it is with the popular poems of Yeats or Eliot, from which Achebe's early novels take their titles and to which we will turn shortly) as something dramatically new that suddenly resolved at once a whole range of representational problems facing African writers of the late 1950s and 1960s.

The power of Achebe's famous (or notorious) article on Conrad has been diminished in a different way by the sheer proliferation of similar criticisms in the more than quarter-century since it was delivered as a lecture in 1975. Viewed unsympathetically, and in the light of the so-called culture wars of the 1980s and 1990s, "An Image of Africa" might seem to be an unfair attack on a great writer who could not possibly have comprehended the African setting of his novella in a way that Achebe—or for that matter any contemporary reader—would have liked. But "An Image of Africa" is misunderstood if it is taken to be about *Heart of Darkness* in particular. It is quite true, as it is sometimes claimed, that Achebe's article adds nothing to our understanding of *Heart of Darkness*: but neither does it take away from it. "An Image of Africa" is more fundamentally about the ideology of interpretation and the relationship between image and meaning; *Heart of Darkness* is merely the ground on which a much more interesting thesis is advanced than that of Conrad's "racism."

The racist content Achebe decries in *Heart of Darkness*—the palpable disgust conveyed in the portrayal of Africans, the explicit denial of their full humanity, the insistence on Africa as the locus of the most atavistic of human possibilities— was never exactly latent. Perhaps our sensitivity to it owes something to Achebe's essay, but the violence of Conrad's descriptions of Africans could not have been entirely missed before Achebe pointed it out. Indeed, as Achebe is aware, his related stylistic criticism of the novella—the observation, touched on in the previous chapter, that Conrad's atmosphere relies excessively on a small group of adjectives expressing the incomprehensibility of the landscape—had been preceded by F. R. Leavis's by three decades. Yet nothing is taken away from our understanding either: Achebe is perfectly mindful—although he is careful to put this attentiveness in the mouths of "students of Conrad"—of the allegorical content of this atavism, the larger claim Conrad's narrative makes about human possibilities. What Achebe managed to do in his short article, however, was to accomplish an overturning of allegorical priority that was decisive for the future of literary criticism. Before Achebe, the image content of *Heart of Darkness* could be considered a mere prop, something that could be discarded once the higher meaning—the horror at the core of humanity's soul—had been reached. With Achebe, the "higher," allegorical meaning becomes more like a distraction, something to attract the eye while the real meaning of the image is picked up like a subliminal advertisement. Achebe's essay is not so much a critique of Conrad as a refusal of a certain repression of racist content. It is a question of which is the real meaning, and Achebe turns the older answer on its head—or perhaps puts criticism back on its feet. For it is the material level of the production of images that counts decisively here, not the idea to which they are supposed ultimately to lead.

Unfortunately, Achebe's insistence on the image, as groundbreaking as it is in itself, has contributed to a critical practice that sometimes arrests the production of meaning at that level so that Achebe's own novels are often seen primarily as rewritings of the precolonial image.[6] As was emphasized in the introduction, this mode of reading is perfectly justifiable as one mode among many. Granted too exclusive an authority, however, it sets up Achebe's novels to be judged in the limited terms of representational justice, thus tending to shut down the possibility of registering their speculative or allegorical content. Of course, that the "correction of the record" is a strong element in Achebe's early novels cannot be denied: *Things Fall Apart* in particular can be partially understood as a passionate cross-genre rewriting of G. T. Basden's 1938 anthropological work *Niger Ibos*,[7] and of course few attentive readers will have missed Achebe's masterful reworking of the road-building episode of Joyce Cary's *Mister Johnson*[8] in chapter 8 of *Arrow of*

God, to which we will return at the end of this chapter. But it will be quite a different kind of meaning that we will be concerned with initially so that when we return, finally, to the level of the image, it will be seen to have a content of its own beyond a mere correction of the record.

Meanwhile, the relationship of Achebe's novels to canonical modernist sources must have an impact on how we read them; but it also reflects back on the modernist works themselves, refreshing their content and adding new layers of meaning. By naming his first two novels after lines from Eliot's "Journey of the Magi" and Yeats's "The Second Coming," Achebe puts the poems into conversation not just with his work but with each other. By juxtaposing the two poems through his novels, he reveals a complex identity between the events that form the pretext of each poem. Both poems are meditations on literally millennial events: the birth of Christ, in Eliot's case, and the second coming, in Yeats's. The event Eliot narrates comes first historically, but at another level it is Yeats that dramatizes the earlier moment: Yeats's poem concerns the approach to Bethlehem ("And what rough beast, its hour come round at last, / Slouches towards Bethlehem to be born"), while Eliot's Magi have returned from there. Yeats's poem reflects on the intimation of a millennial change; Eliot's, on the uneasy phase after the millennial change has occurred (Christ has been born), but has not yet occurred everywhere (the new religion has not yet taken hold). The central element of each is then the fascination with epochal change itself and the way the representation of that change bounces back from the future or the distant past to reflect on the disequilibrium of the present moment. Of course, when Achebe refers to "The Second Coming" and "Journey of the Magi," this "present moment" is suddenly transposed into rather a different context; but the millennial content of these poems, emphasized by their juxtaposition, is carried with them into their new context. It is this content—once again, entirely abstract in the modernist context—that is at the heart of Achebe's novels.

Indeed, the relationship between *Things Fall Apart* and *No Longer at Ease* precisely mirrors that between "The Second Coming" and "Journey of the Magi." The first novel narrates the intimation of the complete disruption of a history and a way of life (the end of village autonomy with the coming of colonialism); and the second narrates the painful interaction between new forms of ethical life (the bureaucratic norms of the modern city) and the old dispensation (older forms of patronage that have not been entirely displaced). When viewed through the lens of Achebe's appropriation, Yeats's poem can suddenly be seen to refer to the coming of Christianity as well as its going: the dissolution it augurs is not just that of European modernity but of all sorts of ethical and religious systems with the increasing reach of the market. Eliot's poem, meanwhile, not only can express a turn toward Christianity as modernity's other but is also a meditation on what we might call the psychology of uneven development.

It is the first, Yeatsian moment of the apprehension of the decisive end of what had been an autonomous history that will concern us here. The central image Achebe takes from Yeats is not, as we might expect of a novel narrating the colonial encounter, one of destruction from without but of the dissolution from within of a society in crisis. This raises the possibility that Achebe's novel is not only what it seems to be, simply the story of the successful "pacification" of Igboland from without, but also the narration of the internal dissolution of Igbo society itself when confronted with the possibility of a radically other civilization, and in particular of the "ways by which larger historical processes come to coincide with internal schisms."[9] If "The Second Coming," besides being the intimation of the death of a society, is also the intimation of a birth, a postapocalyptic existence that "slouches towards Bethlehem to be born," we might begin to wonder whether Achebe's village novels suggest, perhaps in a more utopian way than Yeats's dystopic beast, another kind of apocalyptic rebirth.

Achebe's brilliant *Arrow of God*[10] takes up the theme of *Things Fall Apart* but in an altogether richer and more complex way. We will begin with the second chapter, which flashes back to an event that predates the action of the novel and is a kind of miniature of the central structure of the novel itself. This chapter concerns a land dispute between Umuaro, a community of six villages where the novel is set, and the neighboring polity of Okperi. Ezeulu, priest of Ulu and therefore the chief priest of the six villages, opposes going to war with Okperi over the disputed land, which he claims originally belonged to Okperi along with the rest of the area now occupied by Umuaro. He is opposed by Nwaka, a firebrand who (we later find out) is under the influence of Ezidemili, the rival priest of the god Idemili. Nwaka wins the day, and the village appoints the hawkish Akukalia to take a delegation to Okperi to ask if its leaders want a settlement or war. The marvelous narration of the fate of the delegation raises the tension imperceptibly, sentence by sentence, until it finally explodes in violence. In their impatience the delegation goes on Okperi's market day, a diplomatic faux pas. A difference of custom provokes laughter at the Umuaroans. A man from Okperi accidentally insults Akukalia, resulting in a fight. Enraged, Akukalia splits the man's *ikenga*, his personal god: the man, who has "been made a corpse before his own eyes" (24), shoots Akukalia dead. But this is not the end of the episode: rather than escalating into a war, tensions seem to relax as nobody knows quite what to do with this unprecedented situation. But another difference of custom ignites tensions again, and war is waged for four days.

What happens next is world historical:

> The next day, Afo, saw the war brought to a sudden close. The white man, Wintabota, brought soldiers to Umuaro and stopped it. The story of what these soldiers did in Abame was still told with fear, and so Umuaro made no effort to resist but laid down their arms. (27)

> The white man, not satisfied that he had stopped the war, had gathered all the guns in Umuaro and asked the soldiers to break them in the face of all, except for three or four which he carried away. Afterwards he sat in judgement over Umuaro and Okperi and gave the disputed land to Okperi. (28)

Nothing that occurred in this story was inevitable. The land dispute, the rivalry between Ezidemili and Ezeulu, the diplomatic faux pas, laughter over a slight difference in custom, an accidental insult: none of these need have taken place precisely as they did, and at every moment had things happened differently Umuaro would not have gone to war. And yet we may say that one thing was inevitable in this story: the ultimate outcome, which was quite different than any of the actors had intended. Everything might be imagined differently, except that Umuaro would remain forever autonomous from the new forces resident on Government Hill.

"Umuaro" can no longer be understood only as a discrete fictional entity, but must also be seen to be an allegorical space: as Achebe put it in an interview, the "pacification" and ultimate defection of Umuaro "is not something which one should see in terms of Umuaro alone; it is something one ought to see in terms of the whole movement of world history."[11] This invocation of the "movement of world history" marks the first allegorical level of *Arrow of God*. (The discovery of such content in Achebe's novels is nothing new, and our discussion is preceded in particular by Abiola Irele's admirable essays on Achebe.)[12] In this first allegorical level the story of Umuaro operates on three planes that can be separated analytically but are not rigorously discrete: the political, the religious or ethical, and the material. On the final plane, however, the other two are united, propelling the allegory into a second level that will return us to the question of the image in order to discover the utopian content of the novel. In what follows we will compose all of the internal rifts that constitute Umuaro into a single crisis, to which the subsumption into the capitalist world system becomes both a solution and a repetition.[13]

The first level, again, is that in which disintegration of Umuaro names the particular of which colonial penetration itself is the general. The form this narrative takes, however—a series of contingent acts that nonetheless culminate in an event that seems to have been determined in advance—is a very peculiar one and might remind us (along with Achebe's invocation of "world history") of Hegel's "ruse of History," the idea that History takes place as though it were using individuals for its own ends.[14] World-historical events—the rise of Christianity, the expansion of the Roman Empire, the great bourgeois revolutions, or the British imperial project—have their own logics, deriving from innumerable and contingent individual events and actions that, taken as a whole, seem instead to be at the mercy of the great transformation taking place:

> In world history the outcome of human actions is something other than what the agents aim at and actually achieve, something other than what they immediately know and will. . . . This may be called the *Cunning of Reason*, that it allows the passions to work for it, while what it brings into existence suffers loss and injury. . . . The Idea pays the ransom of existence and transience—not out of its own pocket, but with the passions of individuals.[15]

This "Cunning of Reason" is precisely what Achebe has termed, in a discussion of *Arrow of God*, "Powers of Event": "[T]he '*powers of event*' achieve their own logic. . . . I don't think we should ignore this force or phenomenon, whatever it is, maybe providence. If you are religious, you will call it God."[16] The title *Arrow of God*, then, seems to point to a conception of history whereby "the passions of individuals" only accomplish an end that was somehow determined in advance—by God, by the "Powers of Event," or by History itself. Of course, we can no longer take at face value the notion that what determines history is the unfolding of the Idea; but there are other ways of understanding this structure, not least of which would be the narratological, which would see this apparent inevitability as a by-product of historical narrative (but no less escapable for that), and the systems-theoretical, which would replace the "Idea" with more or less implacable trends of great economic or other processes.[17] The narrative kernel of this apparently paradoxical idea—that what is determined comes about by means of events that are not determined—is encapsulated in a saying that Ezeulu uses, speaking to his friend Akuebue, in discussing who is to blame for the war with Okperi:

> We went to war against Okperi who are our blood brothers over a piece of land which did not belong to us and you blame the white man for stepping in. Have you not heard that when two brothers fight a stranger reaps the harvest? (131)

This proverb sums up the narrative that unfolds in the second chapter, but we find this same proverb expressed somewhat differently in the last pages of the book in another context: this time it is Akuebue who uses it as an argument against Ezeulu.

> "It troubles me," he said, "because it looks like the saying of our ancestors that when brothers fight to death a stranger inherits their father's estate." (220)

We can see that Akuebue doesn't have Ezeulu's sense of verbal economy. Mastery of this kind of subtle modulation of language between characters and situations, so fine as to be almost subliminal, accounts for the restrained brilliance, quite without stylistic fireworks, of Achebe's style. What is important here, though, is that this proverbial theme, central to the second chapter, returns to characterize the larger action of which the second chapter is a miniature. The historical event of the stranger inheriting the estate *is* the content of *Arrow of God*. But in the narrative of the novel as a whole, two priests rather than two villages are the fighting brothers, and the colonial mission inherits the village.

The central dynamic of *Arrow of God* is the conflict alluded to earlier between Ezeulu and Ezidemili, which leads to a disruption in the agricultural cycle and ultimately to a mass defection to the new Christian god. Captain Winterbottom (Wintabota), impressed by Ezeulu's integrity in the dispute with Okperi, calls him to Government Hill to offer him the warrant chieftaincy for Umuaro. Ezeulu goes to Government Hill, against a tradition prohibiting the chief priest from leaving the village, at the insistence of Ezidemili's camp, who win the support of the village. At Government Hill he declines what for him is an absurd proposition, but is imprisoned for his obstinacy. During his captivity he realizes that his imprisonment is a weapon that can be used against Ezidemili and Umuaro. While he is away from Umuaro he cannot eat two sacred yams; when he returns he refuses to call the harvest until the yams are eaten, delaying the harvest by two months. Umuaro faces famine. Finally the Christian mission steps in, offering immunity from Ulu's wrath to anyone who harvests his yams and brings offerings to Christ. Ezeulu cracks, living the rest of his days in the "haughty splendor of a demented high priest" (229).

The intense drama of this rivalry needs no explication, but a close reading of certain passages shows that the antagonism between the two priests goes much deeper than personal rivalry and in fact reveals a deep rift at the heart of Umuaro, a rift that marks a crisis in the unfolding of Umuaro's political history. But this crisis is unexpectedly subsumed by a different history whose presence on the horizon both widens the rift and resolves it: the very move that would have solidified Ezeulu's power once and for all turns out decisively to end village autonomy altogether.

In chapter 2 we learn that Ezeulu's god is a relatively new god:

> In the very distant past, when lizards were still few and far between, the six villages . . . lived as different peoples, and each worshipped its own deity. Then the hired soldiers of Abam used to strike in the dead of night, set fire to the houses and carry men, women, and children into slavery. Things were so bad for the six villages that their leaders came together to save themselves. They hired a strong team of medicine-men to install a common deity for them. This deity which the fathers of the six villages made was called Ulu. . . . From that day on they were never again beaten by an enemy. (15)

If Ezeulu's god has a definite origin within historical memory, the origins of Ezidemili's god are not given so explicitly. In a conversation with Nwaka, Ezidemili claims that "Idemili was there at the beginning of things. Nobody made it" (42). We have no particular reason to believe this claim by the jealous priest, even if it is uttered with a certain sublimity. But finally this view is confirmed by Ulu himself, who appears to Ezeulu late in the novel. " 'Go home and sleep and leave me to settle my quarrel with Idemili, whose envy seeks to destroy me that his python may *again* come to power' " (191, italics added). Idemili predates Ulu, from the time when the six villages "lived as separate peoples."

The conflict between Ezeulu and Ezidemili, then, is the conflict between the priest of an autochthonous god and the priest of a synthetic god, between the village structure, older than historical memory, and a larger political structure that had supplanted it. But the alliance at the core of this political structure has become weakened; in the years after Winterbottom's intervention in the Okperi dispute, Ezeulu's and Ezidemili's villages nearly approach a state of war: "they were at the point which Umuaro people called *kill and take the head*" (39). The embodiment of this new political arrangement, the priesthood of Ulu, is also weakened. Ezeulu's grandfather and father had had the power to change the law singlehandedly, outlawing facial scarification and the practice of enslaving children born to widows, respectively (132, 133). Already, in the flashback to the conflict with Okperi, Ezeulu is unable to stop the war and asks, "How could such a people disregard the god who founded their town and protected it? Ezeulu saw it as the ruin of the world" (15). Praise of the deity itself approaches a conditional tone: "[Ulu] is still our protector, *even though* we no longer fear Abam warriors at night" (27, italics added).

This phrase deserves closer attention: "Even though we no longer fear Abam warriors at night": the danger that had integrated the six villages in the first place—the polity of Umuaro had been forged as an alliance against the Abam— has disappeared. The reason for this disappearance is given with admirable economy a paragraph later, in a passage we have already seen: "The white man, Winta-bota, brought soldiers to Umuaro and stopped [the war]. The story of what these soldiers did in Abame was still told with fear, and so Umuaro made no effort to resist but laid down their arms." (27) The story of the "pacification" of Abame is told in greater detail in *Things Fall Apart* (119–22), but the implication is clear: It is no longer the alliance but the presence of Winterbottom's troops that now protects Umuaro from marauding bands like the Abam. (Historically, raids by the Abam, mercenary soldiers under the Aro, a group who trafficked Igbo slaves, were indeed halted by the British "Aro Expedition" of 1901–2.)[18] The conflict between the two priests comes about because the integrative function of Ulu is no longer necessary, and a submerged power structure based around an older political organization is struggling to reassert itself.

Throughout the novel, Ezidemili claims that Ezeulu wants to be king: "He is a man of ambition; he wants to be king, priest, diviner, all. His father, they said, was like that too. But Umuaro showed him that Igbo people knew no kings" (27). This is plainly not the whole truth, as Ezeulu, whose basis of power is religious, turns down a chance to be secular chief of Umuaro. Further, the strong democratic traditions in Igbo society as portrayed by Achebe (democratic in an older sense, since slaves and women have no official voice) prevent authority from accumulating de jure in the figure of the chief priest. But we have seen that Ezeulu's father and grandfather wielded de facto executive power over the six villages. Indeed, it has been suggested that in certain "impure" forms of stateless society where age grades, priestly offices, and masked societies exist (as they do in fictional Umuaro), "internal disputes combined with a strong external threat tended . . . to bring about state formation."[19] Whether or not this is the case in fictional Umuaro, it is clear that the integrative power of the office of Ezeulu stands opposed to the more segmented political system represented by Ezidemili. Now that, thanks to British intervention, Umuaro is no longer threatened by the Abam, the integrative power wielded by the priest of Ulu is no longer needed, and a rift that had no doubt existed since the new god was installed suddenly emerges as a crisis. But this crisis is quickly subsumed by another history which had, unbe-knownst to anybody, caused the crisis in the first place. Ulu owes its obsolescence not to a return to village autononomy that would reempower Ezidemili, but to a new and greater integrative force on the horizon: the Christian mission and the colonial government.

This synecdochic allegory—the general disruption of autonomous histories figured through a particular political crisis—could be formulated quite differently in religious and ethical terms. (Indeed, these are hardly separable, as it is the priests Ezeulu and Ezidemili who wield political power and represent competing modes of political organization.) Off the scenes a battle takes place of which we only catch the briefest glimpse, when Ulu descends to berate Ezeulu: "As for me and Idemili we shall fight to the finish, and whoever throws the other down will strip him of his anklet!" (191). This conflict is between two gods rather than between two men. The first god, Idemili, remains from a time when each god integrated a village. The second, Ulu, integrates the six villages as a defense against the Abam, leaving the old gods in place but without their former importance. With the coming of colonialism and the pacification of the Abam raiders, the second god has outlived its utility. But this is also because, unbeknownst to either of the first two gods, a third god has appeared on the horizon, a god which, of course, also represents a new and exponentially larger political configuration.

In both *Things Fall Apart* and *Arrow of God*, Christianity plays a central role. Aside from the smashing of shrines and the preaching of the gospel, there is something else that guarantees the success of the Church. This is seen through the figure of Oduche, Ezeulu's son who goes to the mission, but also in Nwoye, the son of the hero of *Things Fall Apart* whose conscience is pricked by the customary killing of twins at birth and the sacrifice of his friend Ikemefuna:

> But there was a young man who had been captivated. His name was Nwoye, Okonkwo's first son. It was not the mad logic of the Trinity that captivated him. He did not understand it. It was the poetry of the new religion, something felt in the marrow. The hymn about brothers who sat in darkness and in fear seemed to answer the vague and persistent question that haunted his young soul—the question of the twins crying in the bush and the question of Ikemefuna who was killed. (128)

This brings us once more to Hegel, for whom Christianity marks the "first place that the right of subjectivity arose,"[20] the first time that individual conscience can make a claim against purely external laws. This, in Achebe's novels, is the real power of Christianity, whatever opportunistic, overzealous, cruel, or absurd forms it might take. Hegel tells another fable of a culture in its twilight, a fable of the intimation of the end of things that is at the same time, secretly, an intimation of the beginning of Christianity:

> Plato was conscious that there was breaking into that life in his own time a deeper principle which could appear in it directly only as something corruptive. To combat it, he needs must have sought aid for that very longing itself. But this aid had to come from on High. . . . This principle dawned in an inward form in the Christian religion.[21]

Converts like Nwoye indeed feel this longing, but it is Ezeulu who occupies the place of Plato in this fable, the wise man of the old order who senses a longing that is not his own—a longing emerging from the rifts and contradictions at the heart of his way of life—but who cannot combat this longing but by the old ways familiar to him. In a moving scene, Ezeulu returns to Ulu's shrine to ask, for the last time, if the harvest can take place after all:

> As he promised the leaders of Umuaro Ezeulu returned to the shrine of Ulu in the morning. . . . As Ezeulu cast his string of cowries the bell of Oduche's people [the converts] began to ring. For one brief moment he was distracted by its sad, measured monotone and he thought how strange it was that it should sound so near—much nearer than it did in his compound.

Ezeulu's announcement that his consultation with the deity had produced no result and that the six villages would be locked in the cycle for two moons longer spread such alarm as had not been known in Umuaro in living history. (209–10)

Ezeulu's consultation provokes no response from his deity because Ulu is dead. In the battle between the god of the village and the god of the alliance, it is the third god who takes Umuaro. Henceforth yams will be "harvested in the name of the son" (230): both in the name of the sons who have converted to the new religion and, of course, of the Son, Christ.

Biodun Jeyifo has shown the importance of Hegel's theory of tragedy for understanding literary representations of the colonial encounter.[22] But as with Jeyifo's initially Hegelian account of Soyinka's "Death and the King's Horseman," the ethical or religious levels must ultimately be surpassed by a materialist reading. The engine of Umuaro's dissolution is a land dispute. The situation that led to this dispute is implicit throughout the novel but could perhaps be clarified here most rapidly by reviewing the more general material background against which the novel is set. The "stateless society" of the Igbo lineage required large amounts of land. The system of titles that has such a prominent place in *Things Fall Apart* and *Arrow of God* prevented any one person from accumulating a great deal of capital, which prevented significant division of labor among free men, who were generally subsistence farmers. But the forest soil, when cleared, could only sustain a yam crop for three or four years before the thin topsoil was eroded away, so that for each plot of arable land there had to be many more recovering from earlier farming. Although "subsistence" is not an accurate term for this form of agriculture, since it did produce surpluses, it did not, even when the environment was cooperative and the social order stable, result in a particularly rich and consistent source of nutrition: throughout *Arrow of God*, the response to polite inquiries after family is " 'We have no trouble except hunger' " (62). However, such an economy was able to sustain a growing population—as long as available land was effectively infinite. But at the time in which the novel is set, population pressure had long ago begun to feed the slave trade and to drive some groups—such as the Abam against whom Umuaro was integrated—to organize into marauding bands. This had been to a great extent stopped, as we saw earlier, not so much by the abolition of the British slave trade in 1807 as by punitive expeditions against the kidnappers.[23] In the crucial second chapter of *Arrow of God*, it can be seen that territorial expansion has run up against its limit: previously unclaimed land has suddenly become a matter of dispute between Umuaro and Okperi.

The defection of Umuaro ultimately has its origins, then, in a material crisis: the famine almost caused by Ezeulu's obstinacy is only the allegorical ground (still on our first level, where the particular contains the general) of a more persistent crisis. Umuaro could not feed itself without acquiring more land, and the aversion of this particular food crisis allegorizes a more general one that is displaced by Umuaro's integration into a world economy that would pay cash for the palm oil—a sustainable crop indigenous to the region—that was used as a lubricant in English factories.[24] "The white man had indeed brought a lunatic religion, but he had also built a trading store and for the first time palm-oil and kernel became things of great price" (*Things Fall Apart* 153). This new economy is a cash economy that can be taxed for roads and other public works, that can buy European and particularly British commodities, that would eventually produce groundnuts and cotton—and, later, of course, fossil oil—as well as palm products. But this is no salvation; this economy is, of course, virtually synonymous with colonialism, which Achebe has characterized, in a neat play on Hobbesian characterizations of precolonial life, as "nasty, British, and short."[25]

And so, once again, we return to Hegel and the problem of history in Africa. While the Hegelian relegation of Africa to a space outside history is untenable, at a certain moment African history and Western history become one: in the words of Samba Diallo's father in *Ambiguous Adventure*, "the era of separate destinies has run its course" (79). From the perspective of the present, the defection of Umuaro—Umuaro considered along the metonymic axis of our first allegorical level—seems inevitable. The great man, Ezeulu, doesn't make history: he finds History waiting for him. In his lyrical preface to the second edition of *Arrow of God*, Achebe gives the story a moral:

> had he been spared Ezeulu might have come to see his fate as perfectly consistent with his high historic destiny as victim, consecrating by his agony—thus raising to the stature of a ritual passage—the defection of his people. And he gladly would have forgiven them. (vii)

But surely this is a strange introduction to a tragic novel: suddenly the most tragic of plots—the decisive end of village autonomy, figured as the destruction of a personality, with the coming of colonialism—is given a strangely positive valence. But this contradiction originates in the assumption that "destiny" ends with the present, that henceforth the entire world is to be "Western" as we know it. But the epochal change that takes place in fictional Umuaro allegorizes another possibility that emerges with the movement toward independence in Africa. When Achebe titled his first novel *Things Fall Apart*, he added a new allegorical level to Yeats's "The Second Coming," which, in narrating the going of Christianity, is suddenly able to represent its coming. This structure is inverted in *Arrow of God*, which, in narrating the coming of colonialism, simultaneously points toward its going.

If the first allegorical level was metonymic, narrating a general historical process through a particular fictional instance, the second level projects the meaning of this instance out into the future. To understand this second level, we need to return to that aspect of Achebe's criticism and his novels usually given priority but here held in abeyance until now: the image. It was mentioned in passing that *Things Fall Apart* could be considered a rewriting of Basden's anthropological account of Igbo life. This recuperative aspect of *Things Fall Apart* has been highlighted by Achebe and glossed by many critics; it is also as much a limit as a precondition of Achebe's first book. *Things Fall Apart* manages to revisit many of the elements that Basden found important: the existence of love, the fate of twins, the meaning of titles, the nature of the masked spirits, the functioning of the oracles, the etiquette of kola, the social function of eloquence, the relationship of the living to the dead, the extremity of human sacrifice, and the significance of the *osu* or outcasts, among others. In every case Basden's account, an extreme objectification of Igbo practice, a frozen instance of pure behavior, mute and incomprehensible, is supplanted by a more supple, narrative representation that not only gives these practices a logic and meaning but translates them into the medium of the novel.[26] What had been objectified in the ethnographic image is suddenly given the right of subjectivity—an effect achieved, paradoxically, by interposing a gulf between the narrative and the motives of its characters.

If one reads Basden after reading Achebe (as most readers of Basden probably do), one is impressed not so much by the datedness or condescension of Basden's attitude toward his object of study as by the poverty of his interpretations; at the same time, one is struck by the possibility that it is this work, and other anthropological works like it, that has determined the altogether richer content of *Things Fall Apart*.[27] In what follows we will return initially to *Things Fall Apart*, which represents a more direct reaction to the colonial image of Africa, before confronting the same issue on the more complex surface of *Arrow of God*.

Examples of the relationship between *Niger Ibos* and *Things Fall Apart* could multiply indefinitely, but a single example will illustrate it. Basden devotes a chapter to what he calls "Day and Night Clubs" (366–76), which have elsewhere been referred to as masked societies. The public activities of these societies—their appearance as ancestral spirits, their dress, their odd voices, the reaction to them by women and children—are described, at the literal level, almost identically by Basden and Achebe. But the interpretations implicit to each are worlds apart. Here, Basden interprets the fact that these spirits are being performed by the men of the society. A new initiate has learned the appropriate techniques:

> What had, hitherto, been accepted in all faith to be a re-embodied spirit proves to be no more than a man, probably a kinsman, masquerading as such. . . . The youth, having experienced the chagrin of being duped himself . . . would find great entertainment in sharing the fun of gulling the non-initiated folk of the village. (375)

In *Things Fall Apart* Achebe interprets the same phenomenon from the perspective of the "duped":

> Okonkwo's wives, and perhaps other women as well, might have noticed that the second *egwugwu* had the springy walk of Okonkwo. And they might also have noticed that Okonkwo was not among the titled men and elders who sat behind the row of *egwugwu*. But if they thought these things they kept them within themselves. The *egwugwu* with the springy walk was one of the dead fathers of the clan. (79)

What in the passage from Basden is a matter of smug duplicity and nearly incomprehensible gullibility is transformed by Achebe into an instance of transubstantiation. Everybody knows that the host in the Catholic mass is a piece of bread, but to refuse to say so and to believe that it is also something else is neither duplicitous nor foolish. The first description takes what is given and interprets it according to a preexisting interpretive scheme, namely the interpretation of children's behavior. The second has its own scheme, which is intimately tied to the assumption that the phenomenon is communicable in the form of the novel.

For Basden the behavior he describes holds no mystery; its interpretation is unitary and commonsense, made without admitting the possibility of other interpretations, including any the actor might have of his own actions. The self-assurance of the prose is evidence enough of this: "the youth, having experienced the chagrin of being duped himself." This is, of course, pure speculation on Basden's part, since, according to his own testimony, to reveal such a thing would be to "court a dreadful death" (366); but the language here is absolutely confident in its appraisal, collapsing all possible explanations into a single reified interpretation. This objectifying gaze is something we are familiar with and goes back to Sartre's concept of the Look[28] (and ultimately back once again to the dialectic of Lord and Bondsman).[29] Despite all that separates Achebe's description from Basden's, it, too, is an interpretation, if a more sympathetic one. The fundamental difference is a formal one and concerns the circumspection of Achebe's language. Okonkwo's wives "*might* have noticed," this or that: "*if* they thought these things they kept them within themselves." Achebe's language refuses to collapse the possible meanings of the phenomenon; an interpretation is suggested but other possible meanings are allowed to freewheel on beyond the text.

Again, this is not an isolated instance but a characteristic difference. The throwing away of twins is given a definitive explanation by Basden (animals have multiple births, making twins less than human) while in *Things Fall Apart* the reason is never fully given. The hospitality ritual is much the same in Basden as it is in *Things Fall Apart*; but in the latter the ritual is subtly different each time, so that the social meanings of a particular instance are never finally available to the reader. In fact, an interesting reading might be made of the kola-nut hospitality ritual as it appears in Basden, in Nzekwu's *Wand of Noble Wood*, in *Things Fall Apart* (where traces of the ethnographic image remain), and finally in *Arrow of God*. In the last, the social meanings of the ritual are finally, as a careful rereading reveals, determinate. But on a first reading, these meanings do not seem determined in advance—as indeed they are not for the fictional participants—and the outcome of the ritual is always in question until after it has taken place. In fact, on a first reading, the breaking of the kola nut does not appear as "ritual" at all: subtle and never determinate social meanings are suggested without the narratorial interpretation that characterizes the ethnographic voice.[30] For Spivak, the possibility of the subaltern subject's "non-containment by the text" is what justifies the privilege of the literary over the ethnographic. Even if one remains wary about ascribing too broad a liberatory potential to the novel as a form, one can see the truth of this statement in *Things Fall Apart*.[31] The paradox of Achebe's writing is that this is accomplished not by stepping toward a more complex and nuanced analysis of character, but through a distance placed between a totalizing narrative and individual agency that is allowed to be infinite and unknowable.

If *Things Fall Apart* can be read as a literary reaction to the ethnographic image, this reading becomes much more complicated with the more elaborate architectonics of *Arrow of God*—even if, as with *Ulysses*, its seemingly effortless wealth of anthropological detail (both in Umuaro and on Government Hill) is in fact a studied effect. Now, when we investigate the meaning of the image in *Arrow of*

God, it will have to be seen in relation to the still open question of the "high historic destiny" at the heart of the novel, the meaning of the world-historical event that is the defection of Umuaro.

As suggested earlier, the postcolonial history of the colonial image cannot be understood without reference to the Look, which had already been translated by Sartre into a postcolonial context, into the dramatic "black men standing and gazing at us" at the beginning of his preface to Senghor's great *Anthologie de la nouvelle poésie nègre et malgache*.[32] Both the contradictions of this essay and its importance to the *négritude* movement have been amply investigated elsewhere, but it is worth rehearsing a few salient points here to draw the contrast with *Arrow of God* more starkly. In "Orphée noir," the essence of colonialism itself is seen to be the colonial image, a violent foreshortening of the dialectic of the Look: "the privilege of seeing without being seen" (which formulation reminds us of the debt Foucauldian surveillance owes to the Sartrean Look). The colonizing Look receives possibly its fullest expression in reifying anthropologies like Basden's, or in semi-anthropological administrative handbooks like the fictive one that closes *Things Fall Apart*, in which the whole story of Okonkwo is reduced to "perhaps not a whole chapter but a reasonable paragraph" of *The Pacification of the Primitive Tribes of the Lower Niger* (179). But the returned gaze that introduces "Orphée noir" is only a negative or reactive moment, the violent assumption of a position that was already given, itself only a reified essence and a partial truth. Theoretically, this incompleteness was to have been self-conscious as the colonial gaze was not; this "antiracist racism" always to have been surpassed toward quite a different relationship:

> Suddenly the subjective, existential, ethnic notion of *négritude* "passes," as Hegel says, into that—objective, positive, exact—of *proletariat*. "For Césaire," says Senghor, "the 'White' symbolizes capital, as the Black, labor."[33]

But what these strategically essentializing notions tended to pass over into—as the champions of *négritude* could not then have known—was not universal revolution but the self-serving "Africanization" of the national bourgeoisies, which accumulated wealth after the colonial manner while maintaining the subordinate status of African economies within the global economy.

Despite initial appearances, then, what is accomplished is not so much a switching of the positions of subject and object, seer and seen, as a change in the valence of terms already given. As Aimé Césaire puts it in his poem "Barbare"— included in the collection that Sartre's essay prefaces—this reversal is "le vrai pouvoir opératoire / de la négation" (56)—the truly effective or strategic power of negation. If we keep in mind the original meaning of this negation in *Being and Nothingness*—the negation of the field of human possibilities by an essentializing gaze that collapses these possibilities into a single, reified actuality—then we can understand this return of the gaze as a change in polarity from (to continue with Sartrean terminology) *shame* to *pride*. The returned gaze is not so much a genuine realignment of terms as a challenge that marks the prideful assumption of a position—or, if one likes, an identity or "object-state"—which had been given in advance as shame.

The point of view *Arrow of God* takes vis-à-vis the colonial Look is quite different from all this. Here it is not a matter of content, of altering the valence of negative representations or exchanging them for positive ones. Instead, it is a matter of form, in particular a matter of narrative totalization. Moments of objectification are present within the text, only to be negated on a different level by the narrative voice itself, which maintains, as we saw above, a certain diffidence in relation to individual motivation. The relationship between the "image of Africa" in *Arrow of God* and the colonial image is best exemplified by the road-building scene, which overwrites a similar scene from Joyce Cary's *Mister Johnson*.

The road-building scene in *Arrow of God* is a remarkable set piece, occupying less than ten pages, in which characters are briefly transposed into another context where they perform entirely different functions. Ezeulu's son Obika briefly becomes the resentful laborer, and Moses Unachukwu, important elsewhere as one of the first Christians in the village, occupies Johnson's position as overseer, the translator and intermediary between Wright and the laborers. Both Achebe's and Cary's scenes take place toward the end of a dry season. It appears, however, as though the road cannot be finished before the rains. The road builder—Rudbeck in *Mister Johnson*, Wright in *Arrow of God*—resorts to unpaid, "volunteer" labor to supplement the paid laborers. But it is the festival season, and none of the young men sent to work on the road is particularly interested in this unpaid work; in fact, most of them are hungover. The seasoned laborers chaff the listless, latecoming "volunteers." In *Mister Johnson*, the tension of this scene is quickly defused: the new laborers are fused with the old (and with the foremen and boss as well) by the magic of a work song in a collective project which, of course, only Rudbeck understands—and he only intuitively and incompletely.

This all plays out differently in *Arrow of God*, where the initial tension explodes into violence at several different levels. Wright, Rudbeck's analog, whips one of the insolent latecomers, who leaps at him in a fury before being subdued and further whipped; the tension between the latecomers and the others plays into the feud between the two villages, resulting in a skirmish; the workers organize a meeting about how to resist the road work, a meeting that itself dissipates in acrimony. The difference between this and the relatively idealized scene in *Mister Johnson* is, of course, significant and restores a dialectic of repression and resistance that is absent in Cary's representation of the colonial project. (Although *Mister Johnson* is certainly not devoid of colonial violence, the exploitive role in forcing labor is put on the village chiefs, and the violence inflicted on Johnson throughout the novel does not emerge in reaction to any conscious resistance on Johnson's part.) But the primary rewriting takes place at the level of the image and is centered around the analogous pair of Johnson and Moses Unachukwu. Now is not the time to enter into a detailed discussion of *Mister Johnson*, whose representation of colonial society itself, without reference to the colonized, is not so different from that of *Arrow of God*, which is remarkable for its complex portrayal of Wright, Winterbottom, and the other residents of Government Hill. But if *Arrow of God* is able to represent these characters without reducing them to an identity or reified object-state, *Mister Johnson* is not able to do so with its central character, who is not so much a character as a pidgin-speaking exuberance.

It is true that any fictional character might be considered as no more than a collection of functional positions occupied in a narratological scheme, and that at certain times—for example, as we shall see shortly, in the fictions of Wyndham Lewis—such a possibility is raised to self-consciousness. But a distinction must be drawn between such self-conscious refusal of illusionistic depth and a phenomenon that has every appearance of resulting from a conceptual blindness. For Johnson is not, like Coetzee's conception of Defoe's Friday in *Foe*, the figure of the colonized as mute and, from the point of view of the colonizer, incomprehensible. On the contrary, Johnson is everywhere heard, and everywhere comprehended. While the narrative series of every other character's actions creates the illusion of being produced by a unity that is never finally compassed, Johnson's behaviors are referred to an immediate understanding: the reasons behind his exultation at marrying Bamu, for example, are arranged in front of us simultaneously with that exultation: "Johnson's idea of civilized marriage, founded on the store catalogues, their fashion notes . . . and a few novels approved by the S.P.C.K., is a compound of romantic sentiment and embroidered underclothes" (4). Johnson is a representational failure not by reference to some external novelistic standard, but by the characterological canon implicit within Cary's novel itself. The problem with Johnson is not that the narrative voice seems to misunderstand Johnson's African mentality but that, like Basden's "Niger Ibos," Johnson has a "mentality" in the first place. Johnson is not, in terms of what he is supposed to represent, misunderstood: instead, he is completely understood—and therefore completely misunderstood.

One of the remarkable things about *Arrow of God*, as few have failed to notice, is its "balanced" or "fair" representation of the contradictions of both the colonial presence and Igbo society. One can see what is meant by this without finding the terms of praise particularly compelling. What this characteristic points to, instead, is the formal totalization Achebe imposes on his material. *Arrow of God* is far less "the gaze returned," which would involve an equal and opposite objectification of the colonial figure, than a synthetic representation of the totality of gazes. Achebe's novel only seems to be the immediately naturalistic story of village life from a perspective that is all too ready to ignore the rich fabric of historical mediations that Achebe presents, and to view it instead as the narration "from below" of a history with which we are already familiar "from above." But, of course, the "below" and the "above" are parts of one thing; and it is this that *Arrow of God* attempts to represent.[34]

To return to the road-building scene in *Arrow of God*: Wright, after the skirmish among the two groups, commands the laborers through Moses Unachukwu, who translates.

> "Tell them this bloody work must be finished by June."
> "The white man says that unless you finish this work on time you will know the kind of man he is."

"No more lateness."

"Pardin?"

"Pardon what? Can't you understand plain, simple English? I said there will be no more late-coming."

"Oho. He says everybody must work hard and stop all this shit-eating." (83)

Here one of Achebe's most achieved effects comes to the fore: the translation of English into "Igbo," an instance of the modulation into different registers of English (which reaches its apotheosis in his technically masterful political drama *Anthills of the Savannah*). At the very least these two registers—Wright's cursory English and the more elegant Igbo into which Unachukwu translates it—mark an incommensurability between Wright's understanding of the situation and that of the laborers'. But there is yet a third register:

> "I have one question I want the white man to answer." This was Nweke Ukpaka.
>
> "What's that?"
>
> Unachukwu hesitated and scratched his head. "Dat man wan axe master queshon."
>
> "No questions."
>
> "Yessah." He turned to Nweke. "The white man says he did not leave his house this morning to come and answer your questions." (83).

For a brief moment, Moses Unachukwu—who a few paragraphs later dresses down an interlocutor with an imperious dignity fully equal to Ezeulu's habitual idiom—is Johnson: "Dat man wan axe master queshon," with a clown-like scratch of the head. It would be wrong to say that the point of view here is Wright's; but suddenly—and only—in speaking to Wright Unachukwu becomes that which Wright estimates him to be: a "native." The single sentence of pidgin English reveals Unachukwu as Johnson, reveals the poverty as well as the inescapability of Wright's interpretation of Unachukwu: Wright could not conceive of Unachukwu other than as Johnson. This is the moment of the colonial image as objectification. But rather than reduce Wright in turn to a crude exploitive intention—Wright is, like Ezeulu, a tangle of conflicting motivations that are no more clear than are the priest's or, for that matter, Rudbeck's in *Mister Johnson*—the narrative steps back to reveal this interpretive poverty in relation to a totality of which Wright has no conception. The image in *Arrow of God* no longer takes part in the agonistic interplay of gazes; it is instead a snapshot of the totality.

As we saw in the previous chapter, the process of totalization, the privilege of Minerva's owl in Hegel's *Philosophy of Right*, is formally retrospective: "When philosophy paints its grey in grey, then has a shape of life grown old. . . . The owl of Minerva spreads its wings only with the falling of the dusk." (13) We find, then, that Achebe's village novels, in narrating the coming of colonialism, unexpectedly bring into being a genuinely postcolonial space, a possible future from which the colonial period could be completely compassed and forgiven. Achebe's generous voice—formally, a perspective from which all of the accounts of the colonial epoch had been put paid—is itself the utopian content of *Arrow of God*, a novel that has sometimes been denounced as "pessimistic." As Achebe has said in response to this critique: the work of art exists to "giv[e] us something that is not already given, something which is not flying around the life of the community, the life of the individual. . . . I think this is what happens when there is *optimism*."[35] Achebe's "optimism," which here explicitly names what we have been calling the utopian aspect, is not something given positively as content but is rather the formal perspective we have been describing. But this perspective can only be occupied imaginatively, not actually, since the colonial dynamic does not end with formal political independence. As the foregoing quote insists, optimism marks the place of a lack, of precisely what is not available in the present.

But this utopian element is not merely abstract, and from this perspective it marks a tremendous leap from the works we have looked at thus far. It is conditioned by a desire made concrete in the bodies of the people of Umuaro. Neither Ezeulu nor Winterbottom, nor Ulu nor the Christian god, is responsible for the village's "defection." It is desire of the village itself—ultimately, nothing more romantic than the desire to eat—that leads to its defection to the new religion, and ultimately from "subsistence" agriculture to the production of cash crops. Ulu and Ezeulu are only its expression. But Achebe hints at something more with a telegram that crosses the desk of the assistant district commissioner: "the weekly Reuter's telegram . . . carried the news that Russian peasants in revolt against the new régime had refused to grow crops. . . . [T]he other packet . . . was a report by the Secretary for Native Affairs on Indirect Rule in Eastern Nigeria" (180). The administrative report Clarke reads fixes the date of the novel at 1921,[36] as does the peasant revolt against the "new régime" of the Soviet government. The era and context remind us once again of Yeats's "The Second Coming," which, as we saw above, already registers the violent passing of Christianity—a passing whose harbinger is the "blood-dimmed tide" of the Russian Revolution. The Europe whose presence is felt in Umuaro is not the Christian Europe of the Conquest; it is a society whose internal contradictions have already exploded in one world war and in revolution. But while in Yeats—and Kane and Ford—the possibility of epochal change only makes a negative appearance as a source of dread, Achebe transforms the disaster that befell Umuaro into a utopian possibility.

Achebe does not allow himself the luxury of an epilogue, only suggesting in a later interview that "[t]he end of a story is only an end in one sense. It is a beginning in another sense. . . . At the end of the page, another page is projected, like an echo or the pebbles you throw in a pond."[37] It is up to us to decipher the meaning of this next page. The peasant revolt to which the telegram refers took place during the famine of 1921: the hunger of the peasantry, which the October revolution had mobilized, began to stir against it when the revolution appeared unable to realize its promise. This immanent power of the masses is what Hardt and Negri have called "the desire of the multitude": at its most basic level, once again, the desire to eat. As we saw briefly in the introduction, Hardt and Negri's work posits this desire as the engine of history. It is also, as we have seen, the engine of *Arrow of God*. The parallel Achebe suggests to Russian history invites us to speculate that the same force that assured colonialism's victory will also rise against it. The hunger that drives the village from Ulu to the colonial economy will also drive mass participation in the resistance to colonialism—and to the neocolonial economy in turn—when that economy proves unable to meet its promise.[38]

But the utopian moment Achebe's voice imaginatively occupies never came, and this historic failure has to reflect back on the voice that prophesied it. If the time has come to make a dialectical turn from the utopian to the ideological content of *Arrow of God*, this can only be carried out with the reminder that Achebe's generation had the extraordinary misfortune of seeing its greatest accomplishment and its greatest failure in a single lifetime. The desire to eat that leads to Umuaro's quiet revolution is indeed concrete; unlike Kane's utopia, Achebe's is backed by a causal force, while the modernist utopias we have seen so far do not even project the possibility of realization. But in another sense it is still abstract—as is Hardt and Negri's "desire of the multitude." It exists in itself, but not for itself, and therefore its only expression can be spontaneous, uncoordinated, and easily perverted. In itself it can never be equal to capital; it can only provoke it. If, as Achebe himself has said, "All art is propaganda, though not all propaganda is art," then the limitations of Achebe's novel lie not with Achebe but with the novel as such, limited by its form (and in the case of Achebe by its language) to speak mainly to the progressive bourgeoisie.[39] The great leap of *Arrow of God* is to have concretely narrated the tremendous power of the desire of the multitude; but there is a contradiction between this leap and the class to which the novel addresses itself. To be equal to capital, the desire of this hungry multitude would have to be organized into a for-itself—pushing us, in a more direct sense than has occupied our discussion this far, into the realm of politics.

PART THREE

Politics

CHAPTER SIX

The Childermass: Revolution and Reaction

In the works we have examined thus far, the absence of a concrete mediation between the subject and history has undermined the utopian impulses of the texts. In our introduction we theorized this mediation as politics, and in the novels of Wyndham Lewis (and in the work of Ngugi wa Thiong'o and Pepetela in the next chapter) politics is the stuff of which narrative is made. For this reason the relationship to the modernist sublime—which, as we saw in the introduction, tends to be antipolitical—is attenuated, though it does reappear in what we will be calling the "embodied clichés" from which Lewis constructs his narratives. To say that Lewis's work is explicitly political does not of course imply that the political building blocks from which these narratives are assembled or the messages that they are presumably meant to convey do not undergo unexpected transformations, reversals, and deformations as they pass into narrative. But while with Joyce or Achebe the canon of immanence is rigorously obeyed, and while the intrusion of partisan perspective into narrative (for example, in some of Ford's less accomplished works) is generally felt to be in violation of that canon, here the narrative and thematic content is explicitly political. Lewis and Ngugi are each concerned with the construction of a political subject, a concrete mediation between the individual subject and history. In Lewis's case, this subject is to be the so-called class of individuals, which turns out to name Lewis's own class fraction, while Ngugi's theater experiments are made in the name of a peasant class consciousness. Surprisingly, Lewis's project in a certain way presupposes Ngugi's—at least, Lewis's own class consciousness is predicated on a reaction to the political subjectivity emerging from the working class, from racial and ethnic minorities, and from the colonies.

With Lewis we face a particularly intense version of the paradox that for Adorno was constitutive for art as such. On one hand, we know very well that an artwork is not a replica of the subject and that art escapes intention the moment it enters history. On the other, the artwork does emerge out of a subjectivity whose individuation and position within social space is given a priori and cannot simply be overleapt at will by the artist. "The situation therefore compels art . . . to undergo subjective mediation in its objective constitution. The share of subjectivity in the artwork is itself a piece of objectivity."[1] This is, of course, no solution to the paradox but only an affirmation of its constitutive character. In the case of Lewis this seeming paradox is all the more fundamental in that it is not unusual to find obvious similarities between Lewis's published political opinions and those of his characters. Indeed, somewhat bizarrely, some of the fictional dialogue spoken by the proto-fascist Hyperidians in early drafts of *The Childermass*[2] finds its way back into Lewis's mouth in his nonfiction treatise *Time and Western Man.*[3] The objectivity of Lewis's fiction cannot be understood without reference to his subjectivity, most consequently his politics as they emerge from a tightly circumscribed and clearly demarcated position in social space. This social determination of Lewis's thought, in turn, returns the subjective content, which might threaten to sink into the merely pathological, to objectivity by establishing the work's methexis in the social totality.

But before we turn to Lewis's political and critical writings, we might take a moment to be surprised that Lewis has not experienced a revival in the past twenty or so years, when we have become increasingly open to literature with explicitly political content, and (one would think) more skeptical with regard to the specific pieties to which Lewis's eye was so perfectly attuned. Considering for the moment only Lewis's writings on the intersections of politics and literature, Lewis's exposure of the class micropolitics of artistic production in his satires of Bloomsbury "bourgeois bohemia," for example, are not so different in content from the more methodologically explicit (and officially Left) analyses of Pierre Bourdieu into various Parisian intellectual and artistic fields.[4] Nor would his critique of the relationship between both "high" and "low" cultural forms and the conditions and needs of capitalist consumption, in its logical outline, seem out of place today. Potentially more interesting in the present context are Lewis's attempts to understand the political implications of literary form, a project he shares with much contemporary literary theory. In these attempts he goes beyond the still current but often facile association of formal rupture with social rupture, reading the most apparently radical departures from conventional narrative as symptoms of a prevailing liberal (and secretly antidemocratic) ideology. We are free to be skeptical about his conclusions, but his formal analyses in *Men Without Art*[5] and *Time and Western Man*—analyses that expose the ties that bind Joyce, Stein, Faulkner, and Hemingway with such writers as Anita Loos, the author of *Gentlemen Prefer Blondes*, in a common exploitation of a pseudo-naïve viewpoint—foreshadow much later critiques of modernism, with the advantage of still bearing the distinctive scent of fresh discovery.

Lewis begins with an accusation that has become a commonplace, namely that mainstream modernism, even at its most apparently avant-garde, is a kind of late variant of Romantic nostalgia.[6] He ends with an understanding of literary form as the by-product of a conspiracy among "High-Bohemia," the " 'revolutionary' rich," and "Big Business" designed to produce happy worker-cretins, and to crush those few exceptional individuals who are not content in their manufactured pseudo-freedom. Plainly, this is where a contemporary analysis, viewing this late romanticism as a symptom of more fundamental social processes, must part ways with Lewis's conspiracy theory of modernism, which really begins and ends with his own precarious position vis-à-vis "High Bohemia." But between these two points, Lewis produces trenchant critiques of the patronizing "cult of *the primitive*" (*Time and Western Man* 53–54); the manufacture of the "public" as an instrument of social control (*The Art of Being Ruled* 79–84);[7] the collusion of scandal and official morality (*Time and Western Man* 15–19); the patriarchal family as an antiquated and repressive institution (*Rude Assignment* 174–77);[8] the existence of the "educationalist state" (*The Art of Being Ruled* 111), prefiguring Althusser's identification of the "educational ideological apparatus";[9] and the ideologies of progressivism (*The Art of Being Ruled* 31–46) and the related notion of a hypostatized human nature (*The Art of Being Ruled* 47). All these are critiques we are accustomed to think of not only as much later developments, but also specifically in terms of Left analyses of liberalism: indeed, as has been pointed out before, it is as a critic of liberalism that Lewis is most sympathetically understood.

This explains to a certain extent Lewis's confusion at times over whether his own politics was Left or Right; in *The Art of Being Ruled* (367–71), for example, he is able to champion the "sovietic system" as the "best," yet recommend "some modified form of fascism" for "anglo-saxon countries" (369), as though Marxism and fascism were merely variations on a single anti-liberal theme (which indeed he claims in "Liberalist Democracy and Authority," *The Art of Being Ruled* 67–70). A twenty-first-century reader of Lewis's political writings, of course, experiences no such confusion. Lewis's politics are, it is true, more complex than our contemporary caricature gives them credit for. Lewis's political and theoretical works—which might be most accurately called works of opinion—are so rich in contradictions, so energetically immune to systematicity, that it is hard to find a statement which does not quickly run up against an apparently incompatible proposition—without, however, providing the ironic spark that might suggest an identity on some other plane.[10] The title of Lewis's own summation of the history of his opinions best qualifies the automatic, almost unconscious character of these writings as representing "A Pattern of Thinking" (*Rude Assignment* 141–219) rather than a coherent philosophy or a worldview. The certainty a contemporary reader has about the political core of Lewis's writings lies in a more formal attribute of Lewis's works of opinion. These critiques of liberalism always seem to break down at the same point, where diagnosis leads to cure, where micropolitics leads to macropolitics, where the insecurity of Lewis's own tenuous position in social space interferes and decisively snaps illuminating critique over into a defensive rant against emerging social changes.

Lewis's public positions on many of the most pressing political issues—Lewis was capable, without embarrassment, of identifying himself with anti-Semitism and other racisms, misogyny, homophobia, the unabashed support of colonial repression, and, most notoriously, Nazism—are beyond apology, but it would be as unfair quickly to identify Lewis with any one of the above attitudes as it would be irresponsible to excuse him of them in the name of some more nuanced reading of his writings. To take just one example: vicious homophobia seems to be a thread that runs through all of Lewis's writings, including his fiction. Yet one is startled to find that, in the late *Rude Assignment* (1950), the idée fixe of the "pansy" turns out to disguise, in admittedly bizarre fashion, the analysis of quite another situation, the obliteration of human differences on the assembly line (174–77). (One is tempted to think that this had "always" been the case: after all, as far back as *The Art of Being Ruled* [1926] homosexuality was merely "a passion . . . [with] a right to rank without comment alongside other forms of sex liveliness" [310]). Feminists—which we had become accustomed to being characterized as the "enemies" in the "sex-war" against the "White European" (understood as male)—are engaged in a legitimate struggle against "the economic injustice imposed on women by barbarous laws" (*Rude Assignment* 176). But, as sincere as these analyses might be, a measure of Lewis's politics must be this: within a page, we have returned to "these ubiquitous perverts" and their unholy alliance with the "embittered, and no longer young" feminist, out to revenge herself on the "he-man, for whom she would no longer be attractive" (177). The ease and consistency with which Lewis's powerful critiques of liberalism are folded back in favor of a bitterly aggressive attempt to defend his own precarious position of relative privilege with regard to women, laborers, the colonized, and so on make him, for us, an unambiguously reactionary figure.

The notoriously celebratory *Hitler* of 1931 gives us a clue as to the source of this politics.[11] Again, it would be unfair to judge Lewis summarily by this book, which was repudiated in an orthodox way in his 1939 *The Hitler Cult*.[12] The hastily written *Hitler* might be most charitably thought of as a kind of slip of the tongue, almost an eruption from the subconscious for it would be pointless to criticize its author but which, nonetheless, serves as symptom of his condition—and of course, not of his alone. The most remarkable thing about *Hitler* is that, taken individually, Lewis's insights—commonplaces today but arrived at without benefit of hindsight in 1931—would seem to expose and discredit Nazi ideology rather than, as he would have it, merely explain it in an "unprejudiced" way (4): the myth of the Aryan is "ethnologically indefensible" (108); the hatred of the Jew is a "racial red-herring" (43) whose only function is to distract from class consciousness (84); "National Socialism" functions through the personality cult of "Hitlerism" (31); and so on. Yet these insights do not lead to a rejection of Nazism, and the supposedly "neutral" tone of the book is nothing of the kind but instead reveals Lewis's enthusiasm—especially surprising in a person who saw himself as "exceedingly skeptical about, and unresponsive to, all 'nationalist' excitements altogether" (5)—for a racist ideology liberal England (or "the intelligent Anglo-saxon" [4]) was already rejecting.

Not just one element among many, it is specifically the racist element of Nazism that attracts Lewis—not with regard to Jews (although elsewhere he is not immune to the stereotyped images of the Jew), but against the "Non-White World," particularly the colonized world. But once again, what is most remarkable is that Lewis's pivotal racism thrives in spite of the fact that its standard ideological underpinnings are completely discredited. There is no reference in *Hitler* to the notions of racial superiority and inferiority that form the customary aura of racialist argument: indeed, Lewis is commendably insensitive to a notion of otherness that (as he was one of the earliest to point out) lay equally behind racist hatred and the liberal love of the "exotic." Lewis's is a completely political racism, almost, paradoxically, a nonracist racism. In *Hitler*, European domination is neither justified by white racial superiority or by the more liberal cultural superiority implied by Europe's "civilizing mission." Instead, "race feeling" is simply a means toward preserving European power and privilege to which they have no inherent right, but simply happen to have. "White Consciousness" is no more than a matter of Europeans' "practical [that is, economic] interests" (121, here with reference to Black Americans):

> Give them all your jobs, exalt them above your own Babbitt-hood, and (being but human) they will surely take advantage of this heaven-sent reversal of status. And they will not then find the Poor White Trash by whom they are surrounded anything like so "romantic" and bewitching as the White American has been persuaded, cajoled, and bullied into finding them. The American Negro, once in power, would probably not be very much troubled by the Exotic Sense! (120)

"White Consciousness," therefore, is purely and explicitly a strategy for the defense of existing privilege, stripped of its ideological aura. What we find here strangely exemplifies one half of Althusser's well-known formulation that ideology "represents the imaginary relationship of individuals to their real conditions of existence."[13] *Hitler* indeed reveals the relationship of an individual to his conditions of existence, but stripped of any justifying imaginary relationship to those conditions. For, as the appearance of the question of employment ("give them all your jobs") clearly shows, this is not fundamentally a racial argument but a racist mapping of a defense of class privilege. Here, with breathtaking cynicism, Lewis openly endorses the logic he discovers in Nazism whereby "the Nationalsocialist is, in reality, attempting to . . . to put *Race* in the place of *Class*" (83). By the same mechanism that drives xenophobic discourse today—only here without pretense—the concept of racial identity functions to disrupt the construction of class consciousness.[14]

Lewis's peculiar politics derives from the fact that his downwardly mobile class trajectory (the son of a wealthy, yacht-owning American wine merchant who left Lewis's mother for a housemaid, the adult Lewis was, in the words of Ezra Pound, "most hampered by lack of funds"[15] and largely dependent on loans from patrons and from wealthier and more commercially successful friends) separates his political interests from those of "bourgeois bohemia" with which he was in direct and lopsided economic competition (precisely a question of "jobs") and makes possible and even necessary his keen insight into the hypocrisies and contradictions of a liberal common sense that can only emerge from a position of relative security. On the other hand, the persistent threat of proletarianization and loss of relative privilege produces a fear of the working class itself as much as of the process that produces it, so that Lewis had as much at stake in distancing himself from the interests of the working class as he found it impossible to identify fully with his professional class milieu. Such a subjective relation to class structures virtually guarantees that class must not be thought as such; consciousness of this double dis-identification would necessarily entail a more systemic understanding than the ad hoc ideological jumble through which Lewis balanced his fluid class allegiances. And in fact class relations throughout Lewis's writings are mystified in a variety of ways, of which the "racial red-herring" is only one. It is this refusal of the category of class, more than anything else, that dooms Lewis's otherwise sophisticated analyses of liberalism to degenerate into conspiracy theory. Despite having nothing but contempt for the petty bourgeoisie—for the supposed imbecility of salaried "puppets" and the anachronistic individualism of the shop-owning "small man" (see *The Art of Being Ruled* 107–9)—Lewis, permanently occupying the same precarious social space as the "small man," shares with him an ideology.

Indeed, Lewis's indictment of the "small man" in *The Art of Being Ruled*—a figure clamoring for a freedom that is "*his* freedom, not ours," anxious to "bite at and checkmate" the bourgeoisie while "protected . . . by that 'civilization' against which he struggles" (108)—reflects rather tellingly back on Lewis himself. Lewis's extreme "elitism"[16]—his desire to replace social class with the "differentiation of mankind into two rigorously separated worlds . . . obtained by an examination system" (*The Art of Being Ruled* 138, 140)—his "statolatry"—his endorsement of "the most powerful and stable authority that can be devised" (370)—and his "status quo anti-capitalism"—his great critiques of bourgeois liberalism combined with vicious defenses of existing privilege—conform all too closely to Nicos Poulantzas's triad characterizing the ideology of the "petty bourgeoisie in revolt"—that is, proto-fascism.[17] These characteristics are not so much the effects of a specific place in the relations of production (salaried employee, shopkeeper, artisan, unsupported artist) as the political effects of an ambiguous relationship to both the proletariat and the bourgeoisie: an abundance of cultural capital in relation to actual capital, a dependence on the state as a bulwark against social upheaval, and an antagonistic relationship to both the bourgeoisie and the proletariat that nonetheless sometimes requires strategic cooperation with one or another against its opponent. Lewis's personal ideology—which will play out in its most interesting form in *The Childermass*—creates the class of the "individual" in opposition to the economic classes of bourgeoisie and proletariat. This is only apparently a category mistake, since "individual" is in fact a name for the intellectual sector of the petty bourgeoisie:

> The "Poor" are detestable animals! They are only picturesque and amusing for the sentimentalist or the romantic! The "Rich" are bores without a single exception, *en tant que riches!*
>
> We want those simple and great people found everywhere.
>
> Blast represents an art of Individuals. (*Blast I* 8)

The point here is not to reduce Lewis's thought to the mere expression of class position. As Sartre once said of Paul Valéry, there can be no doubt that Wyndham Lewis was a petty-bourgeois intellectual—but not every petty-bourgeois intellectual is Wyndham Lewis. When we come to Lewis's fiction and painting (generally more considered productions than his often hastily produced works of opinion) we come up against a whole new complex of problems—primarily having to do with the distanciation and objectification of content involved in the subsumption into narrative and the resultant reflexive moment in Lewis's satire, but also with the peculiar doubling inherent to the critique of *ressentiment*, which, as the famous irony goes, is always its own best example.[18] Nonetheless, the peculiarly circumscribed aspect of Lewis's class situation is an essential element of his fiction, and we must still be concerned with the final and determining element of

Lewis's harmony with the ideology of the "petty bourgeoisie in revolt"—what Poulantzas calls by the paradoxical phrase "status quo anti-capitalism," an anti-capitalist stance coupled with an absolute refusal to consider political alternatives. Whether class is mystified as the privilege of the "White Man," the intellectual, or the member of the "class of individuals" (*The Art of Being Ruled* 354) that will become so important in *The Childermass*, the refusal of social class as an analytical category, its strategic reflection in one or another fun-house mirror, produces a bizarre effect: what is elsewhere in Lewis the criticism of a function of Capital— the creation of "so-called democratic masses, hypnotized into a sort of hysterical imbecility by the mesmeric methods of Advertisement" (*Time and Western Man* 26)—is, strangely but almost inevitably, folded back into an indictment of an imagined communism. In "The Children of Peter Pan" (*The Art of Being Ruled* 184–86), for example, structural infantilization is one of the pseudo-democratic functions of commercial writing (180–83) and, as in the quote above, advertising: it also plays into the ubiquitous conspiracy narrative linking big business, million-aires, and an arms industry only too happy to have reserves of complaisant human "cannon fodder." This infantilization is, in other words, precisely a function of capitalism, and its critique does not appear fundamentally out of line from clearly Left critiques of the culture industry. But in *Hitler* this same rhetoric of the "Peter Pan machine" is, by way of the substitution of race for class, referred back, without comment or explanation, to a spectral communism:

> The Class-doctrine—as opposed to the Race-doctrine—demands a *clean slate*. Every-thing must be wiped off slick. A sort of colourless, featureless automaton—*temporally* two-dimensional—is what is required by the really fanatical Marxist autocrat. Nothing but a mind *without backgrounds*, without any spiritual depth, a flat mirror for propa-ganda, a parrot-soul to give back the catchwords, an ego without *reflection*, in a word, a sort of *Peter Pan Machine*—the adult Child—will be tolerated. (*Hitler* 84)

This antirevolutionary structure, where an imagined communism mysteriously becomes the very distillation of capitalist dystopia, is fundamental to *The Childermass*, and we will return to it shortly. But in this and other works we find also a real commitment to a utopian aesthetic practice. As Lewis said of his paint-erly output:

> It was, after all, a new civilisation that I . . . was making blueprints for. . . . A rough design for a way of seeing for men who as yet were not there. . . . It was more than just picture making: one was making fresh eyes for people, and fresh souls to go with the eyes. (*Rude Assignment* 125)

The old argument that a purely spiritual revolution ("fresh souls") is none other than a reactionary evasion of political revolution is inadequate to explain this contradiction. Lewis's excitement over the machine, his conviction (in "Revolu-tion Rooted in the Technique of Industry" [*The Art of Being Ruled* 9–13] and elsewhere) that changes at the level of production condition the possibility of political transformation, his ambivalent fascination with new collective forms brought into being with mass production, and his confidence that "human na-

ture" right down to the sensory apparatus is radically mutable along with the
social forms in which it finds itself are all evidence that Lewis's thinking of "revolution" is of a totally different nature than the spiritual or conservative "revolutions" to which we are presently accustomed.

We come, then, to a central paradox: in the most ambitious literary work of a
figure universally (and correctly) perceived as reactionary, the literal content is,
again and again, revolution. *The Childermass*, published in 1928, is the first and
most significant book of *The Human Age*,[19] a grand political allegory, originally
conceived as a trilogy, that takes place in a series of afterworlds. The two final
books of *The Human Age*, *Monstre Gai* and *Malign Fiesta*, did not appear until
1955, by which time Lewis's narrative approach had changed considerably from
the first volume. Despite this temporal and aesthetic gap, each of these books
ends in precisely the same way, at the brink of social upheaval in the celestial
sphere. What is remarkable is that in each of these books the social contradictions
that *The Human Age* aims to reconcile on an allegorical plane are never papered
over by narrative sleight of hand; instead, they continue to rub up against one
another until they ignite. But the revolution is never witnessed: at the very moment of upheaval our eye on the action is always spirited away to the next world—
which is never quite the Next World. Instead, we are presented with a potentially
endless series—cut short only by Lewis's death—of u-topias, nowheres, that turn
out to be nowhere else than right here. It is as though, having projected the
contradictions of social life into the afterlife, Lewis was unable to resolve these
contradictions by "honest" narrative means—even when the deus ex machina of
religion itself was abundantly tempting and available—and was continually forced
to defer their resolution. *The Human Age* was to have extended only to three
volumes, but at his death Lewis was contemplating a fourth (*The Trial of Man*)
that would finally have taken place in Heaven itself. But we have no reason to
expect that this utopia would have been any different than the first three: that,
no matter what Lewis might have planned for the fourth volume, it, too, on the
very site of Satan's original rebellion, would have reproduced anything other than
a repetition of these earlier upheavals.

The politics of *The Childermass* present themselves as the politics of the
afterworld. In the middle of a discussion of his political "pattern of thinking"
in *Rude Assignment*, Lewis abruptly brings up *The Childermass* in a gesture that
appears to dismiss it: "A novel—if you can call it that—'*The Childermass*', has
no place in this survey. It is about Heaven: the politics of which, although bitter
in the extreme, have no relation to those of earth, so they do not concern us
here" (199). Considering that the politics of Heaven mirror with some precision
the politics of Earth (at least, as expounded by Lewis in *Time and Western Man*),
these words might seem simply disingenuous. But this dismissal is really no
dismissal at all, but an uncharacteristically sly appraisal of a work about which,
he points out pseudo-offhandedly, "it has often been asserted that this is my
best book" (*Rude Assignment* 199). Lewis continues with an irony that is, for
him, unusually subtle:

Its appearance in 1928 caused no controversy: there were no assailants with whom I have to settle accounts. No one said they were "in it"—nobody claimed to be the Bailiff or Hyperides—there were no claimants to be the original of Satters or of Pulley. It was not put on the Index, as several of my books have been. It can be sold in the Dublin bookshops. Its history has been the most peaceful of any of my books. And blessed is the book without a history. (199)

The phrase "blessed is the book without a history" springs bitterly from the pen of a writer who constantly railed against the conspicuous silence with which his works were sometimes met. As the passage above makes clear, many of his novels did indeed meet with controversy, but primarily for satirical descriptions in which his contemporaries recognized themselves. Like Joyce deriding his printer for refusing to set a few "bloody"s while failing to notice the odd pederast or syphilitic priest, Lewis's point is that this apparently inoffensive book, with no "bloody"s to assail in the form of hidden autobiographical content, in fact deserves to be the most read and most controversial of Lewis's books. Far from being about "Heaven" (a false description that sourly assumes that nobody has read the book: *The Childermass* and *Monstre Gai* take place in two regions without counterpart in conventional theology while *Malign Fiesta* takes place in Hell), *The Human Age* is clearly an allegory of earthly politics: as the Bailiff puts it, "it shall be in heaven as it is on earth" (*Childermass* 287). *The Childermass* stages a confrontation between proto-fascism and the conspiratorial alliance between gangster capitalism and the zeitgeist familiar to us from Lewis's works of opinion; *Monstre Gai* temporarily complicates matters by including the forces of religion and communism, but these terms fall out again in the final confrontation; by *Malign Fiesta*, fascism as well has disappeared, and gangster capitalism is embodied in Satan himself, setting the stage for a final resolution in which he is defeated by God—a defeat that never appears and possibly would not have even had Lewis lived to complete the fourth volume of *The Human Age*.

The adjectivally dense and relentlessly paratactic pages of *The Childermass*, breathlessly unbroken by chapter breaks, initially seem to concern two school friends, Pullman (Pulley) and Satterthwaite (Satters), who have been reunited in a desert limbo inhabited by indigenous "peons" and presided over by the mysterious Bailiff, where the dead await passage into some other region, which may or may not be Heaven. The first half of the narrative bears a family resemblance to Lewis's *Enemy of the Stars* (*Blast I* 51–85) as the two characters wander in a strange landscape, engaging each other in a static series of futile confrontations, rapprochements, and misunderstandings that anticipate the mutual orbiting of Beckett's sparring couples. Surprisingly, however, this relationship, not to appear centrally again until the publication of the second installment of *The Human Age* twenty-seven years later, is unexpectedly reabsorbed into the narrative of the Bailiff and his court. After the Bailiff and his entourage arrive for the day's disputations, the two characters stand aside in favor of what will henceforth be the main action, concerning the makeshift bureaucracy of the Bailiff's court: first, his interactions with and judgments of various British stock characters; later, his confrontation with the proto-fascist Hyperides and his entourage.

The transition between the two sections hinges on a single paragraph that occurs about a third of the way through the book:

> Two characters who have occupied the opening scene, they [Pullman and Satters] conventionally stand aside to observe the entrance of the massed cast in stately procession, Pulman's [sic] manner suggests; withdrawing discreetly a little into the mist, and peering at the massive business of the show as it unfolds itself at the centre of the stage. . . . in attitudes of stylized attention, making the coming of the new event with whispered asides, they stand for the time being aloof puppets. (128)

This passage is characteristic in its employment of what might be called the "embodied cliché," a figure possibly unique to Lewis that characterizes the texture of the entire work. It has been observed before, notably by Jameson, that Lewis's descriptive language is built from the cultural detritus of reified language, but there is a specificity to the cliché in Lewis that can be added to the insights of earlier accounts.[20] While cliché normally refers immediately to language, in *The Childermass* the cliché belongs most immediately to the action: the action is not merely described in stereotyped terms but instead actually performs the cliché. In other words the cliché does not belong, even ironically, to the narrative voice or to some subjective perception of the material; it belongs objectively to the material itself.

In the case of the passage above the stereotyped gesture seems to be performed with a degree of self-consciousness on the part of its actor, as Pullman's "manner suggests" a certain narrative structure that is also, in fact, the structure of the novel, suggesting that (as in *Enemy of the Stars*) the setting of *The Childermass* is in fact a kind of theater and the characters were actually actors playing characters with quasi-Brechtian irony, "conventionally" standing aside, and adopting attitudes of "stylized attention." But in general this Brechtian reading of the ubiquitous embodied cliché does not hold; the irony belongs to the characters as little as the cliché belongs to the narration. The most efficient way of approaching the meaning of this pervasive formal structure is through a very different piece, a strange manifesto of satiric method written as Lewis was working on *The Childermass*. Hugh Kenner was right when he said that "all Lewis's successes" have the air of being accidental:[21] not in the way a team of monkeys or mediocre writers, given time enough, might occasionally tap out something interesting, but as though, like an extraordinarily complex and still experimental machine, it was only sometimes that all of the energies of Lewis's prose were tuned to proper synergy, all mechanical shimmies and grindings adjusted out of existence, the engineer and audience holding their breath lest some unexpected disturbance send the apparatus into self-destructive disarray. "Inferior Religions," an explanatory essay in the form of a prose poem, is one such moment of perfection.[22]

The pretext for "Inferior Religions" is the explication of the method behind the story collection *The Wild Body*, for which "a few of the axioms . . . are here laid down" (233). But most of these stories had been written nearly twenty years earlier, and "Inferior Religions," which was composed while Lewis was working on *The Childermass* in 1927, makes much more sense as a rumination on the method behind this later work.[23] Initially, "Inferior Religions" appears to develop a straightforwardly cynical and elitist theory of existence quite congruous with that of Lewis's works of opinion:

> The wheel at Carisbrooke imposes a set of movements upon the donkey inside it, in drawing water from the well, that it is easy to grasp. But in the case of a hotel or fishing boat, for instance, the complexity of the rhythmic scheme is so great that it passes as open and untrammeled life. This subtler and wider mechanism merges, for the spectator, in the general variety of nature. Yet we have in most lives the spectacle of a pattern as circumscribed and complete as a theorem of Euclid. So these are essays in a new human mathematic. (233)

The apparent elitism of this passage will be familiar to readers of Lewis: "most lives" are little more than ciphers moving in "fascinating imbecility" (232) different only in complexity from that of the pump-driving donkey, only to be resolved into their geometric regularity by the painterly eye of the Lewisian intellectual or "spectator." (The more general form of this problem is hardly unique to Lewis. As Adorno's *Aesthetic Theory* makes clear—but Schiller's criticism already attests to it—the aesthetic prerogative, even when genuinely critical, is always a function of the division of labor.) But the logic of "Inferior Religions," especially what will emerge as the central term of laughter, falsifies this simple reading and sits uneasily with Lewis's usual ideology of the solitary, intellectual "Nature" as opposed to the community of unthinking "puppets."[24]

To begin with, we must consider that Lewis's actual descriptions of the collective social forms hinted at by the hotel or fishing boat suggest a quite different attitude than his nonfiction condemnations of the "puppet" life organized around mechanical production. Indeed, the veneer of condescension belies a real fascination with new forms of collective work. His claim in *The Caliph's Design*—to have elevated and accented in his architectural plans the "hideous foolishness of our buildings, our statues, our interiors"[25] solely to hold them up for ridicule—is of a similar nature to this surface condescension: the secret of this "appetising and delicious idiocy" is that its fascination betrays an investment much deeper than a lust for satire. Nor, in "Inferior Religions," are the more archaic forms of collective labor those that fascinate. The plan of "Inferior Religions" is to expose the logic of a "new human mathematic" (233): the examples of the hotel or the fishing boat, drawn from planned or executed stories in *The Wild Body*, do not adequately reflect the novelty of this fascination, which is more accurately expressed in the mechanical metaphor of humans as "intricately moving bobbins" (233). Indeed, in "Revolution Rooted in the Technique of Industry" (*The Art of Being Ruled* 4–13) it was the new ubiquity of the machine—whose attraction for Lewis the painter is a central fact—that was responsible for the "subtler and wider mechanism" of society itself.

Nonetheless, we would seem to be in familiar territory, where it is the privilege of the solitary intellect to discern these semi-automatic forms. It is as though the methodological skepticism of Descartes had devolved in Lewis into a real solipsism; what is seen from the famous window really is just a collection of hats and coats covering automata.[26] Inasmuch as this *cogito* can be socialized at all it grants full being only to those whose profession it is to think: who thinks, is. Indeed, the "dichotomy of mind and body" on which the "theory of laughter . . . is based" ("Inferior Religions" 243) seems nowhere to be more in harmony with the division of humanity into "puppets" and "Natures"—as always, deflecting class as such into one category and reserving the other for a class fraction to which Lewis belongs—than in the opening paragraphs of "Inferior Religions," where the mechanical scuffling of fishermen exists so that its underlying geometry may be exposed by the observing intellect. But in fact the appearance of laughter disrupts this scheme, to the point that "intellect" virtually disappears.

Section 4 of "Inferior Religions" is a list of the "attributes of Laughter," from which the following are excerpted:

> 1. Laughter is the Wild Body's song of triumph.
> 2. Laughter is the climax in the tragedy of seeing, hearing, and smelling self-consciously.
> 3. Laughter is the bark of delight of a gregarious animal at the proximity of its kind.
> 4. Laughter is an independent, tremendously important, and lurid emotion.
> 9. Laughter is the sudden handshake of mystic violence and the anarchist.
> 10. Laughter is the mind sneezing.
> 12. Laughter does not progress. It is primitive, hard, and unchangeable. (236–37)

Although "Satire" is supposed to be the "great Heaven of Ideas," it turns out to be something else altogether; it is more importantly the home of the "titans of red laughter" (235). It is not the intellect, but laughter, a function of the immutable, archaic, organic substratum of human experience, that "break[s] up the rhythm of our naïveté" (234). Laughter is a reflex, like a sneeze or orgasm of insight that leaves its trace in language. Laughter is the song of triumph of the "Wild Body," that "small, primitive, literally antediluvian vessel in which we set out on our adventures" (237):

> Laughter is the brain-body's snort of exultation. It expresses its wild sensation of power and speed; it is all that remains physical in the flash of thought, its friction: or it may be defiance flung at the hurrying fates.
>
> The Wild Body is this supreme survival that is us, the stark apparatus with its set of mysterious spasms; the most profound of which is laughter. (237–38)

Let us take a moment to appreciate the reversal here. After all the privilege accorded the intellect in the mapping of the Cartesian fissure onto the social division of labor, laughter turns out to be the triumph of the body. The "Wild Body" after which the book is named is the body in its prehistoric, unsocialized aspect, the "supreme survival," the "stark apparatus with its set of mysterious spasms." As we shall see, this does not mean that objects of laughter's object are not historical or that laughter is not a social phenomenon; but laughter itself is material, bodily, and prior to the social form in which it erupts: "laughter does not progress." The theory of Satire is here, in its quasi-poetic form—no matter how thoroughly, in its expository form, it confines Satire to the privileged "intelligence" of the artist (see *Men Without Art* 115–28)—surprisingly materialist. It should come as no surprise, then, that the term "mind" here becomes the "brain-body," and laughter "all that remains physical" of thought. But this "Wild Body," though unsocialized in the sense that it preexists and has the potential to disrupt any particular social "rhythm," is archaically social: "the bark of delight of a gregarious animal at the proximity of its kind."

Laughter is then a matter of relation and not the privilege of any particular perspective—of the intellectual or even the intellect as such: "It is easy for us to see, if we are french, that the German is 'absurd,' or if german, that the French is 'ludicrous' " ("Inferior Religions" 244). The logic of laughter moves out from the relatively small scale choreography of the fishing boat to the norms of national culture (and a reading of *Tarr* will satisfy one's sense that national culture is far from simply a matter of manners or diet).[27] Laughter, far from being the condescending sneer of the intellect at the behavior of the unfortunate puppets, becomes the dizzy recognition of the real precariousness and absurdity—despite the apparent solidity and necessity—of any particular "dance." And the deepest laughter is reserved for the observation that one's own social forms and indeed one's own place in this dance are arbitrary, historical, held in place by flimsy ritual and yet treated by everyone with (and indeed, solidified and made real by) the "devoutness" (234) with which one would respect a god: hence "Inferior Religions." It is in this sense that laughter is the "handshake of mystic violence and the anarchist": "it occasionally takes on the dangerous form of absolute revelation" (245). It is no accident that in *The Revenge for Love*, the least technically adventurous of Lewis's major works, and one in which the world as it is weighs down with unbreachable oppressiveness, red laughter is everywhere replaced by ubiquitous, clattering "cachinnation."[28] Laughter marks the crystallization of the entire social world into something "futile, grotesque, and sometimes pretty" (329) but no more solid than a dance.

This, then, through a roundabout route, is the meaning of the embodied cliché, a form of the modernist sublime that—rather than producing an obscure meaning from the humble detail or turning from that meaning in horror when its content manifests itself—suddenly, by framing a fragment of conventional behavior, defamiliarizes the social totality itself, not only in its aspect of custom and habit but also the entire system of relations that produces it. Cliché in *The Childermass* is not, as in classic moderism, something to be abhorred in favor of *le mot juste*; nor is it, like cliché throughout *Ulysses* but particularly in "Eumaeus," refined to the point where each cliché is paradoxically the perfect specimen of degraded language. Instead, the cliché is only the verbal equivalent of the automatic dance of the fishing boat or hotel: the appearance in language of the stereotyped behavior through which it attains its meaning. The "attitudes of stylized attention" assumed by Satters and Pulley as the Bailiff arrives are nothing ironic in themselves but "conventional" adjustments to a new social ensemble dominated by the baroque theatricality of the Bailiff's court, as here when the fashionable members of the court react to a pseudo-profundity of the Bailiff's:

> The correct façade of the Bailiff's front-row supporters flashes with flattering exchanges of looks of wonder and sympathetic interest in "*Fancy-that!*" poses of strained politeness. (168)

The " '*Fancy that!*' pose" is the essential embodied cliché. The cliché does not belong to the narration: the front-row supporters really are sporting stylized and conventional poses. But the irony of the text is external to the characters. It derives from reference outward to similar performances the reader will have seen elsewhere, which are in turn made absurd by their ironized appearance in the text.

The apparently hallucinatory transformations of *The Childermass*—Satters into the "war-time officer of the Mons Star and mess-kit, in blues" (49), into a "big burning Gretchen" (81), into "Bill-Sikes-Satters" (114); Pullman into the perpetual "Miss Pullman," or "Nurse Pulley," "model Abigail" (27), and so on, but also "Buddha" and "Professor"—are condensed epithetic forms of the embodied cliché, which registers conventional attitudes and actions as fragments that call up the social totality that determines them. The distance between these pseudo-phantasmagoria (which are in fact purposely banal) and the transformations of Joyce's "Circe," which they superficially resemble, is very great:

> BLOOM
> (*A charming soubrette with dauby cheeks, mustard hair and large male hands and nose, leering mouth.*) (536)

Here, the conventional image into which Bloom is quasi-transformed—the "charming soubrette" borrowed from a poster of Marie Kendall that appears in "Wandering Rocks"—is projected into the text from Bloom's private and hyper-idiosyncratic psychology. In *The Childermass*, a similar transformation (here, of Satters as he and Pullman lose their way) operates differently:

> . . . "I can't make out where we went wrong."
> The girl-who-made-the-wrong-turning laughs softly to herself. (45)

The "girl-who-made-the-wrong-turning" is not a hallucinatory projection but refers outside the text to an image that is both the type by which the reader recognizes it and the prototype of Satters's tittering: not that Satters is imitating some Platonic form of the "girl-who-made-the-wrong-turning," but that both the imagined girl of the cliché and Satters are following, like the donkey at Carisbrooke, the same well-worn cultural pathway.

As we saw earlier with the arrival of the Bailiff, however, it is the social ensemble that decisively determines the form of the embodied cliché. When the ensemble is reduced to two, as in the sections that center on Satters and Pulley, the periodic transformation of Pullman into "Nurse Pulley" and so on only has meaning with relation to the transformation of Satters into "The Child": "Big dreamy-eyes and business-like little Miss Pullman, the new governess, out for a pococuranting

stone-kicking promenade, rapt in childhood's dreams away from horrid crowds"
(46). It is not simply that Pullman metaphorically becomes Nurse in relation to
Satters, or that the necessity of solicitude calls up a particular aggregate of nurse-
like behaviors; there is no essential Pullman on whom Nurse Pullman is a mask.
Pullman really is Nurse Pulley and has no existence outside the social ensemble
of Nurse Pulley and Baby Satters. When he attempts to abandon Satters he finds
that he is unable to; not out of any sense of guilt but because he is "not himself"
without Satters. "[I]n his personal economy a vivid loss is registered" (117):

> Pullman is beside himself with the ill-defined sense of loss. What is this missing object
> really? he gropes through all his senses very fussed; continually his mind returns to the
> large staring uncouth bulk of his friend even Satters: that is not what is missing surely?
> Indeed it must be though, since it is always back to that fearsome object that his mind
> is led. (117)

As we shall see in a moment, Pullman has had other such experiences. In fact,
"Pullman" is the sum of the social roles he plays, a "bobbin" in a set of "group
mechanism[s]" (*Childermass* 24)—which term is associated explicitly only with
the peons, apparently the laborers and lumpens of this afterworld. We are seldom
required to take the Bailiff at his word, but here his pronouncements jibe with
Pullman's experience with Satters:

> Those who can combine should do so—that is the rule: it saves time. Also such combi-
> nations ensure the maximum effect of reality—I have known cases of a man being
> completely restored to his true and essential identity after meeting an old friend it's
> most valuable it's the tip we always give the new-comer, dig out the old pal there's
> nothing like it. (137)

"True and essential identity" is of course ironic, since "identity" or subjectivity
has no truth or essence outside the rule of "combination." But the necessity of
the social ensemble to identity is not only a simple matter of relations between
human beings; it also involves the objects that surround them. The modernist
thing puts in a modest appearance as a more mute and material form of the
embodied cliché. Even when the social ensemble apparently consists of only two
people, the entire social world intervenes in the reified form of its material products: the props and physical accoutrements of one's role in the "elaborate civilized
ritual" ("Inferior Religions" 234) of the social world are essential to one's "identity." Pullman's experience with his walking stick suggests as much:

> "Once I left this stick at my kip when I went out. I might as well have left my head! I
> soon went back for it I promise you! That's the way it is. . . . This piece of cloth"—he
> takes up a pinch of his coat sleeve—"is as much me as this flesh. It's a superstition to
> think the me ends here. . . . Even you are a part." (120)

At one point, against Pullman's advice, Satters decides to take off his clothes.
His personality immediately begins to disintegrate: "Satters hears the well-known
Satters-voice, disjoined from him as were the limbs of . . . Professor [Tyndall,
standing before his audience, body in pieces], from just near him, addressing

Pulley" (112). The Satters-Pulley diad turns out to be more complex than it originally had seemed, as the pas de deux is itself determined by a larger choreography
and is thrown into disarray when Satters's clothes, reference points to that choreography, are discarded: "Satters' voice has become so coarse that it has turned
out to be a sort of navvy the young gentleman is up against. . . . The time- and
class-scales in which they hang in reciprocal action are oscillating wildly" (114).
Satters temporarily becomes "navvy" to Pullman's "gentleman" rather than
"baby" to Pullman's "nurse"; but this relationship is nothing privileged, just a
moment in the wild oscillation of reciprocal positions of age and class, no longer
held in check by cultural props.

The point here is not necessarily that there is anything radically new or surprising about the model of individual and social life operative in *The Childermass* but
that it absolutely contradicts the thematic substance of the book, which is Lewis's
ideology of personality. The embodied cliché drastically demystifies the personal
"identity" fetishized in Lewis's expository works—the privilege of the "spectator"
we saw above becomes, for example, an ideology of the intellectual in *The Art of
Being Ruled*—and central among the official contents of *The Childermass*. Here
it is as ephemeral as memory: the embodied memory of one's rote and habitual
relationship to the social world via others and via objects. There is a contradiction
between the formal plane, where the embodied cliché points to the ephemerality
of identity and the historicity of the social world that produces it, and the narrative plane, where strong or "distinct" identity is the essential positive term. (A
measure of this contradiction is the transformation of the Pullman character
throughout *The Human Age*: it is only in *Monstre Gai*, where the narrative becomes more conventional, that the figure of Pullman is able to fulfill the role of
intellectual superman carved out for him, but never occupied, in *The
Childermass*.)

One would have said that the thematic center of *The Childermass* is precisely
the elevation of the principle of the individual intellect or "strong personality"
over the massed "babies" of the Bailiff's court and, more particularly, over the
wraithlike "peons" that do the manual labor in Limbo. Very early in the novel
Pulley and Satters come across these sinister shades, whose existence Pullman
explains to Satters: " 'they are the masses of personalities whom god, having created them, is unable to destroy, but who are not distinct enough to remain more
than what you see' " (28). This theory is endorsed by the narration, which ranks
the peons by the "strength" of their "personality":

> One figure is fainter than any of the rest. . . . He comes and goes; sometimes he is there,
> then he flickers out. . . . He is a tall man of no occupation, in the foreground. He falls
> like a yellow smear upon one much firmer than himself behind, or invades him like a
> rusty putrefaction, but never blots out the stronger person. (22)

Lewis's famous "external approach" (see *Men Without Art* 126–28), formulated
in contradistinction to Joycean subjectivism, forestalls the possibility of inter-
preting this description as projected by Pulley's or Satters's interpretation of the
peons: here the language sorting human types by the strength of their personali-

ties—which is already plainly linked ("of no occupation") to particular positions in the social order—is clearly that of the pure "eye" of the Lewisian spectator.

Pulley's understanding of the peons, fundamentally in line with that of the narration, reappears a few pages later, in nearly the same words as he had used before: " 'No, they are the multitudes of personalities which God, having created, is unable to destroy' " (33). And again, virtually by rote: " 'It is the multitude of personalities which God has created, ever since the beginning of time, and is unable now to destroy' " (37). The logic of the embodied cliché, which had secretly eroded the central category of "personality," here erupts to the surface as the cliché returns to language: Pullman, in dully alluding to what is no less than the thematic center of the text, reveals its status as ideology, a conceptual apparatus that owes its form to a social exigency prior to the *cogito*. Thought itself, Pullman's supposed insight into the nature of the peons, is nothing more than another element in a complex "group mechanism" (24), an unconscious obeisance to something prior to itself like the donkey's path at the wheel at Carisbrooke—or like class interest. The difference in distinctness or individuality between the "peon" and the intellectual is then reduced to nothing:

> Pullman looks up. Satters gazes into a sallow vacant mask, on which lines of sour malice are disappearing, til it is blank and elementary, in fact the face of a clay doll.
> "Why, you are a peon!" Satters cries pointedly, clapping his hands. (37)

This possibility is, however, quickly recontained, so that Pullman's initial statement remains plausible and the later restatements appear to emerge out of some kind of trance:

> Pullman recovers at his cry, and his face, with muscular initiative, shrinks as though in the grip of a colossal sneeze. . . : it unclenches, and the normal Pullman-mask emerges. (37)

The "sneeze" here should remind us of the laugh in "Inferior Religions" ("the mind sneezing"), the bodily reflex that erupts into habitual patterns of behavior. But Pullman's initial statement of the origin of the peons (a theory endorsed by the narrative "eye") cannot escape so easily the fate of its later repetitions, which must inevitably reflect back and cast doubt on their original. When the embodied cliché returns to language and thought—which then become merely forms of practice among others, nothing other than a particular movement of the "bobbin" within the "group mechanism"—the privilege of the thinking subject is yet further eroded: the intellectual or artist, the vaunted "Nature" or individual, becomes little more than a bobbin that performs the clichés determined for it by its place in the social totality. The momentary identity of Pullman's rote speech and the ideology of the text would seem to call into question the official ideological content—the privilege of the strong personality—of the text itself.[29]

Pullman and Satters are dead; perhaps this is no allegory of earthly social life at all but simply the way existence works in Limbo or wherever this is. Or perhaps it is some magic trick pulled by the Bailiff to make his work easier by combining real human intellects into "mindless" combinations. Perhaps this Limbo, rather

than presenting a straightforward allegory of life on Earth as we know it, is supposed to represent what life would be like if the mainstream modernist zeitgeist
embodied in the Bailiff were given free reign. This, indeed, is Satters's point of
view. Pulley has this to say in response:

> "But why magic? Use your intelligence. Did you say *magic—magic*, all the time, in life?
> You never thought of it then yet you should have said *magic* then just as much shouldn't
> you or don't you see that? You think it far-fetched. Wasn't life just as much *magic*?"
> (119)

The apparent solidity of subjectivity and the social world that forms it may be
"just as much magic" as its heavenly equivalent.[30]

Even as the logic of the embodied cliché potentially explodes the ideology of
the strong individual, this possibility is itself ideologically recontained. The title
of *The Childermass* is often taken to refer to the slaughter of the innocents (Mat-
thew 2:16) that was World War I.[31] There is no question that the war is both
important thematically and provides the landscape in which *The Childermass* is
set—Lewis's great 1919 canvas *A Battery Shelled* could be a backdrop for the
action of the first half of the book. But if *The Childermass* is taken to be about
the war in any immediate way it is understood too narrowly. As the novel begins,
in fact, the flow of dead has dried to a trickle:

> With the gait of Cartophilus some homing solitary shadow is continually arriving in
> the restless dust of the turnpike, challenged at the tollgate thrown across it at the first
> milestone from the waterfront. Like black drops falling into a cistern these slow but
> incessant forms feed the camp to overflowing. (10)

Despite the camp being fed to "overflowing," this is not the language of mass
death: "There used to be many more people in the camp than at present" (102).
As his postwar paintings show, if Wyndham Lewis was capable of anything, he
was capable of translating into images the horror of twentieth-century war (one
thinks of the bleak and crowded ink drawings from the 1918 *Guns* exhibition).[32]
In this anti-Inferno the solitary dead cross a parched Mesopotamian landscape;
this is a far cry from the "I had not thought death had undone so many" of Eliot's
more viscerally postwar evocation of mass death. We also know that Pullman was
not killed in the war but "got out just after the Mons show" (109). Undoubtedly
World War I haunts the memory of the text and its characters, as a political
allegory of its time could hardly but have done, and, in a secondary way, the war
is signified by the title. But the "children" referred to in the title are only massa-
cred in a secondary sense; the novel more fundamentally concerns the manufacture of the innocents, who then become the familiar "cannon fodder" for whatever power sees fit to use them. Far from naming something over-and-done-
with back on earth, this "slaughter of the innocents" is what we are witnessing
in the text.

The meaning of the "childermass" is best communicated by quoting a remarkable sentence that relays the experience, without parallel in canonical modernism,
of swinging from word to word across the Lewisian long sentence on the slender
thread of a dimly perceived meaning:

> He [the Bailiff] gives a few intense premonitory coughs of after-dinner-speech mettle: nagging voices at the rear still seek to have at all cost the last word in close theological disputes but the frivolous foreground has put away childish things and disposes itself in a hundred attitudes of more than respectful attention (for the Seeing Eye counting its chickens before they are hatched, a catalogue of all sizes and shapes of kindergarten-lips in which butter-will-not-melt and of eyes that are the peep-of-day—some that do so languish and drip with milky-mouthed naïveness that there is sure no mother's super-Vesuvian bowels burning to litter millions of midgets or billions of bitchlettes on one Ford-pattern, to be driven bleating to the bloody battlefield of the apocolypse, that would not welter and yearn and then burst with 1000° centigrade love all over the shop—it is now a massed babydom, scheduled fused and set to touch off at a feather-trigger contact all the maternal machinery concentrated in the most millennial of communist metropolises, to work double-tides and unending overtime). (208)

In place of the artful subordination of the Jamesian long sentence, we find a mass of independent clauses fused by colons, parentheses, and dashes, joined only to maintain the breathless energy of the prose by refusing it the right to rest on the falling note of a period. After the initial series of embodied clichés, the truly remarkable part of this sentence is the parenthetical description, which moves out from a portrayal of the Bailiff's infantilized audience (from the point of view of the Bailiff? the narrator?) in terms of more embodied clichés—"kindergarten-lips in which butter-will-not-melt"—through a grotesque maternal image that transforms into a nightmare of mass production as the maternal itself becomes something more sinister, through the language of the slaughterhouse and the memory of world war, culminating in a nightmare image of the communist state miraculously coupled with an evocation of capitalist dystopia.

This sentence not only epitomizes the put-on malice of Lewisian satire—the interlude beginning with the trochaic "some that do so languish and drip with milky-mouthed naïveness" virtually requires the lip to raise in a theatrical sneer—but also crystallizes the central meaning of the "childermass." Its logic is nothing we have not already seen in our earlier discussion of the Hitler book, where the properly anticapitalist critique of the consumer-worker-automaton, the "*Peter Pan Machine*—the adult Child" (*Hitler* 84), is strangely projected onto the designs of the "fanatical Marxist autocrat." Here the reproduction of human automata is explicitly referred to Fordism. The manufactured consent of this "massed baby-dom," made imbecilic by the culture industry and by mindless repetitive labor, is what makes possible the literal massacre of the innocents in modern warfare as they are "driven bleating to the bloody battlefield of the apocalypse." It is this process to which the embodied cliché, which submits even the "individual" to its logic, promises us access. But suddenly, as in *Hitler*, before the explosive utopian potential of Lewis's descriptive language can be brought to bear on what would seem to be our own capitalist-dystopic complex, the latter is magically folded over and attributed to "the most millennial of communist metropolises."

This is not the only link between *Hitler* and *The Childermass*: the imagined Limbo of the latter book owes more to the tactical racialism of Lewis's *Hitler* than it might be comfortable to admit. The social structure of *The Childermass* is arranged along two axes. The explicit axis, as we have already seen, is that of the distinct personalities versus the indistinct: it is only the distinct who are supposed to be admitted into Heaven. To be sure, this is the Bailiff's explanation of "the system" (138), delivered in several pages of delightful self-contradictory pseudo-philosophical cant, and it is surely bogus. The Bailiff finally ends up by distinguishing between mere bodily individuality and the necessary criterion of personal existence:

> "The sort of existence we are contemplating in Paradise over there can only mean *personal* existence, that I'm sure you will agree, since mere individual existence would not be worth troubling about, would it?"
>
> An enthusiastic roar of "No!" is released as he ceases. (148)

The Bailiff's criterion of distinct personal existence is plainly mere pandering to an audience that has been systematically deprived of all personality precisely through a myth of "personality." (The expository analog is "The Contemporary Man 'Expresses His Personality' " in *The Art of Being Ruled* [163–68].) Nonetheless, the positive term, once introduced, does not merely disappear; the production of "pseudo-infant-minions" (159) necessarily calls up the positive term of which it is the privative and which in *The Childermass*, the Bailiff, Pullman, and the proto-fascist Hyperides all vie to occupy.[33] The Bailiff, then, is "really" manufacturing nonentities, which presumes some other state of which the Bailiff's subjects are systematically deprived. The Bailiffite ideology *is* the ideology of the text, only reversed: no matter what the rule has been in the past, under the Bailiff's control it is the distinct who will be *refused* admission to the Magnetic City. The Bailiff's version of the doctrine of personality is then a "false" appropriation, within the text, of what is really the ideology of the text.

But beneath this ideology and its Bailiffite pseudo-appropriation, there is another, much more complex scheme in operation: that which distinguishes the "peons" from the rest of the dead. We have already seen that on Bailiffite theory (as parroted by Pullman), it is the distinct who are admitted into the Magnetic City while the indistinct become peons: " 'they are the masses of personalities whom God, having created them, is unable to destroy, but who are not distinct enough to remain more than what you see. Indistinct ideas don't you know' " (28). But if, as we saw above, it is precisely the indistinct who are admitted to the Third City and the distinct excluded, what then is the real explanation for the peons?

Although the logic of the "group mechanism" (24) pertains ultimately, as we saw above, to everything and everyone in *The Childermass*, it is only the peons whose being is explicitly determined by it. The apparently feudal mode of production—the peons carry farm implements rather than working in factories—should not distract from the peons' allegorical status as modern workers, as their instruments of labor unsubtly highlight: "there is the hammer and there is the sickle" (23). As this image suggests, it is not so much class per se as class conflict that they represent: despite being described as "immaterial" (23), "mere upright shadows" (22), they manage to spit very material sputum on Satters and are capable of a "menacing distinctness" (23)—distinctness being, of course, the very quality they were supposed to lack. But over this class aggression race aggression is deftly superimposed: the peons wear turbans (20), the sputum that covers Satters's cheek is stained with betel-juice (25), they speak only fragments of broken English (25), and their color is that of a "yellow smear" or a "rusty putrefaction" (20) as opposed to the pink faces (168) of the Bailiffites. What had appeared to be an evasion of modern relations of production turns out to be motivated after all, as the class terrain is plainly not that of Europe but of the colonies.[34] In relation to them Pullman becomes not the bourgeois or the intellectual but, in another embodied cliché, the white District Commissioner, the seasoned (but liberal) Old Coaster among "his" natives:

> "We must hold our ground," easily he remarks as he does so, without looking at Satters. "Don't show you're afraid of them whatever you do. . . . They're quite inoffensive." (23)
> Calm and masterful in the presence of inferior natures Pullman gives expression to his liberal beliefs.
> "They're too hard on them." (22)

Or again, in a situation that is all too familiar in the context to our own post–cold war indifference to civil conflict on the periphery, Pullman observes the "insect-conflict" of a battle between what are for him undifferentiated groups of peons: "the peons often fight: he sighs: it is no doubt one of their only recreations" (57).

It should be clear that this evasion of social class through the substitution of race, reproducing in advance the logic of *Hitler*, is also part of the logic of colonial racism. As Lenin saw quite clearly (with Engels before him and Fanon after), colonialism remaps the division of labor geographically and racially so that, in terms of the world economy, "the British proletariat becomes bourgeois," or at least it can be convinced that its interests lie more with the British bourgeoisie than with workers in dominated countries.[35] But the geographic and racial displacement of class conflict was nothing unknown to colonialism itself, as Cecil Rhodes made clear in his remarks to a journalist:

> I was in the East End of London yesterday, and attended a meeting of the unemployed. I listened to the wild speeches, which were just a cry for "bread," "bread," "bread," and on my way home I pondered over the scene and I became more than ever convinced of the importance of imperialism. . . . My cherished idea is a solution for the social problem, *i.e.*, in order to save the 40,000,000 inhabitants of the United Kingdom from a bloody civil war, we colonial statesmen must acquire new lands to settle the surplus population, to provide new markets for the goods produced by them in the factories and mines. The Empire, as I have always said, is a bread and butter question. If you want to avoid civil war, you must become imperialists.[36]

Like Lewis's tactical racialism, this passage is cynical enough not to require explication: no "civilizing mission" here.[37]

Some version of this strategy of displacement is the logical political outcome of Poulantzas's "status quo anti-capitalism." (*The Human Age* abundantly displays the rest of Poulantzas's proto-facist ideological triad as well: in the elitism of the negated but still operative ideology of the distinct individual, and the statolatry, throughout the trilogy, of the intellectual Pullman. However, as we have seen, the logic of the embodied cliché erodes the proto-fascist content of Pullman's character in particular by constantly forcing Pullman into the pose of the "intellectual," leaving Pullman [to borrow a chapter title from *Tarr*] "Doomed, Evidently" throughout the three volumes of *The Human Age* to make the worst possible political decisions, always supporting the "wrong" side, finally writing copy for Satan himself.) But as much as the problem of class—which is after all the central problem for Lewis even as it is a category to be feared—is displaced, it must always reappear in another form. (In the second volume, *Monstre Gai*, for example, social class is displaced rather mysteriously onto gender rather than race; women inhabit the urban slum or "Yenery" of the Third City.) Ultimately, it is Lewis's scrupulous refusal to resolve social contradictions by magical means—even by the traditional magic of narrative closure—that leads perpetually to revolutions against the various state forms of the afterlife. The only form that such imaginative resolution takes in *The Childermass* is displacement.

No more than Lewis's narrative displacement can the political displacement that is imperialism permanently defuse class conflict. It can only deflect it into expansionist projects, a process that cannot continue indefinitely before igniting into an apparently quite different kind of conflict, as two world wars made clear. *The Childermass*, whose narrative logic follows the logic of classical imperialism, cannot resolve the contradictions it sets out to resolve, which instead always return in another form. In this sense the perpetual return of revolution in the existing volumes of *The Human Age* forecasts not only another world war but the anticolonial revolutions of the 1960s that mark the "return of the repressed" of a class conflict that was shifted onto colonial domination. Does it need to be said that this conflict, twisted into a brutal and reactionary form by a rhetoric whose logic is the mirror image of Lewis's, returns today in the form of anti-American terror?

The equivocity of *The Childermass*, the opposition between the utopian possibilities embodied in its language and its reactionary content, is itself equivocal. The desire to represent totality—an impossible project that, as Fredric Jameson has pointed out in his discussion of the postmodern "war on totality," must nonetheless be kept faith with if there to be is any hope of seizing some degree of control over human destiny—is in itself the expression of a utopian longing.[38] *The Childermass* approaches the totality through the sublime object of the embodied cliché; the "red laughter" that greets it reveals the fragility and absurdity of social life as we know it. But it will be obvious that Lewis's mode of the modernist sublime, passed over rather quickly in this chapter, is subject to our usual critique. The revelation of the fragility of the social dance is attractive but empty as to content, which is then readily supplied by Lewis's own proto-fascist opinions. As long as the truth of social life—one of structural relations between classes in a global economic system—is not thought as such but only touched on in mystified form, the result is the very opposite of utopia. On the other hand, with Lewis it becomes possible to reverse our usual reversal. Lewis's mystified class consciousness only exists on the basis of his real class situation, which refuses to stop speaking its own truth—the same truth it tries to suppress—in a surprisingly unmediated way. Lewis's class paranoia is precisely reactionary: it only exists on the basis of a perceived threat from below, the prior class identification and "resentment" of the working classes—and of the colonies, to which we will return in the next chapter. The real content of *The Childermass* is not Lewis's self-identification with the "class of individuals" but the aggression of the peons that provokes it. The ideological content of Lewis's novels is, in a more concrete way than his utopian form, their utopian content as well.

CHAPTER SEVEN

Ngugi wa Thiong'o and Pepetela: Revolution and Retrenchment

If even the most explicitly reactionary art can contain within itself a utopian moment, then we cannot assume automatically that deliberately utopian literary works are, in their innermost tendencies, free from the logic of recontainment that we saw in Lewis's fiction. This agnostic attitude is virtually unavoidable with regard to postcolonial literature, when the recent history of the Third World threatens to eclipse with brutal irony the utopian significance of anticolonial culture. The equivocity of this moment for our own is one of the central problems of this book. It is also, of course, a problem for literature itself: how is the period of the African independence movements to be represented now? In the light of the general squalor and disappointment of the neocolonial situation, where nominal political independence masks a crippling economic dependence and a crushing subservience to the demands of First-World-dominated multinational capital, and when mainstream economists can paint a rosy picture of the world system only by finding excuses for leaving Africa out of the reckoning altogether, is there any way to conceive contemporary African history in a way that does not contribute to the very cynicism and disappointment that characterize much of contemporary African literature's representational raw material? Ngugi wa Thiong'o's work with the Kamiriithu theater group in Kenya and the fiction of the Angolan writer Pepetela were not, unlike the African works we have looked at so far, written at the moment of the great surge of African independence movements; rather, that moment, and the dilemma of its historical meaning, are the centers around which Ngugi's and Pepetela's work revolve. The plays staged by Ngugi wa Thiong'o and the Kamiriithu theater group were produced in 1976 and 1982; Pepetela's *A Geração da Utopia* (The Utopian Generation) appeared in 1993. Each, from the perspective of the postcolonial present, attempts to find a way out of this dilemma, which, it should be clear, is equally aesthetic and political. The former draw their content from the Kenyan Mau Mau uprising of 1952–56; the latter, from the long history of the Angolan revolution (the revolutionary Popular Movement for the Liberation of Angola [MPLA] was founded in 1956 but did not form a government until 1975). Each writer's work is intimately bound up not only with representing the promise and failures of the anticolonial movements but with conceiving a mass political subject that would be equal, in the light of that promise and those failures, to new forms of the domination of Capital—the very mirror image and negative condition of Lewis's project, which sought a "class of individuals" to check the emergent mass demands of his own time. In the case of Ngugi wa Thiong'o, this project hinges on peasant class consciousness as the concrete mediation between the abstract "desire of the multi-tude" and real historical possibility.

In his essay "Art War with the State,"[1] Ngugi wa Thiong'o engages in a dialogue with Brecht's "The Anxieties of the Regime":

> Given the immense power of the regime
> . . . .
> One would think they wouldn't have to
> Fear an open word from a simple man.[2]

Ngugi, who was censored, imprisoned, and finally exiled in 1982 by the government of Daniel arap Moi,[3] has more right than anybody to pose anew the question of the "subversive" power of art, a question that had begun to seem—in the context of a European or American intellectual sphere that is ready enough to assimilate the most apparently "transgressive" avant-garde aesthetics under a contemplative attitude toward the object, and a commercial sphere that immediately makes over dissent and subversion into the "alternative" and "shock value"—at best self-indulgent, at worst an ideological mystification. But Ngugi's theater, which was shut down more than once by the Kenyan state and was ultimately razed by state police, permits us to take seriously the possibility that art can be, in more than a metaphorical sense, at war with the state. What indeed was the origin of the regime's anxiety? Was it mere paranoia? Or did Ngugi's theater pose a real threat to the neocolonial state in Kenya?

Ngugi wa Thiong'o's effort to transform the Kenyan theater apparatus began in earnest in 1976 with the origins of the Kamiriithu theater group, a village-based collective of peasants, workers, petty bourgeois, and intellectuals, which produced only two plays (*I Will Marry When I Want* [*Ngaahika Ndeenda*] and *Maitu Njugira* [Mother, Sing for Me]) before being shut down for good by the KANU government (Kenya African National Union, which governed Kenya from independence to 2002). It will be helpful to begin, however, with an earlier work, *The Trial of Dedan Kimathi,*[4] which he and Micere Githae Mugo started in 1974 and was published just before Ngugi began work on the Kamiriithu project. *The Trial of Dedan Kimathi* shares the central preoccupation of the Kamiriithu plays: the attempt to narrate, and in narrating to rethink the meaning of, the Mau Mau uprising of 1952–56, whose role in forging Kenyan independence is still a matter of debate.[5] It already contains, in embryonic form, the problematic that haunts both the Kamiriithu plays and, as we shall see shortly, Pepetela's fiction.

The Trial of Dedan Kimathi begins, appropriately enough, in a courtroom, at the arraignment of Dedan Kimathi, the Mau Mau leader whose capture and execution in 1956 ended the already waning period of Mau Mau resistance.[6] But the courtroom trial only frames the real trials of the play, which are four temptations Kimathi, sequestered in his cell before the courtroom trial begins, undergoes before his martyrdom. Kimathi is first visited by his capturer, Henderson, who offers him the collaborationist option: he may save himself by betraying his fellow fighters in the forest. The second visitation, by a triumvirate of bankers (British, Indian, and African), represents the temptation to trade real victory for a share in the spoils of colonialism. The third temptation is brought by another trio—Business Executive, Politician, and Priest, all African—who represent the hollow nationalization or Africanization of the bourgeoisie, of the political class, and of the Church (and perhaps of the intellectual class more generally). The fourth, as Henderson returns—with gloves off, so to speak—is to capitulate under brutal violence. Kimathi refuses to submit and is sentenced to death.

Interleaved with this narrative is the story of a Boy and a Girl, who first come onstage locked in a deadly battle over a few coins tossed by a tourist. The subplot of the Boy and the Girl represents another aspect of colonialism, as a fourth principal character, a Mau Mau sympathizer named simply the Woman, observes:

> The same old story. Our people . . . tearing one another . . . and all because of the crumbs thrown at them by the exploiting foreigners. Our own food eaten and the leftovers thrown to us—in our own land, where we should have the whole share. (18)

Continuing this allegorical subplot, the Woman ultimately unifies the two in a common effort to free Kimathi, as she asks them to smuggle a gun into the courtroom. The lesson is familiar and clear enough: "tribalism" and other divisions, induced by competition for scraps of colonial power, are only overcome by an armed struggle against a common enemy, forging a new revolutionary and national consciousness. The climax, however, as Kimathi's death sentence is announced, is more ambiguous. The Boy and the Girl, holding the gun together, stand up, crying "Not dead!" and a shot is fired; but darkness falls, obscuring the meaning of the shot. But then "the stage gives way to a mighty crowd of workers and peasants at the centre of which are Boy and Girl, singing a thunderous freedom song" (rendered in Swahili in the English text):

PEOPLE'S SONG AND DANCE
SOLOISTS: Ho-oo, ho-oo great calm river!
GROUP: Ho-oo, ho-oo great calm river!
SOLOISTS: From the west to the east
GROUP: Great calm river
SOLOISTS: From the north to the south
GROUP: Great calm river
SOLOISTS: Hoo-i, hoo-i how the enemy is truly a fool
GROUP: Hoo-i, hoo-i how the enemy is truly a fool
SOLOISTS: He killed our first-born
GROUP: Making him the victor
SOLOISTS: Many more have been born
GROUP: May we celebrate a new birth
SOLOISTS: The last-born, fighting-stick held high
GROUP: May we ambush the new enemy
SOLOISTS: Hoo-ye, hoo-ye workers of the world
GROUP: Hoo-ye, hoo-ye workers of the world
SOLOISTS: And all the peasants
GROUP: Let us all link arms

SOLOISTS: Let us attack the strong man in his weak spot
GROUP: We don't want slavery again
SOLOISTS: Hoo-ye, hoo-ye our unity is our strength
GROUP: Hoo-ye, hoo-ye our unity is our strength
SOLOISTS: We will struggle until the end
GROUP: Stand we but firm, we will win
SOLOISTS: Hoes and matchets held high
GROUP: May we redeem ourselves and rebuild anew.[7]

The first substantive lines of this song celebrate a dialectical turn:

Hoo-i, hoo-i how the enemy is truly a fool
He killed our first-born
Making him the victor

The enemy is a fool because killing Kimathi made him a martyr, a symbol with which to energize the very movement his killing was meant to squelch. The execution of Kimathi is simultaneously defeat and victory. But, like the shot that ends the action of the play, this martyrdom is itself ambiguous. What exactly is celebrated here? For what revolution was Kimathi's death decisive in other but a negative way? Does this poem, in commemorating Kimathi's martyrdom, insist that it ultimately led to real independence?[8] Or does it refer to a future victory, against some "new enemy" that briefly appears a few lines later?

The temporality of these lines is deliberately ambiguous. (In fact, the entire song is temporally ambiguous, tending to gravitate toward the subjunctive.) "Akaua" has been translated here as "he killed," but the -ka- infix denotes not necessarily the past but simply narrative succession. Generally a sequence of verbs in the -ka- tense are preceded by a verb with a more definite temporality (a narrative, for example, would begin in the past tense) but here that is not the case. The following line is temporally indistinct as well, using the -ki- infix that here hinges on the tense of the previous phrase (which, as just noted, has no distinct temporality), an effect that can be translated into English by the progressive. In the context of the play these lines refer to Kimathi; but when the play was first published and performed in 1976,[9] another political martyrdom would have been fresh in the mind of any Kenyan audience: the brutal murder, probably by government forces, of the politician J. M. Kariuki (himself a hero of the Mau Mau period)[10] in March 1975, an assassination that provoked rioting and "the biggest political crisis which the [Kenyatta] regime had ever faced."[11]

It is not necessary to grant this specific (and speculative) interpretation to see that the "new enemy" that appears four lines after this ambiguous martyrdom certainly seems to open up the play to contemporary history rather than to bring the curtain down on the defeat of Mau Mau. But there is a slyness to this line, too, which depends on the worn-out quality of the word umoja, "unity" (literally oneness), a few lines later. A hasty reading or hearing of these lines celebrating the defeat of a "new enemy" with "our unity" might turn up nothing more than the submissive repetition of a constant refrain in Kenyan political discourse: the use of "unity" as a justification for repression of dissidence or, in a somewhat less ideologically suspect context, as a call for the end of "tribalism" (which has also often been, since colonial times, a justification for repression). Here, of course, "unity" in fact names a call for a revolutionary proletarian consciousness as figured by the Boy and the Girl; but "Our unity is our strength" sounds like something that might have come from the lips of KANU politicians as easily as from the pen of Ngugi. Similarly for "May we redeem ourselves and rebuild anew"; on a casual reading, this might sound like the perfectly acceptable Kenyatta-era rhetoric of "Harambee," the antitribalist national slogan of "pulling together."

Of course, the lines

> Hoo-ye, hoo-ye workers of the world
> And all the peasants
> Let us all link arms

recall a quite different rhetoric, paraphrasing as they do the peroration of *The Communist Manifesto*. But the phrase "wafanya kazi wa ulimwengo" has none of the recognizable urgency that the analogous phrase has in English, and "Tushikaneni mikono sote" ("let us all link arms") is less threatening than "Unite!" "Majembe" and "mapanga," a few lines later, are indeed "hoes" and "matchets," which are of course symbols of the peasantry. But, besides being part of the peasant means of production, the *jembe* and the *panga* are formidable weapons: the machete and the Kenyan hoe, which looks more like a long-handled pickax. The peasant with *jembe* held high flips rather easily between a homely and a militant image.

Taken at face value, the song appeals to national unity, to independence as the "defeat" of the colonial power (a vexed issue to which we will return), to the rustic values of the hoe and the matchet. Attended to more closely, it constitutes an appeal to contemporary proletarian class consciousness, to the defeat of the national bourgeoisie, and to a militant peasantry. At this moment, the last moment of the play, the whole of what has passed before suddenly changes meaning. Or rather, it retains its old meaning but gains a new allegorical layer: the drama of the Boy and the Girl over a few coins is still an allegory of colonialism, but it applies equally to a neocolonial situation where "tribal welfare associations" fight over shares in parastatal and multinational ventures. Kimathi's four temptations turn into historical moments that have yet to be overcome: the betrayal of democratic national ideals in order to curry favor with the First-World investors; the scramble for the spoils of the old colonial system; the replacement of a truly egalitarian consciousness with a petty-bourgeois African nationalism; and the smothering of dissent with brutal reprisals. The daring suggestion, which could never have been made in other than this veiled fashion, is that the road not taken by Kimathi is the road taken by Kenyatta. Finally, Kimathi (Kariuki?) is not so much a martyr for independence as a martyr for a peasant revolution still to come.

The Trial of Dedan Kimathi, along with the more radical theater experiments we shall turn to in a moment, calls in its final line for a future utopian redemption:

"Tujikomboe tujenge upya." The verb "kukomboa" is already a dialectical word in Swahili, meaning "to redeem" but more literally "to hollow out," carrying within itself images of both plenitude and poverty. "Upya" here translates most fluidly as "anew," but it is in fact the nominal form of the normally adjectival radical "-pya." Ordinarily, this would signify something like "novelty," but this is obviously too prosaic for the context; perhaps it might be more accurate to translate the last line of the play as "May we redeem ourselves (through hardship) that we might build the New." In its final moment, then, *The Trial of Dedan Kimathi* is not so much the celebration of a revolutionary past (although it is this, too) as the call to a revolutionary future.

But hasn't this "future" already come and gone once already? The allegorical double meaning of the play elides the transition from colonial to postcolonial rule, a transition that cannot in hindsight be viewed as an unambiguous victory for the Kenyan multitude. What difference might there be between the outcome of Mau Mau and some future uprising (such as the failed coup attempts of 1981 and 1982, which only helped Moi to consolidate power)? The question is a practical one and not easily answered; the point here is that this particular allegorical form evades the issue altogether. Left out when postcolonial history is collapsed into a narrative of the colonial period (either this or the reverse occurs also in each of the Kamiriithu plays) are the crucial years between 1956 and 1963 when, with Mau Mau defeated, the British negotiated a transfer of power with favorable terms for the settler and expatriate communities and with little change to existing economic structures. *The Trial of Dedan Kimathi* projects a utopian possibility that is potentially the future of the present, but it does so by animating with the urgency of the present a revolutionary past whose future was far from utopian. If *The Trial of Dedan Kimathi* attempts to represent the genuinely revolutionary possibility of a peasant and proletarian class consciousness, this attempt is frustrated by Kenyan history—the fundamental referent of both this play and the Kamiriithu productions—which turns this utopian possibility primarily into the memory of a missed opportunity. Under these circumstances, is the revolutionary posture any more than an "embodied cliché" of a very different sort than we saw with Lewis?

Ngugi's experimental theater at Kamiriithu, though it develops a similar structure, asks for an altogether different mode of explication than his earlier plays, one that depends less on the text as the origin of meaning and more on reading the circumstances of production as text.[12] Ngugi's Kamiriithu plays address themselves first, in a much more direct way than the works we have seen so far, to a particular social situation at a particular historical juncture. For this reason our own discussion will follow a different trajectory than our earlier ones, hinging more on the immediate historical and political context than in our earlier chapters. The narrative of this situation, and of Ngugi's experience with the Kamiriithu theater group up to 1977, is movingly told in Ngugi's *Detained: A Writer's Prison Diary*[13] which was largely written—on toilet paper—during the author's year in detention for the first production at Kamiriithu.

Kamiriithu is first of all a place, a village in what used to be known as the "White Highlands"; a reader approaching the period of Ngugi's Kamiriithu projects from a perspective that ignores this fact will come away disappointed. The primacy of the local is by now a cliché—though as often as not it serves as an alibi for ignoring more systemic matters—but Ngugi's Kamiriithu dramaturgy is profoundly embedded in a particular and short-lived political situation. At the very least, an understanding of Ngugi's theater in relation to this situation tells us something more generally about the possibilities of art in a period of social unrest; but to begin with the general would ultimately be fruitless. This is not to say that Ngugi's plays themselves contain no wider significations; on the contrary, a reading of his work must come to terms with the fact that what these plays attempt to represent is becoming universal: the dynamic of post-1960s history that goes by the name "globalization." But the function of the particular is different than that which pertains in, for example, the work of Achebe or Kane, where the particular is first and foremost to be understood as an allegory of the general. The fictional histories of Umuaro or of the Diallobé are indeed local histories and derive much of their impact from the violence done to particular modes of life and speech; but they are narrated in such a way that the general situation of which they are the allegory is apprehended almost simultaneously with the particular. Ngugi's work figures this relationship differently, in that the particular through which the universal is to be apprehended has none of the transparency it has in these other writers; it is as though the local, in all its opacity, resonates immediately with the global, without first traversing the general.[14] For a reader or observer outside this context and unfamiliar with Kenyan history, in particular the Mau Mau rebellion and the vexed history of Kenyan independence, the story being told remains opaque, didactic, stereotyped, even clumsy.

For non-speakers of Swahili or Gikuyu, Ngugi does nothing to dispel this opacity by leaving important words, phrases, and songs in Swahili or Gikuyu even in his English and translated works; indeed, now is probably the time to address, briefly, Ngugi's famous "farewell" to the English language in *Decolonising the Mind* and his determination to compose only in Gikuyu and Swahili.[15] One should not take too far, I think, the epistemological argument that African experience can only be captured in African languages (see 4–33). After all, the experience Ngugi narrates above all others is the experience of worker and peasant life under multinational capitalism, "our people's anti-imperialist struggles to liberate their productive forces from foreign control" (29): an experience that does not originate in an African context in the same way African languages do. Similarly, the proprietary view of culture—in which European languages are seen to be stealing the vitality of African languages "to enrich other tongues" (8) in the same way neocolonial economic regimes enrich the First World at the expense of the Third (see also *Penpoints* 127)—has polemical value but does not do justice to the complex dynamics of cultural *métissage*, which tend in almost every instance to refute the simple logic of cultural ownership. From a perspective of "cultural decolonization," neither can this impulse toward "national" languages be rigorously separated from the petty-bourgeois impulse toward cosmetic "Kenyanization" from which Ngugi is careful to distance himself and which, as we have seen from the example of *The Trial of Dedan Kimathi*, is always criticized or lampooned in his plays and fiction.

This is not to dismiss out of hand the question of language; on the contrary, Ngugi's shift to Gikuyu opens up a whole new set of dramatic possibilities and strategies that had not existed before. One might conceive of this shift in terms of audience: how else could a historical and self-conscious awareness of their proletarianization be inculcated in a Gikuyu audience except through their language? But here the word "audience" is already wrong and implies a set of relations Ngugi's theater aims to clear away; further, to leave the matter here would oversimplify the problem by framing in purely ethnic terms what is also an issue of class relations. It is not that the Gikuyu are "addressed" by Ngugi through the medium of the play; composing in Gikuyu makes possible a whole new set of social relations among the intellectuals and peasants, proletarians and bourgeois, that made up the Kamiriithu collective.

We might think of the choice to compose in Gikuyu as a means by which the play "addresses itself" not to an audience but to a situation of which it is the narration:

> *Ngaahika Ndeenda* [*I Will Marry When I Want*, the first play to be produced by the Kamiriithu group] depicts the proletarianization of the peasantry in a neo-colonial society. Concretely it shows the way the Kiguunda family, a poor peasant family, who have to supplement their subsistence on their one and a half acres with the sale of their labor, is finally deprived of even the one-and-a-half acres by a multi-national consortium of Japanese and Euro-American industrialists and bankers aided by the native comprador landlords and businessmen. (*Decolonising* 44)

This is an accurate enough summary by Ngugi of his and Ngugi wa Mirii's own play, at least as it appears at first glance. But *I Will Marry When I Want*[16] is less a representation of social reality than a process or event that both prepares and allegorizes some other historical possibility. Indeed, Ngugi's dramaturgy only makes sense within the context of an historical situation it does not simply represent but addresses in order to change.

Which brings us back to the geographical place on which the drama of the Kamiriithu cultural project was staged: a village in Limuru, in the Kiambu district, part of the former "White Highlands," where the historical ground of the Mau Mau rebellion is almost dizzyingly close.[17] Although the geographical location "Kamiriithu" predates the colonial period, Kamiriithu village was first set up as an "emergency village" during the Mau Mau period. Areas where guerrilla activity was suspected were razed, suspected Mau Mau sympathizers and guerrillas like Ngugi's older brother sent to detention camps or killed, and new, concentrated, easily administered and isolated villages set up in the place of the older, more diffuse communities. The narrative of *I Will Marry When I Want* resonates with this much larger history; but also it frames the memories of the participants themselves. The colonial-era events to which the text of *I Will Marry When I Want* refers took place within living memory; in a particularly poignant example, a prop manager who "made imitation guns for the play at Kamiriithu was the very person who used to make actual guns for the Mau Mau guerillas in the fifties" (*Decolonizing* 55). Within the play this revolutionary memory is vividly and painfully enacted:

> It was then
> That the state of Emergency was declared over Kenya.
> Our patriots,
> Men and women of
> Limuru and the whole country,
> Were arrested!
> . . . .
> Our homes were burnt down.
> We were jailed,
> We were taken to detention camps,
> Some of us were crippled through beatings.
> Others were castrated.
> Our women were raped with bottles. (27)

But it is not only the colonial past and the struggle against it that are inscribed in the very landscape in which the theater sat but the neocolonial present as well. The arrogance of the original settler expropriation of land—the dispossession of the peasants' means of production, which is the original sin of African colonialism and the foundation of modern Kenyan history—was such that near Kamiriithu some of the most fertile land on the continent was converted into hunting grounds, a race track, and a golf course for the entertainment of the European farmers. Twenty-five years after the Mau Mau uprising, when Ngugi engaged in his Kenyan theater projects (indeed fifty years later), the old pleasure grounds—controlled now by the new ruling class, for whom the landless peasants were still a source of cheap labor—remained as powerful reminders of how little had changed with the end of direct European colonialism.

This neocolonial situation is the setting of the play itself, which, as we have seen, represents the present-day continuation of the colonial expropriation of land: "Our family land was given to homeguards. / Today I am just a laborer on farms owned by Ahab Kioi wa Kanoru" (29). The very name of the African landlord—baptized Ahab, after the ultimately humbled King of Israel, of whom "there was none who sold himself to do what was evil in the sight of the Lord like Ahab" (1 Kings 21:25)—is a complex signifier that pulls together both historical moments, the colonial and the neocolonial, in a single figure. Besides appearing to be a transformed version of the settler name "Connor," "Kanoru" simply interposes a syllable into the name of Kenya's ruling (and, at the time of these plays, only) political party, KANU. The form of the name ("wa Kanoru") suggests "son of Kanoru," son of KANU, as well as "son of Connor." Although KANU was originally the more radical of the two parties existing at independence, it gradually came under control of GEMA (Gikuyu, Embu, and Meru Association), a "tribal welfare organization" that controlled much of the land in Limuru as well as interest in manufacturing concerns. The KANU government, allied from an early stage with comprador business interests, was accused of granting foreign multinationals fantastic terms to locate factories in Kenya without instituting any controls on where profits accumulate.[18]

The foreign-owned Bata shoe factory (the major industry in Kamiriithu) is one such entity, referred to here by a character in *I Will Marry When I Want*:

You sweat and sweat and sweat.
Siren.
It's six o'clock, time to go home.
Day in, day out,
Week after week!
A fortnight is over.
During that period
You have made shoes worth millions.
You are given a mere two hundred shillings,
The rest is sent to Europe. (34)

But this contemporary experience refers to the past: the factory alluded to here is dramatized as a part of the characters' contemporary daily life, but the "general strike" (68) that comes up later in the play was actually a 1948 strike at this very factory, well within the memory of many villagers. This event, while not strictly a general strike, was simultaneous with a more general phenomenon with which *I Will Marry When I Want* links it. Mass "oathing," the administration of oaths of unity among squatter populations, began in Kiambu district during this time and spread to the rest of the highland areas. The "general strike" is enacted in the play not through a representation of the strike itself but through an oath administered to the strikers. The militant language of the oath makes it clear that, within the context of the play, this oathing is identical with the Mau Mau movement (indeed, the oathing of squatters during this time, simultaneous with the Bata strike, did contribute to the Mau Mau movement[19]):

If I am asked to hide weapons
I shall obey without questions.
If I am called upon to serve this organization
By day or night,
I'll do so!
If I fail to do so
May this, the people's oath, destroy me
And the blood of the poor turn against me. (69)

The narrative building blocks of the anticolonial struggle—which in themselves could be acceptable content for the KANU government—refer to a moment in history, brief but within memory, when the peasantry and rural proletariat were being formed into a powerful political subject. But, as with *The Trial of Dedan Kimathi* but centered in the present rather than in the past, the contemporary history that dominates the play is narrated in continuity with this older history:

"African employers are no different ... from the Boer white landlords" (20). Moreover, the elision of the moment of independence is thoroughgoing, so that the strike against the Bata plant in 1948 becomes a protest against current conditions, and the Mau Mau oath of unity ultimately becomes a call for revolutionary action in the present, once again projecting, by means of a revolutionary past, the possibility of a future when this appropriation of history by the peasantry and proletariat has indeed taken place:

> A day will surely come when
> If a bean falls to the ground
> It'll be split equally among us,
> For—
>
> . . . . . .
>
> The trumpet—
> Of the workers has been blown
> To wake all the peasants
> To wake all the poor.
> To wake the masses (115)

The elision of the break between the colonial and postcolonial situations is figured not only within the play but, by a twist of fate, between the play and its social context. In a dazzling if depressing irony, the play mentions an old colonial law designed to prevent the swearing of Mau Mau oaths:

> It was soon after this
> That the colonial government
> Forbade people to sing or dance,
> It forbade a gathering of more than five. (67)

This law, stating that "more than five people were deemed to constitute a public gathering and needed a licence" (*Detained* 37), is still on the books: and it is precisely this license that was withdrawn from Kamiriithu by the government in November 1977, ending the run of *I Will Marry When I Want* (58).

But the content of the play forms only part of the allegorical raw material of the play; as with Brecht's learning plays or *Lehrstücke*, the circumstances of its production and the relations among the participants and between the participants and the audience determine the meaning of the play as much as the content itself. In the following pages we will be referring to Brecht's dramatic theory, particularly to the theory of the *Lehrstücke*, but it should be made clear that this should not be taken to represent a thesis on the influence of Brecht on Ngugi's dramaturgy, which would be banal in any case. The importance of Brecht's work for Ngugi is well known, but, as we saw in the introduction, we have every reason to be suspicious of the language of "influence," a force that only works in one direction. The Brechtian language of *Umfunktionierung*—"re-functioning," which implies a kind of retrofitting of older techniques to meet new circumstances—poses a solution by reversing the positions of subject and object: the historical author, rather than projecting a whole complex of anxieties, becomes mere raw material to be refunctioned into something original. After all, Brecht's aesthetic was also one of *Umfunktionierung*, and it should be noted in passing that, particularly in the interplay between old musical forms and new lyrical content, Ngugi's dramaturgy reaches back beyond Brecht to the English ballad opera—whose techniques of course became important elements in the Brechtian aesthetic, but which it would be equally bland and misleading to call simply an "influence" on Brecht.

More decisive to the meaning of the learning play than its content are the circumstances of its production: the relations between the actors and the text, the director and the actors, the actors and the stage, the actors and each other. The *Lehrstück* is not a didactic form if by that it is meant that the audience is simply to be edified by its content; instead, the play is most essentially its rehearsals, in which the meaning of the narrative, and even the narrative itself, is constantly elaborated and disputed. The public performance is secondary, one possible performance among many, which happens, this time, to be witnessed by nonparticipants. The text itself becomes not exactly a pretext but the provocation for a learning process which, even in its formal outlines, has political and philosophical content. The Kamiriithu project dramatizes, to an extent that perhaps even Brecht's theater never did, the possibilities of the *Lehrstück*.

The shape of Ngugi's learning plays begins to emerge with the history of the Kamiriithu center itself. As is suggested by the above passages from *I Will Marry When I Want*, the Kamiriithu theater and its first production developed with explicit reference to a particular manifestation of the neocolonial situation. It is against this neocolonial backdrop that Ngugi helped develop the cultural wing of the Kamiriithu Community Education and Cultural Centre, which began in the mid-1970s as an initiative by village groups for renovating a defunct youth center.[20] In 1976, the villagers who had built the center asked Ngugi wa Thiong'o and Ngugi wa Mirii, the director of the literacy program, to write a play to be produced by the Centre. This play, which ultimately became *I Will Marry When I Want*, incorporated biographies written during the literacy program, which also became a kind of political seminar. The outline produced by the two Ngugis was hammered out by the collective into a working script, which incorporated older songs and dances that were relearned and *umfunktioniert* for their new context. Meanwhile, members of the collective who had renovated the center designed and built an open-air theater—apparently the largest in East Africa—to accommodate the production.[21] Since the theater was outdoors, the rehearsals were public: thus the production was open to critical commentary from the village as a whole. The final product, by Ngugi's account, bore little resemblance to his original script: "[T]he play which was finally put on to a fee-paying audience on Sunday, 2 October 1977, was a far cry from the tentative awkward efforts originally put forth by Ngugi [wa Mirii] and myself" (*Detained* 78). When the production opened on the twenty-fifth anniversary of the beginning of the Mau Mau uprising, it was a towering success: critics from Nairobi refused to believe that the musicians and some of the actors were villagers rather than urban ringers brought in by Ngugi. After seeing the play, several villages sent delegations seeking advice on beginning projects along the lines of Kamiriithu. After nine performances, the play was shut down by the KANU government, its license withdrawn for reasons of "public security." Soon afterward Ngugi himself was arrested and put in detention.

After being held in prison without trial for a year, during which he wrote—also on toilet paper—much of his first novel in Gikuyu, translated into English as *Devil on the Cross*, Ngugi was released, along with all other political prisoners in Kenya's prisons, as suddenly and surprisingly as he had been taken. (Jomo Kenyatta had died, and Daniel arap Moi, who had taken over the presidency, released all political detainees in December 1978. His reasons, it turned out, were far from altruistic; he was in fact releasing mainly enemies of the old Kenyatta-centered power structure, which still threatened his young presidency. These events, as we shall see, are signs of the conditions that led to the possibility of Ngugi's theater.) While Ngugi had been in prison the Kamiriithu group had not languished but had in fact grown both in number and in ambition. When Ngugi completed the outline of *Mother, Sing for Me*, a musical composed in several Kenyan languages, two hundred villagers volunteered for the production. The script, set in the 1930s, was a thinly veiled allegory—so thinly veiled that, as in Brechtian parable, this veiling itself is an impudence—of the betrayal of independence by the new ruling class. Like the earlier play, it was filled in and altered by the group; the ending, as with Brecht's *He Who Said Yes*, switched polarity before the play took final form. It was to premier at the National Theater in March 1982.[22] When the group went to take final rehearsals there, it found the gates locked, with the police standing by. After the play moved to a new rehearsal space at the university, people flocked to the rehearsals; every evening the house was full four hours before rehearsals began (people were sitting on the stage, in the lighting booth, at the windows, down the stairs); Uhuru highway was blocked each afternoon; whole villages chipped in to hire buses to take them in to the city for the rehearsals. According to one estimate, 12,000 to 15,000 people saw the production in ten performances.[23] The show had never been advertised. After ten rehearsal performances, the government banned the play, forbidding the Kamirii-thu group to use the university theater. Soon after, police were sent to Kamiriithu to raze the theater complex to the ground. The two Ngugis and the play's director, Kimani Gecau, were forced to flee the country. Whence the "anxiety of the regime" at the root of such extraordinary reprisals?

Official Kenyan theater under British colonialism and after must be considered somewhat of a special case in that its ideological underpinnings did not need to be discovered by dramatic theory; colonial theater was already explicitly ideological. During the Mau Mau period, popular anticolonial songs and dances were countered by propaganda theater: captured rebels in the countryside or suspected sympathizers were shown sketches and plays demonstrating the relative wages of confessing and not confessing, recanting and not recanting, informing and not informing.[24] Meanwhile, in the capital, there was a more traditional European theater whose function was quite explicitly to help create a national bourgeoisie by bringing together the African, Asian, and European privileged classes under the influence of a shared British culture. As the representative of the British Council in

East Africa from 1947 through Mau Mau put it:

> It was hoped that through the theatre the goodwill of the European community could be gained, European cultural standards could be helped, and, later on, members of the different races [elsewhere, with reference to the Kenya National Theatre, the "leading people of all races" (73)] could be brought together by participation in a common pursuit which they all enjoyed.[25]

This theater continued after independence with its ideological function barely altered: the National Theater in Nairobi, from which Ngugi's *Mother, Sing for Me* was banned, continued to put on a steady stream of bland European fare to which, as Fanon prophesied, the new ruling class fawningly flocked. Ngugi's indignation at the behavior of this class (for example, the "modern African bourgeoisie with all its crude exaggerations of its borrowed culture"[26]) echoes Brecht's famous comment that the bourgeois theater audience assumes the bearing of kings: "One may think a grocer's bearing better than a king's and still find this ridiculous."[27] The bearing of the audience reveals the ideology of the theater apparatus, which was explicitly in the Nairobi of 1978 what it was implicitly in the Berlin of 1929: the audience's kingly attitude of complacent and utterly passive consumption reveals in itself the attitude of pure exploitation. At the same time, this attitude is only a mask that hides the fact that the audience, imitating the imagined manner of a European grand bourgeoisie whose position it can never occupy, is at the same time itself the dupe.

As is well known, Brecht's epic theater—as opposed to his learning theater, to which we will return shortly—addresses itself to this audience in an attempt to transform it. The famous *Verfremdungseffekt* does not merely estrange the play's content from the viewer but reveals the fissures that lie within the logic of everyday life under capitalism. The master trope of the epic theater is the exposure (by text, techniques of acting, and production itself) of the theater apparatus as an allegory of the demystification of production in general. A privileged example would be *St. Joan of the Stockyards*, where the deconstructed stage serves as a platform to map the workings of large-scale economic crises onto the various moments of production itself, while the contradictions in this productive system are shown directly to produce the hypocrisies and real psychological aporia of characters such as the capitalist Mauler. Primarily, the epic theater reveals to the bourgeois audience its contradictory relationship to the social world; it is a critical theater, a theater of negation.

Traces of this structure can be identified in Ngugi's earlier plays, as for example in *The Trial of Dedan Kimathi* where the theatrical trappings of the courtroom trial reveal its status as a kangaroo court:

> Enter Shaw Henderson dressed as a judge. Not in disguise. He should in fact be seen to believe in his role as judge, to acquire the grave airs of a judge. Judge sits down. The audience sits. Clerk gives him the file. Judge looks at it. (24)

But learning theater—both Brecht's and Ngugi's—implies quite another perspective on artistic production, on the "theater apparatus" that ultimately produces bourgeois theater. If the exposure of this apparatus as the exposure of capitalism itself is the trope that governs the epic theater, the governing trope of learning theater is the transformation of this apparatus. Its social goal is not to expose a bourgeois audience to the contradictions of its own ideology but to help create a new political subject. This goal is figured in the production of the learning play itself, which takes on a radically new form regardless of the particular content of the final "product," which is finally not so much a performance as an experience of group practice and a new historical self-consciousness. The central rift in the Marxist narrative of capitalist production—the alienation of the worker from the product of his or her labor—is metaphorically bridged by the unity of audience and performer, consumer and producer. This unity is radicalized in the theater of Ngugi, where the absolutely reified social apparatus of the Nairobi theater is replaced by the Kamiriithu project, where the village that built the theater, that wrote the songs, that acted the parts, and whom the performance was designed to reach—and who, in some cases, had lived the history, fought the revolution, and experienced its betrayal—are all identical.

In the movement of its fundamental trope, then, learning theater is utopian theater. Even if what is represented is a dystopic present, the relations of theatrical production all suggest that the deepest content of Ngugi's learning plays is the experience, in fragmentary form, of a transformed social totality, emerging out of the rifts of our old one. And indeed, in the final moments, against all expectations, *I Will Marry When I Want* calls for such a future:

> The trumpet of the masses has been blown.
> Let's preach to all our friends.
> The trumpet of the masses has been blown.
> We change to new songs
> For the revolution is near. (115)

But the figural fusion of producer and consumer in the learning play, of which Ngugi's theater is a radicalization, here only prefigures a real unification: learning theater is only at home in an historical moment when one can imagine a revolutionary political subject as a concrete possibility. It is a call to a possible future, not an aesthetic compensation for the rift it bridges. Outside of the element of political possibility it is spurious. The metaphor of art as production, which we use so carelessly today—even fashion designers, dwelling at the heart of commodity fetishism, advertise their exposed seams by parroting Adorno—degenerates from metaphor into mere metaphor, returning us all the way back to the aesthetic utopia of the modernist sublime.

However, the metaphor which, post-Brecht, had become cliché, has occasionally been vitally performed when the historical situation permits. Brecht abandoned the learning plays when their historical moment passed, when it became obvious that the possibility of workers' revolution in Germany had been preempted by the rise of the Nazi party. Brecht's learning-play phase, which began with *Lindbergh's Flight* in 1929, ended with his own flight from Berlin after the Reichstag fire. He did produce one later *Lehrstück*, *The Horatians and the Cu-*

riatians of 1934, but the fact that this was a Soviet commission confirms rather than contradicts the assertion that the learning play depends on the possibility of revolution.

Are we any closer to understanding the anxiety of the state when confronted with Ngugi's theater? Moi's government in Kenya seemed so secure for so long that it is easy to forget how tenuous the government's hold on power was in the late 1970s. It must be remembered that when Kenyatta became prime minister of a newly independent Kenya in 1963, he was—despite his accommodation of settler interests and the maintenance, post-1963, of a significant landholding class—a hero of national independence. His anti-imperialist days as the leader of the Kenya African Union had led to his imprisonment as a Mau Mau organizer. As a matter of historical irony, Kenyatta's involvement with Mau Mau resistance, never very deep, was at its lowest when he was detained; however, when he was released it was as a hero of national liberation, and he was regarded as such until his death, even among populations who were hurt by his accommodation of multinational, particularly American, business and military interests. However, the period during which Ngugi was developing the Kamiriithu project (*I Will Marry When I Want* began rehearsals in June 1977, and *Mother, Sing for Me* was scheduled to open in February 1982) was a profoundly precarious one for the Kenyan government. From 1975 on it was obvious that Kenyatta was ill and would not live much longer; the behind-the-scenes politicking that went on over his succession left the ruling party severely factionalized and weakened,[28] while the Left politics of MP J. M. Kariuki (assassinated, as mentioned earlier, during this period) gained popularity and momentum. With remarkable tenacity and some skillful politics, Moi, who had been Kenyatta's vice president since 1967, managed not only to make sure he was appointed interim president after Kenyatta's death in 1978 but to win the 1979 election as well. But the popular support for Moi, who, pre-independence, had been staunchly allied with the settlers while Kenyatta was in detention, could command nothing like the loyalty Kenyatta had earned, and his presidency was bought with patronage that his government could not keep up for long. In August 1982, seven months after *Mother, Sing for Me* was banned from the National Theatre, the air force, supported by university students, staged a coup attempt. The aims of the coup have never been made clear, although it seems certain that it was an attempt to move the country to the Left: at least popularly, the alliance of the highly educated air force with the student community suggested opposition to the single-party system. The appearance of the Kamiriithu project, like Brecht's *Lehrstück* period, took place in a brief window when radical political change seemed to be a possibility. The theater experiments at Kamiriithu perform through their very relations of production a possibility along the lines of that which had opened up historically from 1952–56. However, this new possibility is also ultimately sealed off again. Is the recontainment of utopian possibility entirely external to the Kamiriithu project? Or does it, too, contain the seeds of its own failure?

In *The Trial of Dedan Kimathi*, the allegorical representation of revolutionary consciousness subverts itself by celebrating as heroic victory—the future peasant revolution—what it must simultaneously show to be defeat—the failure of the past peasant revolution. The logic of Kimathi's martyrdom—victory-in-defeat—cannot ultimately be separated from the logic of Kenyan independence: defeat-in-victory. The recontainment of revolutionary possibility is repeated in the final act of *I Will Marry When I Want,* as the impulse of the Mau Mau period is finally brought into the present, though in miniature, in the domestic space of Ahab Kioi wa Kanoru's home. In a scene not unlike the last moment of Sembène Ousmane's *Xala,* the local agent of multinational capital at last receives his humiliation at the hands of the dispossessed peasant, Kiguunda, who bears a sword:

> [*Kioi is trembling with hands raised.*]
> You'll die now.
> Kneel down.
> Kneel!
> [*Kioi kneels down.*]
> Look at yourself, you Nebuchadnezzar.
> You are the one turned into a beast.
> Walk on all fours.
> Walk on your feet and hands.
> [*Kioi walks on all fours.*]
> Eat grass,
> Christ, the Head, is watching you,
> Walk! (101–2)

But in *I Will Marry When I Want,* the humiliation of the landlord is not the final scene. Kioi's wife appears with a gun, trumping Kiguunda's sword (reminding us of the superiority of military technology employed by the British against the Mau Mau in the 1950s). A shot is fired. The next and final scene reveals that although the bullet has missed Kiguunda, he loses his smallhold, is fired from his job, and finally becomes a destitute alcoholic. Although the play ends with an unexpectedly triumphal song, the only result of Kiguunda's revolutionary gesture within the plot of the play is his total abasement.

One is not able—certainly not from the perspective of 1976 or 1982—to say for sure whether socialist revolution was really possible in late 1970s Kenya. As it happened, the "August Disturbances" that put a punctuation mark on the Kamiriithu project ultimately served only to justify Moi's consolidation of power as he continued to transfer police services from executive to party control, including the paramilitarization of the KANU Youth, which answered only to party authority. When the Kamiriithu project began, the populist and relatively permissive government of Jomo Kenyatta was weak and on the defensive; his strong-arm successor had yet to consolidate power, and indeed it seemed unlikely that he could hold onto it; prominent Left politicians were gaining popularity. The project ended when Moi's regime consolidated power and Kenya became a state governed by a single political party with its own paramilitary.

Whether things might have been otherwise, one may express a certain skepticism, as did Immanuel Wallerstein at roughly the moment of the Kamiriithu plays, about the possibilities of radical political and economic transformation in any merely national context as long as "the only *system* in the modern world that can be said to have a mode of production . . . the *world* system . . . is capitalist in mode."[29] Indeed, the fact that the climactic taking up of arms in this penultimate scene of *I Will Marry When I Want* takes place in domestic space, in a restricted sphere surrounded by dogs, watchmen, police, and a court system all poised to reestablish whatever social and economic hierarchy might be overturned within it, can be seen to allegorize the situation of "patriotic" revolution in the context not only of a global economy but of an emerging set of global political structures poised to neutralize local challenges to its hegemony. The plays staged by the Kamiriithu theater group are ultimately returned to tragedy, both in their internal narratives and in their own history. Despite every effort, Kenyan history apparently refuses to be narrated except as tragedy. This recontainment of utopian epic in national tragedy should be thought of not as merely accidental but as exemplifying once again Hegel's Ruse of Reason; though the precise events that returned the Kamiriithu project to tragedy were more or less unpredictable, it is hard to imagine—with, for example, U.S. military bases in Kenya—that a new Mau Mau was very likely.

But this, then, is precisely the point: the reorganization of capital and lines of force prompted by the disintegration of classical imperialism begins to sap the potency of the national narrative. The movements of "national independence" (a rereading of Fanon will remind one how complex this "national" basis really is), besides having taken place in the context of a less thoroughly integrated world economy, also erupted precisely at a moment when the anticolonial struggle was understood to have an international basis.[30] After the defeat of classical imperialism, however, and the reorganization of capital called globalization, national transformation no longer holds the same promise. As Wallerstein had pointed out well before "globalization" became a key word, the potential for transformation at the national level is constricted in an extraordinary way by the world economy, particularly for peripheral economies like those of most sub-Saharan African countries.[31] This is not the place to rehearse Wallerstein's argument in full, but one might consider for starters the difficulty in distributing wealth equitably in a peripheral economy when educated labor is extremely mobile and when, in any case, the structural position of the national economy within the larger system prevents it from dramatically expanding the overall creation of wealth—or the inability of the post-apartheid government of South Africa simultaneously to redistribute land and to satisfy potential investors' desire for stable property relations.

The title of *I Will Marry When I Want*, which seems to have little to do with the crux of the play, might be explained with this in mind. The immediate effect of the title is to call to mind a common trope that stages marriage (generally the marriage of a beautiful, rebellious, contemporary woman who is still dependent on her parents) as the scene of conflict between "tradition" and "modernity." But though the possibility of that plot is brought out by Kiguunda's beautiful and rebellious daughter, it is never performed; instead, the marriage in the play is of the parents, Kiguunda and Wangeci, who are remarried in a parody of a European petty-bourgeois ceremony. Immediately, the title refers to the refrain of a drinking song with a slightly lewd twist that runs through the play, finally being sung in the last scene by a drunk and broken Kiguunda. But "I will marry when I want," restated in a more general form, implies that "I can enter into a social relationship whose form preexists my own existence *on my own terms.*" However, as Kiguunda and Wangeci's remarriage amply shows, one cannot enter into a preestablished form on one's own terms merely by altering the content. The form itself would have to be addressed. Similarly with that set of social relationships called "the nation." The nation itself, particularly the role that the existence of competing national governments plays in maintaining the global division of labor, would have to be addressed. To become a nation, in the world economy, "on one's own terms," is to marry "when I want": a difference that makes little difference.[32]

By now we are familiar with the equivocal structure of an African literature in which utopian desire is oriented toward a real possibility, only to be submerged again by the failure to take into account its own investment in established political and economic structures. In the Kamiriithu plays, this dynamic works out slightly differently. *I Will Marry When I Want*, despite its every intention, is forced back into the genre of national tragedy. This is mainly due to the play's honesty in following to the end the logic of its own insistence on a national revolution—the triumphal song that ends the play is belied by the failure of the revolt within it— but this insistence on the national context is also evident in the dramatic form, which despite the notable popularity of the Kamiriithu plays has limited geographic and demographic reach.

But the narrative of decolonization cannot simply end in tragedy. It is essential to think the moment of decolonization—despite, or indeed because of, the horror and misery that the intervening forty years have witnessed—in other than tragic terms. To fail to do so is to fall into the disillusionment or even cynicism that is part of the national tragedy itself. At one time it may have been possible to think the failure of the African revolutions in strictly national and therefore tragic terms, as though the social body of the nation could be purged of its ills by the pity and fear of the spectacle of the failure of the political class. In this way these narratives could still be said to have presented a kind of "resistance to the present" and a utopian possibility. But if national transformation alone no longer holds the promise it once did, are we forced to concede that the present state of affairs is, more or less, what we are stuck with, both politically and narratively?

Pepetela's *A Geração da Utopia*,[33] a novel that follows the Angolan revolutionary intellectual middle class from its birth among Angolan expatriate students in Lisbon to its agonizing death throes in the 1990s, presents the initial appearance of a national tragedy. But underneath the familiar tragic narrative we can witness another, novel allegory of social forms, indeed of collective life itself, taking shape under the first and hinting at the possibility of a different generation of utopia than that emphasized in Pepetela's title (and, for that matter, a different mode of utopian desire than the ones discussed so far in this book). The fundamental figure of this allegory is the recurring theme of music. *A Geração da Utopia* puts the allegorical potential of music into play in a trio of parables that initially appears only to reproduce the tragic narrative sketched above. In the first of these parables, the hero Aníbal describes a dance where he met Mussole, his fiancée:

> The secret of the dance is in the interaction between the collective and the individual. . . . In the xinjanguila, the collective is fundamental. . . . Everything combined with the movements of shoulders, buttocks, and legs. And the particular? It's in the brief instant in which the person to your left, in coming to the center, invites you stamping her feet or giving a jerk of the buttocks. . . . It's really a constant equilibrium between the habitual collective feeling of the round dance and the particular feeling of a partners dance. The pleasure . . . is in sensing the collective pleasure of the rhythm and in sensing living, thrilling, the body that comes to encounter yours, without touching it.[34]

This is plainly enough an allegory of collective creativity, of the self-production of the social totality not as the exclusion of more private pleasure and production, but as the fullest articulation of particular creativity with that of the collectivity. However, this utopia is not projected toward the future but onto a social organization that is tendentially extinct. On one hand, this is a dramatization of the violence visited on older social forms by the colonial project—a violence figured, in a symbol that is also all too literal, in Mussole's murder at the hands of the Portuguese army. But it is just as plain that this projection of utopia onto a doomed society harmonizes with the central tragedy of the novel.

The second parable replays this narrative structure, this time with both moments—both the possibility of utopia and its death—explicitly represented in musical terms. Near the end of the book, a younger character recalls the moment of independence, the approach of the MPLA:

> I was thirteen years old when Luanda mobilized en masse to greet the heroes of liberation. . . . We marched, we listened to the stories of the elders come from the bush, we sang revolutionary songs, we invented that dance-march that exploded over the entire Country, mixed of patriotic fervor and creative imagination.[35]

This spontaneous expression of collective creativity transports, for the briefest of moments, the utopia of the xinjanguila into the modern urban collective. But Orlando continues:

> And then they wanted to discipline us. They said, you must march like soldiers, you are the future soldiers. We could no longer do those crazy moves that got everyone going, go forward, a step to the side, one to the back, a crazy little twist in the middle. Even during Carnaval, years later, one could only dance like the soldiers, the groups gave up dancing. They liquidated the imagination.[36]

Through the regimentation of the spontaneous dance, it is precisely imagination, the specifically musical possibility of reaching for an order that has yet to be conceived, that is liquidated. The sovereignty of the actual—now donning the very "husk of utopia"—is reasserted.

The final parable is the precise inversion of this middle one in which the creative power of the multitude was subdued, initially in good faith, by the liberating army. In the final parable, a simulacrum of collective joy is manufactured, in bad faith, by a group of former guerrillas hoping to profit from collective misery. Vítor (formerly the guerrilla Mundial) along with his friend Malongo, backs Elias, the Fanonist-turned-Bishop, in his enterprise of starting the new Church of the Hope and Joy of Dominus. It is unclear whether, as a prophet, Elias is completely cynical or all too sincere; but it is clear enough that his backers think of the church principally as an investment in the misery and desperation of the Angolan multitude. The final scene of the novel is the bogus spectacle of Elias's evangelical church, with the Bishop simulating elements of older religions and ideologies, working up the crowd into a fervor of religious joy that is mainly channeled toward filling the coffers of the church with "the money and the few jewels and even the shirts"[37] of the celebrants.

But for all that, this final scene is deeply ambiguous. The energies of this multitude, once released, cannot be so easily recontained, overflowing the boundaries set for them by Elias's church. In other words, Carnaval returns:

> Everybody dancing and kissing and touching each other, dancing belly to belly even in the aisles and hallways and later in the square in front of the Luminar and in the streets nearby . . . toward the markets and the streets, the beaches and the slums, in self-multiplying processions like in Carnaval, leaving the Luminar to reach the World and Hope[38]

This is quite a different sort of utopia than the older imagined Nation, and certainly we must see the "Hope and Joy" of Elias's mercenary church as deeply ironic. But here Elias's slogan is appropriated by the narration in altered form—"the World and Hope"—and the explosive proliferation of the dance must be seen in a different light. Indeed, this scene marks the reemergence of the same collective joy that had been last seen at the moment of independence, fifteen years earlier, when "the multitudes were singing the slogans of independence with equal fervor."[39] But if Carnaval, which had not been seen since that moment, here returns, this is not the disordered space within order that allows order to exist but a space of collective creativity that constantly threatens the bounds that are set for it in advance, multiplying itself without outside impetus or check. (The book, which ends with the passage above, ends without a period.) The power of this allegory, in fact, derives from its ambiguity, precisely from the fact that the creative joy of the multitude is initially organized for profit. In factory production as well, or in colonial domination, the creativity of the multitude is initially organized only to exploit it; but the powers thus magnified then struggle against this arrangement and must, ever after, be either placated or repressed.

This is all very well, but what is the value of this musical utopia when compared to the utopia of national liberation represented by Ngugi, which had behind it the weight of an entire constellation of transformative practice? It is one thing to provide a metaphor or allegory of utopia, but what makes this any different than, say, the religious escapism offered by Elias's church, which only exists to profit from the empty hope it offers? It seems that we have taken a step backward, or perhaps two. At the very least we have retreated from Ngugi's attempt to help bring a political subject into being to Achebe's allegory of the abstract desire of the multitude. At the worst we have merely transposed aesthetic utopia into a different medium.

As for this latter charge, the problem with the utopia of the "aesthetic principle" is that it does not itself overcome any of the problems it resolves internally, but can only present such a solution from within the hermetic interior of the work of art. The situation with music is different. Musical practice does not present us with anything other than itself—it is only at the level of writing about music that performance is transformed into allegory—but rather calls us to a social body that does not yet exist. In Don Ihde's phenomenology of sound, *Listening and Voice*, music names an appeal, a "call" that demands a response of a particular sort:

> If, on the one hand, music is sound calling attention to itself, the temptation then is to conceive of music as "pure body." . . . But what occurs in this engagement is clearly anti-Cartesian. It is my subject-body, my experiencing body, which is engaged, and no longer is it a case of a deistic distance of "mind" to "body." *The call to dance is such that* involvement *and* participation *become the mode of being-in the musical situation* [my emphasis]. The "darkness" of music is in the *loss of distance* which occurs in dramatically sounded musical presence.[40]

What Ihde's formulation implies is that music is essentially that activity by which bodies are synchronized into a social body: "*involvement* and *participation* become the mode of being-in the musical situation." In other words, music enacts fundamentally not just a relationship to the individual body but a relationship between it and the social world. We should consider the strange possibility opened up by Jacques Attali's *Bruits*[41] that music calls us not into our own social order but, like the learning play, to a possible future. Music can run ahead of the particular social order that produces it, reaching for a totality that is immanent in the actual as its negation. In this way classical harmony and time, both based on universal systems of ratios putatively derived from natural law, prefigure the social order only later described by political economy. Music is the presence of the potential within the actual, not a compensation for the world as it is.

As for the former problem, the musical culture to which *A Geração da Utopia* bears witness is, like the defection of the village in *Arrow of God*, an expression of the creativity of the multitude, which only acts spontaneously and unpredictably. But the problem of political subjectivity today is of a different character and order of magnitude than was faced, unconsciously or consciously, by modernism or the anticolonial novel. Popular music, the call to a possible future even in its most debased forms, is—unlike the novel or the learning play form—*addressed to everyone*. Music occupies a different position in social space than literature. Its geographic and demographic reach is much greater than that of drama or the novel; its production much more accessible than film or video; and its potential for mapping and shaping the creativity of the multitude greater than any of these. As we shall see in the next chapter, the flow of musical culture across the globe is less predictable than that of such highly capitalized forms as film, operating in unexpected directions independent of the dominant currents of exchange, and sometimes directly linking political desires. We might think here of the musical exchanges between Cuba and Congo, between jazz and bossa nova, between the music of the Scottish and Kenyan highlands; of the global proliferation of rap music, which has become a universal music of protest; or, indeed, of the Brazilian music the Angolan protagonist of *A Geração da Utopia* recalls from childhood parties. At the end of Pepetela's earlier novel, *Yaka*,[42] a young character, the new protagonist, goes off to join the anticolonial army; not to the tune of the Internationale, nor to a patriotic song, not even to the Ngola Ritmos, but to the sound of Otis Redding. This musical globalization already bears witness to subterranean linkages between the utopian desires of subject populations who as yet have no political connection, only a musical one. The possibilities immanent in the rifts of the present sometimes appear in the open; but sometimes, as now, they are driven underground, living a subterranean existence whose presence, if we keep our ears open, we can sometimes dimly perceive. Aníbal writes in his notebook that, faced with the seeming victory of the ideologies of globalization, "Marx não deve parar de se remexer na tumba, num baile subterrâneo, o pobre Marx num frenético semba" (275): Marx must be spinning in his grave, in a subterranean groove, poor old Marx in a frenetic shuffle.

CHAPTER EIGHT

Conclusion: Postmodernism as Semiperipheral Symptom

baum	ping pong	bim
bim	ping pong ping	bom
	pong ping pong	bim bim bom
baum	ping pong	bim
bim		bom
		bim bim bom
baum		bim bim
bim		é só isso meu baião
		e não tem mais nada não
bim		o meu coração pediu assim
		só

—Friedrich Achleitner, "baum-bim," 195?,[1] Eugen Gomringer,
"ping pong," 1953,[2] João Gilberto, "Bim Bom," 1958[3]

The dynamic we have been pursuing throughout this book has reached a point of exhaustion. To a certain degree this impasse is a logical one. As we saw in the introduction, the rift between the two sides of our larger dialectic deepens as the utopian horizon, moving from subjectivity through history to politics, becomes more concrete. But as soon as this horizon reaches a real point of concretion—the production of a political subject—it begins to cease to be literary. It will have escaped no one's attention that both *The Childermass* and the Kamiriithu plays are deliberately antiliterary projects. The more a work is oriented toward an external political horizon, the less use it has for the internal utopian horizon that we theorized in the introduction as belonging to literature as such. This is not to say—far from it—that these last works are somehow worse than the books we looked at earlier, but simply that they refuse to be evaluated entirely by literary norms and begin to appeal instead to political effectivity. *The Childermass* and the Kamiriithu plays do not, however, cease to be literary; in fact, in our reading of *I Will Marry When I Want* the utopian horizon was seen to be finally recontained, despite the formidable power of the play's political message, within the performance after all. Rather, in these final works literary form begins to work against the very political desires that give it content.

But this impasse is not only logical but historical, as we shall see shortly. Our model for the abrupt transition to this final chapter can be found in Hegel's *Aesthetics*, which repeatedly develops the dynamic immanent in an art form until it reaches a moment of deadlock, at which point the "solution" is a formal and often geographic leap to another art form which, in setting up a new dialectic, resolves the old one. In this case, the leap will be to 1960s Brazil, and to the consideration of music: a leap already made for us by Pepetela's *A Geração da Utopia*, which projects music as a possible medium for utopian desire after the apparent closure, with the end of the cold war and the failure of peripheral political independence, of the twentieth-century political horizon.

We have every reason to be agnostic about the future of the current configuration of the arts, about their relative importance as well as the constitution of the various art forms themselves. On one hand, the last thing we need is another millenarian declaration of the decisive end to this or that aesthetic possibility. On the other hand, it does not take a very strong historicism to note that art forms are born and die, that their constitution and social meaning change over the period of their existence, that an art form may continue to eke out a subsistence even while the social configuration that gave it force has passed into history. And it should not be a particularly radical stance to suggest that literature itself may already have entered this sort of afterlife. This is not to say that people have stopped reading or writing novels and poems, or that they will stop doing so any time soon. Rather, the point is one that those most invested in the value of the literary will be ready to admit: the forms of attention required by the literary object in particular (as opposed to those the novel shares with film or television, or those poetry shares with popular music) no longer come naturally, even to the class for whom literature is still supposed to be the hegemonic art form. Nor is this to say—far from it—that there is no longer any value in these forms of attention. But very few professional teachers of literature will have failed to note that while the vast majority of their students are able easily to generate insights about film and music—right ones, wrong ones, ideological ones, but nonetheless insights appropriate to their object—they often fail to follow even the most overt formal cues in a Wordsworth poem or a novel by Machado de Assis.

As we saw in the introduction, literature's eidaesthetic vocation has not existed uniformly throughout the history of the literary; rather, it has seemed to be taken up most strongly in periods of political crisis and utopian possibility: romanticism and the reorganization of feudal space in the wake of the French Revolution, modernism and the political possibilities that opened up in the wake of the Russian Revolution, the heroic phase of postcolonial literature and the great anticolonial revolutions. To this series, however, we must now add a fourth moment, contrary in tendency to the first three, not obviously marked by a dramatic sense of possibility, and less hospitable to the literary gesture. This would be the shutting down of the utopian impulse shared by these earlier moments and by their literary complements: the end of the cold war and the ideological establishment of the capitalist world market as the ultimate horizon of human history itself. Though this movement toward the closure of the ideological horizon is genuinely global, its temporality has been far from uniform: in some places this transition took place over decades; in others, it took the form of a crisis. We might expect that the foreclosure of utopian possibility would have a profound effect on cultural production. Whether or not, as Badiou suggests, "the age of poets is *over*,"[4] it is fair to speculate that a new hierarchy among the arts may be arising—in the culture at large, has perhaps arisen—in which music and film play a greater role than poetry and fiction.

But, to state the obvious, music and film are not the same thing, and with regard to the question of globalization—with regard, that is, to the present state and possible futures of the world system of Capital—they offer different possibilities. To understand why this might be the case we need to establish a minimal framework for discussing the current state of globalization, of culture, and of the relationship between the two. In a very obvious sense, "globalization means the import and export of culture."[5] But then, as we saw in the introduction, Goethe and Marx both identified the international exchange of culture, in specifically economic language, as a function of then modern commerce, and presumably when we talk about globalization we are talking about more than a mere quantitative change. The problem, then, is also one of the peculiar status of culture in the current configuration of Capital, one that has witnessed the "becoming cultural of the economic, and the becoming economic of the cultural"[6]—one might think here of the decreasing distance between techniques of advertising and those of fine art, or the increasing importance of the culture industry to the U.S. economy—in short, of postmodernity as a mode of production.

In this Jamesonian view, "postmodernism" as the cultural or superstructural aspect of postmodernity (it being understood that one of the features of the latter is the difficulty of separating out the old categories of base and superstructure) is not to be identified with some number of stylistic traits that are then a matter of choice for the artist. Rather, postmodernism names the limits placed on aesthetic practices by the reorganization of Capital in the wake of the disintegration of the old colonial system and the subsumption of the nation-state system into larger, global structures—a movement which is of a piece with the elimination or final subsumption under Capital of hitherto semi-autonomous areas like the aesthetic, or noncapitalist societies. Nonetheless, it is impossible to speak of postmodernism without recourse to such notions as pastiche, which ceases then to be, as it was with Joyce, merely one technique among others, and becomes instead a symptom of the existential possibilities afforded by this latest mutation in the organization of Capital. One of the questions we will be considering in this concluding chapter is whether such techniques as pastiche mean the same thing when deployed from different positions within the geopolitical order, and even whether the words we use to describe the formal attributes of postmodern culture in the

First World can be properly applied to new tendencies in the Third World (or more precisely in the context of this chapter, in the semiperiphery) from which they are formally indistinguishable.

Meanwhile, we need to account for the movement of these forms between the center and the periphery, and in this context it should be noted that postmodern culture is most often seen in terms of the image and its dissemination, which, with notable exceptions, tends to move outward from the dominant economies to the periphery. If postmodernity can be identified with an ideological formation in which, with the end of the cold war, "capitalism and the market should be declared the final form of human history itself," then this end of history in the market also is said to represent "a colonization of reality generally by . . . visual forms which is at one and the same time a commodification of that same intensively colonized reality on a world-wide scale."[7] Postmodernity is, from this perspective, more or less synonymous with a new and particularly virulent form of cultural imperialism.

The flow of musical culture across the surface of the globe, as we saw in the previous chapter, has a more complex and unpredictable relationship with the dominant flows of capital. The reasons for this are many: primary among these may be that the economic barriers to inventing, performing, producing, copying, and distributing music are extraordinarily low in comparison to film and even video (and also literature if one includes the cost of an educational system); in addition, not only is the flow of musical information difficult to control but success in controlling it may in some cases restrict its impact. We have already noted Jacques Attali's suggestion that the emergence of new musical forms—which the past century has seen in abundance—tends to be proleptic, calling us to political configurations that have yet to be invented. If we take up Attali's challenge to examine a world that is "not for reading, but hearing"[8] we might be able to discern a different globalization taking place within the dominant one.

In order to conceptualize this possibility we will turn away from both the periphery and the core toward the semiperiphery, where the circulation of capital is neither self-sustaining as it is in the First World, nor yet in a relation of structural redundancy vis-à-vis First-World capital. This will be in part to fill in a gap in the geopolitical sketch we have been attempting in earlier chapters, since aesthetic and political circumstances represented by the semiperiphery are characterized by the political volatility and experiential immediacy (for certain classes) of a situation in which First and Third World conditions are equally present. More important, however, is the way that in the cultural situation cleaved by the central event of this chapter—the Brazilian counterrevolutionary coup of 1964—the fourth geopolitical and cultural moment of our sketch arrives almost literally overnight, exemplifying with extraordinary starkness the transition from modernism to postmodernism. The 1964 coup was, as Roberto Schwarz has made clear, "one of the crucial moments in the Cold War,"[9] a turning point that marked as an event what was elsewhere felt as a more gradual process of the elimination of socialist alternatives. Although we will briefly consider architecture, drama, and poetry, we will be primarily charting the cleavage between bossa nova—a final modernism—and the post-coup musical movement known as "Tropicália"—one of the first postmodernisms. We will begin by outlining the cultural moment that precedes this break, fundamentally in line in its ambivalent relation to real political possibilities with the modernisms explored in earlier chapters: the great era of a politico-economic formation known as "development populism"—of which Juscelino Kubitschek's promise to accelerate the country through "fifty years in five" is emblematic—and, in the realm of culture, of the invention of new modernisms.

Rather than any of the more obvious ways into this cultural milieu, we will begin with a song released in 1989, temporally quite distant from the politics of 1964 and linked to the emergent music of the pre-coup era only formally. The song "Etc.," by the great Brazilian songwriter Caetano Veloso, introduces the vocal line with a half-measure of guitar that announces the song as a bossa nova, though it differs from and plays on formal convention in interesting ways:

ETC.

Estou sozinho, estou triste etc.
Quem virá com a nova brisa que penetra
Pelas frestas do meu ninho
Quem insiste em anunciar-se no desejo
Quem tanto não vejo
Ainda
Quem pessoa secreta
Vem, te chamo
Vem etc.[10]

I'm alone, I'm sad etc.
Who will come on this new breeze that penetrates
Through the gaps in my nest
Who insists in being foretold in desire
Whom I so fail to see
Yet
What secret person
Come, I'm calling you
Come etc.

We begin with a familiar melancholic lyrical voice whose content is clearly marked as cliché. The lyric immediately announces that part of its content is the depletion of form: the meaning of the first "etcetera" is that we already know everything the bossa nova subject has to tell us about himself. In the next line, however, this sense of depletion is turned around for a moment, since the "etcetera" becomes the opportunity for a clever rhyme (etcetera/penetra) that briefly reanimates the cliché, and the third line does nothing to dispel this expectation. With the fourth line, however, we reach the heart of the song, or what ought to be the heart of the song, where the animating desire of the lyric emerges. But the line itself— "Quem insiste em anunciar-se no desejo" ("Who insists in being foretold in desire")—is extraordinarily awkward, mainly consisting of one repeated note and, as though resorting to a slightly desperate improvisational trick, squeezing too many syllables into each measure. The hopes that ride on this "nova brisa" ("new breeze") seem to outweigh the manifest romantic content; after all, it is not that the desired lover brings an aura but that the breeze itself is full of exciting possibility. The emphasis here is on the desire for the New itself, rather than on any particular new thing, and it may not be too much to see here an echo of 1960s political lyric, where the singer's "tomorrow" is not only a private tomorrow but also a collective and utopian but entirely abstract postrevolutionary future. At any rate, it is clear enough that the central theme of this lyric is not the desired person, who is after all a null quantity, but the desire itself.

But this desire, despite initial appearances, is being conjured, not felt. The emphasis of the next line, "Quem tanto não vejo" ("whom I *so* fail to see") hints at this, but the word "ainda," "yet," which falls on an unresolved note, raises expectations for what will come after the caesura. What follows is the entreaty for the anticipated person to appear; but if the "pessoa secreta" does not appear in the space of the lyric, the real impact of the song comes from the fact that neither did the desire. The final "vem" ("come") is held out on a high note over two bars while chords of increasing tension progress underneath. But this is merely bravado: the final line is a tremendous anticlimax. The song ends with another "etcetera," unrhymed, on a dying note. The meaning of "etcetera" has shifted. It no longer refers to the dispensability of further elaboration but to the pointlessness of continuing to feign desire. It is worth pointing out further that the song, in contrast to most bossa nova compositions—even the very simplest ones, like the one by João Gilberto whose words appear at the head of this chapter—has only one section. The second section paradigmatically serves as a standpoint from which to comment on the first, and here what we get instead in this same lyric, sung again and with identical intonation, is a kind of absolute, unironizable perspective.

This negative evocation of bossa nova as something that is missing or impossible in our own present points to something essential to bossa nova: an atmosphere in which the making of a new music could be viewed as part and parcel of something absolutely new. (The name bossa nova itself means something like "the new thing," and the fact that this name stuck indicates it has meaning beyond a marketing slogan.) But if we begin to ascribe a content to this "new"—in other words a politics—we come up against an objection in the form of a stereotype that views bossa nova as quintessentially apolitical, sunlit, and guiltless; charming music, with its transcendent moments, but easily assimilated to less serious forms of jazz and ultimately to easy listening, devoted thematically to pretty girls, beaches, and the scenic backdrop of a postcard Rio de Janeiro. It is not as though there is nothing to this stereotype, or even that bossa nova's own self-image—together with the commonplace of the Brazilian 1950s as an "age of optimism"—has not contributed to it. Attention to some formal aspects of bossa nova, however, gives specificity to this optimism.

Ordinarily we tend to think of accessibility and technical elaboration as tending in different directions—and not only in the arts. This has everything to do with the progressive segmentation of the labor process and the concomitant specialization of consciousness. The distance between the specialist in a particular field and everyone else tends to widen to the point of incomprehensibility, and this is as true in the arts as it is in engineering, law, or physics. (This cultural tendency is not accidental but a process directly entailed in the logic of the commodity form.)[11] The specialization of consciousness tends to render any attempt at popularization immediately dilutive. The U.S. culture industry, for example, while happy to mobilize certain elements of the technical apparatus to the fullest, purposely leaves others in a state of underdevelopment. Taken as a kind of grand sum or "general intelligence," the tremendous collective talent represented by the culture industry is monstrously out of proportion with the insipidity of its total product. Bossa nova, however, manages at every level—within its own limited sphere—to overcome this antinomy. With all of the commentary about the virtuosity of João Gilberto, who originated the distinctive bossa nova guitar and vocal techniques, what is often forgotten is that these techniques are not only distilled from a popular idiom (samba), but are also, taken separately, extraordinarily simple and, in their basic form, within the reach of anyone who wants to learn them. (The bass line and percussive accompaniment, when they are used, are similarly built up out of simple building blocks.) On the other hand, in the technical execution the interplay between these techniques is dazzlingly elaborated. This is as true for the guitar accompaniment (a relatively simple syncopation that derives its complexity from its interplay with the vocal line) as it is for the vocal quality itself, which eschews decorative embellishment, almost remaining within the compass of ordinary speech, even as this very lack of embellishment requires an extraordinary development of the sense of pitch. The compositional technique of its most accomplished composer, Tom Jobim, exhibits the same dual tendency. On one hand, the emphasis on melody and rhythm makes bossa nova immediately accessible; on the other hand, the building blocks of these melodies sometimes approach dodecaphonic density, and the harmonic base on which they rest provides an apparently inexhaustible supply of ingenious and surprising manipulations of the harmonic system.

Putting this fusion in terms that were surely not on the minds of Jobim or Gilberto, bossa nova fully mobilizes the existing technical apparatus in the service of a popular art form. While not exactly a politics, this aesthetic ideology does not look out of place next to the experiments of Brazilian architecture, which at the time was invested in such massive public projects as the great modernist city of Brasília. If this technological way of describing bossa nova's innovations sounds strange, we should note that it is nothing new in Brazilian cultural criticism; as early as the mid-1960s the concrete poet Augusto de Campos, to take just one example, celebrated bossa nova as a movement that "developed new technologies . . . autonomous, exportable and exported."[12] But the overcoming of this fundamental antinomy between specialization and accessibility—which, like the modernist sublime, overcomes in the work of art antinomies in social life itself—is not emphatic; the world outside bossa nova is still segmented and segmenting, and this persistence inscribes the old antinomy into bossa nova in a new way. (Needless to say this ambivalence applies in a more brutal way to Brasília, built by but not for poor *candango* workers.) Segmentation takes its revenge in the specialized ear of the listener, which must have undergone a certain kind of class training to receive the stylistic development of bossa nova in the proper way. The untrained ear prefers the overblown arrangements, often unevenly performed, that bossa nova supplants, while for the trained ear the chasm between this music and João Gilberto grows ever wider as bossa nova's process of distillation continues.

This ambivalence between the popular imperative and the reinscription of class specialization makes itself explicit in bossa nova lyrics. The beauty and grace supposedly celebrated in bossa nova are paradigmatically inaccessible for the lyrical subject. To take Tom Jobim's most canonical example, one of the mainsprings of the bossa nova stereotype: "The Girl from Ipanema" herself, the symbolic embodiment of the elegance and beauty of the wealthy beach neighborhood of Ipanema, is decisively out of the subject's reach, as is captured perfectly well in the standard translation of Vinicius de Moraes's lyric: "And each day as she walks to the sea / She looks straight ahead not at me."[13] Unconsummated desire is of course a lyrical commonplace that goes back at least to medieval tropes, but here the unattainable desire for a woman is a synecdoche for the desire for her upper-class milieu—in the Portuguese version of these lines, the woman is figured synecdochically as all this "beauty that exists" but "does not belong to me." In Newton Mendonça's "Desafinado" ["Out of Tune"], a kind of manifesto song that introduces the term bossa nova, this structure becomes explicit:

> Se você disser que eu desafino, amor
> Saiba que isso em mim provoca imensa dor
> Só privilegiados têm ouvido igual ao seu
> Eu possuo apenas o que deus me deu.[14]

> If you say I'm out of tune, love
> You should know this hurts me immensely
> Only the privileged have an ear like yours
> I possess only what God gave me.

Although the meaning of "privilegiados" is as flexible in Portuguese as in English, a class reading is made unavoidable by the final line of the stanza, which contrasts the (minimal) god-given talents of the lyrical subject with his lover's class privilege. This reading is confirmed in the following stanza, from which bossa nova takes its name. What is out of tune here is not just the subject's singing but his whole social being, which he excuses by attributing it (falsely, like the "new small talk" in *Pygmalion* but with recognizably urban Brazilian humor), to some new hip way ("bossa nova") of doing things, more "natural" and democratic:

> Se você insiste em classificar
> Meu comportamento de antimusical

Eu mesmo mentindo devo argumentar
Que isto é bossa nova
Que isto é muito natural

If you insist in classifying
My behavior as antimusical
I, though lying, must make the claim
That this is the new thing
That it's quite natural

The music (composed, like "The Girl from Ipanema," by Tom Jobim) both dramatizes the words and introduces a radical disjunction, as the ambiguity we noted in the form ironizes the lyrical content. The first two lines of each stanza end with deliberately awkward intervals, which are meant to perform the awkwardness and antimusicality of the subject—an effect that is lost if the intervals are, in fact, sung out of tune. It only strengthens the paradox that, as we saw above, João Gilberto delivers these lines without glissando or vibrato—an apparently "simplifying" effect, resulting in a more "natural," less ornamented style, but one that requires an extraordinary sense of pitch, since glissando and vibrato allow for miniscule corrections to the pitch after the note is attacked.

What we see then is a tendency within bossa nova to identify the lyric voice with a relatively humble perspective—indeed, in "Desafinado" bossa nova *is* this identification, the equation of this genuinely "new thing" with a simple, unspecialized musical consciousness. Of course it should go without saying that in this relationship bossa nova's composers, lyricists, and performers actually occupy the position bossa nova explicitly rejects, that of the "privileged ear." The popular subjective identification is not complete; it tends to dominate at the level of lyric but to be almost imperceptibly ironized at the formal level. It is against this background that we can best understand the lyric that serves as one of the epigraphs to this chapter, João Gilberto's own "Bim Bom," which in English would look something like this:

> bing
> bong
> bing bing bong
> bing
> bong
> bing bing bong
> bing bing
> my *baião* is just this
> nothing more than this
> my heart wanted it this way
>   just

Nothing could seem sillier and more inconsequential than this little song, the main section of which consists of two notes (one for "bim" and one for "bom") a perfect fifth apart, and which, including repeats, takes up all of one minute and twelve seconds on the 1958 recording. But if we take the time to look at it closely, we note right away that it follows, in miniature, the basic structure outlined above. In fact, the subject of the lyric is specified with remarkable efficiency: not only is he simple and poor, but he's from the Northeast: the rhyme, sense, and meter could have been preserved by any number of words (for example, *canção*, song) besides "baião," which refers to a syncopated dance form from the Northeast. But the second section takes place in a different tonality, expands the harmonic palette, and contains chromatic elements that are plainly beyond the fictional composer of the song within a song. Once again we encounter a split within the lyrical voice—on one hand, an identification with popular simplicity; on the other hand, the slightest tingeing of irony (introduced by the form) that undercuts this identification and introduces a note of pathos that may not be quite legitimate.[15]

The juxtaposition of "Bim Bom" with the two European concrete poems that head this essay is not entirely capricious; the Brazilian concrete poetry of the 1950s shares the ambivalent attitude toward vanguard popularization we have identified with bossa nova.[16] One relationship we might immediately take note of, however, between "Bim Bom" and Achleitner's German example, is that though a similar structure unites these two poems, their content could not be more different. While João Gilberto's deceptively simple song tells a deceptively simple story, "baum-bim" is a minimal linguistic experiment based on the disjunction between "baum" as the German word for tree and as half of an onomatopoetic expression for the sound of a bell. To be sure, this owes something to their formal context— "Bim Bom" is not, after all, a concrete poem—but it also illustrates something we have been seeing all along, which is that forms that appear similar, even those that develop in communication with each other, tend to have different significations as they cross geopolitical fault lines. Even the most apparently "pure" formal experimentation (and in this sense the first section of "Bim Bom" is more formally austere than either of its European counterparts, since the link to onomatopoetic signification is decisively cut) will immediately tend to take on social content in a peripheral situation it tends to resist successfully in a First World cultural context. This phenomenon is also operative between Brazilian concrete poetry and its European counterpart: see, for example, the brutally antisocial (but ultimately utopian) energy of Haroldo de Campos's "Alea I—Semantic Variations" or Augusto de Campos's "sem um número," an apparently empty formal experiment in typographical transformation that turns out to concern the condition of the Brazilian peasantry.[17]

Poesia concreta is most often associated with a later moment in the history of Brazilian popular music, when the concrete poets championed Tropicália against its critics in the mid-1960s. Nonetheless, in a 1968 interview with the concretist Augusto de Campos, in the midst of the furor over Tropicália, Veloso championed "Bim Bom" as one song which, after the banalization of bossa nova, remained unassimilated and vital,[18] and the avant-garde composer Júlio Medaglia singled out this "simple, concrete baião" (one assumes that the word "concrete" here is no accident) as embodying the essence of bossa nova.[19] This relationship between bossa nova and concrete poetry is not accidental; to understand it we should note that the ambivalent democratization of form we have observed in bossa nova, together with its similarly paradoxical semi-identification with a "popular" perspective, can be traced back at least to the Brazilian modernism of the 1920s, particularly the work of Oswald de Andrade. His untranslatable *pronominais* ("pronominal forms"), for example, depends for its force on two different placements of the pronoun "me" ("Dê-me um cigarro" as against "Me dá um cigarro"), the first of which belongs to good students, teachers, and grammar books (and pretentious mulattos, which is another issue), while the second represents not only the "good black and good white / Of the Brazilian nation" but the poet himself, who speaks their language: "Come off it brother / And gimme a cigarette."[20] Concretism marks one possible endpoint of this process. The raw material of concrete poetry is readily accessible to all readers of the language, even the semi-literate: against "expressive poetry, subjective and hedonistic," private and privatizing, Augusto de Campos's "pilot-plan for concrete poetry" proposes a "poem-product: useful object."[21] The "proper" context for his poem "Cidade-cité-city," one enormous portmanteu word, is an electronic signboard in downtown São Paulo, and one can imagine the power his stunning 1961 "Greve" (Strike) might have if put to use, in some suitably monumental context, as propaganda for a general strike.[22] The linguistic element is generally reduced to a few words or even syllables, while emphasis is placed on visual impact and spatial relationships, on "the graphic space as structural agent" rather than syntactical procedures.[23] The relationship to advertising technique is striking, and it comes as no surprise to find direct borrowings from commercial design. Augusto de Campos's handsome red-and-white design from 1972, "VIVA VAIA,"[24] for example, though it looks like a template for one of Lygia Clark's constructivist *bichos*, borrowed its conception from an advertisement for "deluxe ready-to-wear." Aside from parodic possibilities, operative for example in Décio Pignatari's famous 1957 "beba coca cola" (which transforms "drink Coca-Cola" into a cloacal obscenity),[25] concrete poetry at its most interesting confronts us with the power of the advertising image divorced from the necessity of selling shoes: ultimately, with the democratizing edge of capitalism—its unleashing of productive power to the point that this power is, potentially if not actually, "for everyone"—without its exploitive edge, which is immediately entailed by the drive for profit. Once again the impulse is toward the democratization of the vanguard that we saw in bossa nova and modernist architecture; indeed, the "pilot-plan for concrete poetry" quoted above is a direct reference to the "pilot-plan" for the new capital city itself. But the same ambivalence inscribes itself here as well. The use of advertising technique—much closer to industry and the actual functioning of capital than musical technique—brings us closer to a moment when an aesthetic ideology might turn out to be ideology proper. Here the "popularizing" tendency is directly linked to capital, to the fund of available images and stereotypes exploited by advertising, hardly "popular" in a sense worth celebrating. And after all, the difference between "VIVA VAIA" and its commercial model is one of degree, not kind; the democratization of haute couture promised by the claim "deluxe ready-to-wear" is itself not without its utopian aspect, though of course in the falsity of the promise it is immediately belied.

Before we arrive at the historical moment that gives this aesthetic ideology the lie, a theoretical digression is in order. The technical imperative in both concretism and bossa nova, consciously or unconsciously, operates within an Adornian framework where the mobilization of productive forces in the work allegorizes the productive forces outside the work: "Although it appears to be merely subjective, the *totum* of forces invested in the work is the potential presence of the collective according to the level of the available productive forces."[26] The Adornian position assumes a First-World cultural situation, one in which the latest developments in industry—not only production techniques but also the specialization of consciousness—are more or less immediately present subjectively and in the process of artistic production. In a semiperipheral situation, where the national economy cannot be mistaken for the theoretical horizon of the economy as such, matters stand a little differently. From the Adornian perspective cultural production in the classical semiperipheral situation faces an unbearable choice. On one hand, it can ignore its subaltern position and continue to produce "authentic" works in regional traditions. But since cosmopolitan alternatives will always be available to those who can afford them, "authentic" cultural production turns over into its opposite and becomes nothing more than, in a memorable phrase of Oswald de Andrade's often cited by the concretists, "macumba for tourists." On the other hand, it can imitate these same metropolitan forms; but since these forms grew out of particular social formations without equivalent on the periphery, their derivative status will be palpable.

If we refuse to be bound by Adornian absolutism we can allow that beautiful and significant work has been produced under each of these conditions—not because the dilemma is false but because these conditions are rarely met in pure form. Leaving aside the possibility of abandoning the pretension to art altogether, there seem to be two ways out of this dilemma, neither of them easy. The first option is to "join the game," to participate directly in the production of new vanguards, to compete with cosmopolitan culture: that is, to escape, in the restricted realm of art, the restrictions imposed by the peripheral situation. (To return to a question deferred for some time, this is the dominant thrust of the Joycean option.) The second option would be to begin from the fact that impoverishment at the periphery and wealth at the center are aspects of a single process; thus the way the "level of the available productive forces" renders its subjective effects in the periphery is precisely by way of the "uneven development" that impinges on everyday life in unexpected ways. (Even in Joyce, then, the decision is never pure—see the "scrupulous meanness" of *Dubliners.*) This would not in itself imply claiming the semiperipheral condition as an "identity" or a value—which, besides entailing a kind of masochism, would lead us right back to the paradox of authenticity—but rather using the symptoms of the geopolitical order, in however mediated a fashion, as raw material.

It should be clear that these two positions are, in theory, incompatible: the aim of the first is to escape symbolically the limitations imposed by the semiperipheral condition, while that of the second is to occupy this position fully in order to oppose directly the process that produces it. One, undeniably progressive and anti-imperialist, nonetheless remains within the horizon of Capital; the point is not to alter the core-periphery relationship but to represent allegorically the possibility of altering one's position within it. The other position, which begins from the full assumption of all the debilitating effects of the semiperipheral situation, cannot—provided it does not sink into masochistic identification—help but project a social horizon no longer organized around this relationship. This theoretical cleavage, however, does not prevent both tendencies from being present in the same artist, even the same work—indeed, this is may be the case more often than not.[27] In fact this latter impulse is nearly always held in check by the former.

Reaching back to the classic period of Brazilian modernist poetry, a comparison of Oswald de Andrade's famous pair of manifestos, "Manifesto da Poesia Pau-Brasil" ("Manifesto of Brazil-wood Poetry," 1924) and "Manifesto Antropófago" ("Cannibal Manifesto," 1928), elucidates this tension. The liberating importance for the Brazilian avant-gardes of the heroic figure of the cannibal-poet is well known: peripheral anxiety over metropolitan influence is transformed into its opposite in a single stroke, as all culture—American films, psychoanalysis, communism, Tupi myths, Portuguese sentimentality, whatever—is flattened to the status of mere nourishment. But there is something else in Oswald's statement of "cannibal" ethos: "I'm only interested in what's not mine."[28] Cannibal inauthenticity is espoused in the name of an elucidation of the subject, in other words a kind of authenticity: what is most "mine" is the fact of only being interested in what is not mine. The cannibal ethos is then not to be read in contradiction to the earlier demand "to be regional and pure in one's time"[29] but as its expression. The only way to be "regional and pure" is to register the impurity of the semiperipheral situation, which is a function of Capital. In this context the familiar modernist imperative "to see with free eyes" (9) is a rather stronger gesture for Oswald than it is for, say, Lewis, since this "seeing" necessarily contains a geopolitical element.

On the other hand, the figure of "Brazil-wood poetry"—which, like brazil-wood itself, would be "for export" (7)—offers a different metaphor, one that has also had a lasting impact on Brazilian art. The general thrust of the manifesto is toward the development of the technical conditions necessary for the emergence of a vanguard poetry. First among these is "poetry for poets," another familiar modernist refrain that means something slightly different in the peripheral context: not so much the autonomy of cultural producers from the interference of other class fractions as the development of the local division of labor to the point that a specialized artistic class can emerge:

> The return to specialization. Philosophers doing philosophy, critics criticizing . . .
> Poetry for poets. (6)

It is clear that the "technical accomplishment" (8) this demands neither is a mere metaphor nor concerns just artistic technique; it refers instead to the actual development of the national means of production, which requires "engineers, not legal advisors" (6). We have to distinguish, however, between two export economies: the first is the export of raw materials, the hallmark of a colonial economy, and the second is the export of finished products—the hallmark of a core economy (though this has changed in the past three decades). In this context the meaning apparently intended by the notion of "poetry for export"—poetry being, of course, a "finished product"—is undermined by the choice of brazil-wood as an emblem. Rather than entailing a certain "technical accomplishment"—the ideological content of the technical imperative in bossa nova and concretism as well—the brazil-wood economy merely exploits a raw material. The metaphor has a certain aptness, since brazil-wood is the commodity that gave the nation its name. Perhaps it is all too apt, for in a sense the referent of the manifesto, the real basis upon which Brazilian modernism was possible, is part of the old export economy: coffee, which did, for a time, "nourish the initial stage of industrialization," even as it constituted a limit on that process as well.[30]

So on one hand we have the properly utopian perspective of a peripheral subject, consciously situated in its own debilitating relationship to First-World capital, whose horizon must be that abolition of the center-periphery relationship and ultimately all relations of status and domination. (It is not a mere coincidence that the Brazilian modernist movement and the Brazilian Communist Party—of which Oswald later became a member—were formalized in the same year.) On the other, we find the limited perspective of the peripheral bourgeoisie: of coffee money in Oswald's "aperitivo,"[31] where the euphoric atmosphere derives from coffee prices soaring like São Paulo skyscrapers. A certain affective interference takes place between these two positions. Euphoria ("happiness is the acid test")[32] on the first perspective belongs (for everyone) to the future, while on the second it belongs (for a few) to the present. Brazilian modernism's euphoria slides easily from one to the other.

In a kind of paroxysm of vulgar materialism, we might note that the four competing models postulated by the Brazilian sociologist Octavio Ianni for the dominant configuration of the Brazilian economy at the time of the 1964 coup correspond fairly well to the four aesthetic horizons we have outlined.[33] The classic model of "export"—that is, of raw materials—corresponds more or less to the option of producing "authentic" regional art, while the imitative option—the simple adoption of the "finished product" of metropolitan cultural commodities—conforms to the model of full integration with northern capital, the option ultimately imposed by the military dictatorship. Meanwhile, there are two active possibilities in the economic realm, which correspond to the two interpenetrating aesthetic solutions in the manifestos examined above. One is nationalist import substitution, which, as we saw in the introduction, is the more or less spontaneous strategy of the anti-imperialist bourgeoisie. This strategy corresponds to peripheral vanguardism, while the second option, socialism proper, corresponds theoretically to the third-worldist aesthetic solution. In practice, however, just as cultural production tends to blur the distinction between the two latter aesthetic possibilities, the political configuration of pre-coup Brazil tended to oscillate between or conflate the two latter economic options. It should be emphasized, moreover, that the structural correlation between the economic and cultural levels does not mean that one directly entails the other in any personal or public ideology; the point is that the overall formation of aesthetic choices is governed by the field of possibilities generated by tactical compromises between the incompatible positions associated with either capitalist import substitution or socialism.

As we saw in the introduction, import substitution tends to benefit the local owners of capital, and this applies to cultural as well as directly economic capital. Thus the confusion on the part of cultural producers between the utopian anticapitalist desire to engage the creativity of the multitude and a less generous impulse to compete with their First World counterparts is more or less spontaneous. This relatively benign confusion at the level of aesthetic ideology conforms rather precisely—to jump abruptly into a third, political register—to the asystematic development of Brazilian populism described in Ianni's *O Colapso do Populismo no Brasil*.[34] The dominant political configuration in postwar Brazil before the 1964 coup was an alliance between the Left and the "progressive"—that is, urban and industrial—nationalist bourgeoisie. Even the Communist Party endorsed the strategy of import substitution and identified only two contradictions at the heart of Brazilian society, neither of which is the classic contradiction between labor and capital: the conflict between Brazilian national development and U.S. imperialism, and that between industrial progress and the problem of land monopoly.[35] (In fact, the second conflict is a corollary of the first, since both depend on the question of whether the national economy is to center on industrial production or raw material for export.) As Ianni makes clear, not only did this configuration not have a systematic expression, "structuring itself through chance occurrences, through victories and obstacles,"[36] but it could not have had one, since the interests it balanced in uniting the proletariat, the middle classes, and the industrial bourgeoisie were fundamentally incompatible.

All of this is legible—to bring us back full circle—in the aesthetic ideology of bossa nova, for which the dual imperatives to be "popular" and "for export" are not easily coordinated: a genuinely popular audience at home has little in common with bossa nova listeners in the United States. The impulse to join technical elaboration with popular appeal that we have been seeing in the Brazilian arts corresponds to the claim by development populism to be expanding the national means of production via import substitution while at the same time mobilizing them in the interests of the many. (In fact, real material gains were illusory for most.)[37] We can see signs of the populist elision of class conflict in the slight note of illegitimacy we detected in bossa nova lyric. Populism rests on a conflation of the interests of labor and capital into a single, mythical entity: in Roberto Schwarz's words, "an apologetic and sentimentalizable notion of the 'people,' which embraced without distinction the working masses, the lumpenproletariat, the intelligentsia, national industrial magnates, and the army."[38] This pathos of the people emerges in bossa nova, where the position of poverty is taken up by the lyrical voice, but always with a distance, with a benign but ever-present irony. The perspective of the poor is taken up lightly, as though there were no difference between a poor northeasterner and a wealthy resident of Rio—but the difference is maintained nonetheless.

The foregoing sketch attempts to give an account of the relationship between political and economic options and aesthetic ideologies in the Brazilian 1950s. The 1960s tended toward a polarization and coming-to-consciousness of these positions. While the populist configuration more or less absorbed the energies of the Left, the former was of course itself not impervious to pressure from what it had absorbed. The early 1960s saw a tremendous polarization in Brazilian politics, and the Goulart administration seemed to be gravitating toward the socialist alternative.[39] The reasons for this polarization are too complex to enter into here, but it corresponded to the alternatives presented by an emerging economic crisis. As Immanuel Wallerstein has demonstrated, the strategy of import substitution has inherent limitations having to do with its ultimate reliance on imported technology.[40] Despite the symbolic victory of producing new (aesthetic) technologies for export in the form of concrete poetry and bossa nova, Brazil had apparently exhausted the cycle of expansion and faced an untenable debt situation, an economic crisis that led to high inflation and political crisis. Brazil faced a radical alternative: further integration with foreign capital along lines that are familiar today, or a dramatic reorganization of property relations.[41] The Left, having been successful at influencing the existing political configuration, by and large did not take into account the opposition a radical program would face from the "progressive" industrialists and the national bourgeoisie, whose interests naturally did not favor the radical restructuring of property. As can be seen from the Brazilian Communist Party platform cited above, the Left mistook the means—alliance with these progressive elements—for ends in themselves. Partly because they believed, with apparently good reason, that socialism could be imposed from within the existing political configuration, the Left was unable to organize a viable political subject. The failure resulting from this historical error was complete—the military coup met virtually no resistance and indeed appeared to have the support of many sectors of Brazilian society among which the Left had failed to make distinctions.

Before we become immersed in the particularity of this situation, however, we should emphasize once again that what happened in the coup of 1964 was not unique to Brazil; rather, the Brazilian case is a particularly dramatic instance of a global phenomenon of the end of a political modernism grounded in great utopian projects: from the disappointment that followed the apparent seizing of historical initiative by the African independence movements to the dissipation of the First World 1960s countercultures into the "commodified dissent" of alternative lifestyles.[42] The ultimate horizon of the moment we are discussing, in other words, is the turning of the cold war toward the consolidation of a U.S.-led market hegemony, globalization as it is currently understood. What followed the coup was the complete collapse of development populism, along with economic nationalism and the aesthetic ideology that went along with it. For while the technical imperative persisted, the coup reinstated, with a vengeance, the antinomy that this ideology had symbolically overcome and which Brazilian populism itself claimed to be overcoming. For while the military regime was interested in "modernizing" the national means of production, it was plainly unconcerned with the imperative that this expansion be "for everyone."

Roberto Schwarz's insights into this cultural and political nexus are so fundamental that it may not be too much to insist that little consequent can be said about this historical moment outside the framework he constructs.[43] Schwarz's sweeping critique of Brazilian culture during the first years of the dictatorship reveals how profoundly the coup affected the arts. The situation of architecture is emblematic: Brazilian architects, whose formation had been centered around a collectivist, utopian modernism, suddenly had nothing better to do than build single-family houses. The ends being completely out of proportion to the means, the result was architecture ill-suited for living in: formerly "rational" design principles were turned either into a mere sign of good taste or a moralistic symbol of abstract revolution. (This way of putting things implies a value judgment, completely justified in its context, but in a more general sense it is clear that this evacuation of utopian content is the very prototype of the transition from an avant-garde aesthetic economy to postmodern transavantgardism. The current trend toward a "nice modernism" in domestic U.S. architecture, in evacuating everything that would defamiliarize or disturb bourgeois family life, domesticates a transition that is still legible as monstrous and violent in the years following the coup.) Schwarz has similarly important things to say about Tropicália, which we will return to in a moment, but he reserves his most detailed analysis for the theater.[44]

Simplifying Schwarz's discussion a great deal, we might say that there are essentially two possibilities. The first is represented by the Augusto Boal's Teatro de Arena, whose dominant influence, like Ngugi's theater experiments discussed in the previous chapter, was the Brechtian *Lehrstück*.[45] As with the architectural instance (indeed, as with Ngugi's work), the *Lehrstück* techniques, developed in the context of imminent revolution, undergo a certain deformation in the context of the immediate aftermath of a failed one. Indeed, to put it in overly brutal terms, the Brazilian cultural elite, though sincere in its Left politics and opposition to the coup, was "objectively" on the side of the coup, since it failed to take account of the way in which its own class interests coincided with the populist elision of class conflict: "The defeated Left triumphed, without critique, in front of a full house, as though its defeat had not been a defect."[46] Revolutionary artistic technique becomes, at best, a reproduction of the problems inherent in Left populism and at worst a consumable sign of the audience's innocence. It hardly needs to be said that the pleasure of this experience gives the lie to the innocence.

On the other hand we have José Celso Martinez Corrêa's Teatro Oficina, which is more directly relevant to the new music of the period: the military police, at least, gave their association with the Oficina group as a (probably bogus) reason for the imprisonment of Caetano Veloso and his friend and musical collaborator Gilberto Gil, who also had ties with the Arena.[47] The Oficina, particularly its staging of Chico Buarque's *Roda Viva*, represents an entirely different kind of theater experiment based on assault. Grounded in a more critical understanding of the role of the middle classes in the coup, Celso argued that "any understanding between the stage and the house is an ideological and aesthetic mistake."[48] The audience, therefore, is to be insulted by the stage, its habits and choices ridiculed, its very person grabbed by the collar, yelled at, spattered with blood, jostled by actresses fighting in the aisles over a raw ox liver (representing the heart of a television celebrity), jeered out of the theater if they show any resistance. The surprising thing—also the problem—is that the audience enjoys the image of its own humiliation: the show is a tremendous commercial success. But we are not dealing here with simple masochism. In fact, something more sinister appears to be taking place: the audience

> identifies with the aggressor, at the expense of the victim. If someone, after being grabbed, leaves the theater, the satisfaction of those who stay is enormous. The disintegration of solidarity in the face of the massacre and the disloyalty created in the midst of the audience are absolute, and repeat the movement initiated on the stage.[49]

Does it need to be said that that movement initiated on the stage, in turn, repeats the movement of society at large?

There are two ways of evaluating these thoroughly ambiguous experiments. The criterion of the first would be overcoming the contemplative attitude inherent in the "aesthetic principle" in favor of the political value of class consciousness.[50] From this perspective the minimal political cohesion maintained by the Arena productions is preferable to the thoroughgoing "disintegration of solidarity" in the Oficina. The criterion of the second is truth: Adorno's famous "windowless monad," which embodies societal structures without necessarily representing them.[51] In this view the Arena approach becomes simply a lie—the continuation of a Left populist ideology after the point when the illusion that sustained it has ceased to be grounded in appearances—while the Oficina productions, in all their brutality, in fact forecast the actual brutality of the dictatorship (the worst of which was yet to come) and general complacency in the face of it. The point here is not to choose between the two. Such a choice, at any rate, could not be absolute but would have to depend on the political situation in which one finds oneself and how one interprets that situation. At the time these plays were produced, when the part to be played by the student Left, which had begun to take an active role, was still open to the future, one might easily favor the first. In the current situation, in which the possibilities for a genuinely critical art seem increasingly restricted and where, in the U.S. context at least, an unprecedented complacency and ersatz innocence dominate in the face of one global horror after another, there are reasons to be attracted to the antisociality of the second.

At any rate, it is in this context that we should understand the most interesting new music of the period, dubbed Tropicália after an installation by Hélio Oiticica.[52] To ears hearing "Panis et Circenses," one of the title songs to the collaborative 1968 manifesto album *Tropicália ou Panis et Circensis*, some three decades after its release, the arrangement will sound derivative (though no more so than many well-respected British and American albums released during the height of the Beatles' popularity). It might be better in this case to think of this as another example of Brechtian *Umfunktionierung*. For example, "Panis et Circenses" begins with a pompous military fanfare that is clearly inspired by George Martin. But while the meaning of this sort of pastiche is left rather vague in the Beatles' context, deflating older official culture that suddenly seems dated and laughable, in the context of military dictatorship "official culture" takes on a more pointed significance. The title of the song itself refers to "bread and circuses," Juvenal's assessment of what it took to maintain the complacency of the Roman citizenry. The arrangement, imitating circus music, is as rhythmically square as it is possible to be. The misspelling of the Latin reference on the album cover, whether intentional or not, gives a certain parochial air to this particular circus:

PANIS ET CIRCENSES

Eu quis cantar
Minha canção iluminada de sol
Soltei os panos sobre os mastros no ar
Soltei os tigres e os leões nos quintais
Mas as pessoas na sala de jantar
São ocupadas em nascer e morrer.

Mandei fazer
De puro aço luminoso punhal
Para matar o meu amor e matei
As cinco horas na Avenida Central
Mas as pessoas na sala de jantar
São ocupadas em nascer e morrer.

Mandei plantar
Folhas de sonho no jardim do solar
As folhas sabem procurar pelo sol
E as raizes procurar procurar
Mas as pessoas na sala de jantar
São ocupadas em nascer e morrer.[53]

I tried to sing
My sun-illuminated song
I unfurled the sails on the masts in the air
I unleashed the tigers and the lions in the backyards
But the people in the dining room
Are busy being born and dying.

I had them make
A dagger of pure luminous steel
To kill my love with and I did
At five o'clock on Central Avenue
But the people in the dining room
Are busy being born and dying.

I had them plant
Dream leaves in the manor garden
The leaves know how to search for the sun
And the roots to search to search
But the people in the dining room
Are busy being born and dying.

The atmosphere of the arrangement—the entire weight of contemporary recording techniques, the participation of hip avant-garde composers, the use of
tape montage, and so on, brought to bear on a rather insipid little melody, ending
on an anticlimactic authentic cadence, performed in a deliberately stilted fashion—can be read as a specific allegory of a dictatorship that was technically and
economically "modernizing" but mobilized the most "backward" and provincial
elements of the petty bourgeoisie in its support (sundering, in effect, what the
aesthetic ideology of the 1950s had attempted to align). In this context the contempt for bourgeois family life in the first verse is deliberately facile; we are led
to expect a routine denunciation of bourgeois philistinism that would be equally
incisive (that is, not incisive at all) today or a hundred years ago. Indeed the whole
song can be heard in that vein, but the second stanza suggests something much
more wily and sinister, as more than a hint of malice creeps into the singers'
voices and the meaning of the refrain switches polarity. The "I" of the lyric is no
longer an artist lamenting the ignorance of the bourgeoisie but a murderer taking
advantage of it. Suddenly the people in their dining rooms are no longer philis-
tines in the abstract but are of a particular moment when the Brazilian petty
bourgeoisie, mobilized by the dictatorship, closed its eyes and began to join "Family Marches with God for Liberty." The second "I," however, is not marked as
distinct from the first one, so this second, murderous "I" for whom anything is
permitted as long as the peace of dining rooms is not disturbed reflects back on
the first "I," the artist. It cannot have escaped the composers of the song their
own spectacles were (like the Oficina performances) increasingly circus-like, and
of course the album itself is called "bread and circuses"—it, too, is part of what
is required to keep people in their dining rooms. (Caetano Veloso has referred to
pop music generally as "our bread and our circus.")[54] Nobody here is innocent.
Apropos of this Tropicalist effect, which exposes dated, tacky, conservative content
to "the white light of the ultra-modern," Schwarz remarks that it is "like a family
secret dragged into the street."[55]
    The fusion of archaic, "retrograde" elements with modern ones as an allegory
of the dictatorship is a subset of a more general technique in which emblems of
the residual, the actual, and the emergent are thrown together, apparently willy-
nilly. Formally, this is indistinguishable from the "grab bag or lumber room of
disjointed subsystems and random raw materials" that characterize the work of
art in Jamesonian postmodernism.[56] However, here the raw materials are never
quite random, just as the Brazilian concretists never quite succeed in producing
pure linguistic experiments (not that this makes Brazilian concrete poetry inferior
to its European counterpart—quite the opposite). In semiperipheral cultural pro-

duction this kind of juxtaposition is more or less immediately given geopolitical content, since the very texture of everyday life on the semiperiphery consists in the absolute contemporaneity of the residual and the emergent (the integration of Brazil into the world economy via the coffee industry, for example, both maintained quasi-feudal social relationships in the countryside and required a certain level of industrial development in the cities).[57] As with the example of the introductory fanfare cited earlier, so with the McCartneyan juxtaposition of decadent, provincial music hall entertainment with avant-garde studio technique that characterizes the rest of the song: a relatively contentless pastiche in certain Beatles arrangements is unavoidably transformed into an allegory of the dictatorship.

A similar phenomenon concerns the incorporation of aleatory elements in music, which in Jameson's analysis are symptoms of a cultural schizophrenia following on the withdrawal of the signified (that is, History) from the paradigmatic First-World subject. The other manifesto song from the *Tropicália* movement, "Tropicália," begins with a legendary found recording in which one of the drummers, unaware of being recorded, throws off a few lines referring to Pero Vaz Caminha's letter to the Portuguese king describing the discovery of Brazil, terminating with the statement, "And the Gauss of the time recorded it." Given the thematics of the song, which we will turn to in a moment, it seems impossible that this recording could have been accidental, but another example lends the legend credibility. A John Cage composition that cues an unprepared radio is performed in Salvador. When the apparatus is switched on, it immediately announces, in a voice familiar to everyone in the audience, "Radio Bahia, City of Salvador."[58] The Tropicalist effect of exposing parochial content to the ironizing effects of postmodern technique is produced by accident; but it is produced nonetheless, as it could not have been in a performance in the United States. The point here is that the very techniques which, in a First-World context, are symptoms of the withdrawal of History (the evaporation of signification as such in the postmodern artwork) turn out to be, in semiperipheral cultural productions (even in spite of themselves), symptoms of History itself.

There is a more radical way of putting this thesis, which is that the meaning retrieved in semiperipheral performance was always there as repressed content in First-World postmodernism. In a different context (but one in which many of the issues at hand resonate), Reiichi Miura has produced a fascinating reading of Japanese translations of Raymond Carver. Haruki Murakami's immensely popular adaptations, ignoring the cultural resonance of such class markers as, for example, buying carpet at Rug City, tend to "bleach out" the class content of Carver's texts. Miura's point is that this "Japanese misunderstanding of Carver is the correct reading," since class in Carver is a matter of local color, a fetishized cultural identity rather than a mappable position in a transformable social space; it is only a potential reader's intuition of this space that might restore a genuinely realist moment to Carver's work.[59] We might speculate, then, that the aleatory element of the Cage piece was in some sense "about" its own insulation from history, from such problems as an "uneven development" that takes its revenge in the laughter provoked by the Bahian performance.

At any rate, the aleatory moment in Veloso's "Tropicália" is followed by two alternating sections. The first section, of extraordinary density and allusiveness, is sung in quasi-recitative over a stately arrangement by Júlio Medaglia. This part of the song has been analyzed by generations of U.S. and Brazilian critics, so we will not examine it too closely here; but it is worth noting that a central element in the allegory, returning us unexpectedly to the question of architecture, repeats the Schwarzian insight: after 1964 the great modernist city of Brasília itself can only seem like an historical abortion: one finally reaches the heart of the "monument on the Central High Plains" only to find a "smiling child, ugly and dead." The second section has more interest for us at the moment. Here the allegorical elements suddenly become much freer, organized in pairs but detached from any explicit context and allowed to mingle with each other in interesting ways, while the music suddenly breaks into an up-tempo, distinctively Brazilian march whose chord structure contains an echo of the two-note *berimbau*. The juxtapositions, extricated somewhat artificially from their context, are as follows:

Viva a bossa sa sa
Viva a palhoça ça ça ça ça

Viva a mata ta ta
Viva a mulata ta ta ta ta

Viva a Maria ia ia
Viva a Bahia ia ia ia ia

Viva Iracema ma ma
Viva Ipanema ma ma ma ma

Viva a banda da da
Carmen Miranda da da da da[60]

Long live bossa
Long live straw huts

Long live the bush
Long live the mulatta

Long live Maria
Long live Bahia

Long live Iracema
Long live Ipanema

Long live [Chico Buarque's] "A Banda"
Long live Carmen Miranda

The peculiar power of these juxtapositions comes, however, not only from the synthetic procedure of jumbling together examples of technical progress and technical backwardness (bossa nova and straw huts), a procedure which is, after all, a rather simple "linguistic trick."[61] Rather, they share a certain distortion of affect from what this juxtaposition would seem to call forth. On one hand, a "family secret dragged into the street"; on the other hand, a certain tolerance and even affection for this situation ("Long live straw huts"), which is, in its brute form outside the poem or lyric, the effect of a poverty one would not actually want to see perpetuated. Once again one is reminded of Jameson's analysis of postmodernism:

> The exhilaration of these new surfaces is all the more paradoxical in that their essential content . . . has deteriorated or disintegrated to a degree surely still inconceivable in the earlier years of the twentieth century. . . . How [can] urban squalor be a delight to the eyes when expressed in commodification[?][62]

But yet again, the Jamesonian answer does not apply here. In the First-World context this affective quirk gives us a clue to a form of subjectivity for which a horizon other than that given in immediate experience is utterly unthinkable. In "Tropicália," however, it marks something quite different, the transposition of a euphoric, utopian possibility—and we have yet to discover to what in Tropicália this euphoria belongs—onto the dystopic present.

The problem is not so different from what we encountered in Oswald de Andrade, where the euphoria of a utopian future bleeds over into the description of a present which is happy only for a few. Far from being randomly jostled together, in *Tropicália*, the juxtapositions of the second section of "Tropicália" are carefully controlled, kept from becoming outright oppositions or antinomies by forcing the terms to slide between certain registers and not enter others. The anonymous Maria does not get to come up against Carmen Miranda, which would bring in another set of questions; bossa nova doesn't get to come up against "A Banda," which would make the song say something definite about Chico Buarque. (In the existing conjunction of Buarque with Miranda, which is the modern, which the obsolete?)[63] Most significant is the distance that separates "Ipanema" and "palhoça." Ipanema is of course a neighborhood in Rio, Iracema (an anagram for America) the Indian heroine of the eponymous nineteenth-century novel by José de Alencar. Other than the Indian name, which is of course significant for more than the rhyme, nothing seems to unite these two, which reside on different levels of discourse: a neighborhood, a fictional character. On the other hand, if Ipanema also reminds us of the famous girl from Ipanema, then we are dealing with two images of Brazilian femininity; if it refers to the title of Jobim's song (and Iracema to the title of Alencar's work), then with two distinctively Brazilian forms of artistic expression. Ipanema can stand for the trace of the indigenous presence, for sophistication, modernity, Brazilian women, or bossa nova; what it can't refer to is "where wealthy people live in Rio," which would bring it in direct opposition to the straw huts where poor northeasterners live. In a sense this marks the ideological limit of "Tropicália" as a poem. In a moment we will consider whether there is some other content to "Tropicália" that is in fact domesticated by these images, even as it lends them its excitement. Meanwhile, when we consider that this image of Brazil is also a commodity on the world market, we find that a fine line separates the Tropicalist stance—which must empty out much of the baleful significance of the contradictions it maps—from its opposite, a rhetoric that presents a contentless "land of contrasts" for the tourist's contemplation.

The Tropicalist strategy reaches its logical endpoint in Veloso's recent—and very beautiful—"Manhatã," which begins from the conceit, discovered in a poem by Sousândrade, of pronouncing "Manhattan" (originally, of course, the name of a Native American group) phonetically in Portuguese, so that it sounds like "Manhatã," which looks like a Brazilian Indian name.[64] The marvelous first verse reads equally coherently on two radically disparate registers. Each word refers at once to both the island of Manhattan nosing into New York Bay with the Statue of Liberty before it, and an Indian "goddess" in the prow of a canoe on the Amazon. Here the juxtaposition is, as it were, absolute: the archaic and the modern do not simply occupy the same space but are somehow identical. What makes this speculative identity between seemingly incommensurate particularities possible is given with remarkable clarity:

Um remoinho de dinheiro
Varre o mundo inteiro, um leve leviatã

A whirlwind of money
Rakes the entire world, a light leviathan

The operative word here, "varrer," means literally "to sweep," but also to erase: the identity of Manhattan and Manhatã is contained in the movement of Capital itself (in its current phase, centered in a Manhattan in whose direction "all the men in the world turned their eyes"), whose intrinsic disequilibrium has always necessitated perpetual expansion and the incorporation or obliteration of noncapitalist modes of production and ways of life—both Brazilian Indians and the original Manhattans, who sold the island for the equivalent of about a pound of silver. But, as with "Tropicália" and Oswald's poetry, the tone of the chorus (simply "Manhatã," which means both New York and the "sweet name of the girl," repeated over and over again) is paradisiacal—appropriate for a certain experience of Manhattan, but not of course for the contemporary Amazon, and indeed the image we get of Manhatã is plainly cognate with Iracema, not with actual Indians.

All this is not to criticize Veloso's poetry; a more strident tone wouldn't make for better politics but worse poetry. (Indeed, Veloso's explicitly political music tends not to be his best.) This syncretism or pastiche—neither of these words, it should be clear, is really adequate to the Tropicalist approach, though both terms are often used to describe it—is an authentic symptom of the semiperipheral condition; it is just that not everyone is in a position to enjoy this symptom. Not that this problem is easily avoided; if the misery of the Amazon is to be aesthetically represented—and of course refusing to represent it would be ideological as well—then it is, at some level, to be enjoyed. A photograph of present-day Yanomami by Sebastião Salgado, explicitly framed by the real issues of the day and projecting a far more correct representational politics, is nonetheless subject to the same critique.[65]

Despite this ideological limitation, Veloso's work embodies a utopian possibility in a way that might serve as a model for postmodern cultural production. The central fact of postmodern culture, one which must be taken into account at the risk of unforgivable irrelevance, is that for aesthetic production today to have any social effectivity whatsoever, it has to be disseminated through existing channels of distribution. Today there are no channels that do not belong immediately to capital; pockets of genuinely unexploitable amateurism or seriousness, if such exist, are strictly irrelevant. This is the question of the transition from the formal to the real subsumption of (cultural) labor under capital. This transition means that cultural production is always directly, not merely eventually, exploited economically, bought and sold so that somebody can turn a profit. In the contemporary situation, therefore, there is no lag between the potentially "critical" moment of a work of art and its appropriation by the market. The old Romantic prejudice against "selling out," treating art as a commodity on the market, is correct as far as it goes: entering the market necessarily involves compromise and conformism. But the alternative is irrelevance. One can hardly be annoyed at Veloso's constant invocations in *Verdade Tropical* of the Market as the horizon of musical practice; he is speaking remarkably honestly about the conditions under which contemporary artists actually work.[66] Thus, when Júlio Medaglia (who could have been working on his arrangement for Veloso's "Tropicália" at the time) proclaimed in 1967 that there simply was no space outside the market and that heretofore the "artist" was equivalent to the "dilettante," leaving significant cultural production henceforth to the professionals, he was saying something that First World theorists would only come to recognize relatively recently.[67] The ambiguities of this position are deep: on one hand, an abandonment of the notion of the solitary genius in favor of collective production and the obligation to be within the reach of everybody; on the other hand, the culture industry as we know it, an acquiescence to the status quo and the abandonment of the vocation of critique. Veloso himself puts it extraordinarily clearly in the interview cited earlier: "On one hand, Music, violated by a new communicational process, is forced into both innovation and slavery; on the other hand, Music protected and impotent".[68] The problem inherent in Concretism now becomes an unavoidable impasse. We all know by now one result of market absolutism (which by now has to be treated as a fact rather than a mere position—which does not mean that it will always be a fact): any genuinely critical art is immediately commodified and turned into its opposite. The space of transcendence with regard to the market, no matter how slim— and for Adorno, who understood this, it was already slim indeed—is essential for the moment of critique. And this space, as Medaglia et al. recognized long ago, and as Veloso clearly always understood, has disappeared to the point that the culture industry now has to produce its own "critical" art simply to meet demand.

But suddenly we find ourselves on the other side of the coin, since this demand exists. In spite of all the ambiguities entailed in the Tropicalist strategy, there is something beyond this in Veloso's music (and a great deal of other music as well) that is much more fundamental than what happens at the level of lyric. It is significant in this regard that the paradisiacal moments in "Tropicália" emerge not only with a change in poetic tone but when the orchestral arrangement recedes in favor of the drum section, when the recitative bursts into a celebratory march. This march, incidentally, is similar to the rhythm Paul Simon uses on some tracks of his *Rhythm of the Saints*.[69] Simon uses the Afro-Bahian percussion group Olodum as raw material without any content of its own—the postmodern gesture par excellence—as a kind of decorative backdrop to his usual world-weary poetry. Compositionally, the drum section might as well be a single instrument. In Veloso's "Tropicália," on the other hand, this rhythm is used precisely for its own content, the collective joy embodied in the synchronized performance of the drum section. The opposition to focus on at the moment, however, is that between the collective bodily impulse of this march, which is potentially "for everyone," and a poetic gesture that binds this pleasure to the specificity of a class position. The former gives us a clue to the utopian content of Veloso's music, while the latter brings us back to the corrosive ironies of "Panis et Circenses." One might hazard a reading of the title of the album *Tropicália ou Panis et Circensis* here in which the word "or," rather than separating two synonyms, offers a real alternative: on one hand, the dystopian lyrical genius of the Tropicalist image, whose pleasure can only be experienced from a privileged position; on the other hand, an engagement with the creativity of the multitude that represents a real utopian possibility within Tropicália.

Even if culture is now immediately a commodity, it is not a commodity in the abstract but has specific qualities. If the export of Hollywood films is also the export of U.S. comportment, gestures, and consumption habits, then we have to ask a different set of questions about the circulation of musical culture. We suggested in the previous chapter that musical form is related in an intimate way to social form, to the integration of individual bodies into a social body. But the truly radical thing we found in Don Ihde's phenomenological approach to musical form is that it eschews the problematic of representation altogether; as we saw, "*involvement* and *participation* become the mode of being-in the musical situation."[70] Music, rather than representing social form, *is* such form, in the form of a "call" to a possible future. Rather than saying, then, that music itself allegorizes the future, which is a strange thesis if an attractive one, we might say that it embodies the desire for an organization of the social body that does not yet exist. Surely the content of this desire in the music we have been addressing is a value Veloso invokes often: "convivência," conviviality in a very strong sense, universal intimacy.[71] The very opposite of the liberal "tolerance" supposedly fostered by the market itself—which entails precisely a reinforcement of the boundaries between people—such universal intimacy is to be found virtually nowhere in contemporary culture except immanently in musical form and, concretely, in certain kinds of musical performance. The content of the mass music that emerged in the last century—even the worst of it—is precisely this intimacy. The role of the "conscious artist" in this scheme is, in quasi-Brechtian fashion, to refine this content and give it back to us. In order that this "giving back" be as nearly possible "for everyone," the existing channels of distribution must be exploited as fully as possible—which of course involves compromise both with the media themselves and with Capital in the form of marketing niches and so on. And it must not be forgotten that on the economic side this process is none other than our old cultural imperialism, profit derived from the privatization of communal knowledge. Nonetheless we are concerned at the moment to emphasize the desire upon which this process is parasitical. Veloso's omnivorous appropriation of musical forms has been seen in terms of pastiche in the precise Jamesonian sense, with the waning of a parodic impulse that in modernism still had the force of conviction.[72] Although this claim is based on an interesting observation, it is, on the perspective being developed here, precisely wrong. It is true that despite camp expectations there is no irony in Veloso's appropriations of, for example, Carmen Miranda, Vicente Celestino, or late-period Michael Jackson, any more than there is in his composition of bossa novas or trio eléctrico music or Gilberto Gil's distillations of regional forms like the xote or baião.[73] But this is not because they have become mere raw material; on the contrary, what Veloso preserves and distills is the collective joy that is their most essential content.

Let there be no mistake: the kind of immanent desire described here is not political; at best, it is proto-political. For this immanent desire to become political it must, at some crisis point, condense into a position of transcendence. As with the final pages of *A Geração da Utopia*, the current configuration is thoroughly ambivalent. The collective joy to which we are called by this music—a joy which, again, is virtually nonexistent outside of musical practice—is constrained by the media apparatus even as its potential is magnified by it. More often than not it is reduced to an anodyne simulacrum of itself; but its emphatic realization would be Utopia. This ambivalence is not to be overcome without overcoming what determines it. The argument of these final pages is not that music is already in itself a transformative practice, but that music, better than any other medium, embodies the utopian impulse that persists in our postmodern era. In this book on literature and music, we have not even come near to a suggestion of how this Utopia might be brought into being, how the creativity of the multitude might be fashioned into a political subject. As this book is being written the overabundance of human labor power in relation to the needs of capital is beginning to make itself felt in the dominant economies. This crisis may be overcome quickly and, for some, relatively painlessly; or it may expand exponentially the numbers and geographic presence of "monetary subjects without money." In that case, the moment when this question might become urgent might come sooner than we think.

NOTES

CHAPTER ONE

1. It cannot be ignored, meanwhile, that even these genetic relationships occupy a kind of institutional blind spot, to which David I. Ker's *The African Novel and the Modernist Tradition* (New York: Peter Lang, 1997) is a significant corrective, even if its methodology and conclusions cannot be endorsed here. The two sets of texts considered in this book still tend to be opposed along the discredited axis of stylistic innovation versus representational naïveté. Even to ask the question, "What does modernism have to do with African literature?" already presupposes a set of assumptions about literature as such, about modernism, and about African literature that precludes equally fundamental questions that should be turned back on literary study itself: Why should postcolonial literature and literary modernism be isolated in advance? What possibilities are contained by maintaining this boundary? What dimensions of meaning are restricted by the methodological quarantine around each set of texts? Achille Mbembe has memorably pointed out in a different context that this kind of methodological prejudice remains strangely immune to critique: "That such a prejudice has been emptied of all substance by recent criticism seems to make absolutely no difference; the corpse obstinately persists in getting up again every time it is buried and, year in year out, everyday language and much ostensibly scholarly writing remain largely in thrall to [it]" (Achille Mbembe, *On the Postcolony* [Berkeley: University of California Press, 2001], 3). If the hoariest notions of African alterity continue to structure thinking, one has a right to wonder if some material circumstance prevents them from politely receding.

It is tempting to read this persistence in terms of the exclusion of sub-Saharan Africa from the legitimating narratives of market ideology. As a matter of poetry, liberalism's standard metaphor of the global market as a "rising tide that lifts all boats" is patently self-deconstructing, since the tide must be receding somewhere if it is rising here. For the past three decades, poverty in sub-Saharan Africa has increased not only in absolute terms but as a percentage of world poverty, so that the era of globalization is also the era of the "Africanization of world poverty" (see Howard White and Tony Killick, in collaboration with Steve Kayizzi-Mugerwa and Marie-Angelique Savane, *African Poverty at the Millennium* [Washington, DC: The World Bank, 2001], 5, and table 1.2). In fact, "the economic expansion of the post-Second World War period . . . has magnified the economic transfer of surplus from the African periphery to the center far beyond anything that occurred in colonial rule." (Immanuel Wallerstein, "Africa in a Capitalist World," in *The Essential Wallerstein* [New York: The New Press, 2000], 63.) Wallerstein, of course, is not alone in this perspective: the classic texts include Walter Rodney, *How Europe Underdeveloped Africa* (Washington, DC: Howard University Press, 1981), and Samir Amin, *Delinking* (*La déconnexion* [Paris: Éditions La Découverte, 1985]); for a Latin American perspective, see Fernando Henrique Cardoso and Enzo Faletto's work on dependency (*Dependência e Desenvolvimento na América Latina: Ensaio de Interpretação Sociológica* [Rio de Janeiro: Zahar, 1970]). Despite the standard practice of attributing dispiriting statistics to such pathological causes as civil conflict, corruption, or disease (not, of course, straightforward causes of poverty but also effects), even liberal economists like Joseph Stiglitz are waking up to the fact that global capitalism is a rigged and brutal game in which the losers (always the same losers) starve and the winners (always the same winners) take the spoils. Stiglitz's *Globalization and Its Discontents* (New York: Norton, 2002), despite all this, takes the classic liberal position that the system is potentially equitable. Readers of Stiglitz's fundamentally decent text might not be so sure. It may well be, in fact, that capital has reached a level of productivity where it is unable to incorporate the propertyless African masses as labor, incorporating them instead as, in Robert Kurz's phrase, "monetary subjects without money," individuals permanently and systemically redundant to a capitalism that is nonetheless the only existing system for satisfying need. It is this systemically linked "other side" of the global market that must be excluded both from the poetics of liberal apologetics and, by means of the presumption of pathological causes, from the statistical reckoning that supports it.

2. Charles Larson, *The Emergence of African Fiction* (Bloomington: Indiana University Press, 1972); Ayi Kwei Armah, "Larsony: Or, Fiction as Criticism of Fiction," *New Classic* 4 (1977): 38.

3. The "Ana Livia" to whom Armah dedicates *Fragments* is not Joyce's Anna Livia Plurabelle but in fact an actual person named Ana Livia Cordero. Ngugi wa Thiong'o, on the other hand, can be demonstrated to have had an interest in Joseph Conrad as an undergraduate. But the criticism that takes this kind of fact as its point of departure tends ultimately to show up the point of departure as arbitrary. See, e.g., Ker, *The African Novel and the Modernist Tradition*, 75–102.

4. Theodor Adorno, *Aesthetic Theory*, trans. Robert Hullot-Kentor (Minneapolis: University of Minnesota Press, 1997), 19.

5. Paul de Man, "Literary History and Literary Modernity," in *Blindness and Insight: Essays in the Rhetoric of Contemporary Criticism*, 2nd ed. (Minneapolis: University of Minnesota Press, 1983), 165.

6. The most familiar and distinguished example of this genre for a North American audience will be Henry Louis Gates's *The Signifying Monkey: A Theory of Afro-American Literary Criticism* (New York: Oxford University Press, 1988). As remarkable as it is, however, *The Signifying Monkey* does not produce a theory of Black American literature that is notably different from any other kind of literature: "the importance of the Signifying Monkey poems is their repeated stress on the sheer materiality, and the willful play, of the signifier itself" (59). Such statements tell us more about the influence of the French 1970s on the American 1980s than they do about Black American literature. But this is not, of course, to criticize Gates for using the tools at hand. The point is rather that the emphasis on a relatively autonomous "tradition" paradoxically invites a certain blindness to one's own role in producing it.

7. The point of Aijaz Ahmad's critique of the three-worlds vocabulary is well taken, and there is no intention here of resuscitating any of the old uses of these terms that Ahmad emphatically rejects. See Aijaz Ahmad, "Three Worlds Theory: End of a Debate," in *In Theory: Classes, Nations, Literatures* (London: Verso, 1992), 287–318. In this book, the use of "Third World" and related expressions will correspond to the one legitimate use Ahmad allows them, namely as vulgar substitutes for more rigorous language relating the core national economies to those of the peripheral and semiperipheral nations.

8. In English we have Paulin J. Hountondji, "Scientific Dependency in Africa Today," *Research in African Literatures* 21.3 (1990): 5–15, and "Recapturing," in *The Surreptitious Speech: Présence Africaine and the Politics of Otherness 1947–1987*, ed. V. Y. Mudimbe (Chicago: University of Chicago Press, 1992), 238–56; for an overview, see his remarkable philosophical "itinéraire africain," *The Struggle for Meaning: Reflections on Philosophy, Culture, and Democracy in Africa*, trans. John Conteh-Morgan (Athens: Ohio University Press, 2002), especially 223–58, which contains references to the relevant French-language texts.

9. Hountondji, "Recapturing," 248.

10. Chidi Amuta, *The Theory of African Literature: Implications for a Practical Criticism* (London: Zed, 1989), 3.

11. Hountondji, "Recapturing," 248.

12. Johann Wolfgang von Goethe, *Essays on Art and Literature*, ed. John Gearey, trans. Ellen von Nardroff and Ernest H. von Nardroff (New York: Suhrkamp, 1986), 228. Another collection (see note 14) dates the fragment to 1830.

13. See David Damrosch's elegant exploration of the Goethean invention of *Weltliteratur* in *What Is World Literature?* (Princeton: Princeton University Press, 2003).

14. Johann Wolfgang von Goethe, *Goethe's Literary Essays: A Selection in English*, ed. J. E. Spingarn (New York: Frederick Ungar, 1964), 99.

15. Karl Marx, *The Communist Manifesto*, trans. Samuel Moore, ed. Frederic L. Bender (New York: Norton, 1988).

16. Sayyid Abdallah bin Ali bin Nasir, *Al Inkishafi* [Revelations], composed around 1810, trans. William L. Hichens as *Al-Inkishafi: The Soul's Awakening* (Nairobi: Oxford University Press, 1972). The point is that vigilance with regard to the specificity of the concept of literature must be maintained even when referring to a society that plainly does have its own authorized tradition of letters. It should be apparent that it would be no less violent to read the *Inkishafi* as, say, anthropological or historical evidence.

17. Neil Lazarus, *Nationalism and Cultural Practice in the Postcolonial World* (Cambridge: Cambridge University Press, 1999).

18. Karl Marx, *Grundrisse: Foundations of the Critique of Political Economy*, trans. Martin Nicolaus (New York: Penguin, 1993), 408.

19. It must be understood that for the purposes of exposition this process has been greatly oversimplified. Two theses, only apparently contradictory, can be derived from the *Grundrisse* section mentioned here. First, *capitalism always comes from elsewhere*; second, *capitalism is indigenous everywhere*. There is neither any pure capitalist space nor any purely noncapitalist space. Therefore Capital is *always encroaching*, even in the capitalist "West," as it infiltrates as yet uncommodified aspects of social life. But it is also always, as Deleuze and Guattari have pointed out, already everywhere, as the specific nightmare of every social formation that produces social inequalities—that is to say, every social formation. As any number of postcolonial narratives attest, this is precisely Capital's colonizing power. Therefore, each development of capitalism is absolutely idiosyncratic; but this does not make Capital any less universal.

20. At the World's Columbian Exposition of 1893 in Chicago, living Native Americans were displayed in glass cases. The practice is shocking enough in itself, but what is telling about this particular example—something Astrid Boeger has called "extermination by representation" (" 'Did it pull or did it push?' The World's Columbian Exposition and the [Uncertain] Power of Representations" [lecture, University of Illinois at Chicago, February 21, 2003])—is that they were displayed in the prehistory exhibit.

21. What this ignores is that the Taliban's expressed motivations are totally false. What is fundamental in religious fundamentalism is not religion at all but the political instrumentalization of religion—a strategy pursued by the United States in a number of contexts.

22. Ato Quayson makes an important defense of the dialectic in the introduction to his *Calibrations: Reading for the Social* (Minneapolis: University of Minnesota Press, 2003), xi–xl. The approach is rather different than the one taken here but similar in spirit. Quayson is determined to "abandon the unidirectional binaristic fictions of the dialectic" (xxxii). Since the interpretation of Hegel undertaken here centers on the generative power of the negative rather than on positivizing the transitory binaries that it produces, I have been less explicitly concerned with this problem, which I believe the current approach silently resolves.

23. Fredric Jameson, "Third World Literature in the Age of Multinational Capitalism," *Social Text* 15 (1986): 65–88.

24. Not all of the general criticism was fair, however; even in Ahmad's essay the ambiguous but important words "to be read as" are at key moments left out of Jameson's notorious formulation. As such a careful reader of Jameson should have known, Jameson uses allegory primarily to name a practice of reading, not of writing. The excision of "to be read as" (or of their content, which became nearly universal in subsequent criticism of the essay) distorts Jameson's meaning entirely, converting what was quite explicitly framed as an intervention into the way First-World readers are asked to confront Third-World texts— "a new conception of the Humanities in American education today" (75)—into an empirical claim about the texts themselves: a claim so immediately absurd as hardly to merit refutation. On the other hand, it cannot be denied that this misreading is, in a sense, internal to the essay itself: the very ambiguity in the grammar of "to be read as"—by whom? why?—as well as some casual empirical claims about psychic and social life under colonialism, suggest a temptation to which Jameson is not immune. See Aijaz Ahmad, "Jameson's Rhetoric of Otherness and the 'National Allegory,' " in *In Theory*, 95–122. It is tempting to imagine that the twenty-year-old Jameson-Ahmad "debate" is over, but recent exchanges suggest otherwise. See Imre Szeman, "Who's Afraid of National Allegory?" *South Atlantic Quarterly* 100.3 (summer 2001): 803–27, and Silvia López, "Peripheral Glances: Adorno's *Aesthetic Theory* in Brazil," in *Globalizing Critical Theory*, ed. Max Pensky (New York: Rowman and Littlefield, 2005). López's article, like Ahmad's, contains several important critiques of "Third World Literature in the Age of Multinational Capitalism," touching on real weaknesses in the argument for "national allegory," but I still cannot help but feel that these critiques fail to touch on the heart of the matter. Ato Quayson easily admits all of the problems with Jameson's essay while still offering a circumspect defense of what is essential in it in "Literature as a Politically Symbolic Act," in *Postcolonialism: Theory, Practice, or Process?* (Cambridge: Polity, 2000), 76–102, especially 84–86. My thinking on Jameson's essay has benefited greatly from conversations with Szeman, López, and Maria Elisa Cevasco.

25. Ahmad, *In Theory*, 104, 102, 85.

26. See Fredric Jameson, "On Interpretation: Literature as a Socially Symbolic Act," in *The Political Unconscious* (Ithaca: Cornell University Press, 1981), 17–102. In this regard it is also useful to remember that the concept of national allegory was originally invented to describe a possibility intrinsic to modernism. For the original sense of "national allegory," see Fredric Jameson, *Fables of Aggression: Wyndham Lewis, or the Modernist as Fascist* (Berkeley: University of California Press, 1979). This "national" specification of "social allegory," while not essential to the main line of Jameson's argument, is in fundamental agreement with a whole range of writings by Jameson's African contemporaries on the Left. It is important to remember that the larger context for Jameson's essay includes an astonishing surge of Marxist literary criticism in Africa—in the Anglophone context alone one thinks of the remarkable convergence of publications in the mid-1980s by Biodun Jeyifo, Grant Kamenju, Chidi Amuta, Omafume Onoge, Emmanuel Ngara, and of course Ngugi wa Thiong'o, among others—to say nothing of a whole earlier generation of Third-World theorists of imperialism (often political leaders themselves) for whom Marxism was quite simply the medium in which thinking was done, and with whom Jameson is of course intimately familiar. (See V. Y. Mudimbe, *The Invention of Africa: Gnosis, Philosophy, and the Order of Knowledge* [Bloomington: Indiana University Press, 1988], 90.) For all of these critics (and indeed for many non-Marxist African writers and critics as well) what Jameson had to argue about the relationship of Third-World literature to the politics of

the peripheral nation-state was essentially axiomatic. Phanuel Akubueze Egejuru, in her interesting *Towards African Literary Independence: A Dialogue with Contemporary African Writers* (London: Greenwood, 1980), prompts a number of prominent writers to consider other themes than the ones emerging from the national liberation movements. The resistance is varied but universal: see especially her "Africa, the Only Topic of African Literature," 113–20. In reference to Nigerian literature, Chidi Amuta writes that "even the most rabid imperialist critic cannot deny the *national* stamp of this body of literature" (*The Theory of African Literature*, 66). One might prefer his "African Literature and the National Question" (*The Theory of African Literature*, 61–68) to Jameson's more generalized account, but the two perspectives are substantially complementary. As for our own use of the three-worlds vocabulary, see note 7.

27. For reasons that shall become clear, the formal analysis of canonical modernist texts in our own readings will tend to be most intense at the level of the sentence, while the analysis of African texts will tend to intensify at the level of narrative architecture. As we shall see, this is not a matter of reductionism or a double standard, but rather the necessary methodological adjustment required when investigating two distinct approaches to the narrativization of totality—one in the mode of the sublime, the other in the mode of cognitive mapping.

28. Chinua Achebe, "Colonialist Criticism," in *Hopes and Impediments: Selected Essays* (London: Heinemann, 1988), 68–90. For a sublime example, see Harold Bloom's introduction to the "Modern Critical Interpretations" volume on Achebe's *Things Fall Apart* (Broomall, PA: Chelsea House, 2002), 1–3.

29. See Ahmad, "Marx on India: A Clarification," in *In Theory*, 221–42. One is often confronted by claims that Ahmad's critique of Jameson exposes a tendency toward "Left colonialism" intrinsic to Marxism or to the concept of totality itself—a claim that reproduces so many right-wing denunciations of socialism as a "foreign ideology." Needless to say, Ahmad's actual writings refute this theory on almost every page.

30. See Hegel's derivation of Nothingness from the concept of Being in the lesser logic: "First Subdivision of Logic: The Doctrine of Being," in *Hegel's Logic: Being Part One of the Encyclopaedia of the Philosophical Sciences (1830)*, trans. William Wallace (Oxford: Clarendon, 1975), 123–33.

31. Alain Badiou, *Ethics: An Essay on the Understanding of Evil*, trans. Peter Hallward (London: Verso, 2001), 24.

32. Ibid., 24.

33. The more narrowly literary equivalent of Totality would then be simply Irony in the Brooksian sense. This identification has precedent in Hegel's definition of Socratic irony as "the dialectic in a predominantly subjective shape." See Hegel's *Logic*, 117.

34. Quayson, *Calibrations*, xxxi.

35. Omafume Onoge, "The Possibilities of a Radical Sociology of African Literature," in *Literature and Modern West African Culture*, ed. D. I. Nwoga (Benin: Ethiope, 1978), 94.

36. See Wallerstein, "Africa in a Capitalist World."

37. One would not at all wish here to imply that the more radical choice would have been an easy alternative; quite to the contrary, it would have required a herculean and risky effort of international organization.

38. All this is not to say that the contemporary distaste for Hegel is pointless or plain wrong. As Ernesto Laclau puts it, "the characterization of the whole Hegelian *project* (as opposed to what he actually did) as panlogicist can hardly be avoided" ("Identity and Hegemony: The Role of Universality in the Constitution of Political Logics," in Judith Butler, Ernesto Laclau, and Slavoj Žižek, *Contingency, Hegemony, Universality: Contempo-*

rary Dialogues on the Left [London: Verso, 2000], 60). What is most important here appears between parentheses. For even if the Hegelian dialectic imagines itself as the movement of a closed totality, in practice it unfolds in an *open totality*. (It is this possibility of open totality that is rejected by such explicitly antidialectical thinkers as Michael Hardt and Antonio Negri. It almost goes without saying that, like Hegel, Hardt and Negri are practical dialecticians, even as they vigorously oppose what they perceive as the teleological implications of the dialectic. See Nicholas Brown and Imre Szeman, "The Global Coliseum: On Empire," *Cultural Studies* 16.2 [March 2002]: 177–92.) That is, one moment does not derive purely logically from the previous one, and so on into infinity. Rather, not only does all sorts of contingent and empirical material find its way into the transition, but each so-called synthesis produces a new set of tensions and incoherences. But the field of possibilities at any given moment is not infinite: "the panlogicism is still there, operating as a straitjacket limiting the effects of the rhetorical displacements" (63). But of course, as the South African example demonstrates, the empirical field of possibilities is not limitless either.

We might risk an analogy with the natural sciences. If complexity theory has shown us anything, it is that certain phenomena are literally indescribable in their complexity; there is not even a hypothetical set of equations that could predict the state of an element from one moment to the next. The only way to make sense of the system as a whole is to find an algorithm that resembles its functioning and "run the program" from the beginning. Is this not Marx's method in much of *Capital* and the *Grundrisse*?

39. Samuel Johnson, *Dictionary of the English Language* (New York: AMS, 1967).

40. See Alain Badiou, *Manifeste pour la philosophie* (Paris: Éditions du Seuil, 1989), especially chap. 7, "L'âge des poètes," 49–58. Where English translations are not cited, translations from French, Portuguese, and Swahili will be my own. Particularly in the case of literary works I have erred on the side of literalness over elegance, partly because of my own limitations as a translator and partly because poetic movement is better served by providing the original, with the translation as a key, rather than trying to reproduce such movement in English. Where English translations exist (as noted) they have often been helpful.

41. Philippe Lacoue-Labarthe and Jean-Luc Nancy, *The Literary Absolute: The Theory of Literature in German Romanticism*, trans. Philip Barnard and Cheryl Lester (Albany: SUNY Press, 1988), 37.

42. See, e.g., Michel Foucault, *The Order of Things: An Archaeology of the Human Sciences* (New York: Random, 1970), 313.

43. Ibid., 43.

44. Lacoue-Labarthe and Nancy, *The Literary Absolute*, 17, 15.

45. Ibid., 16.

46. Friedrich Schlegel, *Philosophical Fragments* [*Critical Fragments, Athenaeum* fragments, selections from *Blütenstaub*, and *Ideas*], trans. Peter Firchow (Minneapolis: University of Minnesota Press, 1991); *Ideas* 48.

47. *Athenaeum* fragment 238.

48. *Athenaeum* fragment 67.

49. Georg Lukács, "Reification and the Consciousness of the Proletariat," in *History and Class Consciousness: Studies in Marxist Dialectics* (Cambridge, MA: MIT, 1971), 137. Our discussion of Kant will involve a certain deliberate vulgarization that professional exegetes of Kant would likely not admit. For now, however, it is worth pointing out that the ascription of historical content to the production of the category of the Kantian noumenon is not the same as mistakenly finding content in the noumenon itself.

50. Lukács, "Reification," 139.

51. *Athenaeum* fragment 222.

52. *Athenaeum* fragment 216.

53. Fredric Jameson, " 'End of Art' or 'End of History'?" in *The Cultural Turn: Selected Writings on the Postmodern, 1983–1998* (London: Verso, 1998), 84.

54. The history of the interpretation of the Sublime is a history of radical disjunction. Kant's sublime is wildly eccentric with respect to Hume's, Hegel's with regard to Kant's, Žižek's with regard to Hegel. Lyotard, as we have just seen, has to invert the temporality of the Kantian sublime even as he attempts to keep faith with it. Doubtless we could play this game backward to Longinus. The point is that for reasons unexplored here, in this particular language game idiosyncrasy may be the price paid for consequence.

55. Jean-François Lyotard, "Réponse à la question: qu'est-ce que le postmoderne," *Critique* 419 (April 1982): 357–67. A translation by Régis Durand appears as an appendix to Jean-François Lyotard, *The Postmodern Condition: A Report on Knowledge*, trans. Geoff Bennington and Brian Massumi (Manchester: Manchester University Press, 1984), 71–82. Unless otherwise noted, citations will refer to the English text.

56. Lyotard, *The Postmodern Condition*, 74 (translation modified).

57. Ibid., 79 (translation modified).

58. Ibid., 80, 81.

59. Ibid., 82.

60. Thomas Weiskel, *The Romantic Sublime: Studies in the Structure and Psychology of Transcendence* (Baltimore: John Hopkins University Press, 1976), 3.

61. Immanuel Kant, *Critique of Judgment*, trans. Werner S. Pluhar (Indianapolis: Hackett, 1987), 98.

62. Ibid., 111, 117.

63. As many have noted, the possibility of a "sublime object" does not, strictly speaking, exist in Kant, for whom the Sublime refers only to "the attunement that the intellect [gets] through a certain presentation that occupies reflective judgment" (*Critique of Judgment*, 106). The "sublime object" is therefore shorthand for something like "that object the perception of which gives rise to the sublime feeling."

64. T. E. Hulme, "Romanticism and Classicism," in *Speculations: Essays on Humanism and the Philosophy of Art*, ed. Herbert Read (New York: Harcourt, 1924), 118, 131.

65. T. E. Hulme, "Bergson's Theory of Art," in *Speculations*, ed. Read, 147.

66. Victor Shklovsky, "Art as Technique" (1917), *Russian Formalist Criticism: Four Essays*, ed. Lee T. Lemon and Marion J. Reis (Lincoln: University of Nebraska Press, 1965), 12.

67. See, e.g., *Ideas*, 128.

68. Shklovsky, "Art as Technique," 12.

69. Martin Heidegger, *Being and Time*, trans. John Macquarrie and Edward Robinson (New York: Harper and Row, 1962), 28.

70. James Joyce, *Stephen Hero*, ed. Theodore Spencer (1944; New York: New Directions, 1963), 213.

71. Ezra Pound, "A Retrospect," *Literary Essays of Ezra Pound*, ed. T. S. Eliot (New York: New Directions, 1935), 3.

72. William Carlos Williams, *Paterson*, in *Selected Poems*, ed. Charles Tomlimson (New York: New Directions, 1985), 262.

73. William Carlos Williams, "Prologue to *Kora in Hell*," in *Selected Essays of William Carlos Williams* (New York: Random House, 1954).

74. Kant, *Critique of Judgment*, 113.

75. Stephen jerked his thumb towards the window, saying:

—That is God.
Hooray! Ay! Whrrwhee!
—What? Mr Deasy asked.
—A shout in the street, Stephen answered, shrugging his shoulders.

(James Joyce, *Ulysses* [New York: Random House, 1961], 34.) The fact that *Ulysses* itself ironizes this particular mode of the sublime gesture—a warning that prevents us from repeating the category mistake Deasy makes in this same episode—does not negate the argument that follows but, as we shall see in the next chapter, pushes it onto new terrain.

76. See, for example, *Athenaeum* fragment 234: "It's only prejudice and presumption that maintains there is only a single mediator between God and Man. For the perfect Christian—whom in this respect Spinoza probably resembles most—everything would really have to be [such] a mediator."

77. G.W.F. Hegel, *Phenomenology of Spirit*, trans. A. V. Miller (Oxford: Oxford University Press, 1977) 208.

78. Slavoj Žižek, *The Sublime Object of Ideology* (London: Verso, 1989), 209.

79. See Jacques Lacan, "The Agency of the Letter in the Unconscious or Reason since Freud," in *Écrits*, trans. Alan Sheridan (New York: Norton, 1977). As noted above (note 63) Kant's sublimity is not to be found in objects at all; rather, the attribution of sublimity to objects is only a subreption or misattribution of what rightfully belongs to the supersensible substrate. Hence sublimity, which can be (mistakenly) attributed to literally anything so long as it meets the indefinite criterion of being "suitable for exhibiting a sublimity that can be found in the mind" (99), is particularly suited to metonymic displacement.

80. Franz Fanon, *The Wretched of the Earth*, trans. Constance Farrington (New York: Grove, 1968), 314.

81. Lukács, "Reification," 139.

82. See particularly letters I–IX. This is not the time to go into the details of Schiller's argument, which any short quotation would only caricature. At times (see letter IV) Schiller calls for something like a cultural revolution as a necessary counterpart to any political revolution—an exigency that certain historical revolutions have neglected with disastrous consequences. Nonetheless, the aspect Lukács pointed to is undeniable: "we must continue to regard every attempt at political reform as untimely, and every hope based upon it as chimerical, so long as the split within man is not healed, and his nature so restored to wholeness [of which restoration the 'instrument is Fine Art' (letter IX)] that it can itself become the artificer of the State." Friedrich Schiller, *On the Aesthetic Education of Man: In a Series of Letters*, trans. Elizabeth M. Wilkinson and L. A. Willoughby (Oxford: Oxford University Press, 1967), 45 (letter VII).

83. On one hand: "The revolutionary desire to realize the kingdom of God on earth is the elastic point of progressive civilization and the beginning of modern history. Whatever has no relation to the kingdom of God is of strictly secondary importance in it" (*Athenaeum* fragment 222). On the other: "There is no greater need of the age than the need for a spiritual counterweight to the Revolution and to the despotism which the Revolution exercises over people by means of its concentration of the most desirable worldly interests. Where can we seek and find such a counterweight? The answer isn't hard: unquestionably in ourselves . . . and the harmony of all the hitherto isolated and conflicting sciences and arts" (*Ideas* 41).

84. Gayatri Chakravorty Spivak, *A Critique of Postcolonial Reason: Toward a History of the Vanishing Present* (Cambridge, MA: Harvard University Press, 1999), 388.

85. G.W.F. Hegel, *Lectures on Fine Art*, vol. 1, trans. T. M. Knox (Oxford: Clarendon, 1975), 89.

86. It is worth noting that in Hegel's writings the sublime, through all its mutations, is always the sign of a fundamental contradiction arising from the misapprehension of the Absolute—until this misapprehension is overcome and the sublime is reduced to the arbitrary symbol. See *Lectures on Fine Art*, 1:303–426.

87. See Jameson, " 'End of Art'or 'End of History'?" 85–87.

88. Chinua Achebe, *Arrow of God* (1967; New York: John Day, 1974).

89. G.W.F. Hegel, *Philosophy of Right*, trans. T. M. Knox (London: Oxford University Press, 1967), 10.

90. "[O] destino de um sol é nunca ser olhado." "Os mastros do Paralém," in Mia Couto, *Cada homem é uma raça* (Every Man is a Race) (Rio de Janeiro: Nova Fronteira, 1998), 185.

91. All of this is complicated by the Lukácsian critique of Utopianism, which we shall turn to in our final chapter. Briefly, Utopianism in its negative sense names the will to maintain political desire at an abstract level where everyone can agree, rather than submitting it to the concrete mediation of a political program. But this critique must be historicized. While Utopian desire is not yet political, it is nonetheless the prerequisite for any genuine politics, and in our own moment even this prerequisite threatens to disappear.

92. One thinks of Koomson's final escape through a privy in Armah's *The Beautyful Ones Are Not Yet Born* (Boston: Houghton Mifflin, 1968), but also of Nairobi's shit-lined footpaths in Meja Mwangi's *Going Down River Road* (London: Heinemann, 1976), or of the quasi-existentialist *philosophie de la latrine* of "voidancy" in Wole Soyinka's *The Interpreters* (London: Heinemann, 1970).

93. Neil Lazarus, *Resistance in Postcolonial African Fiction* (New Yaven: Yale University Press, 1990), 123. Lazarus is here speaking of a character in Armah's *Why Are We So Blest?*, but earlier in the book (chap. 2) he makes the point powerfully about the anticolonial messianism of a generation of African intellectuals. While Lazarus tends to emphasize the negative aspect of intellectual Utopianism, its positive side seems important to keep in mind in our own historical juncture, where the possibility of dramatic social change seems more remote than ever. If, as Lazarus suggests, the anticolonial moment structurally could not have also been a genuinely revolutionary one, then of course such messianism, though sincere, is culpable through and through. If, on the other hand—and Žižek's theory that there must always be two revolutions is relevant here—the anticolonial movement represents a missed opportunity, then this culpability is rather more ambiguous. It seems to me that this issue is undecidable.

94. For a similar perspective, see Fredric Jameson, "Periodizing the 60s," *The Ideologies of Theory*, vol. 2 (Minneapolis: University of Minnesota Press, 1988).

95. Michael Hardt and Antonio Negri, *Empire* (Cambridge, MA: Harvard University Press, 2000), and *Multitude: War and Dempcracy in the Age of Empire* (New York: Penguin, 2004), especially section 1.3, "Resistance" (63–95). See also Marx's remarks on the development of technology as reactive response to the demands of labor in *Capital I*.

96. See, e.g., Edward Said, *Culture and Imperialism* (New York: Vintage, 1994), 41, 194, 278. In the light of the quote below from Foucault's *The Order of Things*, Said's insistence that "the imperial experience is quite irrelevant" for Foucault is nearly as surprising as his assertion that Marxism "is stunningly silent on . . . oppositional practice in the empire."

97. Mudimbe, *The Invention of Africa*.

98. Jacques Derrida, "Structure, Sign, and Play in the Discourse of the Human Sciences," in *Writing and Difference*, trans. Alan Bass (Chicago: University of Chicago Press, 1978). See especially page 282: "This moment [of the decentering of European thought] is not first and foremost a moment of philosophical or scientific discourse. It is also a moment which is political, economic, technical, and so forth. One can say with total security that there is nothing fortuitous about the fact that the critique of ethnocentrism—the very condition for ethnology—should be systematically and historically contemporaneous with the destruction of the history of metaphysics."

99. The image itself, from the cover of a 1955 *Paris Match*, can be seen in the catalog for Okwui Enwezor's remarkable exhibition of art and images from the period of the African liberation movements. See Okwui Enwezor, ed., *The Short Century: Independence and Liberation Movements in Africa 1945–1994* (Munich: Prestel, 2001), 180, plate 1. It is worth pointing out that in the essay alluded to (Roland Barthes, "Myth Today," in *Mythologies*, trans. Annette Lavers [New York: Hill and Wang, 1972]) the proletariat—the absent cause of an argument in which the one kind of speech that cannot be mythologized is proletarian speech—is displaced toward the colonies: "Today it is the colonized peoples who assume the full ethical and political condition described by Marx as being that of the proletariat" (148n. 25).

100. Foucault, *The Order of Things*, 377.

101. When Deleuze and Guattari claim, for example, that "Oedipus is always colonization pursued by other means, it is the interior colony, and . . . here at home, where we Europeans are concerned, it is our intimate colonial education" (Gilles Deleuze and Félix Guattari, *Anti-Oedipus: Capitalism and Schizophrenia*, trans. Robert Hurley et al. [Minneapolis: University of Minnesota Press, 1983], 170), it must be understood that "colonialism" here is very far from being merely a metaphor.

102. For an excellent account of the relationship between U.S. cold war foreign policy in the Third World, including in Africa, and the development of "global terrorism," see Mahmoud Mamdani's *Good Muslim, Bad Muslim: America, the Cold War, and the Roots of Terror* (New York: Pantheon, 2004).

103. Dante, "Letter to Can Grande Della Scala," in *Literary Criticism of Dante Alighieri*, ed. and trans. Robert S. Haller (Lincoln: University of Nebraska Press, 1973), 99. The fourfold method comes down to us from Aquinas. See Saint Thomas Aquinas, "Whether Holy Scripture Should Use Metaphors?" *Summa Theologica*, part I, question 1, article 10, trans. Laurence Shapcote, revised, corrected, and annotated in *Basic Writings of Saint Thomas Aquinas*, ed. Anton C. Pegis (New York: Random House, 1945), 1:16–17.

104. Saint Augustine, *On Christian Doctrine*, trans. D. W. Robertson, Jr. (New York: Liberal Arts Press, 1958), 2.6.7.

105. The uniquely treacherous aspect of allegory for the exegete—and what prevents it from becoming coercive for everyone else—is that the attainment of the anagogic meaning in itself does not absolutely arrest the movement of the signifier; allegory can continue to function beyond the officially sanctioned meaning. For example, in syncretic festivals Christian saints also represent relatively autochthonous deities, while in North American slave spirituals the anagogic content was turned back toward the political—back, in other words, toward Exodus.

106. Ibid., 1.36.40.

107. Hegel, *Phenomenology of Spirit*, 47.

108. G.W.F. Hegel, *Philosophy of History*, trans. J. Sibree (Amherst, NY: Prometheus, 1991), 27.

109. It should go without saying that the United States' post-9/11 "awakening into history" is, as Žižek has pointed out, in this sense precisely the opposite: an excuse to go back to sleep, to assume the innocence of a national identity without responsibility for the geopolitical situation that engendered Al Qaeda. (Once again, see Mamdani's *Good Muslim, Bad Muslim.*) With regard to History, it is impossible to tell whether the neoliberal twilight is dusk or dawn.

110. Adorno, *Aesthetic Theory*, 85.

111. Roberto Schwarz, "Machado de Assis não havia sido um escritor importante no pré-64," *Seqüências Brasileiras* (São Paulo, Companhia das Letras, 1999), 235.

112. *Athenaeum* fragment 116. Elsewhere the theory of the project as "fragment of the future" (*Athenaeum* fragment 22) confirms this sense of the literary work as perpetually open to history.

113. Fredric Jameson, "On Interpretation: Literature as a Socially Symbolic Act," in *The Political Unconscious: Narrative as a Socially Symbolic Act* (Ithaca: Cornell University Press, 1981).

114. Slavoj Žižek, *The Fragile Absolute—Or, Why Is the Christian Legacy Worth Fighting For?* (London: Verso, 2000), 2.

115. John Mihevc, *The Market Tells Them So: The World Bank and Economic Fundamentalism in Africa* (London: Zed Books, 1995), 27.

116. See Alain Badiou, *Saint Paul: La fondation de l'universalisme* (Paris: Presses Universitaires de France, 1997).

117. Paul de Man, "Literary History and Literary Modernity," in *Blindness and Insight*, 142.

118. Fredric Jameson, *A Singular Modernity: Essay on the Ontology of the Present* (London: Verso, 2002), 210.

119. Alain Badiou, *L'être et l'événement* (Paris: Éditions du Seuil, 1988). See also Peter Hallward, *Badiou: A Subject to Truth* (Minneapolis: University of Minnesota Press, 2003), especially part 2, "Being and Truth," 81–180.

120. The Event that was *Ulysses* needs no further elaboration. For a discussion of the evental nature of Achebe's appearance, see chapter 5.

121. Abiola Irele, "The Crisis of Cultural Memory in Chinua Achebe's *Things Fall Apart,*" in *The African Imagination: Literature in Africa and the Black Diaspora* (New York: Oxford University Press, 2001), 150.

122. The point of each of our engagements will not be at the level of the canon, even if it would be gratifying to see some of the works discussed here achieve greater currency. In defense of this apparent complacency we can do no better than to cite, once again, Chidi Amuta:

> No apologies need to be offered here for the choice of the same overflogged novels, for the object of radical criticism is a transvaluation of received assumptions, not just to ignore those assumptions or accept them as given. Nor is anything to be gained from such ultra-leftism that consigns proven classics to the trash-can simply because those same works have constituted the favorite punching-bags of bourgeois criticism. Our specific challenge is to offer alternative explanations and interpretations of literary works as concrete aspects of the reality which we badly need to change. (*The Theory of African Literature*, 129)

Meanwhile, there are worse things than oblivion; one would almost rather Kane's *Ambiguous Adventure* fade into obscurity than subsist in its current misread state.

123. Walter Benjamin, "Theses on the Philosophy of History," in *Illuminations*, ed. Hannah Arendt, trans. Harry Zohn (New York: Schocken, 1969), 254.

CHAPTER TWO

1. See Franco Moretti, "The Long Goodbye: *Ulysses* and the End of Liberal Capitalism," in *Signs Taken for Wonders: Essays in the Sociology of Literary Forms* (London: NLB, 1983), 182–208. For the Radek and Lukács commentaries on Joyce, see Karl Radek, "Contemporary World Literature and the Tasks of Proletarian Art," in *Problems of Soviet Literature: Reports and Speeches from the First Soviet Writers' Congress*, ed. H. G. Scott (Westport, CT: Greenwood, 1979), 73–182, and Georg Lukács, *Realism in Our Time: Literature and Class Struggle*, trans. John Mander and Necke Mander (New York: Harper and Row, 1964). For an excellent overview of the Left reception of Joyce, see M. Keith Booker, "Joyce among the Marxists, or, The Cultural Politics of Joyce Criticism," in *Ulysses, Capitalism, and Colonialism: Reading Joyce after the Cold War* (Westport, CT: Greenwood, 2000), 19–37.

2. The hyperbolic destruction of North Central Dublin by the citizen's biscuit-tin at the end of the "Cyclops" episode is of course evocative of the British shelling of Dublin in 1916, but formally this is just another correspondence, no more or less connected to the narrative than the Homeric parallel or numerous other moments that can be read both naturalistically and as anachronistic allusions.

3. Colin MacCabe, *James Joyce and the Revolution of the Word* (New York: Harper and Row, 1979), 13. See chap. 5, "City of Words, Streets of Dreams: The Voyage of *Ulysses*."

4. James Joyce, "Ireland, Island of Saints and Sages," in Ellsworth Mason and Richard Ellman, *The Critical Writings of James Joyce* (New York: Viking, 1959), 166.

5. See, e.g., Vincent Cheng, *Joyce, Race, and Empire* (Cambridge: Cambridge University Press, 1995), particularly chap. 2, "The Gratefully Oppressed: Joyce's Dubliners," 101–27.

6. Enda Duffy, *The Subaltern Ulysses* (Minneapolis: University of Minnesota Press, 1994), 181.

7. Another way of putting this is that we cannot simply accuse the infamous Joyce industry of distorting or effacing the political content of Joyce's work and let it go at that. The Joyce industry was Joyce's invention: everything he wrote, even many of the letters, whoever else they were addressed to, were also addressed to "us," to generations who would encounter Joyce once or repeatedly in an academic setting. Jacques Derrida provides an interesting and nuanced account of this relationship in "Ulysses Gramophone: Hear Say Yes in Joyce," trans. Tina Kendall et al., *Acts of Literature*, ed. Derek Attridge (New York: Routledge, 1992), 253–309. The degree to which external commentary is internal to the work is indexed by the fact, so obvious that it is easily forgotten, that the chapter titles are only given in the commentaries, not in the published text. Further, Joyce, far more than most writers, is the author of his own criticism. This is true not only in the way Joyce's great works demand certain kinds of exegesis with extraordinary imperiousness and resist others with extraordinary implacability, but also quite literally. That Joyce assisted others with their critical commentaries on his work is well-known, and Stuart Gilbert's study, in many ways the germ of subsequent commentaries on *Ulysses*, was directly authorized by Joyce. As a side note, it is worth remarking that the anticolonial thrust of *Ulysses* is sufficiently sublimated to have apparently escaped Gilbert, who had been a colonial judge in Burma. See Patrick A. McCarthy, "Stuart Gilbert's Guide to the Perplexed," in *Re-Viewing Classics of Joyce Criticism*, ed. Janet Egleson Dunleavy (Urbana: University of Illinois Press, 1991), 23. While a concept like the Deleuzian notion of a "minor literature" (see Gilles Deleuze and Félix Guattari, *Kafka: Pour une littérature mineure* [Paris: Minuit, 1975])— both more precise and more open-ended than "postcolonial literature"—goes a long way toward accounting for the formal affinities between, say, Franz Kafka and Amos Tutuola,

and while the "scrupulous meanness" of the language of *Dubliners* might be brought under this sign as well, the ambitions of *Ulysses* plainly lie elsewhere. It should be emphasized, however, that this argument about the limitations of postcolonial criticism refers only to *Ulysses*, not to Irish literature in general. The universal aspirations of *Ulysses* represent one choice among several available to the postcolonial writer. We will return to this problem in detail in the concluding chapter.

8. Seamus Deane, "Joyce and Nationalism," in *James Joyce: New Perspectives*, ed. Colin MacCabe (Bloomington: Indiana University Press, 1982), 168–83.

9. Roberto Schwarz makes this point elegantly in a very different context: "If production for the market permeates the totality of social life, as is proper to capitalism, concrete forms of activity cease to have their raison d'être in themselves; their finality is external to them, their particular form is inessential." Roberto Schwarz, "Tribulação de um pai de família," in *O pai da família e outros estudos* (Rio de Janeiro: Paz e Terra, 1978), 24. Schwarz has produced some of the most important work on the relation of semiperipheral culture to metropolitan capital, and we will turn to it in detail in the conclusion.

10. Fredric Jameson, "*Ulysses* in History," in *James Joyce and Modern Literature*, ed. W. J. McCormack and Alistair Stead (London: Routlege, 1982), 126–41.

11. Moretti, *Signs Taken for Wonders*, 264n. 29.

12. While one can wholeheartedly endorse the observation that *Ulysses* "presents all stylistic choices as partial, arbitrary, and subjective" (in other words, ideological), there is an illegitimate leap between this and the notion that "Joyce presents styles and ideologies as purely formal entities, products of an experiment lacking any motivation and purpose" (Moretti, "The Long Goodbye," 207). The inescapability of ideology, as Moretti well knows, does not imply the equivalence of all ideologies, and while *Ulysses* does tend to project such equivalence in straightforwardly parodic episodes—this is the crux of Eliot's remark that "Oxen of the Sun" "show[s] up the futility of all the English styles" (quoted in Virginia Woolf, *A Writer's Diary* [London: Hogarth Press, 1953], 50)—we certainly do not get the same sense from episodes like "Eumaeus" or "Ithaca" or Molly's soliloquy, any more than we do from any of Joyce's other major works, in which style and content are generally understood to have an intimate relationship. Moreover, Moretti's argument is about pastiche, and—leaving aside the question of whether Joyce's stylistic mimicry is pastiche or still carries the ethical sting of parody—it properly applies only to episodes like "Oxen" (or "Nausicaa" or "Cyclops"), which can be described in that mode. Rigorously speaking, it would apply properly to a book that consisted only of such episodes, since pastiche means something different when it is one possibility among many rather than the absolute horizon of stylistic variation.

13. See Hugh Kenner, *Ulysses* (Baltimore: Johns Hopkins University Press, 1987), 129–31; and Jameson, "*Ulysses* in History," 138.

14. Joyce, *Ulysses*, 734.

15. The references are to Martin Heidegger, "The Question Concerning Technology," trans. William Lovitt (trans. altered by David Farrell Krell), in *Martin Heidegger: Basic Writings* (San Francisco: Harper, 1993), 307–41; and *Being and Time*, trans. John Macquarrie and Edward Robinson (New York: Harper and Row, 1962), section 35 (211–14).

16. Under his breath Stephen convicts the philistine Deasy of the sin of identifying character with author in "Nestor," but then commits the same with a vengeance—without conviction but with serious intent—in the following episode; both, of course, in reference to Shakespeare.

17. For the contrast, see John Henry Raleigh, *The Chronicle of Leopold and Molly Bloom: Ulysses as Narrative* (Berkeley: University of California Press, 1977).

18. See Kenner, *Ulysses*, 46–47.

19. The Gabler edition supplies the answer in a passage added to "Scylla and Charybdis": the word is "love," which demonstrates the point. But the excision of this passage in the older editions is preferable, since it lets us find a more Joycean answer in the name of the pub Stephen suggests in "Oxen of the Sun":

> But as before the lightning the serried stormclouds . . . compass earth and sky in one vast slumber . . . till in an instant a flash rives their centres . . . , so and not otherwise was the transformation, violent and instantaneous, upon the utterance of the Word.
>   Burke's! (422–23)

20. It seems to me that Joyce is quite aware of this. See note 19.

21. Foucault, *The Order of Things*, 377.

22. Heidegger, *Being and Time*, 234.

23. Adorno, *Aesthetic Theory*, 130.

24. Ibid., 127.

CHAPTER THREE

1. Cheikh Hamidou Kane, *L'aventure ambiguë* (Paris: Julliard, 1961). Unless otherwise noted, English citations will refer to Cheikh Hamidou Kane, *Ambiguous Adventure*, trans. Katherine Woods (London: Heinemann, 1972).

2. Examples of each tendency are too numerous to list, but a recent example of interest is J. P. Little's erudite and informative reader's guide, *Cheikh Hamidou Kane: L'aventure ambiguë* (London: Grant and Cutler, 2000). Little thoroughly explores both of these interpretive possibilities but tends not to go beyond them; of particular interest is the way the elements of the text that seem most obviously to engage a "Western" literary tradition— the classical prose style and the form of philosophical dialogue—are forced to provide ethnographic information about "the importance of the word in oral societies" (45).

3. William Faulkner, *The Sound and the Fury* (New York: Random House, 1990), 3.

4. *Ambiguous Adventure* is, however, not without thematic similarity to Joyce: one thinks of the themes of exile and return, of the defamiliarizing power of a cosmopolitan education in Paris, and the semi-autobiographical form as allegory of colonized nation.

5. The reviewer complains that *Ambiguous Adventure* is "parfois trop dissertant, et trop bien écrit, car tout le monde, même *la Grande Royale* y parle un langage de congrès de philosophes." P.-H. Simon, "*L'aventure ambiguë*," *Le Monde*, July 26, 1961, cited in Little, *Kane*, 43.

6. "Monsieur Cheikh Hamidou Kane est interviewé par le Professeur Barthélémy Kotchy," *Études Littéraires* 7.3 (December 1974): 479–80.

7. See Vincent Monteil's introduction to the first French edition and also J. P. Little, "Autofiction and Cheikh Hamidou Kane's *L'aventure ambiguë*," *Research in African Literatures* 31.2 (summer 2000): 72. Little's article is very suggestive on the issue of biographical material in Kane's novel.

8. Jean-Paul Sartre, "Orphée noir," introduction to Senghor, *Anthologie de la nouvelle poésie nègre et malgache de langue française* (1948; Paris: Presses Universitaires de France, 1969), ix–xliv, at xxix.

9. Little informs us that the name Diallobé simply refers back to the protagonist's name, meaning something like "Diallo's people."

10. See, e.g., Abiola Irele, "In Praise of Alienation," in *The Surreptitious Speech*, ed. Mudimbe, 203.

11. While the "existential" aspect of *Ambiguous Adventure* and the theme of death have hardly gone unnoticed, the latter has generally been understood in terms that ignore its function as a guarantee of the former.

12. Heidegger, *Being and Time*, 296–304.

13. The real Heidegger and Kane's fictional hero both point to Descartes as the pivotal moment in Western thought—hardly an unconventional view, but the characterization of this moment as a kind of "fall" from religious to scientific certainty is striking in both contexts.

14. Sartre, "Orphée noir," xxix.

15. Vincent Monteil's introduction to the first French edition quotes Kane as saying that "if Islam is not the only religion of West Africa, it is the most important. It also seems to me that it's the religion of [Africa's] heart." *L'aventure ambiguë*, 6–7.

16. Martin Heidegger, "The Origin of the Work of Art," trans. Albert Hofstadter (trans. altered by David Farrell Krell), in *Martin Heidegger: Basic Writings*, trans. of "Der Ursprung des Kunstwerkes," *Holzwege* (Frankfurt am Main: Vittorio Klostermann, 1957).

17. See, e.g., Theodor Adorno, *The Jargon of Authenticity*, trans. Knut Tarnowski and Frederic Will (Evanston, IL: Northwestern University Press, 1973), trans. of *Jargon der Eigenlichkeit: Zur deutschen Ideologie*, 1964, and Pierre Bourdieu, *The Political Ontology of Martin Heidegger* (Stanford: Stanford University Press, 1991).

18. Heidegger, "Der Ursprung des Kunstwerkes," 58.

19. Adorno, *The Jargon of Authenticity*, 7–13 and passim. In other words, what passes for a relationship to Being is in fact a relationship to the social structure. For example, the historically new and precarious situation of the small farmer with regard to capital and the bourgeois society that maintains him for primarily aesthetic and sentimental reasons is revealed to be the real origin of Heidegger's homely nouns: "The subsidies which are paid to the small farmers are the very ground of that which the primal words of the jargon add to that which in fact they mean" (56).

20. Lilyan Kesteloot, *Les écrivains noirs de langue française: Naissance d'une littérature* (Brussels: Éditions de l'Institut de Sociologie de l'Université Libre de Bruxelles, 1965), 270. See also Mudimbe, *The Invention of Africa*, 137. The *Bantu Philosophy* would be a more apt translation, since Tempels seeks to construct a single philosophical system. Quotations from the English will be taken from Placide Tempels, *Bantu Philosophy*, trans. Colin King (Paris: Présence Africaine, 1959). In making his translation King has gone back to the original Dutch to clarify the French. Where reference to the French helps clarify meaning, quotations will be taken from Placide Tempels, *La philosophie bantoue*, trans. A. Rubbens (Paris: Présence Africaine, 1949).

21. Mudimbe, *The Invention of Africa*, 50.

22. Alexis Kagame, *La philosophie bantu-rwandaise de l'être* (Brussels: Académie Royale des Sciences Coloniales, 1956).

23. Heidegger, *Being and Time*, 51.

24. Martin Heidegger, "The Anaximander Fragment," trans. David Farrell Krell, in *Early Greek Thinking*, ed. and trans. David Farrell Krell and Frank Capuzzi (New York: Harper and Row, 1984), trans. of "Der Spruck des Anaximander," in *Holzwege*.

25. Neither thinker develops an explanation for this "fall," a process of segmentation which, from a Lukácsian point of view, appears as a necessary corollary to the development of the commodity form. The diremption of letter and spirit is a consequence of capital's requirement that the law be strictly calculable.

26. Mudimbe, *The Invention of Africa*, 136.

27. Heidegger, "Anaximander," 28, 32.

28. Ibid., 56.

29. Heidegger, "The Origin of the Work of Art," 149.

30. Aimé Césaire, "Cahier d'un retour au pays natal," in *Aimé Césaire: The Collected Poetry*, ed. Clayton Eshleman and Annette Smith (Berkeley: University of California Press, 1983), 68.

31. One is gratified to discover that this is also the original meaning of "aftermath."

32. Without an analysis of capitalism, however, the essay cannot begin to answer it. Heidegger's resort to a deus ex machina, his gnomic insistence that "only a God can save us," is a symptom of the limitation of the notion of *Gestell*.

33. Heidegger, *Being and Time*, 217.

34. Heidegger, "The Question Concerning Technology," trans. of "Die Technik und die Kehre," 1954.

35. "Ambiguë parce que . . . il est décrit là deux voies possibles de l'humanité." "Monsieur Cheikh Hamidou Kane est interviewé par le Professeur Barthélémy Kotchy," 480.

36. Badiou, *Manifeste pour la philosophie*, 49–58.

37. The best known formulation of this phenomenon is from *Capital*: "It would be possible to write a whole history of inventions made since 1830 for the sole purpose of providing capital with weapons against working-class revolt." Karl Marx, *Capital*, trans. Ben Fowles (New York: Random House, 1976), 1:563.

38. Adorno, *The Jargon of Authenticity*, 65.

39. The German text is Robert Kurz, *Der Kollaps der Modernisierung: Vom Zusammenbruch des Kasernensozialismus zur Krise der Weltökonomie* (Frankfurt am Main: Eichborn Verlag, 1991). Neil Larsen's very helpful gloss is in "Poverties of Nation: *The Ends of the Earth*, 'Monetary Subjects without Money' and Postcolonial Theory," in *Determinations: Essays on Theory, Narrative, and Nation in the Americas* (London: Verso, 2001), 55–56.

40. Diallo's death is "une manière de resoudre les problèmes dont on n'avait pas trouvé la solution ici-bas." Quoted in Little, *Cheikh Hamidou Kane*, 81.

CHAPTER FOUR

1. In Frank MacShane, *Ford Madox Ford: The Critical Heritage* (London: Routledge, 1972), 44–46.

2. The first three chapters, interlarded with Vorticist woodcuts and charcoal drawings, appear in Lewis's first *Blast* (Wyndham Lewis, *Blast I* [1914; New York: Kraus Reprint Corporation, 1967], 87–97), under the novel's original title, "The Saddest Story," and under the name Ford Maddox Hueffer.

3. See Max Saunders, *Ford Madox Ford: A Dual Life* (Oxford: Oxford University Press, 1996), 2:151 and passim.

4. Ford Madox Ford, *The Good Soldier: A Tale of Passion* (1915; New York: Alfred A. Knopf, 1951), 31.

5. Joseph Conrad, preface to *The Nigger of the Narcissus* (1897; Garden City, NY: Doubleday, 1914), ix.

6. Ford Madox Ford, "On Impressionism" (1914), *Critical Writings of Ford Madox Ford*, ed. Frank MacShane (Lincoln: University of Nebraska Press, 1964), 33–55.

7. Joseph Conrad, *Heart of Darkness* (1902), in *Three Short Novels* (New York: Bantam, 1960), 41–42.

8. Chinua Achebe, "An Image of Africa: Racism in Conrad's *Heart of Darkness*," in *Hopes and Impediments*, 5.

9. Joseph Conrad, *Lord Jim* (1900; New York: Norton, 1968), 96.

10. A complete analysis of this dynamic is Fredric Jameson's "Romance and Reification: Plot Construction and Ideological Closure in Joseph Conrad," in *The Political Unconscious*, 206–80.

11. Quoted in MacShane, *Ford Madox Ford*, 47–50.

12. Ford returns the favor. Referring to Dreiser's style, he exclaims, "Damn it all, it *is* fun to see that poor old language, that vehicle for conveying moderated thoughts, having the guts kicked out of it, like a deflated football, over all the fields of the boundless Middle West." In Alfred Kazin and Charles Shapiro, eds., *The Stature of Theodore Dreiser: A Critical Survey of the Man and His Work* (Bloomington: Indiana University Press, 1955), 31.

13. MacShane, *Ford Madox Ford*, 50.

14. Hegel, *Philosophy of Right*, 13.

15. Žižek, *The Sublime Object of Ideology*, 69–71.

16. In this context one might think also of the equally "unthinkable" event of the attack on the World Trade Center on September 11, 2001, which had already registered its presence in the social imaginary on album covers and video games long before September. Though these imaginary prefigurations were no doubt signs of malaise, they had nothing to do with a direct desire for the event to happen; instead, each was a manifestation of the sense that History would eventually erupt into the beautiful dream of American social life. The nostalgia expressed in the U.S. press for the world before September 11 was not, then, for any particular historical past, as much as it was truly wished that the attack had never happened. As Žižek has repeatedly pointed out, the desire registered in the mainstream news media after September 11 was not to wake up to its historical responsibility, but to go back to the sleep of unproblematic national identification.

17. Max Saunders, *Ford Madox Ford: A Dual Life* (Oxford: Oxford University Press, 1996), 1:436.

18. Although Ford pretended to repudiate the new title, I would argue that it is intrinsic to the novel and that the change of title is decisive. The rhetoric Ford uses to suggest a new title in a letter to John Lane (see Sodra Stang, ed., *The Ford Madox Ford Reader* [Manchester: Carcanet Press, 1986], 477) pretends to prefer the original title but in fact defends the new name as final. *The Good Soldier* is a carefully considered irony, not a hasty one at all. He suggests "The Roaring Joke," or "anything you like" as a matter of saving face, of denying Lane any artistic authority over his book. But then he carefully cancels out these pseudo-flippant suggestions with a third "that might do," and then shuts down the possibility of any better title: "it is all I can think of." Further, "The Good Soldier" has allusive significance: Saunders reminds us of a particularly apt exchange in *Much Ado About Nothing* ("And a good soldier too, lady." "And a good soldier to a lady, but what is he to a lord?"), and Mark Schorer, in "*The Good Soldier*: An Interpretation" (in Richard Cassell, ed., *Ford Madox Ford: Modern Judgments* [London: MacMillan, 1972]), finds in the title a reference to one of Ford's models, Maupassant's *Fort comme la mort*. And, of course, Edward Ashburnham is referred to early in the book as "a first-rate soldier" (11), then again, twice, in a passage that precisely amplifies the irony of the new title, "a good soldier" (26, 27).

19. Ford Madox Ford, *Parade's End* (1924–28; New York: Alfred A. Knopf, 1950), 366.

20. Adorno, *Aesthetic Theory*, 301.

21. Richard M. Ludwig, ed., *Letters of Ford Madox Ford* (Princeton: Princeton University Press, 1965), 73.

22. Max Horkheimer and Theodor W. Adorno, *Dialectic of Englightenment*, trans. John Cumming (New York: Continuum, 1996), 78.

23. For an account of the transformation of British rural life in the first half of the twentieth century, see Pamela Horn, *Rural Life in England in the First World War* (New

York: St. Martin's Press, 1984), and Jonathan Brown, *Agriculture in England: A Survey of Farming, 1870–1947* (Manchester: Manchester University Press, 1987).

CHAPTER FIVE

1. Georg Lukács, *The Historical Novel*, trans. Hannah Mitchell and Stanley Mitchell (Lincoln: University of Nebraska Press, 1983).

2. Chinua Achebe, *Things Fall Apart* (1958; New York: Knopf, 1992); Achebe, *No Longer at Ease* (London: Heinemann, 1962); Achebe, "An Image of Africa," 1–20. The essay was first delivered as a lecture in 1975.

3. C. L. Innes and Bernth Lindfors, introduction to *Critical Perspectives on Chinua Achebe*, ed. C. L. Innes and Bernth Lindfors (Washington, DC: Three Continents, 1978), 5.

4. See, e.g., D. O. Fagunwa, *The Forest of a Thousand Daemons: A Hunter's Saga*, trans. Wole Soyinka (London: Nelson, 1968), trans. of *Ogboju ode ninu igbo irunmole*.

5. See Nwankwo's *Danda* (London: Andre Deutsch, 1964), Nwapa's *Efuru* (London: Heinemann, 1966), or Agunwa's *More than Once* (London: Longmans, 1967). None of these is purely imitative, but there can be little doubt that *Things Fall Apart* was a necessary condition of their possibility.

6. This is such a common tendency that it does not seem necessary to cite examples, except perhaps Robert M. Wren's fascinating *Achebe's World* (Washington, DC: Three Continents, 1980), which often begins from terms of correct representation but takes these issues in interesting directions.

7. G. T. Basden, *Niger Ibos: A Description of the Primitive Life, Customs, and Animistic Beliefs, &c., of the Ibo People of Nigeria by One Who, for Thirty-Five Years, Enjoyed the Privilege of Their Intimate Confidence and Friendship*, 2nd ed. (New York: Barnes and Noble, 1966).

8. Joyce Cary, *Mister Johnson* (New York: Harper and Brothers, n.d. [1951]).

9. Quayson, *Calibrations*, 142.

10. Achebe, *Arrow of God*.

11. Bernth Lindfors, ed., *Conversations with Chinua Achebe* (Jackson: University Press of Mississippi, 1997), 138.

12. Our own analysis of *Arrow of God* will run in parallel with Irele's sensitive discussion of *Things Fall Apart* in several places: from his identification of Achebe's intuition of history as the core of his genius, to the perception of internal contradiction as the central dynamic of his novels, to the recognition of Hegel (a different Hegel than ours, however) as a necessary touchstone, all the way to the identification of an ultimately utopian meaning (utopian in a specifically Jamesonian sense, but a different Jameson than ours) to the central tragedy of *Things Fall Apart*. The perspective of this chapter, however, is more properly materialist, and in this it is closer in spirit to Chidi Amuta's brief account of *Arrow of God*, which refers the central conflicts of the novel to a confrontation between "antithetical production formations" (Amuta, *The Theory of African Literature*, 133). See Irele, "The Crisis of Cultural Memory," 115–53, and his "The Tragic Conflict in Achebe's Novels," *Black Orpheus* 17 (1965): 24–32.

13. It is worth mentioning that the schematic reading we will produce here does not at all capture the incredible illusionism of *Arrow of God*, which, through its subtle interweaving of narrative strands and significant detail, manages to produce the effect of effortless realism.

14. For the time being, the lessons of Achebe's essay on Conrad and the image will be held in abeyance, both in the reading of Achebe's work and in the framing of the argument

by means of certain Hegelian concepts that seem to be at work in Achebe's novel. Plainly certain of Hegel's texts can be easily assailed along the lines of Achebe's argument, and Irele is justifiably wary about invoking Hegel even as he is compelled to do so ("The Crisis of Cultural Memory," 149, 262n. 26). In the Conrad essay, Achebe decries the belief that there is no such thing as African history, or that history in Africa begins only with colonialism; if this idea did not originate with Hegel, certainly it receives exemplary expression in Hegel's *Philosophy of History*, which begins in the East and "ends" in Europe, with a nod toward the Americas, leaving the continent of Africa outside history. The decision to see a Hegelian conception of History in Achebe's novels requires us to ignore Achebe's lesson and shut away all that we know about Hegel's remarks on Africa: "wild and untamed" Africans with "nothing harmonious with humanity to be found" (150) in their character, eating their enemies, selling their children, and behaving as one would expect of people whose "moral sentiments are . . . strictly speaking, non-existent" (153).

15. G.W.F. Hegel, *Introduction to the Philosophy of History*, trans. Leo Rauch (Indianapolis: Hackett, 1988), 30, 35.

16. Lindfors, Conversations, 117; Achebe, *Hopes and Impediments*, 57.

17. Ato Quayson raises the intriguing possibility that the concept of *chi* in *Things Fall Apart* is formally the same as Hegelian Reason (see *Calibrations*, 145). This anthropomorphization of quite implacable and inhuman processes is hardly unique to Hegel or Umuofia, and we should not assume that either Hegel or the fictional Umuofians are unaware that Reason or *chi* are figures rather than concepts. In Richard Dawkins's idea of the "selfish gene," for example (*The Selfish Gene* [London: Oxford University Press, 1976]), it is understood that the "selfish" is an anthropomorphizing metaphor: natural selection behaves as though it were the genes, not the organisms that carry them, who "wanted" to be passed along to the next generation. Hegelian Reason can be understood in similar terms, where the anthropomorphizing metaphor stands in for the fact that complex sets of phenomena can, on a much longer view, be understood to conform according to a comprehensible logic. This logic does not have to be the "truth" of the phenomena in any too-literal way to be a valuable tool for representing to ourselves phenomena otherwise too complex to admit representation.

18. See A. E. Afigbo, "The Aro Expedition of 1901–02: An Episode in the British Occupation of Iboland," *Odu, A Journal of West African Studies*, April 7, 1972.

19. See Robin Horton, "Stateless Societies in the History of West Africa," in *History of West Africa*, 3rd ed., ed. J.F.A. Ajayi and Michael Crowder (New York: Longman, 1985), 1:87–128, at 127. Horton is careful to avoid the teleological implications of this claim, of which I have been less wary. The implicit teleology of fictional Umuaro is patently quite a different matter than the actual future of societies whose internal development was cut short by British administration.

20. Hegel, *Philosophy of Right*, 268.

21. Ibid., 10, 124.

22. See, e.g., Biodun Jeyifo, "Ideology and Tragic Epistemology: The Emergent Paradigms in Contemporary African Drama," in *The Truthful Lie* (London: New Beacon Books, 1985), 23–45. The role here of the chthonic god echoes that in *Antigone*: "Nor did I think your proclamations strong enough to overrule, mortal as they were, the unwritten and unfailing ordinances of the gods. For these have life, not simply today and yesterday, but forever, and no one knows how long ago they were revealed" (trans. Hugh Lloyd-Jones [Cambridge, MA: Harvard University Press, 1994], ll. 450–56). Hegel's reading of *Antigone*, both in the *Aesthetics* and in *Phenomenology of Spirit*, concerns the conflict between "ethical powers" that are borne by individuals but also represent historical moments. It bears on

Arrow of God in surprising ways, but the reference here to *Antigone* reminds us that, as a tragic figure in the precise Hegelian sense—he makes no choice and bears no flaw, he simply is what he is, "without any inner conflict, without any hesitating recognition of someone else's 'pathos' " (*Aesthetics*, 2:1209)—Ezeulu's destruction could act as a counter-weight to the more metaphysical interpretations of Sophocles's play, starting with Hegel's own.

23. See Ajayi and Crowder, *History of West Africa*, 1:398.

24. See J. E. Flint, "Economic Change in West Africa in the Nineteenth Century," in *History of West Africa*, ed. Ajayi and Crowder, 2:391 and passim.

25. Achebe, *Hopes and Impediments*, 146.

26. This translation is the representational problem that older novelists like Onuora Nzekwu were unable to solve before the appearance of *Things Fall Apart*.

27. Achebe has consistently denied doing any research for any of his novels, claiming of *Things Fall Apart*, like Coleridge of "Kubla Khan," that it was "written straight, without any kind of draft" (*Conversations*, 12). It is possible to interpret this as an implicit claim to some kind of purely intuitive knowledge of Igbo life, but I would prefer to see this kind of denial, like Coleridge's, as excercising the writer's prerogative to refuse to divulge the mysteries of the trade to the uninitiated and to excuse any deficiencies as the necessary limits of a moment of inspiration. *Arrow of God* very clearly takes its central plot device from an anthropological source, but the kind of criticism that has resulted from this discovery indeed makes one wish it had never been made. See Charles Nnolim, "A Source for *Arrow of God*," *Research in African Literatures* 8 (1977): 1–26.

28. Jean-Paul Sartre, *Being and Nothingness*, trans. Hazel E. Barnes (New York: Washington Square Press, 1966), 340–400.

29. Hegel, *Phenomenology of Spirit*, 111–19.

30. In this sense *Arrow of God* enacts a practical critique of anthropology that does not receive explicit expression until Pierre Bourdieu's *Outline of a Theory of Practice*, trans. Richard Nice (Cambridge: Cambridge University Press, 1977), trans. of *Esquisse d'une théorie de la pratique, précédé de trois études d'ethnologie kabyle* (1972). I take Bourdieu's "synoptic illusion" to be the epistemological equivalent of what I have been calling anthropology's objectifying gaze (and is similarly indebted to the Sartrean Look): the "habitus" and the emphasis on strategy the epistemological equivalent of Achebe's narrative technique.

31. Spivak, *A Critique of Postcolonial Reason*, 153.

32. Sartre, "Orphée noir," ix.

33. "Du coup la notion subjective, existentielle, ethnique de *négritude* 'passe,' comme dit Hegel, dans celle—objective, positive, exacte—de *prolétariat*. 'Pour Césaire' dit Senghor, le 'Blanc' symbolise le capital, comme le Nègre le travail" (xl).

34. See Lukács, *The Historical Novel*, especially 206–20, "The Naturalism of the Plebeian Opposition."

35. Lindfors, *Conversations*, 116.

36. See Wren, *Achebe's World*, 120.

37. Innes and Lindfors, *Critical Perspectives on Chinua Achebe*, 50.

38. This is not the place to summarize postcolonial Nigerian history, but for a recent instance one need only think of the resistance to petroleum multinationals and the neocolonial state in the Niger Delta. E. Eghosa Osaghae has described this resistance as a process of the transformation of the Ogoni from a group in itself to a group for itself in "The Ogoni Uprising: Oil Politics, Minority Agitation and the Future of the Nigerian State," *African Affairs* 94.376 (July 1995): 325–44.

39. Quoted in Abiolo Irele, *The Africa Experience in Literature and Ideology* (London: Heinemann, 1981), 1.

CHAPTER SIX

1. Adorno, *Aesthetic Theory,* 41.
2. Wyndham Lewis, *The Childermass* (1928; London: John Calder, 1965).
3. Paul Edwards, *Wyndham Lewis: Painter and Writer* (New Haven: Yale University Press, 2000), 324; Wyndham Lewis, *Time and Western Man* (New York: Harcourt Brace, 1928).
4. The conservative columnist David Brooks has revived the term "bourgeois bohemians," but he seems to think he invented it. He calls them "bobos."
5. Wyndham Lewis, *Men Without Art* (London: Cassell, 1934).
6. See book 1 of *Time and Western Man,* "The Revolutionary Simpleton," especially 35–38 and 69–75.
7. Wyndham Lewis, *The Art of Being Ruled* (London: Chatto and Windus, 1926).
8. Wyndham Lewis, *Rude Assignment: A Narrative of My Career Up-to-Date* (London: Hutchison, 1950).
9. Louis Althusser, *Lenin and Philosophy and Other Essays,* trans. Ben Brewster (New York: Monthly Review Press, 1971), 153.
10. Indeed, as Nicos Poulantzas points out (*Fascism and Dictatorship: The Third International and the Problem of Fascism,* trans. Judith White [London: New Left Books, 1974]) fascist ideology itself—as some of Lewis's works of opinion can be classified—is not susceptible to systematic critique, being little more than "an amalgam of contradictory elements" (253).
11. Wyndham Lewis, *Hitler* (London: Chatto and Windus, 1931).
12. Wyndham Lewis, *The Hitler Cult* (London: J. M. Dent, 1939).
13. Althusser, *Lenin and Philosophy and Other Essays.*
14. This is not to say that this disruption, once it becomes functional, represents the whole truth of racism. Simply because race is pure phenomenon does not mean that, as phenomenon, it does not have real material consequences.
15. Quoted in Paul O'Keefe, *Some Sort of Genius: A Life of Wyndham Lewis* (London: Jonathan Cape, 2000), 259.
16. Throughout this chapter, "elitism" will refer to the real elitism that would rationalize privilege in terms of merit without considering the social determinants of such "merit"—and not to the "elitism" that serves merely as an anti-intellectual slogan. Lewis, it almost goes without saying, considered himself to be anti-elitist—a position he claims two pages after claiming that "the backwards mass drag down and stifle intelligence" (*The Art of Being Ruled,* 184) and so on.
17. Poulantzas, *Fascism and Dictatorship,* 241.
18. Robert C. Elliott has discussed this element convincingly in *The Power of Satire: Magic, Ritual, Art* (Princeton: Princeton University Press, 1960), in a half chapter on Lewis (223–37) titled "The Satirist Satirized." The idea of the reflexiveness of Lewis's satire could easily be adapted to the larger argument of the current work by pointing out that the Archimedean point required by satire posits a utopian space outside the social world ("satire can only exist *in contrast* to something else—it is a shadow, and an ugly shadow at that, of some perfection" [*Men Without Art,* 109]) that is nonetheless corroded by its own action and the mode of its intervention in that social world. Indeed, this is one of the points made by Fredric Jameson in *Fables of Aggression.* The debt this chapter owes to that work will be apparent.

19. Books 2 and 3, *Monstre Gai* and *Malign Fiesta*, are printed together in Wyndham Lewis, *The Human Age* (London: Methuen, 1955). For book 1, see note 2. Book 4, *The Trial of Man*, was never written.

20. See especially Jameson, *Fables of Aggression*.

21. Hugh Kenner, *Wyndham Lewis* (Norfolk, CT: New Directions, 1954), 35.

22. Wyndham Lewis, "Inferior Religions," in *The Wild Body: A Soldier of Humour and Other Stories* (London: Chatto and Windus, 1927).

23. Edwards, *Wyndham Lewis*, 322.

24. For Lewis's gloss on Goethe's distinction, see *The Art of Being Ruled*, 135.

25. Quoted in *Rude Assignment*, 155–56.

26. "Quid autem video praeter pileos & vestes, sub quibus latere possent automata? Sed judico homines esse." "What do I see [from the window] but hats and coats which may cover automata? Yet these I judge to be men." Descartes, Second Meditation, *Meditationes de Prima Philosophia.*

27. Wyndham Lewis, *Tarr* (London: Chatto and Windus, 1928).

28. Wyndham Lewis, *The Revenge for Love* (London: Cassell, 1937).

29. Further confirmation of the opposition between the official content of the "strong personality" and the formal impulse toward its dissolution comes from the fact that the actual individuals in *The Childermass* are far less interesting than the group forms that absorb them, so that all of *The Childermass*'s considerable descriptive energy is focused on the collective scene of the Bailiff's court. Compared to the long sentence quoted above concerning the Bailiff and his "children," or for that matter the antics of the Bailiff's court and the theatrics of the Hyperideans, the language used to narrate the intellectual Pullman is relatively dull, so that while the "horrid crowds" are present, Pullman fades into the background.

30. Even if this Limbo only represented the world "as it would be" if the Bergson or Whitehead characterized in *Time and Western Man* were the authors of its physical and psychological laws, we must remember that Lewis's quixotic lifelong project of refuting mainstream modernism is idealist in the most literal sense. The desire to *refute* Bergson or Joyce seems so bizarre today because we quite readily see cultural phenomena as, if not mere symptoms of social processes, then at least as elements in a much larger social dialectic. But, as Lewis's works of opinion explicitly attest, both his desire for such refutation and the notion that such refutation would be consequent in the first place assume that cultural phenomena are directly determining so that, in the last instance, the world "as it would be" if mainstream modernist assumptions were *true* and the world "as it is" when such assumptions are *dominant* are, in *The Childermass*, far from being easily separable.

31. See, e.g., Daniel Schenker, *Wyndham Lewis: Religion and Modernism* (Tuscaloosa: University of Alabama Press, 1992), 126.

32. See Walter Michel, *Wyndham Lewis: Paintings and Drawings* (Berkeley: University of California Press, 1971), plates 33–37.

33. Always an ambivalent figure, Hyperides, whose name is a homophone for "high parodies," produces a critique of the zeitgeist identical to that of arch-parodist Lewis in his *Time and Western Man*, even as he is himself a caricature of the pseudo-intellectual demagogue. Later, in *Monstre Gai*, the now explicitly fascist Hyperides is unambiguously repudiated and Pullman, who turns out to have been "the greatest writer of [his] time" (*Monstre Gai*, 136), comes to occupy with less irony the role of the great intellectual. Though Pullman with his ashplant was originally modeled after Joyce, there is little question that by the end of the trilogy he much more closely resembles Lewis. It is an accidental but telling reflexive irony that Pullman, discussing the very figure of the demagogic dictator

in the Bailiff, condescendingly pronounces "I like the beggar"—more or less the attitude of Lewis toward Hitler three years later.

34. The word "peon" itself testifies to this. "Peon" comes from the Portuguese *peão*, which is originally the word for "foot soldier" both in the military and in chess, hence "pawn." "Peon" finds its way into English though British imperialism's encounter with the remnants, linguistic and otherwise, of Portugal's great imperial period. It was in Portugal's colonies that *peão* first came to mean "manual laborer," "migrant worker," and indeed something like the English "native." The OED finds the first English uses of "peon" in the seventeenth century with reference to East Indian orderlies and attendants.

35. V. I. Lenin, *Imperialism: The Highest Stage of Capitalism* (New York: International Publishers, 1939), 107.

36. Quoted in Lenin, *Imperialism*, 79.

37. This passage also reminds us that the "desire of the multitude" is not, in itself, necessarily progressive.

38. Fredric Jameson, "Marxism and Postmodernism," in *The Cultural Turn*, 37.

CHAPTER SEVEN

1. Ngugi wa Thiong'o, "Art War with the State: Writers and Guardians of Post-colonial Society," *Penpoints, Gunpoints, and Dreams* (Oxford: Clarendon, 1998), 7–35.

2. Bertolt Brecht, "The Anxieties of the Regime," in *Poems 1913–1956*, ed. John Willett and Ralph Manheim (London: Methuen, 1976), 296–98.

3. Ngugi's exile ended after the KANU party was defeated in 2002. In 2004 he returned to Kenya to give a lecture tour. After a short time in the country, he and his wife were assaulted; the attack may have been politically motivated.

4. Ngugi wa Thiong'o and Micere Githae Mugo, *The Trial of Dedan Kimathi* (London: Heinemann, 1976).

5. The question of whether Britain's handing over of power was a matter of British and world politics or directly due in some way to the Mau Mau uprising is a matter of constant debate. A valuable resource (contemporary with the Kamiriithu plays, but still current) for this central issue is a special issue of *Kenya Historical Review* 5.2 (1977), *Some Perspectives on the Mau Mau Movement*, edited by William R. Ochieng' and Karim K. Janmohamed. See especially Maina Wa Kinyatti, "Mau Mau: The Peak of African Nationalism in Kenya," 287–311, and B. E. Kipkorir, "Mau Mau and the Politics of the Transfer of Power in Kenya, 1957–1960," 313–28.

6. See Ladislav Venys, *A History of the Mau Mau Movement in Kenya* (Prague: Charles University Press, 1970), 63.

7. PEOPLE'S SONG AND DANCE:

> SOLOISTS: Ho-oo, ho-oo mto mkuu wateremka!
> GROUP: Ho-oo, ho-oo mto mkuu wateremka!
> SOLOISTS: Magharibi kwenda mashariki
> GROUP: Mto mkuu wateremka
> SOLOISTS: Kaskazini kwenda kusini
> GROUP: Mto mkuu wateremka
> SOLOISTS: Hooo-i, hoo-i kumbe adui kwela mjinga
> GROUP: Hooo-i, hoo-i kumbe adui kwela mjinga
> SOLOISTS: Akaua mwanza mimba wetu

GROUP: Akijitia yeye mshindi
   SOLOISTS: Wengi zaidi wakazaliwa
GROUP: Tushangilie mazao mapya
SOLOISTS: Vitinda mimba marungu juu
GROUP: Tushambilie adui mpya
SOLOISTS: Hoo-ye, hoo-ye wafanya kazi wa ulimwengu
GROUP: Hoo-ye, hoo-ye wafanya kazi wa ulimwengu
SOLOISTS: Na wakulima wote wadogo
GROUP: Tushikaneni mikono sote
SOLOISTS: Tutwange nyororo za wabeberu
GROUP: Hatutaki tumwa tena.
SOLOISTS: Hoo-ye, hoo-ye umoja wetu ni nguvu yetu
GROUP: Hoo-ye, hoo-ye umoja wetu ni nguvu yetu
SOLOISTS: Tutapigana mpaka mwisho
GROUP: Tufunge vita na tutashinda
SOLOISTS: Majembe juu na mapanga juu
GROUP: Tujikomboe tujenge upya (*The Trial of Dedan Kimathi* 84–85).

8. Ngugi's recent writing seems to endorse this simpler reading. See *Penpoints*, 48.

9. Carol Sicherman, ed., *Ngugi wa Thiong'o: The Making of A Rebel. A Source Book in Kenyan Literature and Resistance* (Borough Green: Hans Zell, 1990), 10.

10. See Kariuki's remarkable memoir, *Mau Mau Detainee: The Account by a Kenya African of His Experiences in Detention Camps, 1953–60* (London: Oxford University Press, 1963).

11. *Independent Kenya* (London: Zed, 1982), 33. *Independent Kenya* was written anonymously, sponsored by the Journal of African Marxists in solidarity with the authors.

12. In discussing the Kamiriithu plays, "Ngugi," like "Brecht" in another context, signifies a number of people in collective effort. The shorthand is, I think, admissible, since Ngugi is, if nothing else, the reason we are aware of these plays. Ngugi himself is always careful to make clear others' contributions to his theater projects, as Brecht was not always concerned to do.

13. Ngugi wa Thiong'o, *Detained: A Writer's Prison Diary* (London: Heinemann, 1981), 72–80.

14. The direct resonance of local struggles with the global structures, identified by Hardt and Negri as constitutive of contemporary dissent and a major point of analysis, may simply be a sign of these struggles' weakness. The direct resonance of the local with the global may in fact be nothing more than the failure of local struggles to do more than provoke Empire, rather than organize into a form that could engage it. This problem reflects back on the Kamiriithu project as well.

15. Ngugi wa Thiong'o, *Decolonising the Mind: The Politics of Language in African Literature* (London: James Currey, 1986), xiv.

16. Ngugi wa Thiong'o and Ngugi wa Mirii, *I Will Marry When I Want* (London: Heinemann, 1982), trans. of Ngugi wa Thiong'o and Ngugi wa Mirii, *Ngaahika Ndeenda*.

17. Much of the information in this paragraph summarizes *Detained*, 72–80.

18. See *Independent Kenya*, particularly chapter 2, "KANU and Kenyatta: Independence for Sale," 13–36.

19. Sicherman, *Ngugi wa Thiong'o*, 74.

20. This narrative of the Kamiriithu Community Education and Cultural Centre is synthesized from accounts in *Detained*, 72–80; *Decolonizing*, 34–62, and Ingrid Björkman, *Mother, Sing for Me: People's Theatre in Kenya* (London: Zed Books, 1989), 51–56.

21. Björkman, *Mother, Sing for Me*, 52, 60.

22. For a more detailed account of the production of *Mother, Sing for Me*, see Björkman, *Mother, Sing for Me*, 54, 57–60.

23. Björkman, *Mother, Sing for Me*, 60.

24. Kariuki, *Mau Mau Detainee*, 128–29.

25. Richard Frost, *Race against Time: Human Relations and Politics in Kenya before Independence* (London: Rex Collings, 1978), 196.

26. Quoted in Björkman, *Mother, Sing for Me*, 73.

27. Bertolt Brecht, *Brecht on Theater: The Development of an Aesthetic*, ed. and trans. John Willett (New York: Hill and Wang, 1964), 39.

28. A lively account of post-independence Kenyan politics is D. Pal Ahluwalia, *Postcolonialism and the Politics of Kenya* (New York: Nova Science Publishers, 1996). See particularly chapters 3–6, which try to make sense of political movements in the period between Kenyatta's illness and the attempted coup of 1982. For a specifically Marxist account, see *Independent Kenya*.

29. Immanuel Wallerstein, "Dependence in an Interdependent World: The Limited Possibilities of Transformation within the Capitalist World Economy," *African Studies Review* 17.1 (April 1974): 7.

30. See, e.g., Fanon, *The Wretched of the Earth*, 64–66.

31. See Wallerstein, "Dependence in an Interdependent World."

32. This explanation was suggested to me by one of my undergraduate students, Alejandro Castro.

33. Pepetela [Artur Pestana], *A Geração da Utopia* (Rio de Janeiro: Nova Fronteira, 2000).

34. "O segredo da dança está na interacção entre o colectivo e o individual. . . . Na xinjanguila, o colectivo é fundamental. . . . Tudo combinado com os movimentos de ombros, ancas, braços e pernas. E o particular? Está no breve instante em que a pessoa da esquerda, ao vir do centro, te convida batendo os pés ou dando um sacão de anca. . . . É realmente um equilíbrio constante entre o habitual sentido colectivo da dança de roda e o sentido particular da dança de pares. O prazer . . . está em sentir o prazer colectivo do rítimo e o de sentir viver, vibrar, o corpo que vem ao encontro do teu, sem o tocar" (*A Geração da Utopia*, 149–50).

35. "Eu tinha treze anos quando Luanda se mobilizou em massa para receber os heróis da libertação. . . . Marchávamos, ouvíamos os relatos dos mais velhos vindos das matas, cantávamos as cancões revolucionárias, inventámos aquela marcha-dança que se espalhou por tudo o País, misto de fervor patriótico e imaginação criativa" (*A Geração da Utopia*, 361).

36. "E depois quiseram enquadrar-nos. Disseram, devem marchar como os soldados, vocês são os futuros soldados. Já não podíamos dar aqueles passos malucos que arrancavam palmas a toda a gente, vai para a frente, um passo para o lado, volta para trás, uma piada no meio. Mesmo no Carnaval, anos mais tarde, só se podia marchar como os soldados, os grupos deixaram de dançar. Liquidaram a imaginação" (*A Geração da Utopia*, 361).

37. "o dinheiro e as poucas jóias e até mesmo as camisas" (*A Geração da Utopia*, 375).

38. "Todo o povo dançando e se beijando e se tocando, se massembando mesmo nas filas e nos corredores e depois no largo à frente do Luminar e nas ruas adjacentes . . . a caminho dos mercados e das casas, das praias e dos muceques, em cortejos se multiplicando como no carnaval, do Luminar partindo felizes para ganhar o Mundo e a Esperança" (*A Geração da Utopia*, 375).

39. "as multidões [estavam] cantando as palavras-de-ordem da independência com igual fervor" (*A Geração da Utopia*, 375).

40. Don Ihde, *Listening and Voice: A Phenomenology of Sound* (Athens: Ohio University Press, 1976), 159.

41. Jacques Attali, *Bruits: Essai sur l'économie politique de la musique* (Paris: Presses Universitaires de France, 1977).

42. Pepetela, *Yaka* (Lisbon: Publicações Dom Quixote, 1985).

CHAPTER EIGHT

1. Emmet Williams, ed., *An Anthology of Concrete Poetry* (New York: Something Else Press, 1967), n.p. (1).

2. Mary Ellen Solt, ed. *Concrete Poetry: A World View* (Bloomington: Indiana University Press, 1970), 92.

3. João Gilberto, *The Legendary João Gilberto: The Original Bossa Nova Recordings* (1958–1961), World Pacific 93891, 1990.

4. Badiou, *Manifeste pour la philosophie*, 51.

5. Fredric Jameson, "Globalization as a Philosophical Issue," in *The Cultures of Globalization*, ed. Fredric Jameson and Masao Miyoshi (Durham: Duke University Press, 1998), 58.

6. Ibid., 60.

7. Jameson, " 'End of Art' or 'End of History?' " 88, 87.

8. Attali, *Bruits*, 7. For an English translation, see *Noise: The Political Economy of Music*, trans. Brian Massumi (Minneapolis: University of Minnesota Press, 1985).

9. Roberto Schwarz, "Cultura e Política, 1964–1969," in *O pai da família e outros estudos*, 73. This piece, along with several of the other essays by Schwarz cited here, are excellently translated in Roberto Schwarz, *Misplaced Ideas: Essays on Brazilian Culture*, ed. and trans. John Gledson (London: Verso, 1992).

10. Caetano Veloso, *Estrangeiro*, Elektra 60898, 1989.

11. The logic of this connection, which cannot be elaborated here for reasons of space, is developed in its classical form in Lukács, "Reification and the Consciousness of the Proletariat."

12. Augusto de Campos, "Boa palavra sobre a música popular," in *Balanço da bossa e outras bossas* (São Paulo: Editora Perspectiva, 1974), 60. The same metaphor was used in negative evaluations of bossa nova as well, which insisted that bossa nova was merely a new kind of jazz. These read less credibly today.

13. Stan Getz and João Gilberto, *Getz/Gilberto* (1964), Verve 314521414–2, 1997.

14. Gilberto, *The Legendary João Gilberto*.

15. We might make a speculative reading of the difference in affective content between the unhappy lover in bossa nova (pathos, helplessness) and in the urban samba of the period (revenge, wrathfulness). If we read the class allegory of bossa nova back into samba itself, the domestication of samba no longer seems so innocent.

16. While the simultaneous and independent invention of concrete poetry is often credited to Eugen Gomringer (Switzerland) and Augusto de Campos (Brazil), it is worth noting that Gomringer was born in Bolivia and wrote many of his concrete poems in Spanish.

17. Solt, *Concrete Poetry*, 105; Augusto de Campos, *Viva Vaia; Poesia 1949–1979* (São Paulo: Ateliê Editorial, 2000), 101.

18. See de Campos, "Conversa com Caetano Veloso," in *Balanço da bossa*, 202.

19. Júlio Medaglia, "Balanço da bossa nova," in *Balanço da bossa*, ed. Campos, 78.

20. *PRONOMINAIS*

Dê-me um cigarro
Diz a gramática
Do professor e do aluno
E do mulato sabido
Mas o bom negro e o bom branco
Da Nação Brasileira
Dizem todos os dias
Deixa disso camarada
Me dá um cigarro

Oswald de Andrade, *Poesias Reunidas* (Rio de Janeiro: Civilização Brazileira, 1971), 63.

21. Augusto de Campos et al, "Plano-piloto para poesia concreta," in *Teoria da Poesia Concreta: Textos Críticos e Manifestos 1950–1960* (São Paulo: Livraria Duas Cidades, 1975), 156.

22. See de Campos, *Viva Vaia*, 111–13.

23. de Campos et al., "Plano-piloto para poesia concreta," 156.

24. de Campos, *Viva Vaia*, 204–5. The literal meaning of the phrase "Viva vaia" is, rather inelegantly in English, "Long live the Bronx cheer." The immediate content is the relationship between the artist and the "public," though of course the nature of this public is unspecified. The historical referent may be the audience response at televised music festivals.

25. Williams, *Anthology of Concrete Poetry*, n.p.; a handsome version in coca-cola red appears in Solt, *Concrete Poetry*, 108.

26. Adorno, *Aesthetic Theory*, 43.

27. See, e.g., Caetano Veloso's fascinating autobiographical account of the Brazilian 1960s, *Verdade Tropical* (São Paulo: Companhia das Letras, 1997), where an explicitly utopian program jostles against the more modest project of diversifying the Brazilian music industry. In Veloso's music, Brazil itself often allegorizes this double horizon, exploiting the "tensions between Brazil-Parallel-Universe and a country peripheral to the American Empire" (16). For an English translation, see *Tropical Truth*, trans. Isabel da Sena (New York: Knopf, 2002).

28. Oswald de Andrade, "Manifesto da Poesia Pau-Brasil," in *Do Pau-Brasil à antropofagia e às utopias: Manifestos, teses de concursos e ensaios* (Rio de Janeiro: Civilização Brasileira, 1972), 13.

29. Ibid., 9.

30. Octavio Ianni, *O Colapso do Populismo no Brasil* (Rio de Janeiro: Civilização Brasileira, 1971), 26. For a somewhat frustrating English translation, see *Crisis in Brazil*, trans. Phyllis B. Eveleth (New York: Columbia University Press, 1970).

31. de Andrade, *Poesias Reunidas*, 64.

32. Oswald de Andrade, "Manifesto Antropófago," in *Do Pau-Brasil*, 18.

33. Ianni, *O Colapso do Populismo no Brasil*, 53–55.

34. Ibid., 122.

35. *Resolução Política da Convenção Nacional dos Comunistas* (Rio de Janeiro, 1961), 15–16, cited in Ianni, *O Colapso do Populismo no Brasil*, 105–6.

36. Ianni, *O Colapso do Populismo no Brasil*, 122.

37. Ibid., 61.

38. Schwarz, "Cultura e Política," 65.

39. For a "moderate" account of this period, see Thomas E. Skidmore, *Politics in Brazil, 1930–1964: An Experiment in Democracy* (London: Oxford University Press, 1967), especially chaps. 7 and 8.

40. See Wallerstein, "Dependence in an Independent World," especially 10–13.

41. See Ianni, *O Colapso do Populismo no Brasil*, 123–24.

42. See Thomas Frank, "Alternative to What?" in *Commodify Your Dissent: Salvos from the Baffler*, ed. Thomas Frank and Matt Weiland (New York: Norton, 1997), 145–61. Many of the other essays in the volume are also relevant to this point.

43. In an article on the Brazilian musical vanguard, Schwarz includes a remarkable footnote: "Generally speaking, incidentally, the arguments I present here are in Adorno's work." (Schwarz, "Nota sobre vanguarda e conformismo," in *O pai da família* 43–48.) Generally speaking, the arguments I present here are in Schwarz's.

44. See also Roberto Schwarz, "Altos e baixos da atualidade de Brecht," *Seqüências Brasileiras: Ensaios* (São Paulo: Companhia das Letras, 1999), 113–48.

45. In fact, there are a number of interesting parallels between the Arena and the Kamiriithu plays. Of particular interest is the musical *Arena conta Zumbi*, in which the dictatorship is allegorized through a narrative of the repression of the famous slave revolt led by Zumbi of Palmares. The narrative and allegorical similarity to Ngugi's *Mother, Sing for Me* is remarkable, but the problems at the heart of the two plays are ultimately divergent. As Schwarz points out, the narrative ambiguity arises from the flexibility of the allegory. In one direction, the slave revolt allegorizes the present situation; and the narrative displacement is a useful way to avoid censorship. In the other direction, the language describing the present situation refers to the slave revolt equally well, driving the narrative into mere moralizing about an eternal struggle between freedom and oppression. The real problem, however, is in the spontaneous agreement between the stage and the audience, neither of which had significant contact with either the peasantry or the proletariat.

46. Schwarz, "Cultura e Política," 83.

47. See Veloso, *Verdade Tropical*, 382–86. Caetano's insistence that he saw nothing explicitly political about *Roda Viva* is surely disingenuous.

48. Schwarz, "Cultura e Política," 85.

49. Ibid., 88.

50. Lukács, "Reification and the Consciousness of the Proletariat," 138–40.

51. Adorno, *Aesthetic Theory*, 43.

52. See Guy Brett et al., *Hélio Oiticica* (Rotterdam: Witte de With, 1993), 121–26.

53. *Tropicália ou Panis et Circensis* (1968), Phillips 512089, 1993.

54. Veloso, *Verdade Tropical*, 272. The third verse reproduces the red-herring structure of the first two. The initial planting of "dream leaves in the manor garden" is a fairly routine, deliberately "shocking" counterculture drug reference. But the emphasis is on the roots, not on the leaves, and we are left with an image of subterranean desires—it is unclear whether they are malign or revolutionary—that perpetually seek outlet. Meanwhile, confirming the ambiguity of the lyric, the people in their dining room get the last word: the refrain accelerates for the coda, culminating in a kind of frenzied repetition of "those people in the dining room" which, rather than resolving, breaks off abruptly into a recorded representation of the dining room itself, where people pass each other dishes to the strains of the "Blue Danube."

55. Schwarz, "Cultura e Política," 74.

56. Jameson, *Postmodernism*, 31.

57. This technique in its linguistic form is nothing new in Brazilian poetry; Schwarz's reading of Oswald de Andrade's group of poems "Postes da Light" ("Electric Poles"—the

title itself, containing the English word "light" in reference to a Canadian company that operated in Brazil, already contains the seeds of the technique) draws out a similar structure. See "O carro, o bonde, e o poeta modernista," in Roberto Schwarz, *Que Horas São?* (São Paulo: Companhia das Letras, 1987). It could be that his engagement with Tropicália gave Schwarz the clue to Brazilian modernism—the article on modernism was written later.

The remarkable thing here is that Tropicália seemed to arrive at this method independently, attesting to the fact that this apparently "postmodern" technique is, as it were, native to the semiperiphery. Caetano Veloso, hardly coy about his influences, insists that he "knew . . . nothing of Oswald" de Andrade (*Verdade Tropical*, 155) until after the similarity was pointed out to him by the Concretists. See also de Campos, *Balanço da bossa*, 204.

58. Veloso, *Verdade Tropical*, 60.

59. Reiichi Miura, "On the Globalization of Literature: Haruki Murakami, Tim O'Brien and Raymond Carver," a talk given at the University of Illinois at Chicago, March 19, 2003.

60. Caetano Veloso, *Caetano Veloso* (1967), Phillips 838557, 2002.

61. Schwarz, "Cultura e Política," 76.

62. Jameson, *Postmodernism*, 33.

63. See Caetano Veloso's defense of Carmen Miranda, "Carmen Mirandadada," trans. Robert Myers and Charles A. Perrone, in *Brazilian Popular Music and Globalization*, ed. Charles A. Perrone and Christopher Dunn (Gainesville: University Press of Florida, 2001), 39–45. In Buarque's "A Banda," a band of musicians passing by can be seen to allegorize a revolutionary opportunity having passed by Brazil. But the allegorical ground of a roving band is decidedly archaic.

64. Veloso, *Verdade Tropical*, 505. The song "Manhatã" appears on Caetano Veloso, *Livro*, PolyGram 536584–2, 1999.

65. In fact, Salgado's images of the Yanomami manage to project *both* the older Romantic ideal of the (female) Indian and the contemporary human-rights ideal, which brings its own problems, different but no less profound. What one sees reflected in many of the most horrible photographs in Salgado's *Migrations* series—and some of them are very horrible indeed—is one's own innocence in face of the massacre: *that horror* is something I could never be responsible for. In the first instance, what one enjoys in these photographs is their great and paradoxical beauty—already far from a simple phenomenon, since they represent the most acute human misery our planet currently has on offer. In the second instance, what one enjoys is one's own innocence, and of course this very enjoyment marks the innocence as spurious. Once again, this is not to say that the massacre should not be represented; there simply may be no "right" way of doing it, and Salgado's unflinching images of, for example, Rwandan Tutsi corpses spilling over the waterfall at Rusumo, give us the massacre with an immediacy that is absolutely necessary in the face of the forgetting demanded by the news media. Nonetheless, one may prefer the comportment of the camera in his *Workers* series (New York: Aperture, 1993). For the Yanomami images, see Sebastião Salgado, *Migrations: Humanity in Transition* (New York: Aperture, 2000), 251–63.

66. It may be that the peripheral condition itself is what allowed the Tropicalists to recognize this before anyone else. Mass culture in its contemporary configuration emerged with extraordinary rapidity in Brazil. A glance at the development of the media apparatus shows that it grew exponentially in the period preceding the Tropicalist moment, quickly outpacing conventional infrastructural development. By 1970, only 12.8 percent of households in Bahia had running water and 22.8 percent had electricity, but 36.6 percent had

radios, which can be shared; the numbers for São Paulo are 58.5 percent, 80.4 percent, and 80.4 percent, respectively. See Christopher Dunn, *Brutality Garden: Tropicália and the Emergence of a Brazilian Counterculture* (Chapel Hill: University of North Carolina Press, 2001), 45.

67. See Schwarz, "Nota sobre vanguarda e conformismo," 43–48. Schwarz's footnote gives 1957 as the date of Medaglia's interview with four vanguard composers, but this appears to be a typo, since Schwarz's response was written in 1967, surely not ten years after the fact.

68. de Campos, *Balanço da bossa*, 200.

69. Paul Simon, *Rhythm of the Saints*, Warner Brothers 26098–2, 1990.

70. Ihde, *Listening and Voice*, 159.

71. Veloso, *Verdade Tropical*, 281.

72. See Dunn, *Brutality Garden*, 90–92.

73. A "samba-provocation" by Gilberto Gil gives a sympathetic reading of Michael Jackson that hints at the kind of non-ironic appropriation described here:

Michael Jackson ainda resiste
Porque além de branco ficou triste

Michael Jackson still resists
Because when he turned white he became sad
"De Bob Dylan a Bob Marley—Um Samba-Provocação," *O eterno deus mu dança*, Wea 703698, 1989.